TROPES AND TERRITORIES

Tropes and Territories

Short Fiction, Postcolonial Readings, Canadian Writing in Context

EDITED BY

MARTA DVOŘÁK AND W.H. NEW

McGill-Queen's University Press

Montreal & Kingston • London • Ithaca

Legal deposit third quarter 2007
Bibliothèque nationale du Québec

Printed in Canada on acid-free paper that is 100% ancient forest tree
(100% post-consumer recycled), processed chlorine free.

This book has been published with the help of a grant from the Canadian
Federation for the Humanities and Social Sciences, through the Aid to Scholarly
Publications Programme, using funds provided by the Social Sciences and
Humanities Research Council of Canada.

McGill-Queen's University Press acknowledges the support of the Canada
Council for the Arts for our publishing program. We also acknowledge the
financial support of the Government of Canada through the Book Publishing
Industry Development Program (BPIDP) for our publishing activities.

Library and Archives Canada Cataloguing in Publication

Tropes and territories : short fiction, postcolonial readings, Canadian
writing in context / edited by Marta Dvořák and W.H. New.

Some essays originally delivered as papers at the conference, Tropes and
territories, held at the Sorbonne Nouvelle, 2005.

Includes bibliographical references and index.
ISBN 978-0-7735-3289-2

1. Short stories, Canadian (English)—History and criticism. 2. Short
stories, Commonwealth (English)—History and criticism. 3. Canadian
fiction (English)—20th century—History and criticism. 4. Commonwealth
fiction (English)—20th century—History and criticism. I. Dvořák, Marta
II. New, W. H. (William Herbert), 1938–

PR9084.T76 2007   C813'.0109054   C2007-902619-2

Typeset in 10/13 Sabon by To The Letter Word Processing Inc.

Contents

READING PRACTICES: TROPES, TERRITORY, TEXTUALITY

RE-READING PRACTICES

Contributors

BRUCE BENNETT is professor of English at the University of New South Wales at the Australian Defence Force Academy campus in Canberra. A member of the Australia-India Council, he has edited ten collections of short stories and is adviser and contributor to the international Reference Guide to Short Fiction. His recent books include *The Oxford Literary History of Australia* (1998), *Australian Short Fiction: A History* (2002), and *Resistance and Reconciliation: Writing in the Commonwealth* (2003).

NEIL BESNER was the Seagram's Chair at the McGill Institute for the Study of Canada in 2001–2, and is currently associate vice-president, International, University of Winnipeg. The author of books on Mavis Gallant and Alice Munro, he has recently translated into English a Brazilian biography of the poet Elizabeth Bishop (2002). Other works include *Carol Shields, The Arts of a Writing Life* (2003), and a co-edited collection of essays on Canadian and Brazilian postcolonial theory (2003).

DIANA BRYDON is Canada Research Chair in Globalization and Cultural Studies at the University of Manitoba, where she teaches postcolonial literatures and theory. Interested early in concepts of expatriation in colonial and postcolonial fiction, she is currently studying global diasporas and the analysis of "travelling theories." A recent co-edited book, *Shakespeare in Canada* (2002), investigates national, regional, ethnic, and feminist appropriations of Shakespeare as an adaptable global icon.

FLORENCE CABARET is a lecturer at the University of Rouen. She has written on Salman Rushdie's novels and the question of the pragmatic status of fictional discourse, and is currently working on Indian literature and children's literature, with the figure of the story teller as the focal point of her study.

WARREN CARIOU is the author of one book of fiction, *The Exalted Company of Roadside Martyrs* (1999), and a prize-winning memoir entitled *Lake of the Prairies* (2002). He also writes criticism of Canadian Aboriginal literature, and teaches in the English Department at the University of Manitoba.

ISABEL CARRERA SUÁREZ teaches Canadian and Caribbean literatures and postcolonial theory at the University of Oviedo, and has published widely on the intersections of gender, postcoloniality, and genre, particularly on the short story. Her most recent books are *En breve: las mujeres del siglo XX en el relato de autoras anglófonas* (2005) and *Post/Imperial Encounters: Anglo-Hispanic Relations* (2005, coedited with J. Tazón).

GWENDOLYN DAVIES is dean of Graduate Studies and associate vice-president (Research) at the University of New Brunswick. A specialist in the literature of Atlantic Canada, she is the author of *Studies in Maritime Literary History, 1760–1930* (1991) and other books on myth, milieu, and literary style. A member of the editorial board of the History of the Book Project in Canada, and an adviser to the Canadian Poetry Database Project, she has also served as president of the Bibliographical Society of Canada.

TAMAS DOBOZY teaches 20th century Canadian and American literature at Wilfrid Laurier University. His first book of short fiction, *When X Equals Marylou* (2002), was followed by the highly praised collection *Last Notes*, published in Canada and the U.S.A. in 2005. His critical writings include studies of Mavis Gallant, Charles Bukowski, John Coltrane, and Philip Roth, and he is currently editing (with Brady Harrison) an issue of *Short Story* that focuses on fictional representations of Canada and the United States.

JEAN-PIERRE DURIX recently retired as professor of English at the Université de Bourgogne in Dijon, and as editor of *Commonwealth*. A specialist in postcolonial literature, he has published widely on Caribbean and South Pacific writings, and has translated into French several works by Wilson Harris, Witi Ihimaera, and Albert Wendt. Recent critical books include *The Writer Written* (1987), *The New Literatures in English* (1993, in collaboration with Carole Durix), and *Mimesis, Genres and Post-Colonial Discourse* (1998).

MARTA DVOŘÁK is professor of Canadian and postcolonial literatures at the Sorbonne Nouvelle, co-director of the Centre for Canadian Studies, and editor of *Commonwealth Essays and Studies*. Recent books include *Ernest Buckler: Rediscovery and Reassessment* (2001), *Thanks for Listening: Stories and Short Fictions by Ernest Buckler* (2004), *Vision/Division: l'oeuvre de Nancy Huston* (2004), as well as *Carol Shields and the Extra-Ordinary* (2007), co-edited with Manina Jones.

CHELVA KANAGANAYAKAM is Professor in the Department of English and also Director of the Centre for South Asian Studies at the University of Toronto. He has edited *Lutesong and Lament: Tamil Writing from Sri Lanka* (2001) and his books include *Structures of Negation: The Writings of Zulfikar Ghose* (1993), *Configurations of Exile: South Asian Writers and Their World* (1995), *Dark Antonyms and Paradise: The Poetry of Rienzi Crusz* (1997), and *Counterrealism and Indo-Anglian Fiction* (2002).

JANICE KULYK KEEFER is the author of more than a dozen works of poetry and prose, including *Marrying the Sea* (1998), *Travelling Ladies* (1992), and *Thieves* (2004), a novel based on the life of Katherine Mansfield. Winner of the 1999 Marian Engel Award and other honours, she teaches at the University of Guelph. Her critical works include a study of Canadian fiction from the Maritimes, *Under Eastern Eyes* (1987), a memoir of her Ukrainian family, *Honey and Ashes* (1998), and a book about Mavis Gallant.

CHRISTINE LORRE is assistant professor at the Sorbonne Nouvelle. Author of commentaries on the fiction of Clark Blaise, Carol Shields, and Nancy Huston, she specializes in Canadian and postcolonial literature, the short story, and writing by women and writers of Chinese heritage. Her work has appeared in such journals as *Etudes canadiennes* and *Journal of the Short Story*.

GERALD LYNCH teaches at the University of Ottawa, and is the prize-winning author of several works of fiction, which include the novels *Troutstream* (1995) and *Exotic Dancers* (2001), and two books of short stories (1989 and 1992). Author and editor of three works on Stephen Leacock, he has also edited *Dominant Impressions: Essays on the Canadian Short Story* (1999) and written an extensive study entitled *The One and the Many: English-Canadian Short Story Cycles* (2001).

LAURA MOSS is associate professor of English at the University of British Columbia, where she specializes in the interconnections between Canadian literature, postcolonial theories, and multicultural policies. The author of articles on Rohinton Mistry, Salman Rushdie, Zadie Smith, Chinua Achebe, and Antjie Krog, among others, she is also the editor of *Is Canada Postcolonial? Unsettling Canadian Literature* (2003) and of a scholarly edition of Frances Brooke's *The History of Emily Montague*.

W.H. NEW is University Killam Professor Emeritus at the University of British Columbia, and recipient of the 2004 Lorne Pierce Medal. Poet, critic, children's writer, he is the author and editor of over 40 books on Canadian and postcolonial writing. These include *Dreams of Speech and Violence* (1987), *Land Sliding* (1997), *Borderlands* (1998), *Reading Mansfield and Metaphors of Form* (1999), *Encyclopedia of Literature in Canada* (2002), *Grandchild of Empire* (2003), *Underwood Log* (2003), *A History of Canadian Literature* (2nd ed. 2003), and *Dream Helmet* (2004).

CLAIRE OMHOVÈRE is assistant professor of English at Université Nancy 2. She has published articles in numerous French and Canadian journals, and contributed chapters on the novels of Robert Kroetsch, Aritha van Herk, Thomas Wharton, Rudy Wiebe, and Anne Michaels to such publications as *When is the Prairies?*, *Writing Canadians* (2002), and *Lecture(s) du paysage canadien*. She is currently interested in investigating "Wandering Tropes," the connections between geography and Canadian culture.

LAURIE RICOU teaches at the University of British Columbia, is editor of *Canadian Literature*, and has published extensively on Canadian writing, as in *Everyday Magic* (1991), on child language and literature, and other books and essays. His most recent books, in which he turns to write eco-criticism, are *A Field Guide to "A Guide to Dungeness Spit"* (1997) and *The Arbutus/Madrone Files: Reading the Pacific Northwest* (2002). Related works entitled *Salal* and *Invader Species* are forthcoming.

ALEXIS TADIÉ is professor of British Literature at the University of Paris 7-Denis Diderot, and is currently director of the Maison Française, Oxford. His books include *Locke* (2000) and *Sterne's Whimsical Theatres of Language* (2003). He has also edited the works of Rudyard Kipling for Flammarion and Gallimard, and published articles on contemporary Indian literature in English.

ROBERT THACKER is professor of Canadian Studies and English and Molson Research Fellow at St. Lawrence University, Canton, New York. Editor of *The American Review of Canadian Studies* (1994–2002), he has contributed broadly to Canadian literary studies and especially to Canada–United States literary comparisons, as in *English-Canadian Literature* (1989, rev. 1996), studies of Willa Cather, Margaret Laurence, and Alice Munro, and *The Great Prairie Fact and Literary Imagination* (1989). His biography *Alice Munro: Writing Her Lives* appeared in 2004.

HÉLIANE VENTURA is professor of Canadian Literature at the University of Orléans. Her research focuses on connections between the verbal and the visual and on the rewriting of myths in contemporary short fiction. Author of studies of Margaret Atwood, Timothy Findley, David Arnason, and numerous other Canadian writers, she has co-edited proceedings from international conferences she co-organized on Word and Image, Robert Kroetsch, and the Invention of Tradition in Canada, Scotland, Ireland and Wales.

LYDIA WEVERS is director of the Stout Research Centre for New Zealand Studies at Victoria University of Wellington, chair of the trustees of the National Library, and a member of the Arts Board of Creative New Zealand. A longtime short story specialist, she wrote "The Short Story" for Terry Sturm's *Oxford History of New Zealand Literature in English* (1991, 1998) and has edited several anthologies, especially of stories by Australian and New Zealand women. Other publications include *Country of Writing: Writing Travel and Travel Writing About New Zealand* (2002), *Travelling to New Zealand* (2000).

MARK WILLIAMS is associate professor at the University of Canterbury, where he teaches New Zealand literature, the modern novel, and the literature of terror. His publications include *Leaving the Highway* and *Patrick White* (1993), "Literary Criticism, Theory and Scholarship" in the *Oxford History of New Zealand Literature in English* (1998), and numerous editions: *The Radical Imagination: Lectures and Talks by Wilson Harris* (1992), *Opening the Book* (1995), *Terror and Text: Representing Political Violence in Literature and the Visual Arts* (2002), *and Writing at the Edge of the Universe* (2004).

Acknowledgments

The editors wish to express their appreciation to Shelley MacDonald Beaulieu, for her care with the typescripts, and to Philip Cercone, Joan McGilvray, and their colleagues at McGill-Queen's University Press for their guidance through the publishing process.

We also wish to thank all those who helped organize the international "Tropes and Territories" conference at the University of Paris III (Sorbonne Nouvelle) in April 2005, on which the current volume is based, especially Christine Lorre and Agnès Vérè for their time and care, and the group of enthusiastic students whose tireless help with daily arrangements proved invaluable. We are also indebted to the Sorbonne Nouvelle, the Centre d'Etudes Canadiennes de Paris III-Sorbonne Nouvelle, the Canadian Embassy, and the Canadian government, who helped with financial and logistical support; to David Arnason, who (with the help of Marie-Christine Lemardeley and Denis Keen) led an ancillary writing workshop for students at the Sorbonne Nouvelle, and who creatively engaged all the participants in thinking about writing; and to the short story writers whose spirited readings added an extraordinary dimension to the critical discussions: Kristjana Gunnars, Janice Kulyk Keefer, Warren Cariou, Tamas Dobozy, David Arnason, and Mavis Gallant. We are especially grateful to Mavis Gallant for her unforgettable generosity with words, wit, laughter, and time, which will continue to be a source of inspiration to us all. We are grateful, too, to every one of the conference participants for the excellent papers that they presented and for their lively discussion; we regret only that not all the participants could be represented here.

We also join with the contributors in extending our appreciation to the various research assistants who are mentioned separately in the

Notes; to Susan Holbrook, for permission to cite her poem "Constance Rooke..." in the essay by Diana Brydon; to Alistair MacLeod, for permission to quote from his personal communications with Gwen Davies, in the essay by her; and to the editors of *Canadian Literature* for their willingness to preprint Claire Omhovère's essay in issue 189 (Summer 2006).

MD & WN

TROPES AND TERRITORIES

MARTA DVOŘÁK AND W.H. NEW

Introduction, Troping the Territory

This collection of essays looks at the narrative and discursive paradigms of short stories, tales, and short fictions that have been written in postcolonial societies, where the genre of short fiction has enjoyed an atypically forceful canonical role. The book brings together the work of over twenty scholars from Europe, North America, and the South Pacific so as to investigate the practices of production and reception in post-imperial spaces, and to theorize on the relations between genre and space when both are perceived as peripheral. The hybrid forms of Canadian, Australian, and New Zealand writing, for example, demonstrate among other things that Indigenous traditions can dovetail with modernist and postmodern practices. But the patterns of composition that they reveal, and the patterns of interpretation that they invite, belong to an even broader critical and theoretical framework. Hence the writers assembled here engage not only with the textual practices of settler-invader societies but also with such issues as the connections between territory and writing, form and function, orality and scripturality, diaspora and home. By studying reading practices as well as textual practices, *Tropes and Territories* aims to elaborate a theory on the postcolonial story as a genre, at various intersections between aesthetics and politics. This book does not propose a unitary model of postcolonial criticism, but argues rather that the interaction amongst the essays will provide a sense of the current debates that bear on the status and the reading of the important genre of short fiction.

Providing the basis for this volume was an international conference held at the Sorbonne in April 2005, attended by a significant number of Canadian, Australian, New Zealand, American, French, and Norwegian writer-academics. Whether addressing critical and theoretical issues directly, or reading from their own or others' fiction, these contributors actively demonstrated how theory feeds textual practices and vice versa, how reading and writing inform each other. We have attempted to replicate this exchange here. For instance, this book investigates several particular textual strategies, but because questions of reception and interpretation interconnect with those of production, it also investigates how meaning is further shaped by cultural paradigms. The contributors to the book are specialists in short fiction, in all its variety, from the often byzantine long story to the prose poem, the vernacular anecdote, and the short-short-fiction which breaks with standard conventions of characterization and narrative line. Readers will consequently find under study the methods and effects of postmodern storytelling, the conventions of traditional storytelling in oral cultures, and also the tactical designs of pre-novel literary production. They will also find a reluctance to treat the postmodern and the postcolonial as simply oppositional binaries. For the writers of the essays collected here are aware of how persistently and effectively stories do cross from one culture to another and of how (sometimes unchanged, sometimes radically reformed for a different context or politics) they reach (or can reach) through history. They are aware also that the currents of critical and creative thought, whether aesthetic or epistemological, can be equally international, cross-cultural, and transhistorical. Hence the essays negotiate what Lydia Wevers identifies as the "shared effects, locations, preoccupations that touch on the territories of postcolonial and postmodern." These notions of difference (or "gap"), and therefore displacement but therefore also of potential overlap are discernible not only in the tropes that are under study, but also in the slippage of the very term "trope" itself. Interestingly, North American critics tend to ground their reading practices in the trope as topos, and explore the motifs of origins, of geographical dislocation, social deracination, or historical dispossession, rife in migrant or diasporic literatures. French critics, by contrast, see tropes as privileged sites of discursive displacement, rhetorical figures that slide and turn: these authors investigate the deviant torsion of irony and the simultaneous yoking and deferral of metaphor and metonymy, grounded in the apperception of the *same* in the *different*. In both cases, informed by a variety of approaches, *territories* prove to be landscapes of the mind, and tropes entail interstitial spaces where cultures and discourses interact.

Hence, while most of the papers at the *Tropes and Territories* conference looked at Canadian literary practice, they did not stop at the national boundaryline. As so often happens when writers get together – an experience we hope to recreate in this volume – discussion moved in multiple directions, always vigorously, often at once. Inquiries into the strategies of narrative texts, the character of oral storytelling, the nature of critical methods, and the implications of cultural theory all began to contextualize each other. Experience in one society led to discussion of parallel or differing issues in another. Writers connected; so did stories; and critical preoccupations began to enter into a dialogue. Our task as editors of this volume has been to suggest what some of these current preoccupations are, how they illuminate our understanding of the short story genre at the present time, and how they help us to read even more closely the history, the words, and the complex social resonance of narrative.

◆

This book comprises six critical sections. The dialectic opening section of critical commentary, entitled "Towards a Poetics of Postcolonial Short Fiction," embodies an implicit dialogue between Diana Brydon and Laura Moss. It is infused with the tensions that postcolonial short stories address or are expected to address, the friction that develops between writer, subject, and social context. Brydon sets out to read across globalization theory and literary studies, placing artistic production against what she terms its sociality, and investigating how stories function in relation to identity-construction and perceived truths. Laura Moss's essay addresses a set of related premises in a different way, critiquing postcolonial criticism and reading practices that are predicated on the socially transformative role of literature (viewed as a site of political engagement). Moss questions the prevalent urge to validate fiction by reading it sociologically or through the expectations of authorial/ethnic identity, and calls for writing and reading that look past political imperatives. The differing lenses of these two papers set the tone for the complexities that the ensuing discussions engage in.

The subsequent sections take up the ramifications of "tropes" and "territories" by looking at particular topics, sites, stories, and social assumptions. In the first of these sections, "Troping Space, Self, and Cultures in Time," a dialogue ensues between general propositions and specific examples. Five critics "place" the idea of territory and demonstrate a series of strategies of troping it, each relating to a different culture: India, New Zealand, Australia, Canada. Chelva Kanaganayakam develops a theory about the roots and characteristics of narrative practice in the Indian subcontinent. Lydia Wevers examines publishing practices in New Zealand, demonstrating how contemporary Maori and Pakeha writers understand and represent the notion of "place" differently, with implications for both narrative practice and social policy. Bruce Bennett surveys Australian narratives of place, showing how the troping of the land in Australian fiction changes over time (embracing the mythic, the documentary, the regional, the imaginary, the self-referential), but showing also how this preoccupation with place and space continues resonantly to evoke a particular social response. With the essays by Janice Kulyk Keefer, on Katherine Mansfield, and Robert Thacker, on Alice Munro, this section of the book turns somewhat away from social space in order to consider psychic, linguistic, and autobiographical space more, with Keefer probing the personality of self and its relation to reading, and with Thacker tracing the cumulative set of tropes that leads one writer to express her profound relation with a place she knows or comes to know as "home."

The four essays in section three, "Dis-placement and Literary Re-placement," consider some of the ways in which writers represent their personal experience of place and of changes in and to place. The focus here falls on Canada and India, and on the political, structural, and visceral interconnections among history, empire, memory, and language. Among these essays are Neil Besner's engaged response to Mavis Gallant and the textuality of conflict, and Florence Cabaret's discussion of the differing compositional strategies of Rohinton Mistry and Salman Rushdie, which works toward a theory of diaspora and reconnection. Other writers include Gwendolyn Davies, who demonstrates the importance of a Highland survival rhetoric in the stories of Alistair MacLeod; and Marta Dvořák, who shows how Emily Carr's metaphorical landscapes and rhetorical displacements trope the language of Empire and freedom, both social and personal. In all these instances, the writers are concerned not only to show how movement away from one place can lead to re-rooting in another, but also to show how language – the patterns of troping – constitutes one medium in which this change works itself out.

Section four addresses even further these questions of culture and form by turning to the contrasts between orality and scripturality and the continuing connections between them. Focussing on Alecia McKenzie's stories, Isabel Carrera demonstrates how feminist diasporic writing from the Caribbean uses oral speech and epistolary form subversively. Warren Cariou's essay speaks of the Métis Rigoreau or trickster stories and of their social, personal, and community implications.

Jean-Pierre Durix looks at the traces of Maori myth that function as tropes in some of Patricia Grace's stories as ways of affirming the presence of the myths and the ancestral past in the lives of those who live apparently fully in the present. Durix also shows how the critic's familiarity with these oral tales can extend the resonance of Grace's stories, and thus inform both the reader and the reading. Gerald Lynch argues that the short story cycle in Canada performs a kind of 'troping' function, demonstrating over time how relationships and understandings are less linear and uniform than they are serial, cumulative, and multifaceted. He argues further that Thomas King's use of this form embodies both a personal take on the world and the recurrent strategy of a society in place. Alexis Tadié looks at the stories of R.K. Narayan, demonstrating how South Indian oral tales constitute the background in the written forms that Narayan characteristically employs, and how the written tales therefore imply the existence of a village-in-place as the site of listening, with which some listener-readers can readily identify but to which the craft of the storytelling nevertheless gives others access.

The five essays in Section five demonstrate some of the reading practices that the questions involved in troping territoriality give rise to. This section reveals, in other words, the specifics of textuality as territory, with the work of eminent New Zealand, Australian, and Canadian writers all in evidence. Christine Lorre analyzes the work of Janet Frame, Claire Omhovère that of Alistair MacLeod, W.H. New that of David Malouf. Héliane Ventura traces Alice Munro's use of visual motifs, and Tamas Dobozy looks at Mark Anthony Jarman's verbal gestures, his paradoxes of principle and disengagement. Within this section, the range of texts and of critical practices begins to work out in a concrete way some of the issues that Diana Brydon and Laura Moss raise at the outset: the tensions between personal trauma and cultural history, between individual stylistic choices and the dimensions of education, between critical practice and critical expectation, text and context, what is said and what is implied, social barriers and social need.

The closing section, "Re-reading Practices," brings together two essays that look towards alternative ways of reading and thinking about postcolonial short fiction. In the previous section, Tamas Dobozy uses the word "spark" to epitomize a moment of recognition; the two essays in Section six pick up on this electric image to probe, once again, the disparities between the two critical positions with which this book

began. Reflecting on Mansfield and Witi Ihimaera, Mark Williams
questions the easy way in which inherited assumptions can come to
be accepted as "traditional" and the equally easy way in which the
practice of critical reading can be equated with a particular politics,
short-circuiting how to understand both people and texts; Williams
then goes on to show how Ihimaera's "Mansfield variations" are
neither facilely parodic nor slavishly imitative (as much critical commentary has averred) but, rather, reverberant – deliberate and highly
charged renderings of a conflicted loyalty. Laurie Ricou's essay takes
a different tack. Beginning by paying close attention to the specifics of
the word – especially the electrifying word "short" in the term "short
story" – he embarks on a set of only seemingly freeform variations
to reflect on what he calls a "botanics of story." In the process (connecting, interestingly, with the metaphysical botanical metaphors of
Emily Carr, discussed in Section three), Ricou reveals how a reader
might begin to appreciate the resonances of language in a postcolonial
world, and how to appreciate, through the medium of story, the intricate interconnections of the world at large. To appreciate the charge
of brevity. The magnitude of the moment. The "territory" of a single
image or a striking phrase. Out of the fragment, or in it, a glimpse of
something more.

◆

We invite readers, therefore, not only to learn from the individual essays collected here but also to engage with the recurrent questions
they ask, to read *across* the separate sections as well as within them, to
see how questions recur in variant forms, to see how critical practice
engages with history, memory, and cultural priorities – the variegated
"territories" of our title – and with the specifics of language, the literary "tropes" or "turns" that structure narrative texts and so direct (or
at least influence) narrative communication. The essays ask these questions in a variety of ways. Some (those by Diana Brydon and Laura
Moss, for example) are implicitly polemical reflections on the role of
the critic and the limitations and possibilities of criticism. Others begin inside the personal experience of the reader, as does Neil Besner's
anecdote about discovering Mavis Gallant, or Warren Cariou's
remembrance of stories told in his childhood. Considering the relation between Gallant and Katherine Mansfield, Janice Kulyk Keefer
insightfully traces the inchoate nature of "influence" in writing; yet

her essay does still more, for it also constitutes an eloquent extended footnote to the composition of her own novel *Thieves* (2004), itself based on episodes in Mansfield's life. Collectively, these essays not only consider the power of a personal response – of experience as a reader's context – they also draw attention to the relevance of life lived: the life of the author, whether in place (Alexis Tadié on R.K. Narayan, Jean-Pierre Durix on Patricia Grace, Gwen Davies on Alistair MacLeod) or out of place, or in another place (Florence Cabaret on Salman Rushdie and Rohinton Mistry, Robert Thacker on Alice Munro leaving and returning to Ontario). By extension, the "lives" of characters also come under examination, as when Héliane Ventura, Christine Lorre, and W.H. New consider the figures who populate the stories of Alice Munro, Janet Frame, and David Malouf, and when Marta Dvořák contemplates the textual Emily Carr.

The tensions that reverberate between stories and their cultural surrounds or that affect publication politics and critical notions of "standards" constitute yet another set of recurrent motifs, which might well be phrased as a series of questions. *What does "home" mean?* (Brydon's question, when she examines the implications of the term "domopolitics.") *Where is "home"?* (Robert Thacker's question about Alice Munro.) *When can a "history" be accepted as taking place in place?* (Bruce Bennett's commentary on Australian short fiction traces recurrent narrative patterns; Gerald Lynch argues for an historical relation between Thomas King's story cycles and those of Stephen Leacock and others; Alexis Tadié specifies how Narayan's South Indian village is particular and concrete.) *What is a "diaspora"?* (one of Chelva Kanaganayakam's and Isabel Carrera's questions).

Kanaganayakam goes on to trace the history of Indian storytelling, to argue that there are "subtextual fields" in narrative that supplement conventional strategies of short fiction, and that these constitute a way of coding an ontology of self, of a culture in place: the very idea of a "cultural context," he suggests, "implies a form of knowledge," and a subtext "suggests a kind of awareness or consciousness." Relatedly, Warren Cariou illuminates the cultural role (and force) of orality in Métis storytelling; Jean-Pierre Durix asks how Patricia Grace (sometimes directly, sometimes obliquely) alludes to Maori creation myths; and Alexis Tadié distinguishes between the local appeal of Narayan's stories and the "universal" nature, the international recognizability, of his character types. Investigating the political implications both of editorial decision-making and the choice and format of places of publication, Lydia Wevers clarifies some of the cultural assumptions that are built into contemporary Maori and Pakeha narrative patterns and some of the paratextual decisions that shape how they reach a readership. The Maori concept of *whanau* ("speaking place") is relevant here: writers and commentators alike write out of geographical place and also out of (personal, communal) social location. This notion of a "speaking place" overlaps, interestingly, with modern western theory, notably when the Russian Formalists identified the concept of an "enunciative position," or when structuralists and poststructuralists heuristically applied the notion to language and discourse analysis, and finally, when postcolonial critics such as Homi Bhabha popularized the term 'the third space of enunciation,' in which the translation of cultural differences unfolds. In line with this notion of a speech act which is deferred with respect to its object of representation, other critics demonstrate how contemporary writing (not necessarily with self-conscious "anxiety") builds upon previous paradigms, as when Neil Besner draws attention to the fact that the "act of memory" (in fiction as in life) *is an act* – a way of reading the past provisionally, of rereading it through its contemporary guises. Inheriting a history is one challenge, that is, of any version of "modernity." Mark Williams shows how a reading of Witi Ihimaera's *Dear Miss Mansfield* draws upon a familiarity with Mansfield's writing but is neither dependent on it nor resistant to it; rather, it brings into scrutiny the ways in which critics (as Williams phrases it) sometimes invest a particular author with the iconicity of a nation.

This question of nationality (and nation*alism*) in literature, and of the short story's connection with political issues, both specific and general, recurs here in a variety of ways. Is the short story an "elitist" form, perhaps? Or is this simply an elitist question, making general assumptions about relations between written language and lived life? Warren Cariou strongly affirms that in Métis societies, storytelling is "community work." Diana Brydon, commenting on the impact of globalization on story telling and story reading, affirms equally strongly that conventional boundary lines are, in the present day, recurrently being crossed or blurred. It becomes clear that there are many ways to "trope a nation" or to trope any configuration of territory; hence gender, family, self, society, hybridity, race, region, and other categories of organization all in due course turn into *both* trope and troped subject. Bruce Bennett comments on the endemic image of the "beach" in Australian writing, a site where two or more versions of power contest for precedence. Other critics focus more on metaphors of movement – kinesis as yet another trope: for an unstable (or at least moving) territory. The call to "read otherwise," or to "read the understory," or to understand the effects of seriation and interruption, or to seek the implications of covert metaphor can all be seen as ways still to affirm some sense of "meaning" in environments where conventional meaning might seem no longer to be relevant or accurate, or to have been lost.

Indeed, one of the most recurrent motifs here involves the tension between a desire for the past to be held onto and a desire to turn away from it towards something better, new, or preferred. Many of the narrative tropes that critics elucidate work to precisely this end: the beach in Australia, as Bruce Bennett analyzes it; the open field in the works of Emily Carr, as Marta Dvořák reads it – both critics asking who holds power and what kind of power can ever be held. While Bennett grounds his reading in the trope as topos, Dvořák explores the metaphor as the locus of rhetorical migration, an interstitial space where cultural discourses interact, providing a place from which both the exilic and the emergent can speak. Further instances of this tension between inheritance and change appear in the essays by Gwendolyn Davies and Claire Omhovère. Davies demonstrates how the "bardic power" in the work of Alistair MacLeod, the circularities of narrative, and the patterns of repetition, all articulate a lost and yet paradoxically continuing connection between Gaelic Scotland and the lives of contemporary Cape Bretoners. Omhovère reaches related conclusions, probing the impact of "refrains" – iteration and analogy – in MacLeod's narratives. Even a passage in one of Malouf's stories is relevant here, as in a scene where a boy turns away from his parents' romantic distortion of an old, elegant, and fictional Europe, in order to find his own life elsewhere.

Elsewhere: it is at once place, no place, a desire – or an imposed or chosen place or process or idea. It can also be configured as an alternative style or manner of shaping worlds into narrative and meaning. For instance, as Tamas Dobozy reads the stories of Mark Anthony Jarman, antinationalism becomes an alternative territory wherein to challenge the contemporary forms of power that go by the name of "the corporation"; Dobozy emphasizes that this is as much a linguistic territory as it is a broadly political one, and he goes on to elucidate how Jarman troubles the conventions of short story form in order to resist any easy absorption into a "corporate" mindset. *Bricolage* becomes the technique of choice. (As the stories of Thomas King also demonstrate – Brydon and Lynch both comment on his work – humour repeatedly functions not only to entertain but also to subvert.) In Jarman's stories, however, as Dobozy argues, the resistance is made more complex by the fact that his characters are beholden to the institutions and the language they make fun of; hence *cliché* in a Jarman story asks to be read not as a failure of language but as a self-reflexive comment *on* the failure of language. As with a number of the other essays in this book, therefore, Dobozy's discussion turns to the intricacies of text; in doing so, it does not turn away from its political implications but finds a way to include, develop, and reapply some of the techniques of close reading. This book thus insists on both the real world issues of postcolonial territories and on the force of the textual language that addresses, conveys, and critiques them.

Still other essays collected here look more closely, as did those of Dvořák and Lorre earlier on, at various forms of textual practice. Héliane Ventura not only analyzes but also theorizes the overlap between the verbal and the visual – the "logogram" – in the stories of Alice Munro; Florence Cabaret distinguishes between the role of metaphor and the role of metonymy in the short narratives of Mistry and Rushdie; W.H. New reads Malouf's ambiguously titled *Untold Tales* for its "understory," arguing that the book adapts conventional storytelling practices in order to affirm the power of recreation and *re*-invention in a world that has learned to celebrate mortality; and Gerald Lynch pursues the history and character of the short story cycle (especially in Canada) for its textual character and for its cultural implications. Such formal devices as interruption, allegory, circularity, and allusion all receive attention. And repeatedly, the interest in the rhetoric of taletelling returns to questions of *how we read, and why.* Alexis Tadié recounts the paradigm that Walter Benjamin uses to clarify two types of short story: the seaman story (the narrative of travel) and the tiller story (the narrative of home). Both forms (and many such stories are the topics of discussion in this book) lead the reader back to the world. To understand it, perhaps: the politics of engagement, the necessity of cultural survival, the challenges to literacy and orality alike. Or to appreciate one's place in it. New argues that mortality is Malouf's ongoing, indirect subject, that Malouf uses the paradigms of fairytale and heroic action less as models of human behaviour than as demonstrations of a misplaced notion of fixity. Human beings are individual. And one of the signs of human individuality is that people must deal with time. They change. Even their language changes. And so do their responses to narrative and silence.

◆

In 1994, the Canadian folk-rock performance group Moxy Früvous released a CD called *Bargainville*. One of the most popular songs on this album, "My Baby Loves a Bunch of Authors," is an anecdotal, comic rendition of a young man's distress that the "honey" he's trying to impress likes reading more than she likes *his* preference, dancing. It is a familiar trope. Here, however, division does not last. Counselling helps the couple, and the song ends up with the man affirming that they'll now be together "for ages," eating and sleeping and "turning pages." Yet before they reach this resolution, there is much angst to be got through, which a series of jocular rhymes manages somehow to turn into a contemporary comedy: "things that she says" rhymes with "García Márquez," "brought the cat would" with "Margaret Atwood," "needs a shave he's" with "Robertson Davies." More to the point, the "friction" between the man and the woman derives in part because "my baby's hooked on / short works of fiction." Which, in an indirect way, is the recurrent subject of this book. *Tropes and Territories* is concerned not so much with the power of singular comic rhymes but with the effects of literary form in general, not with the exclusiveness of reading but with the fascination that the short story exerts upon any attentive reader, not with the divisiveness that literature can introduce into relationships (though critics do read through differing and sometimes contradictory lenses, and will disagree) but with the tensions that short stories address, the friction that develops between writer and subject and social context, or between characters on the page, or in the simple and (therefore) complicated language of storytelling: what this tension implies, and why. The essays in this book consider all of these topics, with specific reference to short stories written in Canada, Australia, India, the Caribbean, and New Zealand, by writers who are aware of a postcolonial frame of reference. The writers behind "Moxy Früvous" are *not* here. But perhaps they could have been, both for the familiar social territory they covered in Bargainville, and for the tropes – the metaphors and other strategies of storytelling – by which they made it new.

Marta Dvořák and W.H. New

TOWARDS A POETICS OF
POSTCOLONIAL SHORT FICTION

LAURA MOSS

Between Fractals and Rainbows:
Critiquing Canadian Criticism

I began my presentation at the "Tropes and Territories" short story conference with the admission that I had written two papers. The first was the one I said I would write – comparing portraits of the everyday in stories by Rohinton Mistry and Eden Robinson. The second – the one I actually presented – came out of my own discomfort with the first. When I read my initial paper, I felt as if I had read it before. I recognized the *pro forma* nature of my original argument. The more I worked through my ideas about critical expectation, the more I found that I was deriving expectations about the stories from what I knew of the authors' biographies. I began, as I set the stories aside, to think about the problems of expectation and the ways in which readers from across Canada have used works by these authors as evidence for sociological and political claims as I myself was doing in the first paper.

There is a problem running through discussions of Canadian literature today. It is linked to a generation of Canadian scholars trained as postcolonialists, now facing the quick decline of postcolonial critical studies, who have (re)turned to Canadian literature as a site of social or political inquiry and engagement.[1] The problem is that reading practices are now heavily predicated on the expectation of an outcome that is socially transformative: literary study as social activism.[2] At the recent "TransCanada: Literature, Institutions, Citizenship" conference, Stephen Slemon began his position paper with the following assertion: "This meditation is grounded in the assumption that what energizes all of us at this conference is a shared commitment to carrying the work of literary critical practice forward to the project of progressive social transformation in both Canada and the world" (http://www.transcanadas.ca/slemon.shtml).[3] While I share Slemon's commitment to social transformation, I worry about what is lost when "literary critical" work is equated with what seems to be a mandated political perspective. Progressive social transformation in the context of TransCanada was highly correlated with the politics of race, institutional reform, and globalization, rather than, say, environmental activism, women's issues, anti-poverty struggles, terrorism, or engaging with the limitations of federalism. As an event meant to mark the state-of-the-field, the TransCanada conference was not concerned with individual texts or authors. But when literature did enter the discussion, the anticipated outcome of social transformation was consistently predicated on the political positioning expected of postcolonial authors.

Expectations based on presumptions about characteristics of authorial identity – whether that identity is defined primarily based on sex, religion, or geography – have long been part of Canadian literary discussions. Writers in Canada have often engaged with readerly expectation based on authorial position. Some writers have marked their awareness of expectation through parody. In her introductory remarks to a reading at the Harbourfront Reading Series in Toronto, Carōl Shields remarked on her frustration at the tendencies of critics to focus on the "ordinary" in her works. In response to this incessant focus she read "Soup de Jour," a story from *Dressing Up for the Carnival*. The parodic story begins:

> Everyone is coming out these days for the pleasures of ordinary existence. Sunsets. Dandelions. Fencing in the backyard and staying home. 'The quotidian is where it's at,' Herb Rhinelander wrote last week in his nationwide syndicated column. 'People are getting their highs on the roller coaster of everydayness, dipping their daily bread in the soup of common delight and simple sensation.' (155)

This is the playful beginning to a sad story about life, love, and obsessive counting. As in most of the other stories in this collection, Shields teases the conventions of ordinariness but she does not relinquish them. By the end of the story we still know all the ingredients required in the soup. By parodying ordinariness but not relinquishing it, Shields confronts the critical expectation that she writes women-centred stories about the quotidian – about something that "smashes" the "useful monotony of happiness" to use her own words from *Unless* (1). I wonder how generic expectation, around the short story for instance, is at least partially dependent on expectations about the author and how authors often sabotage such expectations, quietly or boomingly.

Another way of putting this is to ask why Shields had to protest that her work was indeed sometimes experimental and why a writer like Mistry has to be so emphatic about the ordinariness of his prose.

While the expectations around the work of Shields stem from expectations of gender, critical expectation also comes out of religious positioning, regional affiliation, and ethnic identification. For Shields, expectation means a stress on the everyday. For others, it is geographically determined: Jack Hodgins epitomizes writing from the west coast; David Arnason exemplifies the prairies; David Adams Richards embodies the Maritimes. Matt Cohen proposes, in conversation with Mervin Butovsky in *Other Solitudes*, that "Maybe one of the problems with literature in Canada is that writers are known for their roles rather than their books" (178). Cohen describes the response when he shifted "roles": going from writing about rural Ontario in the Salem novels to writing *The Spanish Doctor* and *Nadine*, about history and about Jewish characters. He also details how he was repeatedly asked when he was going to write Canadian books again. His point in this interview given over fifteen years ago is that *Nadine*, primarily set in Canada with a Canadian cast of characters, is as Canadian as *The Sweet Second Summer of Kitty Malone*. What is un-Canadian about *Nadine* and *The Spanish Doctor* in the 1980s is that they do not conform to expectation arising from Cohen's perceived role as a secular, or quietly Jewish, Ontario writer. The roles of the authors remain predictors of how they will be received. In order to correct such normative assumptions of Canadianness in the 1990s and into this century, critics have actively opened up definitions of "Canadian" by exploring smaller group affiliations.

Recently, in Canadian postcolonial frameworks, the emphasis on identity has centred on ethnicity. Approaching a text through the lens of a specifically ethnicized or racialized representation is the postcolonial version of the enduring trend in interpreting texts based more on who wrote them rather than what is written. Such an emphasis on authorial identity and ethnic-group history occurs particularly frequently with First Nations authors and first generation Canadians, especially those from the major diasporic groups in Canada. A popular approach is to read writers from such groups as engaging with their own marginality in their work, because of their cultural or racial background, without focusing much on the content of their stories, the position they actually hold in the Canadian literature canon, or their own assertions of artistic vision. This has led to Neil Bissoondath's facetious question:

"must declarations of life experience and affidavits of racial and ethnic composition now be submitted with novel manuscripts (not to mention with job or conference applications)?" (171).

Some authors seek roles and others have roles thrust upon them. Some writers, like Dionne Brand and Lillian Allen for instance, have well defined and well articulated political agendas that come out in their critical writing as well as their literary works.[4] Brand and Allen are vocal public intellectuals and artists working for social and political change. Their creative work is part of larger racial, sexual, and gendered emancipatory projects. It would be difficult to completely disentangle their critical work from their creative work or from their personal positioning within both. The genre crossing of these writers further helps to remind the reader of the entanglement of the personal in the literary and yet it also helps to distance the reader from a completely biographical, ethnographic approach. For instance, Brand and Allen variously illustrate the entanglement of ideas and imagination through generic crossovers: Brand's *A Map to the Door of No Return: Notes to Belonging* and *Bread Out of Stone,* and Allen's Dub CD *Revolutionary Tea Party* and essays like "Transforming the Cultural Fortress: Imagining Cultural Equity" confound generic expectation. Brand and Allen are vocal about their own subject positions, how they come out of their personal histories, and how their roles as writers are reflective of their communities' histories. They actively and strategically manipulate audience perception and therefore help to shape readerly expectations.

What about writers who do not want to engage with authorial expectation based on ethnicity? What kinds of roles/expectations are thrust upon them? Two writers who have been outspoken about how they are not trying to be "experts in race relations" are Robinson and Mistry (Mistry, cited in Kamboureli, 387). The work of both authors has invited a questionably welcome focus on their own personal history, ethnic identity, and group identification. Both *Traplines* and *Tales from Firozsha Baag* worry expectations of ethnic mapping from author to characters, and both texts have been read repeatedly as stories that illustrate the struggles of a community. The biographical stress comes with a critical desire to read the stories sociologically rather than as fiction and to read character development and recurrent tropes 'fractally' rather than individually.

A colleague recently introduced me to the mathematic concept of fractals in reference to Tom Stoppard's play *Arcadia*.[5] A fractal is a geometric shape that can be subdivided in parts, each of which is (at least approximately) a reduced size copy of the whole. Fractals are self-similar. This means that "a fractal looks the same over all ranges of scale" (Connors). Independent of scale, a fractal can store, in a small space, photographic quality information derived from a much grander space. Particularly perhaps because of the economy of the form, it seems that the short story invites the reading of a small version representing a larger whole. Fractals also seem a fitting metaphor for recent trends in criticism of stories by writers whose ethnicity is highlighted in the interpretation of their texts. And still, fractals are everywhere in postcolonial Canadian criticism. Whereas with synecdoche, the part *stands* for the whole, with fractals the part *is* the whole. In recent criticism, stories are often interpreted as fractals of whole communities within a nation replicating with self-similarity. The problem is with the simplicity of the articulation of the individual, the ethnic community, and the nation that such an approach is predicated upon.

Reading fractally leads to what I consider to be several types of misreading. First, when a story is read primarily through the author's identity and then related to the author's ethnic community, the emphasis is often on the text as a kind of documentary of diasporic life rather than on the text as fiction. The author is read more as a cultural informant than as an artist. There is also a continuation of the intentional fallacy: where the author is read as intending to represent the community (either in support or in subversion). This is both demeaning to the art as art and demanding of the artist as informant. Second, there are misreadings of formal experimentation when the presence of gaps, temporal shifts, polyphonic narration, or innovative typography is viewed as an inevitable reflection of, for instance, the trauma of diasporic movement, gaps in public memory, or historical dislocation. Third, misreadings evolve when the loneliness/isolation/disenchantment/displacement of a character in a story is read fractally as the loneliness etc. of an entire community. The sadness of one is read as the replication of the sadness of many. Fourth, a fractalic emphasis on the sociology of a story leads to the loss of a sense of play, a sense of humour, a sense of art, and a sense of the ordinary. I believe that it is no longer true to say that mainstream Canadian writing is 'white' and that 'non-white' writers are marginal. However, I do think that there is a double standard of critical expectation where texts by 'white' writers might be read sociologically whereas texts by 'non-white' writers almost inevitably are read in those terms.

One form of reading sociologically is to read fiction as politically motivated fractalic case studies. The politics centre on a movement from the more traditional notions of Canadian literary nationalism into smaller group identifications. The premise is that First Nations, diasporic, or ethnically identified writers are part of a community, are a voice for the community, and therefore write about that community whether or not it is mentioned explicitly in their work. The text is read as a document whereby the reader from outside the community can learn more about that community, as though it exists as a homogenous whole, without actually visiting it, or the reader from inside can see herself reflected in it.

Reminiscent of Frank Davey's claim about thematic critics in *Surviving the Paraphrase*, contemporary postcolonial critics are sometimes more interested in what texts "say" about groups within Canada than what they are doing individually (Davey 3). Although the critical framework has shifted and my argument here is not with the thematic critics at all, Davey's scathing criticism of "bad sociology" still holds: "while the social scientist is content to describe society and predict the effects of specific events or interventions, [D.G] Jones attempts both to describe Canadian culture and prescribe how it should change. His sociology is extra-literary, normative, and polemic" (5). Now three decades later the nationalist aim of Jones, at least as configured by Davey, is no longer dominant. It has been replaced by an insistence on multiplicity or, as Imre Szeman points out, on an insistence on the unfeasibility of the nation. Szeman asserts that "the novels after 1967 reveal not characteristic qualities of Canadian culture and nation, but rather that the nation has disappeared, in other words, novels continue to be seen mimetically reflecting the national situation, even if what they reflect is that the 'national-ity' of this situation has been placed in jeopardy, if not dissipated entirely" (160).[6] Postcolonial critics often engage in criticism that is 'extra-literary, normative, and polemic' as they focus on the ethnicity of the author or her place of origin. Generally, they are not as interested in the unfeasibility of the nation in so much as they are interested in recognizing its very dissociated parts. One unity, Canada, has been replaced by another, the ethnic subject from a specific group within Canada. Although there is a pretense at specificity, generalities still predominate.

An over-emphasis on the ethnicity or personal history of an author often leads to the overly simplified pairings of literary theories with texts. The popularity of theoretical engagements with hybridity (through Homi Bhabha, Nikos Papastergiadis, and Robert Young etc.), diaspora (through Avtar Brah, Arjun Appadurai, Rajagopalan Radhakrishnan, Daniel and Jonathan Boyarin, and Stuart Hall etc.), and trauma (through Cathy Caruth, Judith Lewis Herman, Dominick LaCapra, and Sigmund Freud etc.), has led to a preponderance of mappings of hybridity, diaspora, and trauma theory onto texts. Criticism of Mistry's stories serves as an illustration here. *Tales from Firozsha Baag*, with the stories "Swimming Lessons" and "Squatter" in particular, is repeatedly read as a text articulating the third space of hybridity and the intricacies of diasporic movement. The argument almost inevitably rests on tracing the autobiographical elements of Mistry in his characters. Nilufer Bharucha's *Rohinton Mistry: Ethnic Enclosures and Transcultural Spaces*, for instance, begins with a long and interesting chapter on the Parsi diaspora. On the one hand, this is essential information to contextualize Mistry and his characters: particularly the tenants of Firozsha Baag. On the other hand, it leads to assertions about the characters' motivations and actions based on the author's heritage (because Mistry is Parsi, his characters act thus). There is a tendency for critics to collapse Kersi, from *Tales*, within the story and Mistry outside the story because both have travelled between an immigrant community in Ontario and a Parsi community in Bombay. Kersi/Mistry is read as embodying a version of Bhabha's third space of hybridity where he is *in* and *between* both India and Canada. In such a reading the character of Kersi is a fractalic embodiment of Mistry's own history, the history of the Parsis in India, and the history of South Asians in Canada. The critical trajectory is thus: from character to author to theory to society.

While Sharmani Patricia Gabriel points to the conjunction of the Canadian narrative and the Indian one in Mistry's work and thus tries to complicate notions of doubled diasporic movement as a complex mediation between "here" and "there," "present" and "past," she still relies on the identity of the author in order to make comments about the text. She cites Mistry from Smaro Kamboureli's headnote to "Swimming Lessons" in *Making a Difference*.

I think they feel that when a person arrives here from a different culture, if that person is a writer, he must have some profound observations about the meeting of two cultures. And he must write about multiculturalism. He has an area of expertise foisted on him which he may not necessarily want, or which may not necessarily interest him. (387)

Gabriel logically concludes that "what Mistry specifically objects to is the tendency to read multicultural literature through racial or ethnic labels affixed to its authors" (31). And yet although she notes its perils, she reads through the lens of authorial identity, when she reads the *Tales* as doubly diasporic stories that illustrate the issues of diasporic movement in the character of Kersi who "comes close to being the fictional equivalent of Mistry himself" (36). Gabriel concludes that the "strategy of narrative self-reflexivity destabilizes reader expectation; it undermines the distinctions between writer/text/reader" (36). Here is the clear connection between author, character, and community that I have been speaking of. By drawing Mistry into her argument, she almost inevitably enacts what she herself argues Mistry does not want enacted. Gabriel is in a difficult position here because she is stuck between respecting the autonomy of the artist and making a valid and important cultural point. Although I do not want to privilege Mistry's own reading of his work, I do think it necessary to listen to his frustration at what is clearly an expectation based on a trend in theoretical criticism. It is not so much the approach itself, but the predominance of the approach that has rendered it ineffective. Overuse has made the 'third space' argument and the doubleness of diaspora argument so predictable that they have lost the critical bite and political urgency that once accompanied them.

What such theoretical mappings also lack is an awareness of the humour in Mistry's stories. Take, for instance, the oft cited passage from the end of *Tales from Firozsha Baag*, in the story "Swimming Lessons":

> The last story they liked the best of all because it had the most in it about Canada, and now they felt they knew at least a little bit, even if it was a very little bit, about his day-to-day life in his apartment; and Father said if he continues to write about such things he will become popular because I am sure they are interested there in reading about life through the eyes of an immigrant, it provides a different viewpoint; the only danger is if he changes and becomes so much like them that he will write like one of them and lose the important difference.

This passage is often read as a commentary on the commercialism of immigrant narratives and the problems of assimilation. It is also a very funny passage in which Mistry anticipates the critical desire to read the story as representative of the life of an immigrant by gently ridiculing the reading practices of the parents. Throughout the story there is a Socratic dialogue between the parents. While the mother responds to her son's stories with emotion, the father responds with intellectual engagement. Mistry is satirizing both types of readers. He is challenging the readers outside the text to read beyond the autobiographical as the readers within the story do. While I am not advocating reading the story as a romp through Don Mills and I recognize that Mistry's satire often has political implications (think of the portrait of a Multiculturalism Directorate with devices to enable assimilation into Canadian society through eating Wonder Bread in "Squatter"), I am noting that criticism derived from expectations based on the author's identity or theoretical trends tends to ignore elements in which the author is playing, experimenting, or drawing on literary precedent (satire in this case).

Theoretical approaches are not alone in producing critical expectation. Marlene Nourbese Philip points out that "questions of community raise complex issues of audience and conflicting values for immigrant and minority writers in Canada. If writers shape community values, they are also shaped by them in nurturing and imprisoning ways" (cited in Dawson and Stone, 57). Although Philip concentrates on the choice of compositional language for the immigrant writer, the paradox of nutrition and confinement also holds for authorial expectations –what to write and who to speak for. These expectations, Philip points out, come from both inside and outside an author's ethnic community. Similarly, Arun Mukherjee notes the negative response from a "South Asian Canadian women's group" for "betraying the community by being negative about one of 'our' writers" when she criticized *Such a Long Journey* for sexist portrayals of women (37). She writes: "what I am pointing out is the phenomenon where the writer becomes either an icon of community pride or a target of community anger" (37). To realize the variations of expectations placed on a writer and a text, one need only think back to the criticisms of *Running in the Family* as romanticizing Sri Lanka/Ceylon and the question of Michael Ondaatje's responsibility to Sri Lankan politics that played out with South Asian Canadian and non-South Asian Canadian critics alike in the 1980s. There was more criticism of Ondaatje from within the Sri Lankan Canadian community than from without because he was seen to have shirked his responsibility to take a stand in a volatile political context. For Philip "there is also the 'nostalgia factor' and its conundrums for immigrant writers to negotiate" (cited in Dawson and Stone, 58). She continues, "their own cultural communities can be so starved for anything evocative of 'home' and the valuing of its traditions that artists can be constrained by the pressure to meet such expectations" (cited in Dawson and Stone, 58). I read these expectations as enacting a kind of communal ownership and valuation as well as creating an imagined community. As Mukherjee points out, communal expectation can lead to celebration for fulfilling a role, or it can lead to condemnation for failing to fulfill a role leading to an expected outcome.

Eden Robinson's work also invites speculation based on her refusal to conform to expectation determined by her identity as an Haisla author. Cynthia Sugars notes that "numerous critics have pointed out how difficult it is to pinpoint the racial identity of Robinson's characters, or how, in some cases, she only subtly hints at their aboriginal and/or white identity" (79). Sugars cites Robinson's statement in an interview that she strategically withholds identity markers because "she does not want to be pigeon-holed as a Native writer, someone who *must* write about Native issues only" (80). In a footnote, Sugars expands on her reasons for exploring "Dogs in Winter" partially through the identity of the author: "there are enough details in the text to support an interpretation of Lisa and Mama as aboriginal, and of course, Robinson's aboriginal ancestry, combined with the subject matter of her other writings, cannot help but influence one's interpretation. When an aboriginal author uses motifs of savagery, they carry extra cultural weight" (89). She is right. In the current theoretical and political climate, one can not help but take these contextual facts into account. Her argument rests on the vital note that whether or not the characters in the story are "identified as Native," Robinson is "appropriating" the expectations of savagery "conventionally assigned to Native peoples and reworking them here" (89). This is another prime example of an author playing with readerly expectation. Sugars persuasively argues, "Readers, then, are challenged to sort out the racial/cultural identity of her characters, and are in a sense led to enact their own performances of colonialist violence on the texts" (80). But I wonder what it is that compels us to sort out the racial or cultural identity of the characters in Robinson's stories. The answer lies with a linking of critical expectation based on authorial identity and an expected socially transformative outcome.

Many postcolonialists in Canadian criticism today find themselves between a rock and a hard place. It is the challenge that we all face as responsible critics: struggling to do justice to the context of a work – to the socio-cultural framework of a text – but not to provide an over-determined reading based on that context. The struggle sometimes leads to two of the shortcomings of contemporary postcolonially-inflected criticisms of literature: that is to read fiction as a case study of sociology and/or to read it through the expectations of authorial identity. Since these shortcomings are so prevalent, it is useful to hypothesize where they might come from. First, there seems to be a desire to make literary discussions relevant in light of the Social Sciences and Humanities Research Council of Canada (SSHRCC) restructuring and valorizing of the 'human sciences' over the arts. Reading sociologically validates reading in a politically fraught climate where literature departments are trying to maintain relevance within the wider framework of institutional restructurings. This shifting institutional framework was the focus of the most productive criticism at the TransCanada conference. Critics have constructed links between literary texts and social ones to show the literary as contributing politically, and importantly, to the social. Literature is relevant as a marker of culture and community. It is important that this is never forgotten. Second, the emphasis on authorial identity comes out of the need to validate a range of writing by a range of writers in order to make sure that the canon keeps evolving in its diversity and show that it is becoming more representative of Canadian demographic shifts of the past few decades. Third, there is a recognition of how dynamic Canadian literature is and there is a need to disconnect contemporary literature from a nation-focused version of Can Lit. In this case, Canadian literature reflects a multiplicity of communities rather than a singular national entity. Fourth, there is a worry about depoliticizing or decontextualizing a text without a thorough treatment of the author's background: a very real worry about an assimilationist kind of reading where stories are judged on the basis of artistic merit alone. The very reasonable quests for relevance, validation, recognition, and politics have led to a crisis in criticism, however, in my own work and in the work of others, because they have cut short other kinds of conversations about some exciting and important works of literature.

So, if I think there is a problem, what do I think we should do about it? When interviewed, many writers discuss how there is both a pressure on them to write about racial or ethnic "topics" and a clear prevalence of what Albie Sachs, in the context of South African anti-apartheid protest writing in 1990, but also relevant here, dismissively calls *solidarity criticism* or criticism that fails to look past the politics of a work of literature, or beyond the author's identity, to allow for artistic freedom. After nearly a decade of living in a State of Emergency and after more than forty years of apartheid practices, Sachs proposed, albeit somewhat tongue-in-cheek, a ban on "saying that culture is a weapon of struggle" for "a period of, say, five years" because such an approach to art both detracted from the art being produced and from the struggle (19). I am tempted to say that a similar moratorium in postcolonial Canadian criticism might lead to better criticism and to better art – art that is approached without readerly expectations. However, in order to get away from the confines of expectation, I wonder if too much would be lost if we were to take the political imperative off the table for a short while. What if we were to read blind in the same way that refereed journals provide blind reviews of articles to help with impartiality? Is this possible or productive? Is this suggestion too contradictory for someone who holds that literature is highly socially relevant and who tries to attend to literary, historical, social, and political context in her own reading. It might be, but it is also crucial to think about what would be gained if we were to approach a text through the text itself rather than through the role of the author.

Am I again siding with Davey from *Surviving the Paraphrase* where he calls for criticism that attends "specifically to that ground from which all writing communicates and all themes spring: style, structure, vocabulary, literary form, and syntax – of writing" (7)? No, not only that. I would like critics to attend to such formal "ground," while at the same time remembering the context of a work. It should be important to read literature closely in order to join context and content. By context, I also want to go well beyond authorial identity and social impact to consider such things as the text's historical context, the literary history surrounding a genre or a theme, the location in time and space of the text's production, the foci of the text's marketing, and its critical reception. I want to disentangle the expectations arising from the authorial, and the political, and the social context of a work of fiction from the work itself. I want to have literary critical practices that are socially transformative at the same time as I want there to be room for literary critical practices that look at such things as animals in literature, various modes of storytelling, gothic haunting, or even short stories.

Marlene Goldman, at the TransCanada conference, argued in her presentation that "While I am not suggesting that the author is dead, I do feel that attempts to essentialize and identify the authenticity of the diasporic subject/author are less valuable than attempts to attend to diasporic narratives." Therefore, for instance, Jane Urquhart's *Away* fits within what she calls a "hermeneutics of diaspora." I like this solution. Goldman's response to a search for authenticity is much like my own response to what I see as reading literature in search of social truth claims. When expectation is based on the author's identity, it is limiting because the work of fiction is too often read as the "true" story of a community. Such a critical desire for truthful representation or a need for authenticity is fractalic, where the part *is* the whole.

The multiplicity of truth is missed in the search for socially representative authenticity. Although it was written in a dramatically different context, perhaps we can again turn to South Africa and look to the report of the South African Truth and Reconciliation Commission for another reading approach. Deborah Posel notes how the report deals with the complexity of competing testimonies by creating a "rainbow of truths" (154). The "solution in the report is to differentiate between four notions of truth: factual or forensic truth; personal or narrative truth; social or 'dialogue' truth ... and healing and restorative truth" (154). The Commission thus distinguishes between the truths of stories, memories, communities, and the truths of facts. Posel criticizes the Commission's attempt at qualifying truth, arguing that the "grounds for differentiating the four types of truth are poorly specified and remain largely opaque" (155). Still, the concept of a multiplicity of different types of truths is a valuable starting point for acknowledging the roles that stories play in social and individual interactions.[7] Just as there are different types of truths, there are different roles stories and storytellers play. The same, I hope, might be said for contemporary readers and postcolonial critics.

NOTES

1   While this paper is not meant to be read as confessional, I am among the postcolonialists I refer to. I direct my criticism at myself as well other postcolonial scholars. I wish to thank Diana Brydon, Héliane Ventura, Travis.V. Mason, Tunji Osinubi, Gillian Jerome, and John Moss for helpful feedback on versions of this paper, and Marta Dvořák and Bill New for their editorial guidance.

2   This is not to undermine the value of interdisciplinary approaches to literature. I am not talking about the very valid intersections between soci-

ology and literature, such as the kind of research that looks at public arts policy and sees the effect on literary production and cultural formation. This is also not to say that there are not instances when fiction is used to illustrate a sociological point. In "Fiction in the Scientific Procedure," Erna Brodber, a sociologist by training, states that her novel *Myal* is a fictional case study of the dissociative personality. Brodber asserts that her fiction writing is a means of filling the void in information on Caribbean history: "I must fill this gap in a way that the findings [can] be immediately translated into action" (165). But whereas Brodber is explicit in linking spirit thievery with colonialism, the link between incidents in a story and incidents in an author's personal or ethnic history is not always evident.

3   The "TransCanada: Literature, Institutions, Citizenship" Conference co-organized by Roy Miki (SFU) and Smaro Kamboureli (Guelph) was held at The Morris J. Wosk Centre for Dialogue, Simon Fraser University, June 23–26, 2005. The conference was organized to go "beyond the troubled legacy of nationalism, the domestication of the postcolonial, and an acquiescent engagement with globalization." See www.transcanadas.ca for position papers and on-going dialogue.

4   Interestingly, Bissoondath's comment above is in direct response to his citation of Brand's criticism of him for "validating Eurocentric discourse" in his portrayals of "women and blacks" (168).

5   Thanks to Christina Lupton for introducing me to fractals in reference to *Arcadia*.

6   Robert Lecker is more direct: "Today we seldom see examples of Canadian literary criticism that actually suggest a relation between the literature and the country. In fact, the very suggestion is often treated as a sign of bad taste, mainly because it is rooted in the disgraced mimetic assumption that literature reflects life or in assumptions about the relation between literature and culture that are rooted in Arnoldian humanism" (12).

7   In *Country of My Skull*, Antjie Krog outlines how the first independent body formed after the 1994 democratic election in South Africa was the Truth and Reconciliation Commission. Created by an Act of Parliament known as the National Unity and Reconciliation Act, the TRC was a legislated attempt to redress gaps in public knowledge and memory. In total, close to 21,000 statements from victims of Human Rights violations – defined by the Commission as murder, attempted murder, abduction, torture, or severe ill treatment – and their families were submitted to the Truth Commission and over 7,500 people applied for amnesty. See

my "'Nice Audible Crying': Editions, Testimonies, and *Country of My Skull*" (*Research in African Literatures* 37.4 (2006): 87-104) for a more detailed discussion of the problems of the TRC and Krog's mixed genre representation of it.

WORKS CITED

Bharucha, Nilufer. *Rohinton Mistry: Ethnic Enclosures and Transcultural Spaces.* New Delhi: Rawat, 2003.

Bissoondath, Neil. *Selling Illusions: The Cult of Multiculturalism in Canada.* Toronto: Penguin, 1994.

Butovsky, Mervin. "Interview with Matt Cohen" in *Other Solitudes: Canadian Multicultural Fictions.* eds. Linda Hutcheon and Marion Richmond. Toronto: Oxford University Press, 1990: 172-178.

Connors, Mary Ann. "Fractals." http://www.math.umass.edu/~mconnors/ fractal/fractal.html, accessed March 28, 2005.

Davey, Frank. *Surviving the Paraphrase.* Winnipeg: Turnstone, 1983.

Dawson, Carrie and Marjorie Stone "The Art of the Possible: Literature, Citizenship and Canadian Multiculturalism in a Global Context" *Canadian Diversity.* 2:1, (Spring 2003): 56–59.

Gabriel, Sharmani Patricia. "Interrogating Multiculturalism: Double Diaspora, Nation, and Re-Narration in Rohinton Mistry's Canadian Tales." *Canadian Literature* 181 (Summer 2004): 27–41.

Goldman, Marlene. "The Cultural and Textual Politics of Canadian Anthologies in a Diasporic Age," *TransCanada, Literature, Institutions, Citizenship* Conference. Simon Fraser University, 2005.

Jameson, Fredric. "Third-World Literature in the Era of Multinational Capitalism." *Social Text* 15 (1986): 65–88.

Kamboureli, Smaro. *Making a Difference: Canadian Multicultural Literature.* Toronto: Oxford University Press, 1996.

Krog, Antjie. *Country of My Skull: Guilt, Sorrow and the Limits of Forgiveness in the New South Africa.* New York: Three Rivers Press. 2000.

Lecker, Robert. *Making It Real: The Canonization of English-Canadian Literature.* Toronto: Anansi, 1995.

Mistry, Rohinton. *Tales from Firozsha Baag.* London: Faber and Faber, 1992.

Mukherjee, Arun. *Postcolonialism: My Living.* Toronto: Tsar, 1998.

Posel, Deborah. "The TRC Report: What Kind of History? What Kind of Truth?" *Commissioning the Past: Understanding South Africa's Truth and Reconciliation Commission.* Deborah Posel and Graeme Simpson. eds. Johannesburg: Witwatersrand University Press (2002):147-72.

Robinson, Eden. *Traplines*. Toronto: Knopf, 1996.

Sachs, Albie. "Preparing Ourselves for Freedom." *Spring is Rebellious: Arguments About Cultural Freedom by Albie Sachs and Respondents*. Eds. Ingrid de Kok and Karen Press. Cape Town: Buchu Books, 1990. 19–29.

Shields, Carol. *Dressing Up for the Carnival*. Toronto: Vintage, 2001.

– *Unless*. Toronto: Vintage, 2002.

Slemon, Stephen. "TransCanada, Literature: No Direction Home" http://www.transcanadas.ca/slemon.shtml, accessed June 29, 2005.

Sugars, Cynthia. "Strategic Abjection: Windigo Psychosis and the "Postindian" Subject in Eden Robinson's "Dogs in Winter." *Canadian Literature* 181 (Summer 2004): 78- 91.

Szeman, Imre. *Zones of Instability*. Baltimore: Johns Hopkins University Press, 2003.

DIANA BRYDON

Storying Home: Power and Truth

In many ways, home is an image for the power of stories. With
both, we need to live in them if they are to take hold, and we need
to stand back from them if we are to understand their power. But
we do need them; when we don't have them, we become filled with
a deep sorrow. That's if we're lucky. If we're unlucky, we go mad.
(Chamberlin 77)

The Oscar-nominated *Hotel Rwanda* is one of several movies and
novels about the genocide. But is it fair to reduce events of such
magnitude to a single dramatic entertainment? Can telling a story
ever be the same as telling the truth? (Jason Cowley, *The Observer*,
Sunday, February 27, 2005)

The tension between these two epigraphs frames my paper. "Home
is an image for the power of stories" (Chamberlin). "Can telling a
story ever be the same as telling the truth?"(Cowley). What links
home, story, and truth? Can we assume that truth is singular, or that it
can be reduced to mere information only, as Jason Cowley's comments
seem to imply? Surely postcolonial literature tells us otherwise. How
do power, conflict, and the search for truth meet in story, especially
in postcolonial and globalizing contexts?[1] Conventional short story
theory and criticism provide little help in answering such questions. In
privileging the formal properties of the short story in its written forms
and in developing modes of thematic analysis, short story criticism has
not addressed the larger properties of story with which Chamberlin
seeks to engage. My approach therefore finds more support in Deepika
Bahri's chapter, "Geography is not History: The Storyteller in the Age
of Globalization," the concluding chapter of her *Native Intelligence*
(200–46). I will explore the implications of Bahri's endorsement of

Adorno's notion that in thinking philosophically about aesthetics, "it is the status of artistic production *in a dialectic with its sociality* that must command our attention (204–05). For Bahri, such a process involves modifying Walter Benjamin's European understanding of modernity and tradition as presented in his essay "The Storyteller" and elsewhere, through opening a dialogue between such canonical formations and postcolonial alternatives. My interest lies in bringing contemporary Canadian feminist and indigenous short story practices and theories of story into dialogue with globalization studies, including contemporary postcolonial theorizations of planetarity as an alternative mode of what I am calling "storying home."

This paper asks what happens when you bring these two worlds, of the social-scientific and the literary-creative imaginations, into dialogue. I suggest that feminist political scientist Bonnie Honig and creative writer Salman Rushdie not only illuminate each other but push our understanding further when brought together in this way.[2] Similarly, Alice Munro's "Runaway" and Margaret Atwood's "Faster" provide valuable correctives to the analysis of Anthony Giddens in *Runaway World*. In framing my project around this dialogue, I hope to illuminate the relation between short story and story, placing this discussion within the larger context of postcolonial reconsiderations of the legacy of modernism and focussing on some of the ways in which contemporary appeals to story move beyond the modernist aesthetics of the short story form as perfected by writers such as Poe and Mansfield.

In thinking about the postcolonial short story through "tropes and territory," my argument here derives from a larger project on imagining home. Home is a concept that globalization has pushed to the fore in ways that have encouraged social scientists to address these questions through coining new terms such as domopolitics (Walters on the politics of home) and domicide (Porteous and Smith on the deliberate killing of home) and through reading political arguments through literary frames, as Bonnie Honig does in *Democracy and the Foreigner*. Writers work through evoking powerful symbols from popular culture, as Salman Rushdie does in "At the Auction of the Ruby Slippers," or elliptically, through evoking actions from the everyday, as Alice Munro does in "Runaway." But whatever the generic mode of engagement, reimagining home is part of what is at stake in globalization. It has implications for how tropes and territory are understood in every dimension of human activity. My concern in this paper is with the role of stories in naming and embodying home. If home is an image for the power of stories, what kind of image will it be? William Walters coins the term, domopolitics, to describe the dangerous trend toward "a reconfiguring of the relations between citizenship, state, and territory. At its heart is a fateful conjunction of home, land and security. It rationalizes a sense of security measures in the name of a particular conception of home" (241). The stories of domopolitics circulate as a "common sense" of our times. The stories told in literature may confirm or trouble such notions.

Domopolitics create an ideological space with implications for the kind of civic society that can be imagined within communities and nations and across the world. By mapping the threatened bourgeois nuclear family onto nation as the image of home, domopolitics naturalize stories of threat in which anxious citizens seek security through shutting out the unfamiliar, including immigrants, building walls and seeking refuge from the world in an illusory private sphere while at the same time directing this quest for security outward into taming and conquering what lies beyond this controlled space. Postcolonial imaginings of planetary community, such as those advocated by Paul Gilroy and Gayatri Spivak, devise an alternative to domopolitics by refusing to accept its founding premises. Instead, they reimagine home *and* the stories with which it is associated. Spivak proposes "the planet to overwrite the globe" (72) as a way of bypassing globalization's claims to the tropes and territory of inevitable progress through positing conquering as the only mode of inhabiting the earth. For this reason, she claims that planetarity "is perhaps best imagined from the precapitalist cultures of the planet" (101), not in a spirit of nostalgia for what has been lost (as in Benjamin's "Storyteller"), but as a way of keeping "responsibility alive in the reading and teaching of the textual" and a way of inscribing what she cryptically terms "responsibility as right" (101–02). Spivak seeks a mode of reading that can counter globalization as "a time and place that has privatized the imagination and pitted it against the political" (37–38). Domopolitics is a term that nicely captures this dimension of globalization: its capacity to expand privatization into the most intimate spheres so that the political itself is transformed and shrunk. To counter the assumptions of the domopolitical, this essay employs strategies described by Spivak as "reconstellation" (91) and recasting women not as a "special case" but as representing the human (70); in other words, by employing "gender as a general critical instrument" (74). This is important because domopolitics often reinforces patriarchal as well as ethnocentric values, mapping the hierarchies of a particular kind of home onto the nation.   -

Just as imperial strategies of ordering, classifying, naming, and judging delegitimized indigenous namings of home, territory, and community, so they also devalued, deformed, and bowdlerized indigenous story. Literary studies, in its late twentieth-century aspirations toward achieving a scientific status for its discipline, continued such imperial strategies by other means. Nationalist literary criticism is not exempt from such temptations. Neither is the diasporic. Teachers of English need to ask: what is being done in the name of our discipline and our nation? Postcolonial fiction and criticism have a role to play in reclaiming tropes and territory for a planetary imagination that reimagines home, releasing it from the defensive narrowing of possibilities provided by domopolitics into a respect for different modes of belonging to the world and inhabiting space and time. Postcolonial theorists know that how to inhabit the world as home and how to inhabit stories are related challenges. Beyond the indirections of story, we may not yet have the resources to express this relation.

Alice Munro suggests that for her, reading a story is more like inhabiting a house than following a road (1982: 224). These differently oriented processes remind us that home is always a contested term. Domopolitics shift how the space of the house and the national home are experienced and narrativized. In defining the short story as an imaginative construction, which shapes "the elements of experience into an artful composition," the *Harper Handbook to Literature* notes that "Often it imitates the texture of ordinary life close to home" (432). In Munro's short stories, the texture of ordinary life close to home explodes the lies of the domopolitical-- and related critical attempts to define the constituent elements of the "artful composition." Objecting to J. Hillis Miller's confidence that "'in fictions we order and reorder the givens of experience,'" Aritha Van Herk queries what these givens might be, asking: "Are they doing what they pretend they're doing: in either life or fiction?" (102). For Van Herk, the link between domopolitics and generic prescription is clear and must be contested. "I want to explode writing as prescription, as a code for the proper behaviour of good little girls," she writes (131). The policed boundaries of gender and genre lead her to desire the "story ungoverned" (103) and to cast the fictioneer as "an outlaw of words, on the lam and on the run" (14). Is this just a feminist version of romantic orthodoxy, or could it also be intuiting, as Spivak hopes, that "Literature is what escapes the system; you cannot speed read it" (52). Although Munro seldom makes comments as explicit as Van Herk's, her work also seems to question the givens of experience and the rules for narrating these. If Spivak is correct in suggesting that Literature cannot be controlled by the domopolitical urge to police boundaries, then what is the role of the literary critic? Too often, it has been to redomesticate the story, locking it back into modes of diminishment.

This struggle, serious as it is, is delightfully enacted in Susan Holbrook's poem, "Constance Rooke, author of *The Clear Path: A Guide to Writing English Essays*, and Home Inspection Consultant Brad LaBute converse, with rude interruptions by Walt Whitman." A brief extract from the end of the poem makes my point:

> My criticism of Version 2 is not so much that the essay lacks a thesis
> And I know the amplitude of time.
> As that the implicit thesis is not sufficiently interesting from a literary point of view.
> Unscrew the locks from the doors!
> Unscrew the doors themselves from their jambs!
> The S-trap should be upgraded to a P-trap.
> The topic of this paragraph is love (70).

Here both technocratic and metaphysical prescriptions for the literary collide with the iconoclastic practice of the literary imagination itself. How does the literary critic unscrew the locks and reconnect analysis with imagination? At a time when home has become heavily overdetermined as a signifier of security, it is useful to remember the runaway in all its manifestations, not just the refugee seeking asylum but also those fleeing increasingly constricted notions of a privatized national home. This paper employs the trope of the runaway to complicate theorizations of story as home, such as Chamberlin's, which turn to indigenous theorizations of story but without incorporating a gendered analysis.

Home in the contemporary imaginary, as the narrator of Salman Rushdie's story, "At the Auction of the Ruby Slippers," complains, is a "scattered, damaged various concept" (93), now fetishized, sentimentalized, and commercialized, frozen into the form of Dorothy's magic slippers, locked "behind bullet-proof glass" (88). Rushdie's story illustrates the ways in which both sickness and cure for the maladies of home have been misdiagnosed through the rise of what Walters calls domopolitics. Walters states: "Whereas political economy is descended from the will to govern the state as a household, domopolitics aspires to govern the state like a home." For him, two conclusions follow. First, "domopolitics and liberal political economy exist in tension with one another." Secondly, and this is where my paper comes in, "we need new forms of comparison if we are to adequately map domopolitics" (237). I argue that those forms of comparison may be found through reading across the roles played by story in oral cultures, short fiction, political theory, and media imagery. These routes are being charted in the work of anthropologists, literary critics, feminist political theorists, and creative writers but little has yet been done to pull their insights together. How can we begin to read across globalization theory and literary studies? This paper tests one way in a very preliminary fashion.

It is my impression that much critical work devoted to the short story has been concerned with categorization and explication. In 1997, Susan Lohafer suggested that the field was moving away from asking what a short story is and what is allowable in the genre toward asking questions about how identity is constructed through the form and technique of the story (172). This paper tries to push further. What if we turn from the storyteller to the interactive contexts out of which the story is generated, not just at its first moment of production but also at each new reading?

In advocating such an approach, I wish to move beyond attempts such as Peter Stummer's, in *The Story Must Be Told: Short Narrative Prose in the New English Literatures* (1986), which seeks to remedy a lack of critical attention devoted to the postcolonial short story by identifying five aspects of what he terms a functional view: interpreting the story in the context of a collection or anthology; treating it as practice for writing a novel; focussing on the medium, such as a magazine, in which it appears; addressing situational factors such as oral traditions; and focussing on therapeutic functions, in which he includes what he terms both "private compensation and a political propaganda component" (8). W.H. New provides a more thoroughly elaborated and nuanced overview in *Dreams of Speech and Violence: The Art of the Short Story in Canada and New Zealand* (1987). He discovers three definitions by form (by length, by technique, and by type) and several by history and cultural origin. None of these are flexible enough to address the contexts that New sums up in the title of a later book, *Land Sliding*.

In *Dreams*, New concludes that "Each of the theoretical approaches that critics have taken ... is implicitly an appeal to authority and an appeal for order" (17). These appeals were the product of their times, representing the desire of former colonies aspiring to what Toronto now terms "world-class status" and the desire of literary critics to have their work accorded scientific status. As such, they work against the instincts of writers from many communities and against the recognition of alternative notions of story. Joy Asham Fedorick asserts that First Nations stories "do not necessarily have a beginning, middle and end ... Our stories," she says, "are not 'formula' oriented" (32–33). Teaching such stories in the classroom, I still encounter stubborn rejections of such texts from Honours English students who have learned the rules, are following the clear path, and will tolerate no deviance from it. This despite the insistence of writer-critics such as John Metcalf, who notes: "The old high school division into plot, characters, setting and theme are false divisions and a genuine barrier to understanding" (176). To Christina Stead, praising the "ocean of story": "The short story can't wither and, living, can't be tied to a plan. It is only when the short story is written to a rigid plan, or done as an imitation, that it dies. It dies where it is pinned down ..." (10). These are not anti-intellectual rejections of analysis but recognitions that story resists the domesticating urges of the categorizer as genre police. Just as a certain kind of critic seeks to secure the boundaries of story, so domopolitics seeks to secure the national home from outside entry and internal rebellion.

In thinking about how the domopolitical poses challenges to the postcolonial and the planetary, I have found Bonnie Honig particularly helpful. Drawing on feminist theory, she suggests that democratic theory must be recast so as "to give up on the dream of a place called home, a place free of power, conflict, and struggle ..." (1996: 258). Nationalist literatures, both imperial and decolonizing, may be tempted by such a dream. Diasporic literatures, too, may be seduced by its nostalgic simplicity. But postcolonial theorists tend to warn against it. Postcolonial theory embraces home as inherently a place of power and struggle. Order cannot always trump dissent. Unlike the critics enumerated by New, I remain wary of appeals to authority in framing the story. Instead, this paper asks, with Honig: what if we "switch the questions" (2001: 1–14)?

What if we turn from the storyteller to the interactive contexts out of which the story is generated? If criticism often makes meaning through ordering, literature disturbs such designs. More attention to this interplay and its implications for judgment is necessary. In *Democracy and the Foreigner*, Honig argues that political theorists, like literary critics, read for narrative patterns that are constructed generically. Neither she nor I argue against this tendency. My desire is to understand how it operates and what interests such decisions serve. Honig asks: "What if we read democratic theory gothically instead of romantically?" She argues for this shift because gothic modes of reading press us "to attend to the people's perpetual uncertainty about the law and their relation to it" (9). In her view, this uncertainty is better suited than romantic certainties for negotiating democratic politics today. By reading gothically, Honig switches the questions and recasts the foreigner as founder rather than threat to American culture. As conventionally accepted ideas of authority are increasingly challenged by intellectual, social, and political developments, whether one terms these postmodern, postcolonial, planetary, or globalizing, these challenges carry implication for how we read tropes and territory, within and beyond postcolonial short fiction.

Because New's concern (in *Dreams*) lies in how to write and read within a settler colony, he identifies three problems of story-telling that arise in colonial contexts: "whose story to tell, whom to tell it to, how to tell it" (22). At one time, this focus was encapsulated in the opening sentence of Rudy Wiebe's "Where Is the Voice Coming From?": "The problem is to make the story" (135). That problem is now yielding to the urgency of other dilemmas, or at least different ways of phrasing the compelling connections between story, community, and life. More urgent for me, in my vocation as critic, is the question of how to read, especially when critics of the postcolonial are increasingly reading across conventionally established boundaries.

With the rise of postcolonial and indigenous theories, the questions and claims around story have shifted. Thomas King begins each story-lecture in his 2003 CBC Massey Lectures, *The Truth About Stories: A Native Narrative*, with the claim: "There is a story I know" (1, 31, 61, 91, 121). There is a story I know. The knowledge-claim is clear. It is a form of truth-claim but not a claim to absolute, imperial truth. What he knows is complex, sure in its values yet shifting in its surety. "Stories are wondrous things. And they are dangerous" (9), he warns. (A point also stressed by Rushdie.) As King tells his opening creation story five different times, the details shift to acknowledge location while the substance remains. This opening claim is followed by another assertion: "The truth about stories is that that's all we are" (2). This too is repeated with variation throughout the series of lectures-as-stories. King's interest is not in categorizing, aesthetically evaluating, or even interpreting the story. But he is interested in redefining the relation of story to identity, place, history, and community. His interest lies in what Julie Cruikshank terms "the social life of stories": their performative functions, their capacity to imagine and shape the world within and beyond its current constraints. Anthony Giddens believes that "building a democracy of the emotions is one part of a progressive civic culture" (95). Markets cannot create that, he insists. Perhaps stories still can.

The two epigraphs that head my paper provide radically different approaches to the power of stories, based on different assumptions about how they function in relation to identity-construction and the nature of truth. These delimit part of the terrain of story today. Ted Chamberlin's book, *If This is Your Land, Where are Your Stories?*, argues that the assumptions governing the second epigraph are wrong, even if the force beyond the question asked there means that we need to keep asking it. Telling a story and telling the truth are <u>not</u> *the same*. Postmodern relativists confuse the issue when they imply that stories and truth are interchangeable. None the less, their relation is much more complex than the journalist in my second epigraph assumes. It would be a further mistake to follow his lead in equating telling a story with entertainment and telling the truth with realism. King demolishes both these myths with humour in *The Truth About Stories*.

These category-mistakes are prevalent enough that they cannot be left unchallenged. In Chamberlin's view, if our schools are teaching us that we need to make a choice between reality and imagination, then that choice is false (127). What we value in language, he argues, is its ability to show us "the point where mystery and clarity converge" (124). Storytelling may take us to that point. When telling a story is defined as performative, or in anthropological terms, as "communication-based social action," its relation to the communicative construction of community becomes its privileged function (Cruikshank 155). In multicultural and globalized contexts, this is the dimension of story that becomes most challenging for story teller and story reader (or listener) to negotiate.

Chamberlin's book strives "to give the reader a sense of how important it is to come together in a new understanding of the power and the paradox of stories" (239) because that task has implications for the future of our world. That new understanding, as I see it, will be found in a postcolonial poetics of story. Such a poetics might follow Charles Bernstein's lead in extending "Shelley's dictum that poets are the unacknowledged legislators of the world and George Oppen's revision that poets are the legislators of the unacknowledged world" (vii). Instead of labelling and policing generic markers, including assigning writers to an ethnic or national origin, the critic might ask how a writer's stylistic choices may imply political meanings within its various contexts of production and reception. In what sense can postcolonial short fiction be seen to legislate the unacknowledged world? That word, legislation, might give some readers pause. Van Herk's desire was for "the story ungoverned." I read this phrase, possibly against the grain, as Van Herk insisting on the story's right to self-governance, the basic principle of democracy: "that those subject to the laws also be their authors" (Benhabib 221). Patriarchal bourgeois homes, nations governed along such models, and generic rules for writing "proper" stories have not operated according to such principles, yet they remain an important ideal for each.

King argues that stories not only imagine alternative worlds but can actively contribute to bring them into being – or to destroy them. In *The Truth about Stories*, King re-legislates the unacknowledged world of Native storytelling through adapting form and function to the circumstances of the occasion and blurring the boundaries between lecture and story, oral and written, imagination and reality. He questions these categories of separation from a Native perspective. Like Chamberlin and Cruikshank, King brings indigenous storytelling traditions into dialogue with those of critics as varied as Walter Benjamin, Mikhail Bakhtin, and Harold Innis (critics whose insights Cruikshank finds compatible with Yukon indigenous traditions). To read short fiction today, we need to ask why and how stories matter. Chamberlin, Cruikshank, and King give similar answers to this question. In Cruikshank's words, stories matter because they have the power "to sustain social life" (xiii) and "to inform and enlarge other forms of explanation," even across boundaries designed to separate one group from another. As Cruikshank puts it, "a story can reframe a divisive issue by providing a broader context" for evaluation (xv). For Chamberlin, stories can lead antagonists to common ground, beyond divisions of them and us. King warns, however, that stories are medicine: they can injure as well as cure (92). And story is everywhere. It is not limited to the category of short fiction although what we call short fiction can convey truths not easily grasped in other media.

For purposes of my own research, I am especially interested in Cruikshank's argument that "academic narratives – about cultural categories, about narrative forms, about historical periodization – can be enlarged if we take seriously the stories people tell about themselves" (xiv-xv). Those stories proliferate in many forms beyond that particular genre that we label short fiction. Questions about the relation of stories to truth find themselves embroiled in questions about knowledge and its category constructions. Neither truth nor stories are transparent. Eventually, it all comes back to the audience: as reader, listener, or spectator. Stories in the form of short fiction have devices at their disposal for calling their readers into being, for opening spaces that readers can enter for the duration of the tale and encouraging them to open themselves to difference, but these devices remain dependent on convention, the "literacy" of the audience, and the particular pressures of the time and place.

Literacy itself is produced through community. When community is fissured, fragmented, or weakened through globalizing processes, what happens to the power of story? Ted Chamberlin argues that "We need a new way of looking at stories and songs that balances the artifice of their conventions with the naturalness – or the truth – of their representation of the world" (21). I do not find this formulation helpful. Opposing artifice and the natural confuses things further. I do agree, though, that literary criticism needs to rethink how it situates its work within the world.

Globalization theorist Anthony Giddens argues that the renewal of self-identity through story-telling becomes a more urgent necessity in globalizing times, whether that remodelling of the self through story is performed through therapy, self-help groups, or other means, such as, I would add, reading postcolonial short fiction. Storying home is essential to constructing identity but in these contexts may as often tend to reproduce a form of identity that reinforces normative assumptions about people and their place in the world as to challenge these, even when the writers themselves wish to do so. Stories are one way of coping with what Giddens terms our "runaway world." Giddens asserts "There is a global revolution going on in how we think of ourselves and how we form ties and connections with others" (69). Although he locates the family as the site of these struggles, his argument implies that family, home, and story are not easily disentangled. How we think of ourselves and how we form ties with others. How we name home. We do that through story.

The story of Giddens' *Runaway World*, despite its surface advocacy of democracy, cosmopolitanism, and equal rights for women, depicts a world from the point of view of those who have always been in control and do not want to lose it now. Giddens claims: "we can and must find ways of bringing our runaway world to heel" (23). This is the rhetoric of securitization and domopolitics. That runaway world, as he describes it, is constituted, in part, by the dynamic between feminist and postcolonial emancipation from traditional structures *and* fundamentalist reactions against them. For Giddens, the runaway world is "a society living after the end of nature" and "a society living after the end of tradition" (61). This narrative of ends dominates and eventually overwhelms his attempt to theorize beginnings. Although he has a powerful argument to make, he is not fully in control of the meanings that his metaphors generate.

To read Margaret Atwood and Alice Munro through the lens of Giddens' analysis is to understand more fully King's suggestion that the magic of literature is not in the themes – "it is in the way meaning is refracted by cosmology, the way understanding is shaped by cultural paradigms" (112). With globalization, cosmology and cultural paradigms are in flux but through their changes they continue to refract the meanings that stories make and unmake. The two stories I will now discuss engage the domopolitical and globalizing imaginations to re-legislate aspects of their unacknowledged worlds.

Alice Munro's short story "Runaway" and Margaret Atwood's short short story "Faster" address different aspects of the runaway world through different techniques of making the story. Munro's story is realistic and detailed (what we might identify as the conventional short story at its best) and if it has an argument to make, it is that life is too complex to categorize. Atwood's two-paragraph fiction is closer to the parable. Yet she too succeeds in taking readers to that point where mystery and clarity converge.

Giddens' runaway world takes individualized shape in Munro's runaway girl and her runaway goat in the opening story "Runaway" in the volume of the same title. Munro's story gives material and psychic substance to Giddens' contention that "The dark side of decision making is the rise of addictions and compulsions" (64). Carla makes the decision to run away from her parents but then becomes trapped in a compulsive relationship with Clark. When she tries to run away from him, she finds that she has lost her capacity to imagine herself outside the frame of the couple, however dysfunctional it has proved to be. In

Giddens' terms, "Addiction comes into play when choice, which should be driven by autonomy, is subverted by anxiety" (65). This is a story about living with anxiety, and about the subversion of autonomy – the power to legislate for oneself. Carla can remain where she is only by refusing to know, refusing to investigate what has happened to Flora, and thus refusing to acknowledge to herself the deceptions on which her relationship with Clark is built. Flora's death images the death of Carla's runaway self, now trapped within the stationary mobile home. Instead of resolving her anxiety, Carla learns to live with it, by cutting herself off from Flora's world. Through her own position within the triangulated relation of Clark, Carla, and Flora the goat, Sylvia works out her own autonomy after the death of her poet-husband. And the reader's capacity for choice may be enlarged by being made privy to the entire web of these dynamics.

In Atwood's "Faster," the reader is more immediately implicated in the "we" of the story. Atwood's use of "we" in this context echoes Giddens' belief that the "we" now worrying about globalization is "all of us" (45), even if the impacts are differentially distributed and the anxieties are not the same. The anxiety generated by keeping up, speeding up, moving ahead is the theme of this story. Its question and answer structure creates a dialogue that functions to construct a communicative model of community, however minimal. "Our" running seems initially to be merely a quest for speed. The story begins: "Walking was not fast enough so we ran" (41). By the second sentence, we have found faster modes of travelling. By the second paragraph, more information is disclosed: "We want to get there faster. Get where? Wherever we are not" (41). We are back in Giddens' runaway world. And once more, the push faster and faster forward is matched by a pull backwards. The pull recalls Tolstoy's story, "How Much Land Does a Man Need?": "But a human soul can go only as fast as a man can walk, they used to say" (41). Another voice queries: "In that case, where are all the souls?" (41). The ominous answer seems almost nonchalant: "Left behind" (41). The soulless bodies explain: "we're way ahead of them, they'll never catch up. That's why we can go so fast: our souls don't weigh us down" (42). Those final chilling words, in invoking the amoral triumphalism of neoliberal globalization, also imply their opposite: the need that Giddens believes every person has for a moral commitment that stands "above the petty concerns and squabbles of everyday life" (68). Without the tethering soul, the other self races into a void, giddy and foolish. Wandering souls vainly seek their groundings. They are lost in the marshes, abandoned in the quest for speed. Through "Faster," readers are taken a long way from home to reaffirm King's belief that stories are what we are.

Chamberlin's prescription for the critic is to learn to live in stories and to stand back from them. At a time when the social life of stories is complicated by the pushes and pulls toward and away from the domopolitical, we need to switch the questions that we ask of stories and of ourselves, and to continue to question the ways in which home, story, truth, and power are defined. From a feminist and postcolonial standpoint, globalization may be less a runaway world than a continuation of empire by other means. I have argued that literary criticism's twentieth-century aspirations toward scientific authority undervalued the genuine links between science and art that are forged not through categorization but through the imagination. Contemporary modes of storying home create a contested terrain. We may not always wish to follow Chamberlin in seeking common ground, but we may need to redraw the boundaries that have restricted the research imagination from engaging in more equitable forms of knowledge construction.

NOTES

1   I am grateful to Jessica Schagerl and Cheryl Suzack for crucial feedback on an early version of this paper, and to Marta Dvořák and Bill New for inviting me to write and deliver it. Comments from conference participants have substantially helped me to develop my argument. Support from the Social Sciences and Humanities Research Council of Canada has been essential for the conduct of the research behind the paper and a grant from the Dean of Arts and Humanities at the University of Western Ontario enabled my travel.

2   Honig engages explicitly with Rushdie's interpretation of the movie of *The Wizard of Oz* (15–16, 131–32) in *Democracy and the Foreigner*.

WORKS CITED

Atwood, Margaret. "Faster." *Bottle*. Hay: Hay Festival Press, 2004: 41–42.

Bahri, Deepika. *Native Intelligence: Aesthetics, Politics and Postcolonial Literature*. Minneapolis: University of Minnesota Press, 2003.

Benhabib, Seyla. *The Rights of Others: Aliens, Residents and Citizens*. Cambridge: Cambridge University Press, 2004.

Bernstein, Charles, ed. *The Politics of Poetic Form: Poetry and Public Policy*. New York: Roof, 1990.

Chamberlin, J. Edward. *If This is Your Land, Where Are Your Stories? Finding Common Ground.* Toronto: Alfred Knopf, 2003.

Cruikshank, Julie. *The Social Life of Stories: Narrative and Knowledge in the Yukon Territory.* Lincoln & London: University Nebraska Press, 1998.

Fedorick, Joy Asham. "Fencepost Sitting and How I Fell Off to One Side." *Give Back: First Nations Perspectives on Cultural Practice.* North Vancouver: Gallerie, 1992: 27–46.

Giddens, Anthony. *Runaway World.* New York: Routledge, 2000.

Gilroy, Paul. *Postcolonial Melancholia.* New York: Columbia University Press, 2005.

– "'Where ignorant armies clash by night': Homogeneous community and the planetary aspect" *International Journal of Cultural Studies.* 6.3 (2003): 261–76.

The Harper Handbook to Literature. New York: Longman, 1997.

Holbrook, Susan. "Constance Rooke, author of *The Clear Path: A Guide to Writing English Essays,* and Home Inspection Consultant Brad LaBute converse, with rude interruptions by Walt Whitman." *Open Letter.* Twelfth Series. No. 5 (Spring 2005): 67–70.

Honig, Bonnie. *Democracy and the Foreigner.* Princeton: Princeton University Press, 2001.

– "Difference, Dilemmas, and the Politics of Home." *Democracy and Difference: Contesting the Boundaries of the Political.* Ed. Seyla Behnhabib. Princeton: Princton University Press, 1996. 257–77.

King, Thomas. *The Truth About Stories: A Native Narrative.* Toronto: Anansi, 2003.

Metcalf, John. "Building Castles." *Making It New: Contemporary Canadian Stories,* ed. John Metcalf. Toronto: Methuen, 1982: 175–79.

Munro, Alice. *Runaway.* Toronto: McClelland & Stewart, 2004.

– "What is Real?" *Making It New: Contemporary Canadian Stories,* ed. John Metcalf. Toronto: Methuen, 1982: 223–26.

New, W.H. *Dreams of Speech and Violence: The Art of the Short Story in Canada and New Zealand.* Toronto: University of Toronto Press, 1987.

Porteous, J. Douglas and Sandra E. Smith. *Domicide: The Global Destruction of Home.* Montreal: McGill-Queen's University Press, 2001.

Rushdie, Salman. "At the Auction of the Ruby Slippers." *East, West.* New York: Vintage, 1994. 85–103.

Siebert, Hilary. "An Interview with Susan Lohafer." *Speaking of the Short Story: Interviews with Contemporary Writers.* Eds. Farhat Iftekharuddin, Mary Rohrberger, & Maurice Lee. Jackson: University Press of Mississippi, 1997: 167–180.

Spivak, Gayatri Chakravorty. *Death of a Discipline.* New York: Columbia University Press, 2003.

Stead, Christina. *Ocean of Story.* Ed. R.G. Geering. New York: Viking, 1985.

Stummer, Peter O., ed. *The Story Must Be Told: Short Narrative Prose in the New English Literatures.* Wurzberg: Konighausen & Neumann, 1986.

Van Herk, Aritha. *In Visible Ink: (crypto-fictions).* Edmonton: NeWest, 1991.

Walters, William. "Secure Borders, Safe Haven, Domopolitics." *Citizenship Studies.* 8.3 (September 2004): 237–60.

Wiebe, Rudy. "Where Is the Voice Coming From?" *Where Is the Voice Coming From?* Toronto: McClelland and Stewart, 1974: 135–44.

TROPING SPACE, SELF, AND CULTURES IN TIME

CHELVA KANAGANAYAKAM

Configuring a Typology for South Asian Short Fiction

The publication of Shyam Selvadurai's *Story-Wallah* (2004) reinforces a fundamental assumption that frames this paper, namely, that it is not altogether whimsical to attempt a typology of South Asian fiction in English.[1] In some senses, this anthology edited by Selvadurai is the first of its kind, although the collection itself is not so much a "celebration of South Asian fiction in English" as it claims on its cover as a collection of recent South Asian diasporic fiction. There is no overt statement about why "the very best of South Asian fiction" (dust jacket) scrupulously avoids "local" or "stay-at-home" writers, but they are, unfortunately, not represented. Selvadurai's thoughts about diaspora, culture, identity, and short fiction are brought together in his introduction. This paper is partially a response to the anthology, but is more centrally about cultural continuity, typology, and literary practice.

Selvadurai's introduction follows from the basic premise that the South Asian diaspora needs to be understood in all its historical complexity, and it is the manner in which the global dispersal of South Asians happened over two centuries that determines the questions of identity that run through this body of writing. Indenture thus becomes an originary moment in his conceptual framework. He is quick to distance himself from what might well be construed as a Marxist approach. "I was not interested in including message-driven or propagandist stories," says Selvadurai. And he adds that the stories that interest him "take you into their world by the strength of their voice and hold you there by offering multi-dimensional characters with interesting dilemmas and conflicts" (13). Historical specificity thus gives way to a form of universalism and aesthetic appeal. At the end of the introduction, however, he moves back to a circumscribed frame by claiming that the overall "effect created was a marvelous cacophony that reminded [him] ... of those South Asian bazaars with the bargaining, carnival-like milieu. The goods on sale in this instance being stories hawked by story-traders: Story-Wallahs" (14). Selvadurai's closure, rather than his discussion, with all its suggestions of orality, multiplicity, collectivity and a sense of community, serves as a useful take-off point for this paper.

Any attempt to identify specific attributes that recur in South Asian writing often runs the risk of leading to quasi-essentialist statements. However, despite all the dangers of positioning oneself along such lines, it is necessary to assert there are some identifiably South Asian traits about South Asian short fiction in English. And that is not simply a matter of thematic preoccupation or, in conventional terms, setting and background. To say that South Asian writing is about South Asia is, for the most part, nothing more than pointless tautology. The assertion about an identifiable or pervasive South Asianness, however, nudges the edges of essentialism largely because South Asia implies more than a region, and being South Asian may not imply, in many cases, anything more than brown skin. To claim a measure of uniqueness about Canadian or Australian short fiction is, in some respects, more reasonable than to talk about South Asian writing as a homogenous category.[2] A grouping that sees a commonality among writers from, say, Trinidad, Fiji, Malaysia, Canada, India, and Sri Lanka, for instance, must inevitably go beyond historical circumstance or racial identity.

Historians such as Kapil Kapoor, critics such as A.K. Ramanujan and more recently anthropologists like Dipankar Gupta have made claims about foundational or primordial Indian characteristics from very different perspectives. Kapoor advances a Sanskritic frame – an epistemological scaffolding – that explains and surrounds the notion of Indianness. The India of the Vedas has for him preserved a line of continuity that pervades modernity. Ramanujan goes with notions of context-sensitivity to demonstrate the mindset of India. Gupta advances the idea of root metaphors as a significant marker for identifying Indianness.[3] Each one identifies a particular pan-Indian trait that serves as a frame for advancing a totalizing argument. All three are convinced about the existence of a substratum of subjectivity that links India, although they espouse different perspectives. Such stances can be difficult to defend, largely because they might well flaunt objectivity while masking hegemonic and ideological concerns, but to be dismissive about such claims might well amount to throwing out the baby with the bathwater.

A fundamental premise of the present paper is that it is possible and necessary to claim an identifiable South Asianness, but that its origins might well lie in the Bhakti movement of the medieval period, and in the coming of modernity together with colonialism. The Hindu religious movement that swept across India from the sixth century to about the twelfth, together with the arrival of modernity in the seventeenth and eighteenth centuries, gave a distinctive character to South Asia. These are two defining – Renaissance-like – moments that shaped the idea of South Asianness. To make this claim is not to deny the local and the situational. Religion, ethnicity, and landscape matter, but they do not disturb the substratum or *Weltanschauung* of South Asia. The diaspora, for example, is a crucial moment of transition and a constitutive aspect of cultural identity. One cannot ignore the role of, say, Islam, Buddhism, or Christianity in shaping South Asian cultural values. The fact is, however, that the Bhakti movement made South Asia religious in a profoundly cultural and even secular sense. It draws from a number of traditions that predate the medieval period, but the manner in which it manifested itself allowed for a profound cultural transformation across India. Over a period of six centuries, as the movement spread across India, it not only established religion as central to the ontology of the country, but also set up a whole cultural system that drew its strength from what started ostensibly as a religious movement. If religious epistemology appeared in India much earlier, and even moved to other parts of Asia, it did not emerge as a populist enterprise or a cultural phenomena until the Bhakti movement orchestrated a metamorphosis. And when the West arrived in the sixteenth and seventeenth centuries, it brought with it both secularism and modernity that interacted with, complemented, subverted, and in the final analysis, co-existed with the religious ontology cemented by the Bhakti movement.

At some level, to juxtapose Bhakti and modernity in this manner does not amount to anything more than a familiar postcolonial gesture. Time and again, postcolonial theory has reinforced the need to adopt an approach that accommodates the claims of tradition and colonial presence. What makes the Bhakti movement different is the manner in which it accommodated and shaped the secular and retained its role as an identifiable subtext among those who belonged to very different regions and spoke languages that were noticeably different. It provided a national and transnational base for modernity to interact with and produce a way of life.

Locating the Bhakti movement as a defining, transformative moment also raises a number of troubling questions. Is Sri Lanka, to which migration occurred long before the Bhakti movement took place, an anomaly? How would one expand the notion of a pervasive South Asianness to include Sri Lanka when the migration took place several centuries before the Bhakti movement? Is the spread of Hinduism before the sixth century a matter of less relevance? More significantly, how would it be possible to use the Bhakti movement as a watershed without privileging Hinduism in a region that includes a large number of Muslims and Christians? Of these questions, the last one is probably the most crucial. For the present purpose suffice it to mention that regardless of the religious underpinning of the movement, that fact is that a social and economic framework facilitated the genesis of this religious revival, and in turn the movement gradually constructed a cultural matrix with the temple as its central structural and spatial focus. The cultural dimension persisted, despite the vicissitudes of time. The Bhakti movement reinforced a way of life that was both religious and secular. Hence its power to withstand the more pronounced secularism of the colonial period. Colonialism facilitated the spread of this consciousness and helped link it with the idea of a nation state.

In practical terms, the idea of South Asianness operates as a subtextual field of meaning, regardless of ethnic, class, caste or even religious differences. Space, for instance, is an aspect of this consciousness that functions in ways that are often complex and contradictory. Public and private space, sacred and secular space are defined in a manner that implies a strong sub-textual layer of meaning. Where people gather, as strangers, acquaintances, friends, or family would depend on how space is configured. Friends who belong to one caste may not meet where other castes gather. Secular spaces get transformed into sacred spaces on specific occasions, and for specific times.[4] One tries not to violate these codes, and if modernity makes adjustments necessary, it does not eclipse the weight of meaning that lies within these conventions. Modernity brought about secular notions of space based on economic and utilitarian grounds. But modernity did not replace the pre-modern; instead it found a way of co-existing with the past.

The argument of this paper rests on the assumption that these conventions are real and that they shape literature. They are present in all literature, in the lyric, the novel, and the epic, but in short fiction their presence or absence is often quite crucial. Given the formal constraints of the short story, the intertextual components and the allusive elements tend to occupy a central space. Short story theorists have drawn attention to the possibility of thinking about the short story in spatial rather than linear terms.[5] Short stories in South Asia may well achieve a similar effect by drawing on a set of shared cultural assumptions. It is possible to argue that if short fiction in the vernacular languages has had spectacular success in the past several decades, it might well be that these writers were able to adapt an alien form in unique ways. The relation between the vernacular short story and short fiction in English is a productive area of inquiry, but one that lies beyond the scope of this paper.

Short fiction in English has been, admittedly, less prominent than the novel. But there is a corpus of writing in India, Pakistan, Sri Lanka, Singapore, Malaysia, and in Europe that amounts to a substantial body of work. The number of anthologies listed in *Telling Stories; Postcolonial Short Fiction in English* (2001)[6] offers a fair sampling of what is available. Add to this the work of Caribbean and African authors of Indian origin, and the literature becomes even more impressive. Any typology that attempts to find a pattern of recurrence in this varied body of work is likely to be tentative at best, but it is a necessary undertaking. Exceptions are present everywhere, and one only needs to read, say, the stories of G.V. Desani to realize that writers have a disconcerting tendency to destabilize the paradigms that critics so painstakingly advance. They do not realize that we too have to make a living![7]

That said, writers such as R.K. Narayan, Raja Rao, even Anita Desai, despite all their differences, rely heavily on a subtextual field to supplement what emerges through the more conventional strategies of short fiction. The stories written by "local" writers are not necessarily inaccessible to one who has not acquired – and I use the term "acquired" rather than "inherited" quite deliberately – the ontology of South Asianness, but the subtext is an essential tool to decode what might well appear to be otherwise contradictory or opaque. To make this point is not to restate in a convoluted way that without a sense of cultural context implied meanings are often lost, regardless of where the short story originates. Would the stories that make up *Dubliners* be meaningful in the absence of some knowledge of Irish history, or would one recognize the nuances of, say, Frank Moorhouse without an awareness of the social intersections that characterized Australia in the 1960s and 1970s? Cultural context implies a form of knowledge and subtext suggests a kind of awareness or consciousness. One important difference might be that it is difficult to conceive of so many language groups, so many ethnicities who may not even have a common language to communicate with each other, recognizing certain markers as being significant. These markers, together with the role they play in determining cultural life, may well be in conflict with modernity that insists on a very different scheme, often a rational scheme for determining social relations. The challenge, however, is that the subtext cannot be discussed without appearing to be essentialist, ideologically fixed, or even wrong-headed. But it is a presence, one that negotiates its own significance in ways that lie outside the reach of everyday language. A longer work, such as Arundhati Roy's *The God of Small Things* (1997) or Mulk Raj Anand's various novels, would find numerous ways of articulating the levels that lie below the surface. Short stories simply accommodate them as part of the discourse. Even writers as varied as R.K. Narayan and Anita Desai, despite all the explication they provide, fall back on values that are implied but hardly ever stated. Some of the finest short stories in the vernaculars resist translation primarily because they rely so heavily on these shared assumptions.

A few years ago, I had occasion to visit a writer in rural South India. Sundara Ramaswamy, who writes only in Tamil, and has never really lived outside his village, very kindly offered to show me around. As we walked through the main street with its shops, cafes, and all its bustling activity, he pointed to a Tamarind tree and said that this was the tree about which he has written so much. I was aware of the tree through his fiction, even a novel entitled *The Story of a Tamarind Tree* (1996), but this was a moment to actually see it and reflect on what a tree might mean in that culture. All the rituals, superstitions, legends, myths, together with local anecdotes, became a reality in ways that are distinctive. The tree is local and situational, but it is also cultural and mythical. It is a spatial trope that implies layers of meaning and identity. South Asian short fiction, if it is not to be considered part of a universal monolithic entity called the short story, may well be a result of this particular dimension.[8]

The diasporic author – and here again generalizations are likely to be misleading in a globalized world – works with a consciousness that has been formed in South Asia, but writes from a perspective that is distanced in many ways. Precise definitions of who qualifies as a diasporic author are probably less relevant than the fact that the diasporic writer is one for whom belonging and citizenship occupy two different spaces. Realism of a particular kind is not often the forte of the diasporic author who subscribes to the world view that one identifies as "South Asian" but is less cognizant of the ways in which this intersects with quotidian realities. Realism as convention and realism as reflection of an identifiable referent are very different matters and it is easy to confuse one with the other. Writers such as Rohinton Mistry or Selvadurai are insistently referential. But Selvadurai claims in his introduction that he has written "Canadian novels set exclusively in Sri Lanka" (2). It is possible to argue that the diasporic writer thematizes what lies below the surface and finds a social context that would exemplify that layer of meaning. It may well be that this distinction sets up a binary that is not always accurate. "Local" and "foreign" are deeply troubling terms in contexts where all generalizations may be true or untrue. But diasporic authors – one thinks of, say, Salman Rushdie, Zulfikar Ghose, Vikram Chandra, Suniti Namjoshi, Amitav Ghosh, Michael Ondaatje, are identifiably different from R.K. Narayan, Mulk Raj Anand, Khushwant Singh, Amit Chaudhuri, and Jean Arasanayagam. Immediate realities are erased by time, but memory retains subliminally the markers that define South Asian culture. They often reappear as legend, ritual, myth, or formalized behaviour. Quite often the spatial configurations in diasporic stories masquerade as secular and realistic when they are in fact religious and symbolic. In short, there is a shift in diaspora as the unstated dimension of local writing gets articulated as mythical or symbolic space. The differences between local and diasporic writers often get articulated in spatial and temporal terms, but a crucial distinction might well be that while the local writer uses, quite overtly, the repertoire of implied meanings, the diasporic author transforms those meanings into mythical or symbolic structures.

An example of the manner in which the referential becomes symbolic occurs in Zulfikar Ghose's remarkable short story "The Savage Mother of Desire." The opening paragraph is particularly striking:

The mangoes fallen from the trees during the last monsoon rain had turned black and on the rising slopes, which half a mile away became the foothills of the mountain range, the coconut trees bore a new crop of fruit. Ramchand sighted the steamer from Bombay as it came round Rocky Point, a long mass of granite extending into the ocean to form a natural sea wall, its outer end, where the rock tapered into the water, smoothed by the waves into a cylindrical shape with a red light glowing at the point, and watched for a moment a cloud of black smoke disperse from the steamer into thin lines, reminding him of charcoal marks some vandal had scored on the temple wall. 'No,' he said to the fruit vendor, putting down the papaya that he had been weighing in his hand, caressing it as he placed it back on the pile, 'I think not.'

A quotidian moment, one that announces itself as very traditional in its evocation of mood and setting, takes on a special significance as the story progresses, and the elements that make up the introductory paragraph become constitutive aspects of a larger narrative that involves sexuality, ritual, fertility, and religion. The referential continues to be necessary, but it quickly becomes subservient to the symbolic and the mythical. Ghose re-articulates the subtext as myth and ritual in a manner that demonstrates the role of memory.

A third category – one that is likely to become increasingly important in the future – concerns those writers whose knowledge of South Asia lacks the inwardness that underlines the other two categories. Second-generation authors almost always belong to this category. Again, defining who belongs here is a complex task, but these writers mark the limits of South Asianness. Their presence changes a dyadic structure into a triadic paradigm in ways that are crucial. The fact that these writers do not have ready access to a South Asian ontology is not so much a limitation as a difference. And when they write about South Asia they do not have an awareness – unless they have chosen to acquire it – of the subtextual field that is instinctually grasped by members of the community. Inevitably, they project spaces – domestic and public – in ways that imply a very different scheme of values. Land and landscape are, by the same token, represented differently. These writers are products of modernity whose affiliation with South Asia is more a matter of stance and identification rather than identity. Jhumpa Lahiri is an author who quite clearly succeeds as a short story writer, but her success is achieved on her own terms. Despite Tanuja Desai Hidier's title *Born Confused*, these authors are not necessarily born or raised confused. In their work South Asianness accommodates itself to modernity in a manner that clearly demonstrates a paradigmatic shift. If Lahiri's stories that are set in the United States are more successful than the ones that are set in India, it is probably because Lahiri's characters are more comfortable with the secularism and modernity of the West. The temporality of such stories works much better than the spatiality of her Indian stories.[9]

In 1964, Zulfikar Ghose, together with B.S. Johnson, put together a collection of stories called *Statement Against Corpses*. The preface claims that the short story as a genre is in decline, and that "this book represents a joint attempt, through demonstration of the form's wide technical range, to draw attention to a literary form which is quite undeservedly neglected." Whether the stories in the collection helped to recuperate a dying form or contributed to the overall moribund condition is not entirely clear. However, thirty-five years later Ghose brought out another collection entitled *Veronica and the Gongora Passion*. Subtitled "Stories, fictions, tales, and one fable," it implicitly acknowledges the dangers of making easy generalizations. More importantly, the stories themselves are a striking example of how the best of diasporic South Asian fiction configures itself. Juxtaposed with, say, the work of Lahiri and Narayan, the collection serves as a strong reminder that there are major differences and similarities among South Asian writers of short fiction that make a typology necessary and perhaps timely too.

In postcolonial studies, local and diasporic have often functioned as a convenient binary to explore differences. Local writers have stayed and diasporic writers (to use Salman Rushdie's term) "flown." Very little effort has been made to tease out the implications of this binary or transcend its assumptions. If the present argument holds, then it is important to recognize that South Asian fiction accommodates at least three different strands, namely, the local, the diasporic, and the new, and in order to understand the various intersections that unite and divide them one needs to go back to two historical moments, the Bhakti movement and the coming of modernity, that, in the last fifteen centuries or so, made South Asia identifiably South Asian.

NOTES

1   Similar attempts have been made to establish a classificatory system for women's writing in India, but these have been largely thematic in their approach. For example, see Urvashi Butalia and Ritu Menon, ed. *In Other Words: New Writing by Indian Women* (1992) and Geeta Dharmarajan, ed. *Separate Journeys: Short Stories by Indian Women Writers* (1993).

2   Of particular interest here is the comparative study of the short story in Canada and New Zealand by W.H. New. The author quite rightly draws attention to the "separate shifting tensions between individual artistic

commitment and an unfolding social context" (25) as a way of establishing connections and discontinuities. For a detailed discussion, see *Dreams of Speech and Violence* (1987).

3   For a more detailed discussion see, Kapil Kapoor's *Literary Theory: Indian Conceptual Framework* (1998), A.K. Ramanujan's "Is There an Indian Way of Thinking? An Informal Essay" (1990), and Dipankar Gupta's *Culture, Space, and the Nation State* (2000).

4   There is, for instance, a story such as N.K. Ragunathan's "Let's Chat in the Moonlight" which relies heavily on the reader's understanding of the relation between space and caste in Sri Lankan Tamil society. The ironic mode of the story requires that explanations be kept to a minimum. The effect of the subtext, then, depends heavily on the reader's awareness of cultural context. For a translated version of the story, see *Lutesong and Lament*, ed. Chelva Kanaganayakam (2001): 12–14.

5   Suzanne Hunter Brown's essay on "Discourse Analysis and the Short Story" is an example of a theoretical essay that makes use of this binary. See Susan Lohafer and Jo Ellyn Clarey, 217–48.

6   See pages 459–60.

7   The stories in Desani's *Hali and Collected Stories* (1986) do necessarily destabilize the notion of South Asianness, but they do not fit easily into the typology that makes a distinction between the "local" and the "diasporic."

8   Sundara Ramaswamy lives in a small village called Nagercoil in Tamil Nadu.

9   Take, for instance, two stories such as "A Temporary Matter" and "A Real Durwan" in *Interpreter of Maladies* (1999). While the latter appears contrived, the former comes across as perfectly natural.

WORKS CITED

Bardolph, Jacqueline. *Telling Stories: Postcolonial Short Fiction in English.* Amsterdam: Rodopi, 2001.

Butalia, Urvashi and Ritu Menon, eds. *In Other Words: New Writing by Indian Women.* Delhi: Kali for Women, 1992.

Desani, G.V. *Hali and Collected Stories.* 1986; Delhi: Penguin, 1998.

Dharmarajan, Geeta, ed. *Separate Journeys: Short Stories by Indian Women Writers.* London: Mantra, 1993.

Ghose, Zulfikar. *Veronica and the Gongora Passion: Stories, Fictions, Tales and One Fable.* Toronto: TSAR, 1998.

Ghose, Zulfikar and B.S. Johnson. *Statement Against Corpses.* London: Constable, 1964.

Gupta, Dipankar. *Culture, Space and the Nation-State*. New Delhi: Sage, 2000.

Hidier, Tanuja Desai. *Born Confused*. New York: Scholastic, 2002.

Kanaganayakam, Chelva, ed. *Lutesong and Lament: Tamil Writing from Sri Lanka*. Toronto: TSAR, 2001.

Kapoor, Kapil. *Literary Theory: Indian Conceptual Framework*. New Delhi: Affiliated East-West Press, 1998

Lahiri, Jhumpa. *Interpreter of Maladies*. New York: Houghton Mifflin, 1999.

Lohafer, Susan and Jo Ellyn Clarey, eds. *Short Story Theory at a Crossroads*. Baton Rouge and London: Louisiana State University Press, 1989.

New, W.H. *Dreams of Speech and Violence: The Art of the Short Story in Canada and New Zealand*. Toronto: University of Toronto Press, 1987.

Ramanujan, A.K. "Is There an Indian Way of Thinking? An Informal Essay." In *India Through Hindu Categories*. New Delhi: Sage, 1990: 42–58.

Ramaswamy, Sundara. *Oru Puliyamarathin Kathai*. Nagercoil, India: Kalachchuvadu, 1996.

Selvadurai, Shyam, ed. *Story-Wallah*. Toronto: Thomas Allen, 2004.

LYDIA WEVERS

What Should the Reader Know?: Culture, History, and Politics in Contemporary Short Fiction from Aotearoa New Zealand

How does the very contemporary New Zealand short story enunciate national and cultural space? Or perhaps, to be less grandly ambitious about it, what does the short story have to say to us, in the early years of the twenty-first century, about Maori and Pakeha and the place in which they live. I have chosen not to look at collections of short fiction, the bulk of which are produced by mid-career writers, in order to traverse the bumpier, harder-to-read ground of recent serial publication with its editorial politics and role in the, if not canon, then 'literature' formation. Because the short story has historically been a highly privileged genre in New Zealand literature, with a forceful canonical role, you cannot read it 'blind', but I have chosen to consider stories published very recently as a way of avoiding the context of commentary and reception, and focus instead on the way short stories express the politics of the social, or to put it another way, why and if stories matter. So this paper looks at the last five years of two publications – one broadly speaking Pakeha, the biannual journal *Sport*, and the other Maori, the biennial anthology *Huia Short Stories*.[1]

The predominance of the short story as a genre choice in New Zealand literature has been attributed variously to the ascendancy of Katherine Mansfield and Frank Sargeson, to a kind of literary adolescence (our writers are still practising), and to the colonial condition. That is, the textual space of the short story, in Sargeson's case, often only a page, is metonymic of the space of New Zealand's colonial and postcolonial history and correspondingly its grip on large claims of narrative, geography, modernity, and nation. It is no coincidence that the short texts of literary nationalism are full of a language of childhood, of traces, beginnings, solitude. The whole bloody, tangled, imperialist contest of the nineteenth century was pushed aside so that New Zealand modernity could recolonize, as James Belich has argued, newly emptied islands.[2] But that's the European or Pakeha story. If the name 'Aotearoa' is substituted for 'New Zealand,' the role of the short story in articulating a nation space takes on a different resonance, hints at the back- or perhaps the under-story of Polynesian migrations and descent groups, pre-European oral traditions, worldviews and aesthetics, and the storytelling of deracination, displacement, silencing and dispossession. It's not so much a short as an interrupted story.

Bridget Orr has noted that the Pakeha domination of New Zealand literature existed alongside but mostly in ignorance of substantial and continuous Maori oral and written cultural production (Orr, 78). When the so-called Maori Renaissance occurred in the 1970s it brought literature by Maori writing in English to a wide reading public and made it integral to canon formation, but it is still the case, as Orr commented in 1999, that with rare exceptions Pakeha critics do not engage much with Maori literary production. This may be because of what Dorothy Driver calls the "nervous condition." Talking about black female South African writers, Driver adapts Jean Paul Sartre's epigraph about Frantz Fanon – "the condition of the native is a nervous condition" – to describe her own reading position:

> I read from another kind of nervous condition … that of a white middle class academic feminist aware of the history which speaks through each of those labels, trying not to speak for black women who of course speak for themselves, but to listen learn, and pass on in order to learn again. (Driver 87)

In the particular case of the short story in New Zealand the "nervous condition" of the academic postcolonial critic is compounded by the immediately visible existence of a short story production with radical cultural difference. Orr has justly remarked that Pakeha critics mostly fail to address texts written by Maori in the terms they themselves propose. Instead a critical double standard reinscribes Pakeha texts as embodiments of excellence while Maori writing is "treated … as the aesthetically unsuccessful epiphenomenon of cultural conflict" (81).

In this paper I step away from questions of aesthetic judgment (with their monolithic critical implications) to pay attention to what, as a reader, I can learn. What is being negotiated in the pages and in the literary production of these journals?

Sport, a biannual journal, was founded in 1988 and quickly established itself as the New Zealand equivalent of *Granta* or *Meanjin*. *Sport* is the leading outlet for new literary writers. Its byline is New Zealand new writing and on its website, *Sport* invites submissions from New Zealand writers or writers with a New Zealand connection. The short story is not a privileged genre – it jostles for space with poetry, essays, memoirs, and photographic essays. Many commentators see *Sport* as having a house style. Like *Landfall* before it the nexus between a publishing house and a magazine has a powerful effect on the shape of new New Zealand publication. The *Huia* anthology is produced by Huia Press, a publishing house devoted to publishing Maori writers as part of a literature of Aotearoa (Heiss 202) and is selected from the entries in the Huia short story competition. Initiated in 1995, the Huia competition is run every two years in four categories including stories written for children, for adults, and in te reo Maori. There are about 350 entries each competition. Huia's competitions arose from the deliberate objective of increasing what Brian and Robyn Bargh, the publishers, refer to as the catchment of Maori writers. The competitions are advertised everywhere there might be Maori writing stories, to all marae, secondary schools, kohanga reo, libraries, kapa haka festivals and on Maori radio.[3] Stories published in the anthology reflect this broad and diverse production, both in their poetics and modes, and in their content. Many are first time writers who report on experience. One of the explicit aims of the Huia imprint, as Robyn Bargh has said, is to convey Maori as "contemporary, active participants of society" (Heiss 202), and the short story competition, which includes stories written entirely in te reo Maori, is the genre in which this occurs. *Huia* was the place of first publication for a number of writers who have gone on to win prizes and be recognized as members of a literary elite – Paula Morris, James George, Phil Kawana, and Kellyana Morey. The last two *Huia* anthologies have started to show some crossover with *Sport* though this traffic is always one way – *Huia* is restricted to Maori. But in a range of ways the distance between *Sport* and *Huia* is large and visible, marked partly by their names (and markets and design styles) and shown by the very different social, political, and cultural contexts each publication reflects and negotiates.

It is tempting to describe this difference by resorting to the terminology of postmodern and postcolonial, except that both categories disguise more than they reveal, and import a misleading binary. The idea that New Zealand, known to some Maori as Occupied Aotearoa, is "postcolonial," smoothes over real political contradictions and tamps down the range of modes, from traditional storytelling to contemporary hip, in short story production by Maori. Similarly lumping the stories in *Sport* into "postmodern" gives a troubling consolidation to the intensely contested and perhaps outmoded uses of that term, and ignores the way fiction by Maori or Pakeha moves around the various fields of posts. However there are ways in which each publication coheres around some shared effects, locations, preoccupations that touch on the territories of postcolonial and postmodern.

Sport 29, Spring 2002, opens with a story by new writer Julian Novitz called "My Real Life":

One Friday afternoon, I open my front door and see my bachelor's degree jammed halfway into the letter box.

'We should film this' says Ev, my flatmate, when I bring the envelope back into the house. He runs off to fetch his camera. (28)

The narrator finds he doesn't want to appear as himself in Ev's film – "Up till now I have just been a disembodied voice, narrating or asking questions" – so they film him interviewing Shane, a friend, who holds the narrator's degree and answers questions, facetiously, as if he is the narrator.

It hardly seems necessary to rehearse the ways in which Novitz's story has displaced social in favour of representational identities; the story's humour and point resides in the reader's recognition of these familiar postmodern gambits. At its close Ev and the narrator are driving north from Christchurch.

Ev and I drive in silence until we are six or seven miles out of Christchurch and then Ev says:

'This is like the end of a movie. The heroes heading off into the distance, their work done, their tale finished.'

'No' I say. 'This feels like the start of a movie. A long empty road. A man from nowhere travelling into uncertainty.'

'Either way' says Ev, 'we've got to get this on tape.'

I nod and pull over. Ev gets out of the car with his camera and stands by the roadside, filming me as I drive away.

After a while, I put on some music. (36)

The reader here is both a spectator and a player – watching real life reel away. The reader knows the game of deferred meaning mediated through the multiple displacements of the story, from its title to the slyness and reflexivity of its humour – travelling into uncertainty is the best game in town. Of course the game-playing reader is standard equipment for the literatures of postmodernity. As another *Sport* fiction writer, R. Carl Shuker observes in a story about a French boy in Tokyo, the "play plays the players and not the other way round" (*Sport* 31: 125).

Two observations are germane here. First, fictions in *Sport* display surprising similarity of mode and location. They focus on young New Zealanders, mostly Pakeha but also Maori, who are always in a state of mobility and often travelling in other parts of the world, awash in signs and representations, watching themselves being watched, aware of being intertextual, allusive, displaced. And secondly, many "stories" are actually segments of novels, which reflects a corresponding tendency in the novel to be a series of stories, for example Julian Novitz's story "My Real Life" became an episode in a novel of the same name, published in 2004. The relation between the short story and the novel has shifted, as it has more widely in literatures in English, under pressure from markets and electronic publishing. Indeed in many literatures the short story is perceived to be under threat of extinction.[4] In the New Zealand case, the short story is no longer the primary genre in which Pakeha New Zealanders express and represent locality, nationality, or local/cultural identifications. Indeed "nation" is only one of a number of formerly potent identifiers now threadbare and exhausted – the idea of a local culture is similarly outworn, or redundantly discrete. The question to ask is what is being negotiated here?

Owen Marshall, doyen of the short story in New Zealand literature through the 1980s and 1990s, author of many mordant, super-, and hyper-realist stories of small town New Zealand life and culture, has a story in *Sport* 28 (Autumn 2002) called "The Language Picnic." An English department fraught with the usual discontents and professional anomie, picnics at a lonely windswept beach, redolent of signature New Zealand fictions – Janet Frame, Frank Sargeson, Maurice Gee, even Katherine Mansfield. The feuds, boredom, and melancholy of this group project out to a reader who is able to recognize the disaffections it embodies – which are significantly to do with place (a number of the English academics are disappointed in their expectations of bigger brighter universities) as well as feeling adrift from intellectual trends.

The displacement in this story is only geographically different from the displacement which is the focus of stories about New Zealand students in Japan, or Kiwis in London or Ghana, or stories which project themselves into historically or imaginatively remote worlds. What they have in common is the erasure of origin, of location. Marshall's story suggestively links beach, literature, and academic work, or location, culture, and intellect, through the occasion of the picnic, a recreational event that turns out to be as full, possibly more full, of protocols and obligations than the routines and hierarchies of daily life, but is also marginal, empty, and pointless – an unsettling and temporary occupation of an inhospitable and disappointing space. This is, of course, the European or Pakeha side of the postcolonial ledger – discomfort, illegitimacy, unsettlement, unmeaning meaningfulness. Many of the stories in *Sport* negotiate these conflicting and uncomfortable apprehensions about home, about location, history, intellectual and social configurations, through a postmodern inscription of identity as spectatorial, nomadic, coded, figural, consumerist, decentred. In the playful fictions of *Sport*, New Zealanders can be, and are, anywhere, and the same intense but disconnected meaningfulness surrounds them. The nationalist, colonialist effort of the 1930s to find a special and local reality has been replaced by "New Zealand" like a ball in play, volatile, only notionally tethered.

Switch to *Huia*. Straight away the reader is given some signs, as clear and unequivocal as the carved barge boards fronting a wharenui (ceremonial meeting house). The huia, a legendarily beautiful bird, is now known only from museum specimens – it speaks of loss but also of the hope for recovery. *Huia* 3, 1999, opens with an introduction by the editor, John Huria, which begins "E nga iwi, e nga reo, e nga mana, tena koutou," a greeting which folds in tribes, language, "mana"[5] and by extension nation. The greeting invites the reader into Maori territory. What the non-Maori reader knows in the *Huia* collections, is quite simply the force of that fact. Later anthologies do not carry introductions – the reader's self recognition is conducted through the activity of reading. It is deceptively easy at this point to rehearse some characteristics that distinguish short fiction by Maori which replicate broader cultural distinctions that operate both in daily life and in the mythologies and stereotypes that surround cultural difference in Aotearoa. The stories are full of wounded people – they express the pain, damage, psychic and material loss of colonialism, the fracture of tribal identities and their often painful reconstructions, the remnants of oral traditions, the diversity of contemporary Maori life, what has been called neotribalism sitting alongside more familiar and disheartening representations of social statistics, and the enduring and resistant networks of Maori social and cultural organization. They also show Maori as nomadic, urban, and transcultural like other inhabitants of Aotearoa, but much less interested in reading life as "text," as game, as play.

I want to consider here two features of the imaginary of the *Huia* anthologies that don't change much over time. The first is the persistent return to death as the story subject. Death ceremony, the tangi, is the cliché of fiction by Maori as numerous commentators, including Patricia Grace, have noted.[6] Death is at the heart of literary production as it is at the heart of Maori social statistics, cultural experience, and postcolonial identity. If you are Maori you are twice as likely to smoke as non-Maori, three times as likely to die of lung cancer, and five times as likely to die of Sudden Infant Death Syndrome. Maori have higher suicide rates and injury and accident rates. Life expectancy is lower by about seven years. Short fiction by Maori repeatedly maps this colonial and contemporary ground. But death practice is also an inexhaustible cultural location. A story by Paula Morris in *Huia* 4, "Many Mansions," plays with the cliché of the tangi as a cultural reassertion by focussing on a separated Maori woman flying to the funeral (in Dunedin, a very Pakeha city) of her Pakeha mother-in-law. As she bustles about providing cups of tea, longing to wail in church and make the dead hear her, giving her gift of food and memory and laughter to the bereaved, a different set of cultural practices is evoked. But it is not just the difference in (missing) cultural practice which resonates in this story. Like the narrator in Novitz's story who is configured in camera shots, dialogue, and displacements, Ra has little biographical presence. But while the narrator in "My Real Life" is understood to be an effect of representation, the absence around Ra meaningfully glosses the role she occupies as a Maori. Ra is on the edge of the family, and the death, but provides both material and emotional sustenance. The other characters are drawn to her because she offers comfort. The cold emotionless funeral is countered by Ra's memories of her warm close relationship with her ex-mother-in-law. She is the story's expression of emotion. As social observation the story is finely crafted; as postcolonial observation it is piercingly subtle. Ra is positioned to supply services and attributes which set off and sustain the larger, richer, Pakeha group. The political and cultural dynamic, with its freight of history, is delicately but unavoidably evoked. Further, Ra is a word that means sail, or sun, or day or light. It is a word with a long Pasifika etymology, which makes what Ra brings to the Pakeha world brilliantly clear – metaphorically and culturally. It is important to note however that Morris doesn't deal in simplistic binaries. The Pakeha world she describes is not itself homogenous, and while broad cultural differences have a depth and resonance, the story's fine differentiations produce a complex and not fully known world.

The second aspect of *Huia* short fiction I want to note is related to the first and that's the focus on family. Roma Potiki has observed that of the various myths about Maori the most dangerous is that all Maori people belong to a loving and caring whanau (Potiki 317). Representations of the social family in *Huia* 3, 4 and 5 belong to as wide a range of modes and configurations as social practice. The point I think is not that representations of the family counter, in their variety, the politically dangerous unitary myth Potiki describes, but that the enunciative position of short fiction by Maori is the whanau. Behind the whanau lie the connections or ruptures of whakapapa, the deep structures of collective identity with all its internal variants.[7]

Short stories by Maori enunciate a worldview in which the whanau, whatever its condition, however violently damaged or damaging, articulates the people, their history, ancestors, gods, their dispossessions and retentions, their political and social realities. Whanau is the speaking place and maps the cultural politics. In contrast, in the contemporary short New Zealand story displayed in *Sport*, family is scarcely a category of identity. Not only can it be moved around on the field of sport or culture or language as another referent, another sign, it is no longer an enunciative space. Christine Johnson's story "Mixed Blessings" in *Sport* 32 elegantly makes the point. A woman whose husband has died in an accident is trying to contain her grief. The story heightens its effect by taking the form of a list as she counts her poignantly inadequate blessings – the sun rises, the toast is made. Each accumulated detail intensifies her solitude – the system by which she tries to order an unorderable grief, the disconnection between her material life and its psychic emotional storm. There is no family, only the devastated self and its objects.

So, to conclude, what as a reader do I see here? Boldly generalizing I would say that the short story is no longer as central to Pakeha writers as it once was. Pakeha writers – and most publishers – no longer see the short story as a valuable apprenticeship form, let alone as something of value in its own right. Quantitatively it is diminished. Nor is it a shaping force in the construction of a "New Zealand" national literature. Short fiction by Pakeha is more interested in representing the effects and strategies of postmodernity than anything which might fall into Curnow's category of local and special reality.[8] Nor does it articulate "identity" except as a category of representation. Even more significantly, short stories by Pakeha writers are more and more solipsistic – they offer almost no sense that there is a Maori world. Instead the reader's attention is directed to story as a sign among signs, whose politics are those of representation, globalism, and consumption. Short fiction by Maori writers is, on the other hand, still a nursery for growing an indigenous literature. It is also far more interested in representing the social, cultural, and emotional distinctiveness of contemporary Maori and of indicating a landscape which might be the literature of Aotearoa. And it is centrally interested in identity structures rather than representations.

I am not suggesting that short fiction by Maori does not represent Maori as members of an international, technological, consumerist, postmodernity. But the predominant *Huia* mode is realism, and postmodernity is more likely to appear as cultural and economic knowledge than as a fictional strategy or as an endless displacement into text. In Anton Blank's story "Queen" (*Huia* 3) the narrator is in Sydney, cruising Oxford Street with Brendan, a Maori dragqueen he knows from back home, when they pause to look at a nightclub poster and see Brendan under his stage name Barbie Q.

> Barbie is there, wearing a kowhaiwhai one-piece swimsuit, and she has a moko painted onto her chin. Muscled dancers in piupiu surround her.
>
> At home I adopted a pretentiously postmodern stance during the debate over Paco Rabanne's use of the koru, and the Spice Girls' infamous haka. Live and let live I said, and in this day and age what culture can claim to be truly authentic? We're all trading cultural symbols left, right and bloody centre. But looking at this poster of Barbie Q doing the pukana I feel overwhelmed with sadness and I don't know why. (17–18)

While the narrator ironically notes the appropriation and recontextualisation of cultural symbols as a feature of postmodernity, he cannot completely dissociate them, or himself, from their emotional and historical weight, from their accumulated meaning. And this seems to me to be where the line is. In the *Huia* collections the short story has presence and energy, it enunciates changing social and cultural space, but also demonstrates that in the literature of Aotearoa cultural and emotional meaning has a location and a history. In contrast the short story as a Pakeha mode and poetic is always leading somewhere else – to another genre, another context, another deferral.

NOTES

1 I have chosen *Sport* rather than *Landfall*, New Zealand's oldest literary journal and historically an agent of canon formation, because *Landfall* has returned to its initial format of being a journal for literature and the arts, and the short fiction content has fallen accordingly.

2 James Belich *Paradise Reforged* (2001) makes this argument around the economy but with cultural implications. In nineteenth-century New Zealand literature Maori are the constant narrative focus but literary nationalism constructs a monocultural landscape.

3 A marae is the meeting place of a tribe; kohanga reo are preschools teaching Maori language (te reo Maori); and kapa haka are Maori dance groups.

4 A British campaign Save Our Short Story (http://www.saveourshortstory. org.uk/) begun in 2002 has explicitly tried to raise the prestige and profile of the short story in the UK with online publishing and solicited stories from high profile writers.

5 Mana is a word which is very difficult to translate. Williams' *A Dictionary of the Maori Language* gives eight meanings, but it is generally understood to mean authority and power, and has a spiritual dimension.

6 Anita Heiss, asking "Is there a Maori style?" quotes Patricia Grace saying that content often identifies writing by Maori: "Then there's the cliché, the tangi – the death ceremony pops up all over the place" (198).

7 Whanau is immediate family; whakapapa is genealogy. The recitation of whakapapa, which can go back many generations, is the base of Maori identity, knowledge, and culture.

8 The phrase used by New Zealand poet Allen Curnow in the introduction to *The Penguin Book of New Zealand Verse* (1960) to describe what New Zealand poets should do.

WORKS CITED

Belich, James. *Paradise Reforged*. Auckland: Allen Lane/Penguin, 2001.

Curnow, Allen. *The Penguin Book of New Zealand Verse*. Harmondsworth: Penguin Press, 1960.

Driver, Dorothy. "Unruly Subjects in Southern African Fiction: Writing and Regeneration in the Fiction of Bessie Head, Zoe Wicomb, Tsitsi Dangarembga and Yvonne Wera," *CRNLE Journal* (2001): 65–93.

Heiss, Anita. *Dhuuluu-Yala To Talk Straight* Canberra: Aboriginal Studies Press, 2003.

Huia Short Stories 3. Wellington: Huia Publishers, 1999.

Huia Short Stories 4. Wellington: Huia Publishers, 2001.

Huia Short Stories 5. Wellington: Huia Publishers, 2003.

Orr, Bridget. "The Maori House of Fiction." *Cultural Institutions of the Novel*, ed. Deidre Lynch and William B. Warner. Durham/London: Duke University Press, 1996: 73–95.

Potiki, Roma. "The Journey from Anxiety to Confidence." *Te Ao Marama* 2, ed. Witi Ihimaera. Auckland: Reed, 1993: 314–19.

Sport 29. Wellington: Fergus Barrowman, Spring 2002.

Sport 30. Wellington: Fergus Barrowman, Summer 2003.

Sport 31. Wellington: Fergus Barrowman, Spring 2003.

Sport 32. Wellington: Fergus Barrowman, Summer 2004.

Williams, H.W. *A Dictionary of the Maori Language* (7th ed.). Wellington: Government Printer, 1971.

BRUCE BENNETT

"Crossroads of Circumstance": Place in Contemporary Australian Short Fiction

INTRODUCTION

When considering place in literature, and short fiction in particular, it is difficult to look past Eudora Welty's comments in 1956:

> It is by the nature of itself that fiction is all bound up in the local. The internal reason for that is surely that *feelings* are bound up in place. The human mind is a mass of associations – associations more poetic even than actual. I say, "The Yorkshire Moors" and you will say, "*Wuthering Heights*," and I have only to murmur, "If Father were only alive" – for you to come back with "We could go to Moscow," which is certainly not so. The truth is, fiction depends for its life on place. Location is the crossroads of circumstance, the proving ground of "What happened? Who's here? Who's coming?" – that is the heart's field.[1]

Has the power of place in literature, and short fiction especially, remained as strong as it was for Welty in America's Deep South in the first half of the twentieth century? Presented in her dramatic and lyric modes, the Mississippi of Welty's upbringing was the principal setting of all but four of her short stories. Her only short story cycle, *The Golden Apples*, describes the interconnected lives of the inhabitants of Morgana, Mississippi, over a period of forty years. This is the literary record that has made Welty's name, in company with William Faulkner, Flannery O'Connor and others, almost synonymous with concepts of place (Werlock 438–40).

The main purpose of this essay is to test the work and example of a number of Australian short story writers since the 1970s against Welty's precepts, with a view to pursuing the role of place, region and community in contemporary short fiction. In so doing, I acknowledge Bill New's work, especially *Dreams of Speech and Violence*, his book on short fiction in Canada and New Zealand. I also acknowledge the example of Mavis Gallant, whose ninth collection of stories, *In Transit*, suggests a kind of counterpointing of some of Eudora Welty's notions. If entrapment is a major theme of much place-related fiction, another powerful theme is the transition from one place, or state of being, to another.

AUSTRALIAN CONTEXTS – BUSH AND CITY

The young Turks of Australian short fiction in the 1970s saw themselves as harbingers of a new, experimental, urban writing which finally dislodged an older Australian nationalist tradition. That older tradition seemed to be embodied in writing of the bush and backblocks by Henry Lawson and Steele Rudd. Lawson's much anthologized, praised and parodied story "The Drover's Wife" contains his archetypal description of the Australian bush:

> Bush all round – bush with no horizon, for the country is flat. No ranges in the distance. The bush consists of stunted, rotten native apple trees. No undergrowth. Nothing to relieve the eye save the darker green of a few she-oaks which are sighing above the narrow, almost waterless creek. Nineteen miles to the nearest sign of civilization – a shanty on the main road. (*Short Stories and Sketches* 47)

The nullity of this landscape is conveyed here by the repeated negatives. The verblessness suggests a lack of human energy, perhaps fatalism in the face of a physical environment that dwarfs the individual. For Lawson, the shanty was a necessary sign of civilization but nineteen miles is a long walk. Lawson's stories are notable for the kind of "up country" loneliness they engender, especially for women but also for the itinerant swagmen seeking food, drink or just human company. The interconnections of human lives in Lawson's bush are more wayward and fleeting than those in Welty's Mississippi, reflecting the sparsity of settlements and communities.

So infectious was Lawson's rhetoric of the bush (later in his work capitalized as Bush to indicate its iconic status) that this setting and its associated characters, with their particular ways of speaking (in abrupt, laconic or garrulous modes) could be used to continue stereotyping perceptions of a "real" Australia. Such images of the Australian bush, and its eccentric characters, still persist in the popular imagination through television and internet advertisements for such Australian essentials as beer, or four-wheel drive vehicles with roo-bars which are generally found in the quieter garden suburbs of capital cities.

By the late 1960s and 1970s, a definitive transition was made from Lawson-style "outback" realism to different and more various forms. Academic and fiction writer Michael Wilding spoke up for the new movement in his afterword to *The Tabloid Story Pocket Book* (1978), an anthology of Australia's "young ... experimental story tellers." In Wilding's view, the weight put upon Lawson's 1890s by the new nationalist critics of the 1930s, 1940s and 1950s, such as P.R. Stephensen and Vance and Nettie Palmer, produced a version of the "bush realist" literary tradition which gave a particular reading of that decade undue influence. To counter this influence, Wilding "discovered" a predecessor of Lawson, Marcus Clarke, whose fiction, including his short stories, had been neglected (Wilding argued) because Clarke was not born in Australia and his stories varied from realistic, up-country sketches, in a pre-Lawson mode, to melodramas and "experimental, metaphysical and fantasy stories" (*Tabloid* 303).

But the literary magazines and anthologies in the 1960s and 70s still reflected the old orthodoxies, Wilding claimed. Hence the need for the *Tabloid Story* experiment whereby a new generation of writers in their twenties and thirties could strut their wares in a packaged short story magazine supplement to other, more mass produced magazines and newspapers. The new experimentalists of the early 1970s hoped to attract new audiences and the breakdown of an "old elitism." The *Tabloid Story* experiment as devised by Wilding, Frank Moorhouse, and Carmel Kelly ran from 1972 to 1975 in Sydney before it transferred to Melbourne, where it lost some impetus and stopped publishing in 1980. Apart from stories by the editors, *Tabloid Story* brought to wider public notice new work by emerging writers such as Murray Bail, Peter Carey, Elizabeth Jolley, Laurie Clancy, Peter Mathers, and Vicki Viidikas. *The Oxford Companion to Australian Literature* has conveniently summarized the fiction in *Tabloid Story* as urban oriented and "characterised by its sexual explicitness, the radical, politi-

cal and social stance of many of its writers, and its eclecticism of form
and techniques, including fabulist, process and confessional stories"
(*Oxford Companion* 736).[2]

THE BUSH REINSCRIBED:

FRANK MOORHOUSE

Of the Sydney revolutionists of the 1960s and 1970s, Frank Moorhouse was the most "grounded" in his appreciation of place in contemporary fiction. Less attracted by fantasy, fabulism, and the process
story than Peter Carey and Wilding, Moorhouse renovated and rein-
vigorated realism for the new generation. His experience as a journalist for country newspapers and urban underground magazines helped
him in this. Moorhouse's anthology/memoir of the 1970s, *Days of
Wine and Rage*, while it drew on aspects of a national imaginary, was
a "homage to Sydney," where Moorhouse had lived for twenty years
after a childhood and youth in Nowra on the New South Wales south
coast (*Days* xiii). But Moorhouse's Sydney in this volume, as in many
of his "discontinuous fictions," is a provisional city viewed through the
eyes of a country boy. His ironic chronicles of the Sydney Push – one
of Australia's versions of post–1968 urban social and cultural activism – at parties, pubs, beaches or in bed contain a running dialogue
between country and city ways of seeing.

The story by Moorhouse which perhaps best exemplifies his sense of
location as a dialogical construction is "From a Bush Log Book I" in
his collection *Forty-Seventeen*. When it was first published in *Meanjin*
this story was called "Going into the Heartlands with the Wrong Person at Christmas."[3] The semi-autobiographical narrator in the story
returns with his old sexual friend, Belle, to commemorate Christmas
and his turning forty in the Budawang Ranges in south-eastern Australia. The times are not propitious. His much younger girlfriend, with
whom he is obsessed, has left him for another lover in London. Other
pressures are at work in him too:

> He also had some home-yearnings which came on at Christmas.
> His family was not in town for this Christmas, but anyhow his
> home-yearnings had been displaced over the years away from his
> family in the town to the bush about fifty kilometres away from,
> but behind, the coastal town where he had grown up – the Sassa-
> fras bush in the Budawang Ranges. (*Forty-Seventeen* 23)

Moorhouse's alter ego and Belle know each other well enough to engage in ironic banter about what the bush means to them:

"I don't go into the bush for views," he said.
"Tell me – what do you go into the bush for?"
"I go into the bush to be swallowed whole. I don't go into the bush to look at natural formations – I don't marvel at God's handiwork." (24)

Here as elsewhere, Moorhouse is a Montaigne or Voltaire-style doubter in search of belief. Belle's role in the narrative is to counter the Moorhouse figure's tendency to theorize his experiences. She makes a camp fire while he opens a bottle of 1968 Coonawarra Cabernet Shiraz, which they drink in the Guzzini goblets he's bought for camping. Despite the flies, and led by Belle, they have sex on the rock. They play with the idea of primitiveness. After a night in their tent, and clearing up in the morning, Moorhouse's narrator feels that a mistake has been made:

The disquiet came because Belle had been moved *out of place* in his life. The Budawang bush was the place of his childhood testing, his family's bush experience, touching base, touching primitive base. He had learned his masculinity here.
She did not belong in that album.
He looked back at her up the trail, plodding through the swampy part in her Keds dripping wet from the moisture of the bushes. He saw her again at the camp fire, primitively squatting. He felt a huge fondness for her. (29)

Yet the thought haunts him that coming to this place with her has been a disaster:

By bringing Belle with him on his fortieth birthday and on Christmas he had left an ineradicable and inappropriate memory trace across the countryside. (29)

Lying behind this disquiet is a sense of his lost love – and youth – that may be impossible to recover.
When the Moorhouse character and Belle return to their comfortable motel on the coast, the narrator spreads out a map of southern New South Wales on the floor and tries to discern where he belongs:

These are my heartlands, he showed her, the English damp green
tablelands of Bowral and Moss Vale, the old goldfields, the lakes of
Jindabyne, the new snow resort, down to Bega where my father introduced me to the man who had a library of a thousand books of
mystery and the supernatural, to Kiama where my girlfriend from
school and I went for our miserable honeymoon after we were
married in the hometown Church of England. (30)

He tries to place Belle in his great-grandmother's territory, but realizes
she cannot enter his heartlands or any personal or family story he can
create. In order to "erase the mistake," the Moorhouse character returns two weeks later and camps in the same place, alone. But instead
of erasing the memory, he finds he has only inscribed it more deeply.
The writer's log book, perhaps his most important reason for the
camping trip, records a man at a crossroads in his life, out of joint with
his time and place, uncertain of where he belongs, and with whom.

Despite the misgivings and uncertainties, Moorhouse's bush remains
a stabilizing influence in his sense of self. He represents it as a different zone of his personal symbology than Lawson did. While Lawson's
rhetoric of the bush presented it as representative Australia in an act of
radical differentiation from the mother country, Britain, Moorhouse
associates his identity with a particular region and *chooses* to go there
at a time of identity crisis. He is not fatalistic, but remains open to
experiment and change.

In some respects, Moorhouse has become in this story a *connois-
seur* of the natural environment, who has not cut himself off from the
traditions represented by Lawson and Rudd but has drawn from them
in order to contemplate the new selves that seem possible in contemporary Australia. In Moorhouse's work as a whole, his bush traveller is
the one who tries to understand himself in terms of a "natural" identity with links to the land and family. In later collections, such as *Room
Service* or *The Inspector-General of Misconception*, Moorhouse shifts
his focus from more or less stable referents of the Australian natural
environment to ironic and humorous reflections on signifiers of international transit zones – a pattern he had foreshadowed in his widely
anthologized 1970s story, "The Airport, the Pizzeria, the Motel, the
Rented Car, and the Mysteries of Life" (*Tales of Mystery* 59–69).

PLACES OF SIGNIFICANCE: THEA ASTLEY, DAVID MALOUF, ROBERT DREWE, MANDY SAYER

Since the 1970s, Australian short fiction writers have written from, and often of, a wide range of Australian cities and suburbs and their wider geographic regions. For example, Helen Garner is mainly associated with inner-city Melbourne and Geelong, the town where she was born 74 km west of Melbourne, with occasional excursions to Sydney, the Gold Coast, and Paris. Other prominent short story writers of this period primarily associated with certain cities or regions include Tim Winton (coastal Western Australia), Carmel Bird (Hobart), Peter Goldsworthy and Barbara Hanrahan (Adelaide), and Marion Halligan (Canberra).

I have written elsewhere of Herb Wharton and Dewi Anggraeni as short story writers whose Aboriginal and Indonesian immigrant backgrounds respectively give them particular perspectives on place in Australia ("Some Dynamics of Literary Place-making" 102–03). Here, I will focus briefly on work by four writers of literary merit since the 1970s who have left their signatures on Australian places or regions. The four writers are Thea Astley, David Malouf, Robert Drewe, and Mandy Sayer. Their literary places are, respectively, a tropical rainforest, a suburban house, the beach, and a notorious urban red-light district. The troping of each of these territories, I suggest, evokes a particularity of location, a certain *goût de terroir*, and also projects them onto a wider stage of place-making with mythic dimensions that makes them accessible to those who do not know these territories first-hand.

THEA ASTLEY'S TROPICAL NORTH

The tropical rainforests of North Queensland are a well known Australian tourist destination, but Thea Astley reverses the advertising imagery in her volume of stories *Hunting the Wild Pineapple* (1979). The stories are focused chiefly on old-established Queenslanders or misfits from across the border down south – "Mexicans," as they are sometimes called. In fact, Astley's North shows her indebtedness to makers of the American Deep South such as Faulkner, Flannery O'Connor, and Welty. Yet her own signature is everywhere apparent in a sardonic, satiric style which reveals the darkness of souls and the brutality of bodies in a lapsed, tropical Eden.

Astley's essay "Being a Queenslander" notes that "the Parish is the heart of the world" and that "literary truth is derived from the Parish" (Astley 255). Her fictional parish of North Queensland derives in part from the Catholic iconography with which she was raised. Astley's eccentric male narrator in the stories that comprise *Hunting the Wild Pineapple* is a long-time denizen of the North who presents his region as a "slovenly" Eden and does not refrain from moral judgments about its inhabitants, old or new.

For all its gothic horrors, however, Astley's tropical North offers her narrator Leverson scope to indulge in a strain of elegiac posturing which sets a mood. The town of Mango is presented metonymically like this, for example:

> Once this town panted under a miasma bubbling with gold-light; but it's a waste now, howling for time ... Time wins out. The place stands still; and if it waits long enough, just blinking now and again in the humid weather, the landscape becomes what it once was. (*Hunting* 65)

Astley's juxtapositioning of natural and human environments reveals gaps between a cornucopia of forest, fruit and natural fulfilment and the reality of living at the fag end of civilization:

> At six the pub verandahs are filling up with the seedy, the old, the sun-blasted discards of the tropics; and here we are, the lot of us, gulping our beers and pushing the conversation across flat decades of memory while the wavering atmospherics of the place suggests another drink and another. (*Hunting* 169)

Astley's North is a men's world which not only the women but also the educated men find difficult. The lazy hippies from the South add little to the culture. The failure of men to understand women in Astley's "parish" is exemplified in the volume's opening, scene-setting story, which introduces a 67-year-old itinerant labourer nicknamed Fixer (because he generally can't fix anything). The narrator Leverson describes Fixer's approach to girls:

> I've driven Fixer down to Reef Town sometimes and when he's spotted a pretty girl he's leant out of the window of the car and clapped, ever so nicely. He told me once he was in a van with three

of his mates, and when they sighted this marvellous sort dawdling along the strand they pulled up and gave her a round of applause. No words. Just applause. "I used to say congratulations once," he said. "But they took it wrong." (*Hunting* 20)

Fixer considers himself a poet and sometimes takes his doggerel to the pubs, where the real drinkers rapidly escape his clutches, but for a time the hippies make him their guru, listening to his awful verse as the guitars clunk and joints are passed around (*Hunting* 21). The story evokes both ridicule and a degree of pathos when the inept Fixer is taken up for a time as a lover by the drugged-out Lilian, who then leaves him. But the author's satiric eye sees them both as odd relics of the game of love.

The real lament in Astley's North is for the loss of souls. "It's a kind of carpet-bagger's paradise," remarks Leverson (*Hunting* 162). Like Patrick White's satiric attacks on Australian suburban materialism and greed in essays, novels, and stories, Astley's satire simultaneously portrays a search for a paradise of mind and spirit, and its antithesis in her fallen North.

DAVID MALOUF: HOUSE AND SUBURB

A novel approach to depicting Australian suburban life as a "crossroads of circumstance" was taken by David Malouf in his 66–page "essay story" *12 Edmondstone Street* (1985). This form, which combines the characteristics of both story and essay, is one of a variety of ways which Malouf has used to shape, texture, and mythologize Brisbane, the city of his birth. The novelty of *12 Edmondstone Street* lies in its brilliant and ingenious interweaving of the autobiographical narrator's memories of a house and its environment. Malouf's remarkable achievement is to use techniques of short fiction such as description, narration, dialogue and imagery in the service of what James Tulip has aptly called "a kind of Morality Play where the self or soul of the writer discovers itself as it moves from room to room on a journey through life" (Tulip 11). The story gains poignancy from the recognition that the actual one-storey weatherboard house of childhood has been destroyed and can therefore only ever be a product of memory and imagination.

12 Edmondstone Street is also about family, especially the writer's relationship to his Lebanese grandfather, his parents and his sister, and their relationship to Brisbane and a wider Australia. Each individual plays a part in the narrator's Morality Play. For example, the Malouf character's father betrays his Lebanese father by adapting himself so completely to the new country and growing up "Australian" (7) in the years before the Great War. While the narrative follows the movements and perceptions of a single body remembering particular rooms, their furniture, the verandah outside and the under-the-house area, the narrator occasionally pauses to generalize:

> Each house has its own topography, its own lore: negotiable barriers, spaces open or closed, the salient features ... The house is a field of dense affinities, laid down, each one, with an almost physical power ... (9)

This "field of dense affinities" – the "heart's field" in Welty's terminology – is explored through a single, authorial self in Malouf's story. The central intrigue, and search, is for the marks one made, and were made on one, in the childhood home. As Malouf remarks, "We are drawn back magically, magnetically, to our own sticky fingerprints" (9).

The subdued lyricism of *12 Edmondstone Street* is enhanced by the rapt attention given by the middle-aged narrator to his child self. The metaphors of inside and outside are mediated by the liminal space of the verandah, as Malouf notices:

> Verandahs are no-man's-land, border zones that keep contact with the house and activities on one face but are open on the other to the street, the night and all the vast, unknown areas beyond. (20)

Fiona Giles has shown in her anthology *From the Verandah* that the verandah was an actual and metaphoric space for romance tales by women in colonial Australian society. For the young Malouf, it was a half-way house to the world outside where, the older narrating self reminds us, people such as Aborigines and migrants also lived. This is the world too, from which the personified but never named Burglar came to steal objects from the house. Family pressures are intensely concerned with remaining "inside" the home. The perils of stepping outside are obvious:

> Forbidden to use local slang, or to speak or act "Australian," we grew up as in a foreign land, where everything local, everything

outside the house that was closest and most ordinary, had about it the glow of the exotic. (33)

ROBERT DREWE: THE BEACH

By contrast with the miasma of Astley's tropical North and the inner spaces of Malouf's Brisbane home of childhood, Robert Drewe's collection of stories, *The Bodysurfers* (1983) reconstructs the outdoor spaces of Australian *beaches* as major sites of pleasure-seeking and self-discovery. The metaphor of bodysurfing (i.e. surfing without boards or other artificial aids) serves to accentuate the sensual and physical aspects of self-discovery. *The Bodysurfers* became one of the best known titles of short fiction produced in Australia when it was subsequently dramatized for television, film, radio, and the stage.

The appeal of *The Bodysurfers* was partly that Drewe detected, explored, and popularized notions of the beach, which had been a relatively neglected site for representations of contemporary Australian experience (Bennett, *Australian Short Fiction* 253). Drewe's interest in reversing notions of the Australian interior as the iconic place for self-exploration is evident in his story "The Last Explorer" (*Bodysurfers* 147–53). The protagonist in this story is an old bushman explorer of the 1930s nearing the end of his life in a beachside hospice, who is interviewed by a reporter about the meaning and value of his inland explorations. He can view the Indian Ocean from his bed. At the end of the story, the old man manages to turn his bed around so that he is facing the desert. "The Last Explorer" neatly reverses the seaward gaze of most stories in *The Bodysurfers* and reinforces a view that generational change is occurring. Drewe further reinforced his sense of beaches as a fruitful location for contemporary storytelling when he edited *The Picador Book of the Beach* in 1993 with contributions from other Australians such as Tim Winton, Glenda Adams, and Frank Moorhouse, together with a raft of international fiction writers including Raymond Carver, Keri Hulme, Ian McEwan, Nadine Gordimer, Graham Swift, and John Updike.

Robert Drewe's seaside locations range from Western Australia to New South Wales and Queensland. For him, they offer places where tension, conflict, and occasional epiphany occur. Most often, they suggest sites for the testing of a precious but ever-threatened Australian brand of innocence. The white beach sands west of Perth are especially significant for sexual rites of passage, and dangerous waves, rip-tides, and hidden rocks suggest perils beneath the surface and the accidents of living.

The tantalizing opening story in *The Bodysurfers* recalls a Christmas dinner from the first-person narrator's childhood at a beachside hotel near Perth. The boy's mother has died six months earlier and his father has decided that he, his sister Annie, and brother should celebrate this Christmas by the sea. Across the water the holiday island of Rottnest is visible from the hotel dining room, but what remains in the narrator's memory is a mirage which seems to divide Rottnest into "three attenuated islands that seemed to be sailing south" (13). The memory of this mirage gets associated in the narrator's memory with his observation as a boy of his father flirting with the hotel manageress. The boy has realized with a shock that he loves his father. His mother has died and the divided feelings of the child dealing with false hopes, jealousy, and betrayal are revealed poignantly and economically.

Robert Drewe's oceans and beaches provide "the crossroads of circumstance" for a variety of men and women who retreat there for refreshment, relief, thrills, or escape. The author's deft evocation of sense impressions reveals the attraction of the beach for actual bodysurfers:

> The electric cleansing of the surf is astonishing, the cold effervescing over the head and trunk and limbs. And the internal results are a real wonder. At once the spirits lift. (*Bodysurfers* 158)

But the beach is also a place to escape to, as in the story "Shark Logic," about a headmaster who has left his school, feigned suicide, changed his name, and taken up residence in a flat near the beach. But the man's paranoia follows him, he imagines sharks everywhere and goes to see them in an aquarium. Having apparently cut himself off from family, school, and society, he is walking on the beach one day when he sees a fisherman being dragged out to sea by the currents and brings him in to safety. The story poses the question of whether this incident will enable him to find a way back to human fellowship.

Drewe's compassion for such lonely and bereft figures is allied with a sharp sense of humour and irony. In his story "Baby Oil," Anthea, a journalist, has started a new sexual relationship with Max at her beachside unit. Her speciality is Johnson's Baby Oil for sensuality and lubricity. When Max begins to suspect that the levels in the bottle are diminishing further between their meetings, he is haunted by suspicion and jealousy. The author watches on wryly, without comment upon this novel variant on the long-established tale of sexual jealousy.

MANDY SAYER'S KING'S CROSS

Sydney's Montmartre – the notorious red-light district, Kings Cross – provides the chief framing device of place in Mandy Sayer's collection *15 Kinds of Desire* (2002). Kings Cross is not virgin literary territory, as the anthology edited by Sayer and Louis Nowra, *In the Gutter ... Looking at the Stars: A Literary Adventure Through Kings Cross* (2000), amply reveals. (The title comes from Oscar Wilde's remark: "We are all in the gutter, but some of us are looking at the stars.") But Sayer's is a fresh, younger voice with an intimate knowledge of the physical and socio-economic topography of her chosen place through having lived there as a child and returning there again in the 1990s and early 2000s after a period in the USA.

In "True Story," the concluding piece in *15 Kinds of Desire*, Sayer reveals that Kings Cross offered her unconventional, jazz drummer father, and later herself, a pleasure in escaping "the boredom and conformity of [Sydney] suburbia" (219). When her mother and father were briefly reconciled in Kings Cross, the place seemed to offer, for a time, a "precarious paradise" (221). She recalls a moment from that time:

> I sat on the lip of the El Alamein Fountain, and instead of marvelling at the puff-ball orbs of water, I looked up to see a high-speed car chase roaring up Macleay Street and along Darlinghurst Road. Immediately I was intrigued by the place, by the oscillating neon lights, the ornate buildings, the jazz leaking up from the basement clubs. (215)

Sayer's deeply embedded image, like others canvassed in this essay, arises from her experience of childhood or youth.

Sayer's opening story in *15 Kinds of Desire* introduces a child called Scarlet who is forced to grow up fast in the urban jungle of Kings Cross. An eleven-year-old redhead, Scarlet looks after her drug-addicted mother and her similarly afflicted maternal grandfather, Grant, who is a transvestite. Sayer interweaves her contemporary story of urban exploitation, misery and survival with elements of the Little Red Riding Hood tale. She presents Scarlet as a voracious reader of Enid Blyton's Famous Five adventure stories. In her red jacket on which she has embroidered a perfect "S," she sets out on a mission of mercy to take "medicine" to her grandfather/mother but the medicine is smack cocaine. The journey takes her through the dark, wet streets of a topographically recognizable Kings Cross past derelicts, perverts and drunks. She is accosted by a number of men on the way including a policeman, but she rejects his offer to take her through the dangerous park, remembering from family folklore that all police are "pigs," to be avoided at all costs. What happens when she arrives at her grandfather/granny's house will not be divulged here: suffice to say that little Scarlet has learnt how to deal with big bad wolves in disguise and survives another night in this urban jungle.

Sexual mobility and the scope for identity change are recurrent features of Sayer's Kings Cross. Her story "Ash" tests these possibilities in its depiction of the brothels of the red-light district as a magnet for visiting American sailors on R & R. The story's narrator is a boy who has dropped out of high school to work as an assistant and cleaner at a brothel, a job his mother used to do before she died. Curious, and envious of the American sailors' popularity with local women, Ash steals the white uniform and cap of one of them while the sailor is otherwise occupied in the brothel, and goes out on the town. He makes some surprising discoveries, including the one that not all young women are "snowed" by the American sailors.

Mandy Sayer's Kings Cross is a place of surprising discoveries. She does not approach her subjects or their urban environments as a moralist but as a fiction writer intrigued by impersonation and disguise – the making of illusions. Her main theme is desire and the crazy forms it can take. In this context, most settled forms of living, including marriage and living in the suburbs, seem illusionistic and love is "a crazy roulette game" (172).

Like the other Australian short fiction writers of the contemporary period discussed in this paper – Moorhouse, Astley, Malouf, and Drewe – Mandy Sayer has a sophisticated awareness of the literary contexts in which she works. She reveals this in one of the stories in *15 Kinds of Desire* which shifts the setting from Kings Cross back to representations of the Australian bush. She calls the story "The Drover's Wife" and this produces the latest in a series of parodic regressions which lead back to Russell Drysdale's painting with that title and Henry Lawson's iconic story.[4] Sayer's story refers most directly, in fact, to Murray Bail's story called "The Drover's Wife" from *Contemporary Portraits and Other Stories* (1975), which employs the Drysdale painting to show a suburban dentist's obsession with the wife who has left him and who, he believes, has run away to the bush and become the drover's wife depicted in Drysdale's famous painting. Sayer's story accepts aspects of Bail's tale of a suburban dentist who dreams of the bush to which he believes his wife has escaped. But Sayer takes the point of view of the woman, who follows her desire by escaping from suburbia to work as a snake charmer in a circus (with all the sexual connotations evoked by that vocation).

CONCLUSION

Contemporary Australian short fiction writers have found their "crossroads of circumstance" in a variety of unusual locations. Their representations of place differ from Lawson's in drawing widely from Australian and international literary traditions, and showing that a variety of Australians now have the luxury of choosing their places and the constructions they put upon them. With the possible exception of Thea Astley, Australian short fiction writers since the 1970s have rejected the kind of fatalism that many of Lawson's or Faulkner's characters express in their environments. But just as Lawson and Faulkner sought to render the "character" of a place or region, so have Moorhouse, Astley, Malouf, Drewe, and Sayer striven to show the special qualities of their fictional environments, which are based on memory, imagination, and a wide cultural exposure of contemporary urban media including television and film. Literary places that have a depth of emotional connotation, as in the work of these writers, are often infused with memories of childhood; for, as Eudora Welty showed, such places, renewed and recast in memory and imagination, are often "the proving ground of 'What happened? Who's here? Who's coming?' – that is the heart's field."

NOTES

1   Eudora Welty, "Place in Fiction" from *Critical Approaches to Fiction.* Ed. Shiv K. Kumar and Keith McKean. New York: McGraw-Hill, 1968: 249–264.

2   It can be argued that journals such as *Westerly* and *Meanjin* did publish some of the new, experimental short fiction, but the circulation figures of these literary magazines were in the low thousands.

3   Frank Moorhouse, "Going into the Heartlands with the Wrong Person at Christmas," *Meanjin* 40.2 (1981): 152–60.
4   Other authors who have written their own parodic versions of "The Drover's Wife" include Frank Moorhouse, Jack Hodgins, and Barbara Jefferis.

WORKS CITED

Astley, Thea. "Being a Queenslander: A Form of Literary and Geographical Conceit," *Southerly* 36.3 (1976): 252–64.
– *Hunting the Wild Pineapple.* 1979; Ringwood, Vic: Penguin, 1981.
Bail, Murray. "The Drover's Wife." *Contemporary Portraits and Other Stories.* St. Lucia: University of Queensland Press, 1975.
Bennett, Bruce. "Some Dynamics of Literary Placemaking: An Australian Perspective." *ISLE: Interdisciplinary Studies in Literature and the Environment.* 10.2 (Summer 2003): 97–109.
– *Australian Short Fiction: A History.* St Lucia: University of Queensland Press, 2002.
Drewe, Robert. *The Bodysurfers.* Darlinghurst: James Fraser, 1983.
– Ed. *The Picador Book of the Beach.* Sydney: Picador/Pan Macmillan, 1993.
Gallant, Mavis. *In Transit.* Markham, ON: Viking/Penguin, 1988.
Giles, Fiona. Ed. *From the Verandah: Stories of Love and Landscape by Nineteenth Century Australian Women.* Melbourne: McPhee Gribble/ Penguin, 1987.
Lawson, Henry. *Short Stories and Sketches 1888–1922.* Vol. 1 Collected Prose. Ed. Colin Roderick. Sydney: Angus and Robertson, 1972.
Malouf, David. *12 Edmondstone Street.* 1985; Harmondsworth: Penguin, 1986, 1–66.
Moorhouse, Frank. *Tales of Mystery and Romance.* London: Angus and Robertson, 1977.
– *Days of Wine and Rage.* Ringwood, Vic: Penguin, 1980.
– *Room Service.* Ringwood, Vic: Viking/Penguin, 1985.
– Ed. *A Steele Rudd Selection.* St. Lucia. University of Queensland Press, 1986.
– *Forty-Seventeen.* Ringwood, Vic: Viking/Penguin, 1988.
– *The Inspector-General of Misconception.* Sydney: Vintage/Random House, 2002.
New, W.H. *Dreams of Speech and Violence: The Art of the Short Story in Canada and New Zealand.* Toronto: University of Toronto Press, 1987.
Sayer, Mandy. *15 Kinds of Desire.* Sydney: Vintage/Random House, 2001.
Sayer, Mandy and Louis Nowra. Eds. *In the Gutter … Looking at the Stars: A Literary Adventure Through King's Cross.* Sydney: Random House, 2000.

Tulip, James. "Essaying Stories," *Age Monthly Review* 5.10 (March 1986): 11.

Welty, Eudora. "Place in Fiction." 1956; repr. in *Critical Approaches to Fiction*. Ed. Shiv Kumar and Keith McKean. New York: McGraw-Hill, 1968: 249–264.

Welty, Eudora. *The Golden Apples*. 1949. New York: Harcourt Brace, 1988.

Werlock, Abby H.P. Ed. *The Facts on File Companion to the American Short Story*. New York: Facts on File, 2000.

Wilding, Michael. Ed. *The Tabloid Story Pocket Book*. Sydney: Wild and Woolley, 1978.

Wilde, William H., Joy Hooton and Barry Andrews. *The Oxford Companion to Australian Literature*, 2nd ed. Melbourne: Oxford University Press, 1994.

JANICE KULYK KEEFER

La Dame Seule Meets the Angel of History: Katherine Mansfield and Mavis Gallant

In one of Mavis Gallant's early stories, "Virus X," the central characters, ladylike grad student Lottie, and bohemian drop-out Vera, Canadians temporarily resident in Paris, are fishing about for something to do.

'Katherine Mansfield's grave, how about that? Remember Miss Pink? She fed us old Mansfield till it ran out of our ears. She's buried around Fontainebleau. Mansfield is, not Miss Pink ...'
  'She was my favourite author until I specialized', said Lottie primly. 'Then, I'm sorry to say, I had to restrict my reading'.
  Vera dug into her rice as if looking for buried treasure. 'Right,' she said. 'We'll go out to the grave.' Lottie consented to nothing of the kind. (HT,180)

I begin this paper with a reference to these less than passionate pilgrims to make two points: one, that Mavis Gallant does not suffer academics gladly, and two, that it's a tricky business, tracing influences on writers – the nature and effect of that influence may be far more complex, ambivalent or simply playful than the academic might wish. So, caveat professor, and let's begin.

Katherine Mansfield died at the age of 34, by which age Mavis Gallant had only just embarked on her vocation as a full-time writer living, like Mansfield, as a colonial expatriate in Europe. To date, Gallant's writing life has extended at least four decades beyond Mansfield's, and it would be foolish to argue that the New Zealand writer's work has been a unique or comprehensive influence on the Canadian's oeuvre. Yet much of Gallant's early fiction and some of her finest, mature work not only make direct reference to Katherine Mansfield, but also explore and extend some of Mansfield's most characteristic motifs – the displaced "dame seule," for example. And though the two writers' oeuvres are quite different, Gallant's aesthetic shares crucial elements with Mansfield's. In their extraordinary mastery of the "divine detail," and their concern with deracination and isolation, particularly as they affect women of different cultures and social classes, the works of these two writers compose a continuum in which the possibilities of short fiction as a genre have richly flowered.

What interests me principally, however, is the way in which one writer influences another, not by copying, but rather by learning, one from the other, while recognizing similarities of vision and perception. I am intrigued by the passion with which an emerging writer embraces the work of an established artist and then, just as passionately, establishes her independence. I say passionately, not anxiously, for there need be no Bloomian killing-off of influence; the metaphor I prefer – one particularly suitable for Paris, where Gallant has made her home, and where Mansfield spent some of the most important periods of her writing life – is one of apparel. It's as if one writer deeply influenced by another were to dress in the clothes, not only of her words, but also of her way of seeing the world. The body does not change through the donning of such garments; rather, the cloth and cut itself alter with wear: seams are let out, stitches unpicked, new material let in, hems slashed and sleeves lopped or added. And in time, the garment itself may be taken off, given or thrown away, but often – at least in this particular case – a remnant is kept, a sample of the fabric or detailing, to be sewn into what has become the writer's own, independent and characteristic mode of dress.

◆

Katherine Mansfield was strongly influenced by Chekhov, whom she read as a teenager, borrowing copies of his short fiction from the parliamentary library in Wellington, New Zealand. One of the most contentious events in Mansfield's writing life is her reworking of a Chekhov story, "*Spat' Khochetsia*" (often translated as "Sleepy Head" though the Russian means "I Want to Sleep"). "*Spat' Khochetsia*" became, in Mansfield's version "The Child Who Was Tired," and appeared in her first published volume, *In a German Pension*. Critics and biographers differ as to whether "The Child Who Was Tired" should be construed as outright plagiarism or treated as an imaginatively independent "translation" of the original. Whatever the case, Mansfield refused to have *In a German Pension* reissued, not only because she was reluctant to stoke anti-German hysteria during the First World War, but also, it may be, because the "fit" of the Chekhov original now appeared uncomfortably tight. Mansfield herself became a significant influence on her arch-rival Virginia Woolf – at least, Woolf was preoccupied with the idea of rivalry vis à vis the colonial's work. No one who reads "The Garden Party" and then *Mrs Dalloway* or *To the Lighthouse* on the heels of "At the Bay" can escape the perception that the publisher of *Prelude* learned a great deal from the writer whom Woolf described both as a civet cat who had taken to street walking and the only writer of whom she had ever been jealous.

I have never asked Mavis Gallant about her relationship with the work of Katherine Mansfield, but have found more than "a scrap of the New Zealander's dress" in the fabric of the Canadian's stories. One could argue, for example, that there are traces of "The Little Governess" in "The Four Seasons," both of which deal with the plight of pitifully young servant girls stranded in foreign parts. In fact, much of the two women's work has to do with what used to be called "the servant problem," though from an unaccustomed perspective: Mansfield's "Life of Ma Parker" and "The Lady's Maid," and Gallant's "An Alien Flower," and "An Unmarried Man's Summer," for example. In reading "The Moabitess," that story of Miss Horeham, a skint elderly spinster exiled and alone in the south of France and obsessed with a dead father, it's hard not to think of "Miss Brill," as well, of course, as "The Daughters of the Late Colonel." The portrayal of children's vulnerability, their being at the mercy of adults who are too incompetent or lackadaisical to look after them, but also the acuity of intelligence which human beings possess in childhood, when they have all their wits about them – these form additional links between the writing of Gallant and Mansfield. The Kezia of "Prelude" and "At the Bay" and "The Doll's House," and the child Linnet Muir in the eponymous suite of stories, can be called sisters under the skin – I use that analogy knowingly, as someone who has, and has often sparred with, a sister. The orphaning of Mansfield's Fenella in "The Voyage" and the obscure parentage of "The Fenton Child," the shocking precocity of Hennie and his unnamed sister in "The Young Girl" and their counterparts in "The Statues Taken Down"; the coldness, even cruelty of mothers and their substitutes: Linda and Beryl Burnell, Mrs Sheridan; Charlotte Muir, Linnet's chilling progenitrix, and the mother in the story "The Wedding Ring" – these are only a few of the thematic *semblables* in Gallant's and Mansfield's oeuvres. Finally, the title as well as the gist of Mansfield's early story, "An Indiscreet Journey," could well describe countless fictions of Gallant's, in which so many "permanent movables" are set in rash, bittersweet, or sorry motion.

But there is more to the reality of influence than subject matter although I remember how enthralling that particular discovery can be. When, as a fledgling writer, returned to Canada after nearly a decade in England and France, I chanced upon a copy of *From the Fifteenth District* in Ottawa's Ogilvy's department store, I forgot all about the warm gloves I was supposed to be buying, and stood reading for a good half hour before I finally realized that I could, after all, buy the book and take it home with me in my bare but happy hands. An idea kept lighting up my head as I read the stories of Carmela and Alec Webb and Piotr/Potter – you can be a Canadian writer and set your fiction in German or Italy or France where I had last lived; you can write about things other than death in the snow, wheat fields, and northern lakes awash with singing paddles and still be a Canadian writer.

Subject and matter and style, of course, are inextricably bound up with a writer's vision. And while a certain narratorial detachment, a wickedly subtle use of irony, and a flair for satire are to be found in Gallant's and in Mansfield's best fiction, the shared stylistic feature on which I wish to focus is something more fundamental. It is what I would call perceptualism, the exercise of sensuous apprehension to produce what Mansfield's contemporary, Viktor Shklovsky, termed *ostrananie* or "making the familiar strange."

Katherine Mansfield is a past master at "making the stone stony," and thus creating not only a freshness of perception in her readers, but also a means of returning them to something like an originary moment of perception – that experience we had as children of really seeing and truly knowing something for the first time. I believe that this is what Mansfield refers to when she writes, in a reference to Blake, of the artist's need to make "that divine spring into the bounding outline of things" (KMLJ, 84). There's a famous, half-joking letter to the painter Dorothy Brett, in which Mansfield describes stopping at an apple stall and staring until she felt herself to be "changing into an apple, too" or a duck, or Tolstoy's Natasha – whatever happened to be in her physical or mind's eye. And yet this transformation or identification with the object perceived is, Mansfield insists, "only the 'prelude.' There follows the moment when you are *more* duck, *more* apple, or *more* Natasha than any of these objects could ever possibly be, and so you create them anew" (KMLJ, 84).

Sensuous apprehension, for Mansfield, was a source of delight and sometimes distress. What other word but uncanny is there to describe her recreation, in exact detail, of the smell and look, the sensuous materiality of an evening at the beach, or her account of an imagined ride in a cab, on a wet night, to a house drenched in damp? In a letter to the Russian émigré Koteliansky, she admits:

> The queer thing is that ... I can't help living it all, down to the smallest details – down to the very dampness of the salt at supper that night and the way it came out on your plate, the exact shape of the salt spoon ...
>
> Do you, too feel an infinite delight and value in *detail* – not for the sake of detail but for the life *in* the life of it. I never can express myself ... but do you ever feel as though the Lord threw you into eternity – into the very centre of eternity, and even as you plunged you felt every ripple that flowed out from your plunging – every single ripple floating away and touching and drawing into its circle every slightest thing it touched. (KMCL, I, 192)

In some of her fiction, characters are shown to possess an alarmingly acute ESP: thus Kezia and Linda experience, in *Prelude*, the sense of mere things coming alive. Alone in the emptied house, Kezia is menaced by something she calls "IT ... just behind her, waiting at the door ... hiding in the passage, ready to dart out ..." (KMSS, 43). And her mother's deep ambivalence about sexuality and her own fertility is expressed as she traces the poppies on the wallflower, and feels

> the sticky, silky petals, the stem, hairy like a gooseberry skin, the rough leaf and the tight glazed bud. Things had a habit of coming alive like that ... They listened, they seemed to well out with some mysterious, important content ... they were members of a secret society and they smiled among themselves. Sometimes, when she had fallen asleep in the daytime, she woke and could not lift a finger, could not even turn her eyes to left or right because THEY were there: sometimes when she went out of a room and left it empty, she knew as she clicked the door to that THEY were filling

it. And there were times in the evenings when she was upstairs, perhaps, and everybody else was down, when she could hardly escape from them. Then she could not hurry, she could not hum a tune; if she tried to … THEY were not deceived. THEY knew how frightened she was, THEY saw how she turned her head away as she passed the mirror. What Linda always felt was that THEY wanted something of her, and she knew that if she gave herself up and was … silent, motionless, something would really happen. (KMSS, 54)

♦

Precision of detail, as well as acuity of observation, are dominant characteristics of Mansfield's and Gallant's work. Compare, in *Prelude*, Kezia's tear rolling down her cheek and how "she caught it with a neat little whisk of her tongue and ate it before any of them had seen" (NZS, 97) with Peter Frazier brushing snow from Agnes Brusen's clothes, on a dark Geneva street, then licking snow from her hands in a gesture "formal as a handshake, in "The Ice Wagon Going Down the Street" (MGSS, 207). Both writers seem to have the gift of absolute recall, with Mansfield summoning up the look of cut glass doorknobs, and the smell of Worcester sauce from the sideboard in one of her childhood homes, and Gallant remembering, via Linnet Muir, the deliciousness of "breathing inside knitted wool … warm, moist, pungent when one had been sucking on mint candies …" (MGSS, 708). Yet in the best of their work, defamiliarizing detail and moments of intense sensuous perception serve the deeper, larger vision of each writer. In a review of Dorothy Richardson, among others, Mansfield emphasized the limitations of the "quivering moment of suspension" favoured by what she called the dragonfly school of writing fashionable among her contemporaries:

For them the whole art of writing consists in the power with which they are able to register that faint inward shock of recognition … There is a quality in the familiarity of these experiences or in their strangeness which evokes an immediate mysterious response – a desire for expression. But now, instead of going any further, instead of attempting to relate their experiences to life or to see them against any sort of background, these writers are … content to remain in the air, hovering over, as if the thrilling moment were enough and more than enough … .

But what is the effect of this kind of writing upon the reader? How is he to judge the importance of one thing rather than another if each is seen in isolation? And is it not rather cold comfort to be offered a share in a secret on the express understanding that you do not ask what the secret is – more especially if you cherish the uncomfortable suspicion that the author is no wiser than you, that the author is in love with the secret and would not discover it if he could? (NN, 137–38)

What, then, are the secrets which Mansfield and Gallant explore, how do they relate their perceptual experiences to life, and against what sort of background do they assume significance?

◆

It's hardly surprising that Mansfield, a chronic invalid from her early twenties on, with untreated gonorrhea as well as pulmonary tuberculosis, should have been acutely aware of her own mortality. It is more surprising, perhaps, to learn from a perusal of her juvenilia, that the child Kassie Beauchamp seemed obsessed by Death. Her earliest notebooks are full of stories in which Death appears as a desirable young woman to whom the living are in thrall, or as the Grim Reaper trying to seduce a child – there is always something erotic about its approach. In her world – one, we must recall, without antibiotics – children and infants – like her baby sister Gwen – die with a pitiful regularity.

In contrast to Kassie Beauchamp, Katherine Mansfield's understanding of mortality, that ultimate experience of isolation which makes all of us *dames ou hommes seul(e)s*, acquired a far more sophisticated erotic edge and became profoundly nuanced. In a letter to the young writer William Gerhardi, about her story "The Garden Party," she explains how she tried to convey

[t]he diversity of life and how we try to fit in everything, Death included … [Laura, being so young] feels things ought to happen differently. First one and then the other. But life isn't like that. We haven't the ordering of it. Laura says, 'But all these things must not happen at once.' And Life answers, 'Why not? How are they divided from each other?' And they *do* all happen, it is inevitable. And it seems to me there is beauty in that inevitability. (KMSL, 250)

This beauty coexists with, is perhaps the condition for, that sadness Mansfield discerned at the core of life: not sorrow, which passes, but sadness, "deep down, deep down, part of one, like one's breathing" (KMSS, 362). It is, if not unthinkable, unspeakable. "The Daughters of the Late Colonel," her masterpiece – and the last piece she ever wrote, "The Canary" – are haunted by this inexpressible awareness. What Constantia longs for when she lies outstretched in the chill moonlight; what she can't explain to her sister, what she forgets to say, just as it seems she is about to speak herself into life, her own life, at long last. And what the old woman in "The Canary" understands to be at the core of life, "something which is like longing, and yet is not longing" (KMSS, 360). "What is it?" she asks, erasing the question with her response: "One can never know." The only bearable response, perhaps for the knowledge that the mystery we sense at the heart of life is emptiness: a far less acerbic apprehension than that voiced by one of Gallant's more caustic characters, Bea Armitage, in "Malcolm and Bea": "'Mystery' had been her word for Roy unborn. But why hadn't anyone warned her the Mystery was so very ugly? Birth was another ugly mystery. Death was ugly. Her mother, dying ..." (EW, 118). If Mansfield's wrestling with mortality is the dark sky which gives substance and significance to her dragonfly details, then history performs the same function in the work of Mavis Gallant. History understood as both act – and failure to act – and memory, that medium for the obfuscation, revision, and sometimes the merciless record of action – the pin through the dragonfly, into the board.

The key event of Katherine Mansfield's short life was the First World War, in which her young brother Leslie perished in a particularly gruesome way, "blown to bits" while demonstrating to his men the use of a (defective) grenade. One of Mansfield's most famous aperçus stems from this experience: in a letter to Jack Murry, she outlines the only honest way to write, now that the war has seeped into the fabric of day-to-day life. She cannot speak "bang out" about Death and "deserts of vast eternity," she says, but must write in a new way, acknowledging the background of death to all life's small and seemingly trivial occurrences – a woman combing out her hair by a window, a boy eating a bowl of strawberries. "Now we know ourselves for what we are. In a way it's a tragic knowledge: it's as though, even while we live again, we face death. But through life; that's the point" (KMLJ,150). Seeing "'the common things of light and day'" against, as it were, a black scrim, restores our sense of wonder at, our discovery of mystery in, the lives we

lead – the only lives we have. For Mavis Gallant, this scrim was provided by the Second World War, and, unforgettably, by the experience
of being assigned, as a young reporter for the *Montreal Standard*, the
task of creating captions for the first photographs to emerge from the
Nazi death camps. (A task, I must add, which she would not perform.)
Refusing to speak "bang out" about a form and scale of horror that
would, perhaps, have shocked even Conrad's Kurtz, Gallant turned
instead to the pathos of Walter Benjamin's "angel of history" under
whose aegis memory functions not as nostalgia, or passive reflection of
the past, but as the painfully active desire to remain in place, resurrect
the dead, and rebuild the ruins. Gallant's is a pathos braced by irony
as in this sentence from the story "Forain": "It was remarkable ... the
way literate people, reasonably well travelled and educated, comfort-
ably off, could live adequate lives without wanting to know what had
gone before or happened elsewhere" (MGSS, 630). Among the literate
are journalists who substitute "a few names, a date looked up, a notion of geography" (MGSS, 631) for any sustained form of historical
consciousness.

Any such consciousness is, of course, dependent on memory, which,
as Gallant's oeuvre has so convincingly shown, is notoriously capri-
cious and yet which remains crucial to the preservation of human de-
cency and dignity. It is the bane – or perhaps the salvation – of Netta
Ross in "The Moslem Wife" that she possesses a "dark, an accurate, a
deadly memory" (MGSS, 35). It makes her see, during her rendezvous
with her blithely amnesiac husband Jack, who has spent the war safely
in the United States, the partisans hanged from the arches of the Place
Masséna in Nice, and in particular "a poor lad's bound, dangling feet"
(MGSS, 33). Jack's "short memory, his comfortable imagination" have
always infuriated and attracted Netta; this ambivalence both prevents
her from sending Jack the letter in which she shows "how much [she]
know[s] of the truth, the truth the truth" (MGSS, 32) of war and life,
and allows her to walk off with Jack at the end of the story, her arm
held, her steps guided: not so much a Moslem wife, again, as a Moslem widow.

◆

I'd like to end this paper with a glance at two works, from the "middle
period" of each writer's oeuvre: Mansfield's "The Man Without a
Temperament"(1920) and the aforementioned story of Gallant's,

"The Moslem Wife" (1976). Both deal with "the woe that is in marriage" or to put it another way, "the mystery of what makes a couple,"
particularly a couple that, against all odds, persists in the embrace of
marriage. They are stories of two Jacks, though in Mansfield's text he
is called Robert, the thinly-disguised model for Robert Salesby being
John Middleton Murry, Mansfield's husband. The difference between
the original and the fictive version is perhaps as great as the difference
between Robert Salesby's and Jack Murry's nicknames – Boogles and
Bogey. "The Moslem Wife" is also, primarily, the story of Netta Ross,
née Archer, and in some ways Netta seems a dead ringer for Katherine Mansfield: not only does she possess that writer's deadly accurate
memory, but she resembles her uncannily in her physical appearance
as well: "She ... had the dry, burned-out look of someone turned inward. Her dark eyes glowed out of a thin face. She had the shape of a
girl of fourteen" (MGSS, 7). Spectacularly unlike Mansfield, it would
seem, the newly married Netta is "intensely, almost unnaturally happy" (MGSS, 9) though, in tune with Mansfield, "[h]er happiness had
always been great enough to allow for despair" (MGSS, 18).

Netta's Jack is in some ways the contrary of Robert Salesby. While
both are Englishmen, Robert is perceived as repellent by the guests at
the Italian hotel where he is keeping his invalid wife company; Jack
Ross, on the other hand, is the compleat charmer, at least to the female
guests and neighbours of the Hotel Prince Albert and Albion. But both
are men with absolutely nothing in the world to do; Robert because
of the unconscionable amount of time his wife takes dying, and Jack
because it's his métier. Both men fail their wives – who adore and are
devoted to them – egregiously. As we have seen, Netta Ross outgrows
her passionate dependence on her Jack; Jinnie Salesby, however, must
rely on her husband to dole out her medicine, fetch her cloaks, and
even squash the mosquitoes tormenting her under the netting round
her white and solitary bed. So heavy is her dependence and so demanding her illness, that when Robert addresses to his wife the one
word with which the story ends, we sense a grisly double entendre:
"Rot! he whispers"(KMSS, 154).

We shouldn't be shocked when Netta takes her prodigal husband
back at the end of a horrendous war, for earlier on, we discover that
she'd realized "to a certainty that if Jack were to die, she would search
the crowd of mourners for a man she could live with. She would not
return from the funeral alone" (MG SS, 24). In effect, the day that Jack
returns to her is the day of the funeral of Netta's lover, the Italian com-

mander who'd protected her during the war, and who was later seized by the Germans. It's an imagined rather than actual funeral: when Netta gropes, through the clasp of her husband's hand, for the "other, invisible hand" of her Italian lover, it dissolves: "It was a lost, indifferent hand; it no longer recognized her warmth. She understood: he is dead ..." (MGSS, 35). Jack Ross has become the stranger she picks out of a sparse crowd, to live with.

"The Man Without a Temperament" is not Mansfield's finest story – by a long shot that crown belongs to "The Daughters of the Late Colonel" to which the opening paragraph of the "The Moslem Wife" refers. (There are other sly quotations from "Daughters" in "Wife," for example the Maharajah's daughters' governess with her pretentious articulation: shades of Nurse Andrews and her comments on Lady Tuke's butter dish in "Daughters.") Yet there are threads of "The Man Without a Temperament" in "The Moslem Wife." Both stories are set in hotels, and when we learn that Netta and Jack Ross "never make the conjugal sounds that pass for conversation and that might as well have been bowwow and quack quack" (MGSS, 10) we may recall the General's "loud caw" and the two Topknots shrieking "Mr Queet" like deranged parakeets in Mansfield's story. But one of the most noticeable differences between the two stories is that the sole reference to the first war in "Temperament" is the name of the American guest's dog, "Klaymongso" – a far cry from that mention of a dead lad's dangling feet, in "Wife," and the details of life under occupation which Netta offers in her unsent letter to Jack. Moreover, the following reflection by Netta should be read against Mansfield's comments about how the war had utterly changed life, or the way we respond to life: "Death made death casual" (MGSS, 30). Perhaps it's not so much a rejection of Mansfield's belief that death enhances, intensifies, and illuminates "'the common things of life and day'" (KMLJ, 150); perhaps it's more in the nature of an alteration, in the way one "turns" a dress so that the unworn side of the fabric is exposed to view.

◆

Let's return, in closing, to the reluctant Lottie of "Virus X," who believes she may die at the same young age as Mansfield due to "asthma, colds, low blood pressure" and to Vera, whose commitment to Mansfield, we are told, stems from "an old crush on Miss Pink ... [that] had led [her] to read this one writer when she never read anything else, or wanted to. Now that she was away from the Miss Pinks of this world, she read all the time" (HT, 182). The grave they visit is in a walled cemetery lidded with sunless sky: it is "a block of polished granite weigh[t]ed upon a block still larger." Droningly, Vera reads out the inscription chiselled into the granite, stopping to puzzle less over the meaning of the epitaph – Hotspur's paradox vis à vis nettles and safety – than the tacky, china rose adorning the granite:

'You can't just abandon people that way, under all that granite. It's less than love. It's just considering your own taste.'
  'She is not abandoned, Vera; she is buried.'
  The orator heard only herself. 'The stone is even moss-resistant,' she said. But no, for the first wash of green crept up the granite step and reached a capital 'M.' (HT, 185)

But Vera is right: Mansfield was abandoned in this stark square of arid ground, bordered, I might add, by a railway line and what seems to be a small factory. Abandoned by her husband, whose name appears prominently on her grave, and who knew how much she loathed noise and loved flowers. One of the less appealing faux pas of Jack Murry was to forget to pay the upkeep on Mansfield's grave, so that a year after her death she was dug up and put into a *fosse commune*. (Her Canadian brother-in-law, who'd come on his own pilgrimage to the cemetery, arranged to have her dug back up and put into a permanent grave of her own. Katherine Mansfield, restless even in death.)
  Vera horrifies her companion by breaking off the "puritanical" (HT, 185) china rose and replacing it with a handful of yellow pansies filched from another grave in a gesture that seems "suspect" to poor Lottie. For Lottie is doomed, like her literary cousin Carol in "The Other Paris," to marry, safely, one of her own kind. Vera, on the other hand is a classic *dame seule*; she has been exiled to Europe by her Winnipeg family because of an inconvenient pregnancy, just as the pregnant Mansfield was exiled to a Bavarian spa by a monster-mother who cut her errant daughter out of her will as soon as said mother returned to New Zealand. Vera's plans to hang out in Rome with a shiftless Polish-Canadian named Al seem hardly less restrictive, in the end, than Lottie's reunion with her staunch fiancé Kevin. But Gallant isn't making us choose one fate over the other, to plump for reckless Vera (is it an accident that Jack Ross's deadly-dotty mother in "The Moslem Wife" is also a Vera?) over stolid Lottie. Instead she projects the

fates of these representative Canadians – one the child of Ukrainian, the other of German immigrants – against the catastrophic screen of public as opposed to personal history: World Wars I and II, suggested by the other pilgrimage in the story, to the Maginot line, and by the upcoming Algerian war, suggested by the "shack" full of Arabs, across from Lottie's Strasbourg hotel. For the space of this story, Lottie and Vera both are dames seules, far from the terminal safety of a moss-encroached grave, and plunged into a chaotic, dangerous, insistent world in which the angel of history longs to mend what has been smashed, turning her back to all the fresh calamities waiting in the wings.

WORKS CITED

Mavis Gallant:

EW. *The End of the World and Other Stories.* Toronto: McClelland and Stewart, 1974.

HT. *Home Truths: Selected Canadian Stories.* Toronto: Macmillan, 1981

FD. *From the Fifteenth District: a Novella and Eight Stories.* Toronto: Macmillan, 1983.

MGSS. *Mavis Gallant: The Selected Stories.* Toronto: McClelland and Stewart, 1997.

Katherine Mansfield:

NN. *Novels & Novelists.* Ed. John Middleton Murray. London: Constable, 1930.

KMSS. *Katherine Mansfield: Selected Stories.* Ed. D.M. Davin. Oxford, Oxford University Press, 1981.

KMCL. *The Collected Letters of Katherine Mansfield, Vol. I.* Ed. Vincent O' Sullivan and Margaret Scott. Oxford: Clarendon, 1984.

KMLJ. *Katherine Mansfield: The Letters and Journals, a Selection.* Ed. C.K. Stead. Harmondsworth: Penguin, 1988.

KMSL. *Katherine Mansfield: Selected Letters.* Ed. Vincent O'Sullivan. Oxford: Oxford University Press, 1990.

ROBERT THACKER

Alice Munro's Ontario

Alice Munro begins "The Love of a Good Woman" (1996) with a list
of items to be found in the Walley, Ontario, museum – photos, churns,
horse harnesses, and porcelain insulators. The next paragraph adds:

> Also there is a red box, which has the letters D.M. WILLENS,
> OPTOMETRIST printed on it, and a note beside it, saying, 'This
> box of optometrist's instruments though not very old has consider-
> able local significance, since it belonged to Mr. D.M. Willens, who
> drowned in the Peregrine River, 1951. It escaped the catastrophe
> and was found, presumably by the anonymous donor, who dis-
> patched it to be a feature of our collection.' (3)

"The Love of a Good Woman," extremely long even for the *New Yorker* where it first appeared, was recognized immediately as a *tour de
force* story – Munro critics seized it as a crucial text and several essays
(e.g. Duffy, McCombs) immediately probed its intricacies. Highlighted
in its *New Yorker* presentation by a lurid cover image and subtitled
with gothic flourish ("A Murder, a Mystery, a Romance"), "The Love
of a Good Woman" constructs Alice Munro as the preeminent writer
she is. Margaret Atwood may well be English-Canada's leading novelist, but there is little doubt that Munro is its leading storyteller and
even, perhaps, its leading writer – frequently cited as among the best
writers working in the English language.

While another analysis of "The Love of a Good Woman" might
well be justified, I begin with it here only to introduce its subject as
my own, "Alice Munro's Ontario." A.S. Byatt has written, aptly, that
Munro "has learned to depict whole lives from a distance in the same
strangely unworked-up and unaccented way [as did American novelist
Willa Cather], while also making it entirely new, as her landscape and
moeurs are new" (53). In the passage just quoted from "The Love of a

Good Woman," Munro manages to "place" the stories of several persons' lives in critical relation to the box of optometrist's instruments now on display in the Walley museum with which she begins. And having done so in extended detail (the book version is over 70 pages long), Munro still manages to avoid telling her reader just who was responsible for getting, and just how whoever it was actually got, that box of instruments into the Walley museum. Its mystery still evident, held, the box both opens "The Love of a Good Woman" and stands at its end a talisman, a trope glowing with meaning yet still withholding unequivocal explanation. Indeed, contextualizing Munro's rural Southwestern Ontario home place, "The Love of a Good Woman" is also extended demonstration that no single contemporary Canadian writer has rendered her subjective relation to a place more complexly than has Alice Munro – Tracy Ware's description of Munro's recent work is apt; he calls it "bewilderingly complex." That is certainly so in "The Love of a Good Woman."

Beginning in 1950, Munro's published stories have been rooted in her autobiographical Huron County (Ontario) home place. Now, over fifty years later, they still are. As "The Love of a Good Woman" demonstrates, that connection is both detailed and profound. Betweeen 1968 and 2006, Alice Munro published twelve volumes of stories and a putative novel. In these collections are some fifty-one stories that first appeared in the United States' premier venue for short stories: the *New Yorker*. Complex and detailed, Alice Munro's stories proclaim her "connection" to Ontario as both a place remembered and one she has lived in and knows well.

Indeed, Alice Munro's Ontario is a complexly rendered fictional territory, one borne in the first part of her career of distance and imaginative return (1951–73) and, since 1973, a place intimately known and long meditated. As John Weaver has argued, it is possible to read the whole of social history of Huron County, and of rural southwestern Ontario generally, by reading Munro's fiction chronologically. This is so because Munro has textured her prose with the surface details of her Ontario place, details at once commonplace and alluring. She has long and freely admitted that she is "excited by what you might call the surface of life," and she has deprecated her writing by saying that she "can't have anybody in a room without describing all the furniture" (Gibson 241, 257). Rendering fictional contexts in such detail may also be traced through her use of repeated figures; take, as a key example, Munro's use of the Maitland River, which flows through her home town of Wingham (Ontario) on its way to nearby Lake Huron. In a brief 1974 essay, "Everything Here is Touchable and Mysterious," Munro once wrote:

> There is a short river the Indians called the *Menesetung*, and the first settlers, or surveyors of the Huron Tract, called the Maitland. From the place where the forks join, at Wingham, it winds about 35 miles, to flow into the lake at Goderich, Ont. Just west of Wingham it flows through that straggling, unincorporated, sometimes legendary non-part of town called Lower Town (pronounced Loretown) and past my father's land and Cruikshank's farm, to make a loop called the Big Bend before flowing south under Zetland Bridge, and that is the mile or so I know of it. (33)

Such passages as this are typical of Munro: she knows the details of her home place, and she uses them precisely. Equally, too, these details yield the meaning she seeks, as is evident in the essay's final lines:

> Because I am still partly convinced that this river – not even the whole river, but this little stretch of it – will provide whatever myths you want, whatever adventures. I name the plants, I name the fish, and every name seems to me triumphant, every leaf and quick fish remarkably valuable. This ordinary place is sufficient, everything here touchable and mysterious. (33)

Munro returned to this river in a story, "Meneseteung" (1988), where she creates a narrator who is researching the life of a local nineteenth-century "poetess," long dead, an "old maid" named Almeda Joynt Roth. The story is mainly concerned, though without real logical provenance, with the narrator's imagined near-courtship of Roth by a local eligible widower, Jarvis Poulter. Among Roth's poems is one entitled "Champlain at the Mouth of the Meneseteung" (Friend 52). Imagined, such a tableau characterizes Roth's old maid's mind – at one point she is thinking of "Champlain and the naked Indians" (70) – but in Munro's creation of Roth, and especially through the narrator's research into the poetess's life, Munro is indeed creating a myth along the Meneseteung. And if the essay's details demonstrate one central aspect of Munro's writing, the penultimate paragraph of "Meneseteung" offers another. Looking for Roth's gravestone, wondering over a reference in one of the published poems, the narrator finds the name Meda

written on a gravestone, and reflects that she is perhaps not the last
person to make the connection between poet and poem, for people do
"put things together ... in the hope of ... making a connection, rescuing
one thing from the rubbish." The last paragraph follows:

> And they may get it wrong, after all. I may have got it wrong. I
> don't know if she took laudanum. Many ladies did. I don't know if
> she made grape jelly. (*Friend* 73)

These last questions refer to incidents in the story proper but their
exact meaning is less important than the effect of the final paragraph
– one that Munro reinstated in the story after the story's first publication in the *New Yorker*. This paragraph compromises the narrator's
authority if not dashing it altogether and welcomes us to Alice Munro
– where everything is both "touchable and mysterious," a world in
which each character, especially those who narrate or serve as centre
for Munro's wonderings, is raptly aware of myriad difficulties in the
"hope of seeing this trickle in time," or in "making a connection"
(Thacker, "Introduction").

Focusing on this same story, Pam Houston raises the relation between Munro's narrator and the character she describes, Almeda
Roth, and asks "'Does the landscape, then, exist separately from the
way these women see it?' And neither woman can answer. The two
women have momentarily become one voice, bound together by the
metonymic qualities of language, and by the inability of metaphor to
speak to them" (89). The metonymy Houston deduces here is crucial
to the definition of Alice Munro's Ontario, although I would argue
that her notion of "two women becoming one voice" is better applied
to Munro herself and the speaking voice in her stories – sometimes this
is a first-person narrator, but more often she is not, since third-person
narration has predominated in recent years.

What I mean by this is that Alice Munro's Ontario is constructed
along the line – if line it is – between fiction and memoir. It is a world
rooted in the times and the touchable surfaces and characters of Huron County, Ontario, a place lived in since the early 1800s by Munro's
ancestors (a time she has been taking up, more and more, first signaled
by "Meneseteung"), one which she has taken in all its depths (Thacker,
"Introduction"). "A place that ever was lived in is like a fire that never
goes out," Eudora Welty wrote in "Some Notes on River Country,"
and Munro's focus on the area around "this little stretch" of the Men-

eseteung/Maitland River has certainly proved her assertion that it is an "ordinary place sufficient" for her work, one that she is probing even yet, as "The Love of a Good Woman" demonstrates.[1]

◆

Given these contexts, I wish here to look at what I take to be a key instance of Munro's method: a memoir she published in 1981 entitled "Working for a Living." Because it began as a fiction but – for various reasons – became a memoir, the piece is an apt demonstration of Munro's method and of her Ontario-rooted art. As such a transformation suggests, what Munro has done in her stories has been to define and probe factual complexities, wondering ever, herself, over what she has called "the rest of the story" (Introduction xvi). Before I take the memoir up, however, I need to contextualize it by some brief discussion of Munro's methods and some brief mention of other works.

As in "Everything Here is Touchable and Mysterious," Munro has several times addressed the relation between the factual and the imaginative in her fiction. In another essay, "What is Real?" (1982), she asserts her unshakeable doubt that "Every final draft, every published story, is still only an attempt, an approach, to the story." To illustrate, Munro cites her story, "Royal Beatings," from *Who Do You Think You Are?* (1978); rejecting any pretense of using an incident "to show anything," she says rather that she "put this story at the heart of my story because I need it there and it belongs there. It is the black room at the centre of the house with all the rooms leading to and away from it. That is all." She continues:

Who told me to write [the character, Hat Nettleton's] story? Who feels any need of it before it is written? I do. I do, so that I might grab off this piece of horrid reality and install it where I see fit, even if Hat Nettleton and his friends are still around to make me sorry.

The answer seems to be as confusing as ever. Lots of true answers are. Yes and no. Yes, I use bits of what is real, in the sense of being really there and really happening, in my story. No, I am not concerned with using what is real to make any sort of record to prove any sort of point, and I am not concerned with any methods of selection but my own, which I can't fully explain. (36)

Trying to explain, though, Munro rejects the notion that a story is "a road, taking me somewhere." "It's more like a house": "I go into it, and move back and forth and settle here and there, and stay in it for a while" (5).

By speaking of "the black room at the centre of the house," Munro posits not so much an essentialism as a core mystery informing each story. In "The Love of a Good Woman," it is Mr. Willens' talismanic box of optometrist's instruments: how did it get into the Walley museum yes, but more variously, what human relations occurred to produce Willens's death? In "Meneseteung," it is the inferred actions of Almeda Roth of a Saturday night and Sunday morning, a moment transfixed in the story, that might have brought connection and, with it, transformation. It does not. As these instances suggest, Munro places a crucial fact at the core of her stories – these facts are, like Mr. Willens' instruments, both evident and mysterious, leaving us seeing but also leaving us wondering. "It's the fact you cherish," Munro wrote at one point in a 1994 essay entitled "What Do You Want to Know For?" (208). For her, such cherished facts are the beginning of the story, the wonderings that produce the imaginative wanderings, about the imagined house, that create the story at hand.

◆

For Munro, no literal house has been the site of more imaginative wondering, the site of more imaginative wandering, than her family home in Wingham has been. There she grew up, living in the house from 1931 to 1949, when she moved away to attend university and then, in 1951, to move to Vancouver with her new husband, James Munro. Although the next twenty-two years were spent mostly a continent away from Ontario, "Home," Munro was ever imaginatively beckoned back to Wingham and its circumstances, and especially to her family home where her mother, until she died in 1959, fought the debilitations of Parkinson's Disease. A direct result of her mother's death was "The Peace of Utrecht" (1960), a story that Munro once called "her first really painful autobiographical story ... the first time I wrote a story that tore me up ..." (Metcalf 58). It treats a visit made by the narrator, Helen, home to Jubilee to see her sister, Maddy, after their mother had finally died from a long, lingering illness. Helen is the sister who got away to a life of her own while Maddy stayed behind to nurse their "Gothic Mother." The story's details are less important here than is its parallel to Munro's own life and also a phrase describing Helen's recalled feelings on earlier trips home, seeing once more the town's familiar details: "feeling as I recognized these signs a queer kind of oppression and release, as I exchanged the whole holiday world of school, of friends and, later on, of love, for the dim world of continuing disaster, of home" (*Dance* 200, 191).

Thus the circumstances of this story suggest that Munro got away from her "home place," Ontario, only to return repeatedly in her imagination; more than this, Munro literally returned home to stay in the mid–1970s, long after her mother's death in 1959 but before her father's death in 1976. This return to Ontario and to Huron County from British Columbia, where she had lived since 1951, occasioned a perceptible shift in Munro's work. It was seen initially in the circumstances surrounding *Who Do You Think You Are?* (1978; see Hoy) – that might well be described in Munro's own phrase, "the dim world of continuing disaster, of home." Munro has, certainly, returned repeatedly to the circumstances surrounding her mother's lingering death – "The Ottawa Valley" (1974), "Home" (1974), "The Progress of Love" (1985), "Friend of My Youth" (1990) – but since her return to Ontario a deepened analysis of the cultural history of her home place has been predominant. Her own family's history has been seen as derived from, and connected to, the larger history of Huron County, a place first settled in the earlier nineteenth century as the Huron Tract (see Thacker, "Connection," "Introduction"). The "continuing disaster" Munro has drawn upon in her fiction since *Who Do You Think You Are?* has been less a matter of literal disaster than it has been one of a sense, again in Munro's own phrasing, of "a devouring muddle" – that is, a recognition that any understanding is contingent, its clarity apparent only, apt to disappear upon further reflection into "Sudden holes and impromptu tricks and radiant vanishing consolations" (*Open* 50).

This sense may be seen developing in "Home," a rendering of a trip Munro made to Wingham in 1973, just after her return to Ontario from British Columbia, to visit her father, who was then living with his second wife and who was suffering from the heart disease to which he succumbed in 1976. One of a handful of stories Munro published separately but for many years chose not to include in a collection, "Home" may be reasonably paired with "The Ottawa Valley," also first published in 1974.[2] That is another story that takes up Munro's mother's illness and, like "Home," in it, too, Munro herself breaks into the narrative, commenting metafictionally on what she has done. In "The Ottawa Valley" she steps back from the concluded story and writes, "I had been making a proper story out of this, I would have ended it, I think, with my mother not answering and going ahead of me across the pasture." This is the moment when, in response to the narrator's question, "'Is your arm going to stop shaking?'", her mother does not respond, "For the first time she held out altogether against me. She went on as if she had not heard, her familiar bulk ahead of me turning strange, indifferent" (*Something* 246, 244).

Throughout "Home," however, Munro is more venturesome with her authorial interjection, punctuating the narrative with italicized authorial second thoughts: *A problem of the voices, the way people talk, how can it be handled? It sounds like parody if you take it straight, as out of a tape-recorder. My own attitude, too; complicated and unresolved"* (142). Yet these interjections confirm the literal truth of the memories offered as fiction from the home place – that it is actually memoir. Munro's final paragraphs suggest this connection. *"There was something else I could have worked into an ending,"* the narrator writes, *"the setting of the first scene I can establish as a true memory in my life."* Particular details follow: a flight of steps, a black and white cow in 1935, warm clothes, a three-legged milking-stool. Then she adds:

> *You can see this scene, can't you, you can see it quietly made, that magic and prosaic safety briefly held for us, the camera moving out and out, that spot shrinking, darkness. Yes. That is effective.*
> *I don't want any more effects, I tell you, lying. I don't know what I want. I want to do this with honour, if I possibly can.* (152–53; italics in original)

The tension here is palpable, between what Munro remembers – memoir – and "effects," "lying" – made fiction. Munro's decision not to collect this story until 2006 owes to her rejection of such metafictional techniques and, as well, to her use of the "characters" and situation in "Home" as a basis for Flo and her husband in *Who* as well as another rendering of her father in "The Moons of Jupiter" (1978). Finally included in a book, *The View from Castle Rock* (2006), "Home" reappears without its metafictional commentary.

This crux, and the evident tension between memory and fiction in "Home," point also to "Working for a Living," a memoir about her

parents, especially her father, Munro published in 1981. Its provenance is also indicative, since it reveals Munro just at the point of
what might be called "deep empathy" with her home place, with its
well of memories. Munro began "Working for a Living" as a story but,
as I have indicated, it became a memoir. In the story version – which
exists in a variety of drafts in Munro's papers at the University of
Calgary, and which was rejected by the *New Yorker* – the character
Janet has an argument with the Bursar at the beginning of her final
year at university and, rather than compromise as she had in previous
years, she leaves school and goes home. Arriving there, she sees it differently through her now-educated eyes as a place from *Winesburg,
Ohio* or a Russian village from Chekhov. Such illusions fade fast, as
Janet continues:

> I saw my parents' life as a tragedy ... But when I came home this
> time I threw myself into that part of life you never see in stage
> tragedies, rarely read about. While the speeches are being made,
> the emotions twisted, the truth laid bare, who is keeping the back-
> ground in order, washing the sheets and towels and sweeping the
> floor? It seemed essential to me that the tragedy be played out in
> cleanliness, in comfort, that the piled-up mess disappear from the
> porch and the torn, dusty plastic curtains be taken down. I house-
> cleaned ferociously and impatiently, kept the incinerator smok-
> ing all day, scrubbed down to the bedrock of poverty, which was
> the torn linoleum and the sheets worn out in the middle. (AMP,
> 38.10.36.f8)

Here is Munro, creating fictional "effects" out of her own experience,
out of her parents' experience. The draft continues with the returned,
housecleaning Janet settling back into life in Dalgliesh, taking charge
at home in view of her mother's illness, getting work, and at one point
visiting her father who worked then in the local foundry.

   In the published version of "Working for a Living," Janet is gone.
She is replaced by Munro speaking as herself, matter-of-factly, analyti-
cally, beginning "In the first years of this century there was a notable
difference between people who lived on farms and people who lived in
country towns and villages" (9). Taking up her parents' lives – there is
no mistaking here that she is describing Robert E. Laidlaw (1901–76)
and Anne Chamney Laidlaw (1898–1959) – Munro places them within the social history of early twentieth-century Huron County and,

retrospectively, dissects their lives through representative, though not minute, detail. In transforming "Working for a Living," Munro made something of a "glorious leap" from fiction to memoir, a leap which, if not characteristic, seems nevertheless to have been demanded by the factuality she presents, a factuality that accords with the personal family history Munro has told through her fiction: "Connection. That was what it was all about" ("Author's" 125, *Moons* 6). Here, however, a reversal of her usual practice asserts that connection.

Placing her father within both social and family contexts – there is a great deal of detail about his parents, some of which echoes material seen in such stories as "Chaddeleys and Flemings" (1978–79) and "The Progress of Love" – Munro describes his education through "the Continuation School in Blyth"; these were "small high schools, without the final fifth form, now Grade Thirteen; you would have to go to a larger town for that" (10). Her father had, Munro writes, "a streak of pride posing as humility, making him scared and touchy, ready to bow out, never ask questions. I know it very well. He made a mystery there, a hostile structure of rules and secrets, far beyond anything that really existed. He felt a danger too, of competition, of ridicule. The family wisdom came to him then. Stay out of it" (10–11). While he might have gone on in school, Laidlaw did not; instead, during high school "he began to spend more and more days in the bush" and, when the time to decide came, "he turned his back on education and advancement. They had the farm; he was the only son, the only child" (11). Even so, he read, and "would certainly have read Fenimore Cooper. So he would have absorbed the myths and half-myths about the wilderness that most country boys did not know" (12). Munro continues, detailing her father's path imaginatively and practically, accounting for his life:

> My father being a Huron County farm boy with the extra, Fenimore-Cooper perception, a cultivated hunger, did not turn aside from the these boyish interests at the age of eighteen, nineteen, twenty. Instead of giving up the bush he took to it more steadily and seriously ... He was edging away from the life of a farmer ... The life in the bush, on the edge of the farms, away from the towns; how could it be managed? (13)

Here Munro is wondering over the same question that informs her meditation on the American novelist Willa Cather in "Dulse," a story she wrote concurrent with "Working." There, her character wondering about Cather, she writes: "But was she lucky or was she not, and was it all right with that woman? How did she live?" (*Moons* 58). And as with the fictional Lydia's wonderings over Cather, here too Munro is focused on facts: her parents, especially her father, were actual people, not characters. Thus from this passage Munro details her father's move from trapping into fox farming, and the subsequent visit of a "young woman," "a cousin on the Irish side, from Eastern Ontario. She was a school-teacher, lively, importunate, good-looking, and a couple of years older than he. She was interested in the foxes, and not, as his mother thought, pretending to be interested in order to entice him": "She looked at the foxes and did not see their connection with the wilderness; she saw a new industry, the possibility of riches. She had a little money saved, to help buy a place where all this could get started. She became my mother" (17).

Adept as she is at describing salient human characteristics, Munro's meditation on her parents' characters and motives, and of her own understanding of each, over time, is detailed, tentative, and ultimately profound, imaging them as youthful, "helpless, marvelously deceived" – but realizing that she does so as much to imagine herself as a child born out of real, rather than "stingy" or "half-hearted" affection (17–18). As part of a detailed accounting of her parents' personal characteristics, Munro focuses on two memories, indicative of each of them, of her own in the balance of "Working for a Living." The first, her mother's triumph by retailing their best furs at a hotel in Muskoka – Munro and her father drove to get her there in a rickety automobile that should not have been on the highway so, she later inferred, her father took back roads as a precaution. He had little money to take on the trip, so they all depended on Munro's mother's success. Because of the sales "gifts she had," Anne Chamney Laidlaw had the money they needed (27). In "those later years" after she had died, Robert Laidlaw "would speak of my mother's salesmanship, and how she had saved the day, and say that he didn't know what he was going to do, that time, if she hadn't had the money when he got there. 'But she had it,' he said, and the tone in which he said this made me wonder about the reservations [about her mother] I had assumed he shared. Such shame now seems shameful. It would be a relief to me to think he hadn't shared it" (28).

As this episode suggests, things were tight in Laidlaw's fox-farming business and, in 1947, it failed. "When my father went looking for a job he had to find a night job, because he had to work all day going out of business. He had to pelt all the stock and sell the skins for what he could get, he had to tear down the pens." "He got a job as a night-watchman at the Foundry, covering the hours from five in the afternoon till ten in the evening" (28, 29). One evening in 1949, while he was working there, "the last spring, in fact the last whole season, I lived at home, I was riding my old bicycle ... to give a message to my father" at the foundry (28). This visit is the central incident shared by the fictional and memoir versions of "Working for a Living." In it, Laidlaw gives Munro a tour of the foundry – where she has never been – and she, for her part, realizes the nature of his job (he mops the floor there, for example, something he would never have done at home). Munro moves from this incident to an account of a practical joke the supervisor played on a worker there and, from that, to her father's account of his enjoyment of his work at the foundry: one night, gathered in the caretaker's room, the men discussed the question "what is the best time in a man's life? When is a person the happiest?" A variety of views were offered. "Then my father said, 'I don't know, I think maybe right now'" (36).

Along with this story, Munro's father also told her of a midnight when, leaving the foundry, he found "a great snowstorm in progress." Leaving his car where it was, he began to walk the two miles home and, almost there, was stopped by the storm:

He thought of his death. He would die leaving a sick crippled wife who could not take care of herself, an old mother full of disappointment, a younger daughter whose health had always been delicate, an older girl who was often self-centered and mysteriously incompetent, a son who seemed to be bright and reliable but who was still only a little boy. He would die in debt, and before he had even finished pulling down the [fox] pens; they would be there to show the ruin of his enterprise.

"Was that all you thought about?" I said when he told me this.

"Wasn't that enough?" he said, and went on to tell how he ... had got home.

But I had meant, didn't he think of himself, of the boy who had trapped along the Blyth Creek, and asked for Sign's Snow Paper; the young man about to be married who had cut cedar poles in the swamp to build the first fox-pens; the forty-year-old-man who had thought of joining the army? I meant, was his life now something that only other people had a use for? (36–37)

Munro then breaks the text and, taking it up again, unites her parents in a final paragraph to mark them "off, to describe, to illumine" but not at all "to *get rid*" of them (*Something* 246):

> My father always said that he didn't really grow up until he went to work in the Foundry. He never wanted to talk much about the fox-farm, until he was old and could talk easily about anything that had happened. But my mother, as she was being walled in by the increasing paralysis, often wanted to talk about her three weeks at the Pine Tree Hotel, the friend and money she had made there. (37)

Rather, Robert Laidlaw and Anne Chamney Laidlaw are here, together, in "Working for a Living," textualized, their daughter's words having caught something of their lives, having imprisoned their beings – even though they are gone and still wondered over yet – in her text.

Yet, as Munro's changed "Working for a Living" demonstrates, a fictional persona such as Janet is a mask sustained at cost – the illusion that none of this happened, that all of it is fiction, "made up" or, if portions did happen, they did not occur in just the way invoked by the author's words on the page. As Munro wrote in "Dulse," "That is what" Lydia said to her "doctor. But is it the truth?" (*Moons* 55). Working on "Dulse," pondering versions of "truth" – fictional, factual, and (given Cather's presence in the story) biographical, Munro had also been working at about the same time on "Working for a Living." That piece, by collapsing into fact, by eliding fictional personae, defines the deep empathy lying behind Munro's fictions, an empathy derived from her intimacy with, feeling for, and long contemplation of, her own home place, in resonant detail. Technically, too, "Working for a Living," like "Dulse," shows Munro moving across the putative line between memory and imagination, finding words that, when arranged in their most satisfactory order, recreate on the page the connections of being – connections to persons, to places, to memory, to the present moment: that is, to the very nexus of identity. Those connections are "what it was all about" in the work of Alice Munro (*Moons* 6); they do demonstrate that, in Munro's words, "This ordinary place is sufficient, everything here touchable and mysterious." For Alice Munro, "here" is "Home," "Home" is Huron County, Ontario.

◆

A final quotation, one that encapsulates this whole imaginative process. Connection is "what it was all about" in Munro's story by that title and, as she ends that story before taking up her father's side of the family in its second part, "Chaddeleys and Flemings: 2. The Stone in the Field," Munro returns to the image of long-gone people singing, recalled through memory, "a mould in which to imprison for a moment the shining, elusive element which is life itself" (Cather, *Song* 254). There, she has the narrator remembering her younger self hearing her mother's visiting cousins, singing together as sleep draws near, "*Row, row, row your boat / Gently down the stream.*" The song, the voices, the people singing in such high spirits: all are clear – until memory fades out like the song itself, like life. "[T]o my surprise – for I am surprised, even though I know the pattern of the rounds – the song is thinning out, you can hear the two voices striving," 'merrily' turning into 'dream', and then only "one voice alone … singing on, gamely, to the finish … *Life is*. Wait. *But a*. Now, wait. *Dream*" (*Moons* 18).

NOTES

1   Alice Munro's relation to her Ontario home place is of major consideration in my *Alice Munro: Writing Her Lives: A Biography*, a book which was written subsequent to this essay.
2   In 1980, Munro corresponded with Douglas Gibson, her editor, about "a kind of family book I want to do someday" (see Thacker *Alice* 367–68). That book is *The View From Castle Rock* (2006), which among other pieces includes "Home" – without its metafictional commentary (285–315) – "Working for a Living" (also revised, 127–70) and "What Do You Want to Know For?" (also revised, 316–40).

WORKS CITED

The Alice Munro Papers: Second Accession. Ed. Apollonia Steele and Jean F. Tener. Calgary: University of Calgary Press, 1987.

Byatt, A. S. "Justice for Willa Cather." Rev. of *Willa Cather and the Politics of Criticism*. By Joan Acocella. *New York Review of Books* 30 November 2000: 51–53.

Cather, Willa. *The Song of the Lark*. 1915. New York: Penguin, 1999.

Duffy, Dennis. "'A Dark Sort of Mirror': 'The Love of a Good Woman' as Pauline Poetic." Thacker, ed. 169–90.

Gibson, Graeme. "Alice Munro." Interview. *Eleven Canadian Novelists.* Toronto: Anansi, 1973: 241–64.

Houston, Pam. "'A Hopeful Sign': The Making of Metonymic Meaning in Munro's 'Meneseteung.'" *Kenyon Review* 14.4 (1992): 79–92.

Hoy, Helen. "'Rose and Janet': Alice Munro's Metafiction." *Canadian Literature* 121 (1989): 59–83.

McCombs, Judith. "Searching Bluebeard's Chambers: Grimm, Gothic, and Bible Mysteries in Alice Munro's 'The Love of a Good Woman." *American Review of Canadian Studies* 30 (2000): 327–48.

Munro, Alice. "Author's Commentary." In *Sixteen By Twelve: Short Stories by Canadian Writers.* Ed. John Metcalf. Toronto: Ryerson, 1970: 125–26.

– "A Conversation with Alice Munro." *Journal of Canadian Fiction.* With John Metcalf. 1.4 (1972): 54–62.

– *Dance of the Happy Shades.* Fore. Hugh Garner. Toronto: McGraw-Hill Ryerson, 1968.

– "Everything Here is Touchable and Mysterious." *Weekend Magazine* [*Toronto Star*] 11 May 1974: 33.

– *Friend of My Youth.* Toronto: McClelland and Stewart, 1990.

– "Home." *New Canadian Stories: 74.* Ed. David Helwig and Joan Harcourt. Ottawa: Oberon, 1974: 133–53.

– Introduction. *Selected Stories.* By Munro. New York: Vintage, 1997: xiii-xxi.

– *The Love of a Good Woman.* Toronto: McClelland and Stewart, 1998.

– *The Moons of Jupiter.* Toronto: Macmillan, 1982.

– *Open Secrets.* Toronto: McClelland and Stewart, 1994.

– *Something I've Been Meaning to Tell You: Thirteen Stories.* Toronto: McGraw-Hill Ryerson, 1974.

– *The View From Castle Rock.* Toronto: McClelland and Stewart, 2006.

– "What Do You Want to Know For?" *Writing Away.* Ed. Constance Rooke. Toronto: McClelland and Stewart, 1994: 203–20.

– "What is Real?" *Canadian Forum* September 1982: 5, 36.

– *Who Do You Think You Are?* Toronto: Macmillan, 1978.

– "Working for a Living." *Grand Street* 1.1 (Fall 1981): 9–37.

Thacker, Robert. *Alice Munro: Writing Her Lives: A Biography.* Toronto: McClelland and Stewart, 2005.

– "Connection: Alice Munro and Ontario." *American Review of Canadian Studies* 14 (1984): 213–26.

– "Introduction: Alice Munro, Writing 'Home': 'Seeing This Trickle in Time.'" Thacker, ed. 1–20.

– "So Shocking a Verdict in Real Life: Autobiography in Alice Munro's Stories." In *Reflections: Autobiography and Canadian Literature.* Ed. K.P.

Stich. Ottawa: University of Ottawa Press, 1988. 153–61.

– ed. *The Rest of the Story: Critical Essays on Alice Munro*. Toronto: ECW Press, 1999.

Ware, Tracy. E-mail. 2 December 1999.

Weaver, John. "Society and Culture in Rural and Small-Town Ontario: Alice Munro's Testimony on the Last Forty Years." *Patterns of the Past: Interpreting Ontario's History*. Ed. Roger Hall, William Westfall, and Laura Sefton MacDowell. Toronto: Dundurn, 1988: 381–402.

Welty, Eudora. "Some Notes on River Country." *The Eyes of the Story: Selected Essays and Reviews*. 1944. New York: Vintage, 1979: 286–99.

DIS-PLACEMENT AND LITERARY RE-PLACEMENT: EMPIRE, MEMORY, LANGUAGE

GWENDOLYN DAVIES

Alistair MacLeod and the Gaelic Diaspora

In Alistair MacLeod's "The Closing Down of Summer," Gaelic-speaking Cape Breton miners carry sprigs of spruce from Cape Breton with them "to Africa as mementos or talismans or symbols of identity." "Much," argues the narrator, "as our Highland ancestors, for centuries, fashioned crude badges of heather or whortleberries to accompany them on the battlefields of the world. Perhaps so that in the closeness of their work with death they might find nearness to their homes and an intensified realization of themselves" (*As Birds* 11).

The miners' action – an act of resistance to threats of geographical and cultural erasure – assumes added resonance when contextualized by MacLeod himself. Indicating in various interviews that "Cape Breton is where I grew up and it is the landscape I care the most about" (Martin D9), MacLeod has none the less argued that, although "I think of myself as coming from a particular place and a particular time, I do not think of myself as anything like an 'instant' North American, not sure of his mother's maiden name" (Nicholson, "Signatures" 97). When his ancestors immigrated to Inverness County, Nova Scotia, in the eighteenth century, he notes, they traveled "in family groups from individual islands, like Eigg, and intermarried, and carried with them the whole body of whatever it is that people carry with them – folklore, emotional weight." Therefore, he adds, "if you look at my ancestry and my wife's ancestry, there's no-one who's not from the Highlands and Islands of Scotland. All of our ancestors bear those names: MacLeod, MacLellan, Macdonald, Rankin, Beaton, Walker, MacIsaac, Gillis, MacDonnell, Campbell, MacPherson, MacLennan ... this is still who we are. This is why there is this felt affinity on the part of those who emigrated for those who remain" (Nicholson 92). To this end, MacLeod has described how, when his Cape Breton father-in-law visited his ancestral area of Moidart in the Highlands in the mid-1980s, he spoke Gaelic with an accent immediately recognizable to local residents.[1] It is a scene repeated in *No Great Mischief* where the narrator's sister, Catriona MacDonald, visits Moidart, the MacDonalds' ancestral Highland home two hundred years earlier, and encounters an old woman on the beach who salutes her: "You are from here." Catriona joins a kitchen gathering where "I began to speak to her and to them in Gaelic as well. I don't even remember what I said, the actual words or phrases. It was just like it poured out of me, like some subterranean river that had been running deep within me and suddenly burst forth" (*No Great Mischief* 160–63). The dogs, always a cultural link between old and new in MacLeod stories, recognize her by her smell, and the old man and the neighbours – in a kitchen not unlike her grandparents' kitchen in Cape Breton – assure her: "It is as if you had never left ... You are home now" (164–67).

It is scenes such as these in *No Great Mischief* or in the short story "Vision" that give resonance to the argument that the "regional" in MacLeod's work is less Cape Breton and more the *Gaeltacht* itself[2] – that Gaelic diaspora where the next imagined island in the chain of the Hebrides is Cape Breton, and, the clan, with its real and constructed oral history, is the centre of resistance against a dominant English culture no matter where branches of the clan might be physically located. As "textual geography," notes Colin Nicholson, MacLeod's Cape Breton setting "becomes inseparable from, because identified through, Scottish experience. Personal memory and historical recall merge in these tellings to forge a landscape of the mind out of a territory of fact. In these ways, the 'regional' transcends its physical boundaries as a wider collective experience re-connects the disconnected and re-roots the displaced" (Nicholson "Regions" 131). Or, as MacLeod illustrates in "Vision" where he collapses the two islands of Canna (Scotland and Cape Breton) into tales within tales: "That was a very long time ago ... over thirteen hundred years ago. But, yes, sometimes I feel I know him and I think I see him as well ... we carry certain things within us. Sometimes there are things within us which we do not know or fully understand" (*As Birds* 149–50).[3]

"The history of the Gaels," notes Cape Breton Gaelic singer Mary Jane Lamond, "is written in their poetry." It is here that one finds "a true reflection of their lives and societal changes" ("Celtic Spirit"; see also "Interview"). And it is in the early bardic poetry of outmigration, travel, and exile that one finds the roots of the "tradition bearers," cultural patterns, memory, and orality that inform the Cape Breton and Gaelic diaspora about which MacLeod writes. Early Scottish-Canadian emigration poems such as the "Emigration of the Islanders" by Bard Calum Bàn MacMhannain (Malcolm Ban Buchanan) or "You Have Been Loud and Boastful" by Bard Allan Macdonald (Allan the Ridge) who sailed to Prince Edward Island and Cape Breton in 1803 and 1816 respectively, demonstrate the colloquial tone, strong rhythms, spontaneity, and sincerity that marked bardic poetry. As Kurt Wittig has pointed out in *The Scottish Tradition in Literature*, Gaelic poetry challenges the expectations of those trained in the tradition of Western European literature, for it lacks the organic structure, underlying intellectual system, or moral dimension often associated with readers' conceptions of poetry (188). By contrast, in the Gaelic tradition, there is a seeming lack of structure in the poem because of the colloquial first-person voice. "The canvas is ... small," notes Wittig, the subject is "one that the poet knows intimately," and the subject is "turned round and round till all its possibilities are exhausted," creating "a series of exact pictures, each adding some fresh detail" (189). The traditional Gaelic poet "enabled his audience to participate in their culture; to act out culturally reinforcing roles," adds Donald MacAulay in his introduction to *Modern Scottish Gaelic Poems*: "The poetry was largely oral-based; much of it was meant to be sung ... The measure of a poem's success was largely its acceptance by its audience. This alone ensured that it survived and was disseminated beyond its local place and time, at least until it was written down" (46).

"The Emigration of the Islanders" by Bard Calum Bàn Mac-Mhannain (Malcolm Ban Buchanan) of Skye and Cape Prim, Prince Edward Island, is a case in point. The bard knew the "shores of his native Skye with an intimacy typical of Hebrideans," notes Margaret MacDonell in *The Emigrant Experience: Songs of Highland Emigrants in North America*: "Moreover, he was keenly attuned to the sounds and signs of impending storms and to the hazards of sailing" (105). The first stanza is rich in geographical touchstones and conversational dialogue as the immigrants to the Maritime Provinces sail out of Portree harbour, leaving their mourning clansfolk on shore:

When we set out
from the harbour at Portree
there were many sorrowful people on shore;
they gazed across intently

with their eye on the vessel
as she headed for Rona.
Said MacFadyn from Digg
as he shouted to me,
'She will veer down towards Trodday;
let the most skillful
be at the helm
until she reaches beyond Soain.'

As the ship "hums along," the next stanza continues the poem's emphasis on narrative, orality, and topographical detail. In doing so, it also reinforces a sense of the particularity that Charles W. Dunn in *Highland Settler: A Portrait of the Scottish Gael in Nova Scotia* defines as characteristic of this kind of poetry: "The bards were connoisseurs of the beauties of crag and cliff and possessed in their mother tongue a rich vocabulary descriptive of the varied types of hills and knolls, peaks and mountains, which every day they saw around them. *Aonach, bac, beinn, braighe, carn, cnoc, coire, creag, cruach, fireach, leathad, mam, monadh, sgorr, sliabh, slios, stuc, tolm, torr* – such specialized and almost untranslatable terms offer a sample of the words at their disposal" (9). Or, as David Buchan puts it in *The Ballad and the Folk*, such poems "became a vehicle for the expression of a regional ethos and identity" (10):

A north wind arose
when we were above Fladda-Chuain;
then she hummed along
moving rapidly
as she tacked around
to take the main she knew so well.
I glanced behind me
towards Rubh' á Chàirn Leith
and saw only mist over it.
Then MacPhail spoke
As he gazed upwards,
'I do believe it is the top of Storr.'
    (MacMhannain/Buchanan, "Emigration" in MacDonell 107–13)

This is familiar physical territory to all who are leaving on the ship, and the perilous currents of Rubha Hunish or the lambing on Rigg are personally and graphically recorded so that the images, scents, and scenes will survive for centuries in the memory banks of descendants who will hear this poem recited by tradition bearers. In addition, as Kurt Wittig notes in his analysis of Gaelic poetry, it is pictorial, flashing together both "the precise description ... of the thing perceived" and the image which it creates in the mind of the viewer (190). Thus, in the "Emigration of the Islanders," MacPhail comments at the end of stanza three on Storr, one of the promentories that they are passing, and the poem then moves in stanza four from the "precise description ... of the thing perceived"(Storr in the mist) to the images or memories that that perception triggers – visits to the grazing land of Rigg, the cattle, the month of March, the grasses and flowers, and the "sporting and leaping, / giving birth to young lambs in early May" – that will forever be embedded in the clan memory of the exiles because of this poem. In keeping with the conventions of Gaelic verse, there is also a quality of understatement in the text (Wittig 196). In stanza five, the speaker and his clansmen are leaving not because they want to but because "A new master has come / into the land, / a sad, woeful matter. / The people are leaving; / their possessions have dwindled. / They haven't a cow to put to graze." As Wittig notes, "sorrow and pathos" in Gaelic poetry is usually expressed in language of unaffected simplicity" (196). Here, suppressed emotion prevails.

In his own way, MacLeod continues the tradition of the bardic poets. His 1985 poem, "The Road to Rhu and *Cairn an Dorin* (The Cairn of Sorrow)," published in *The Antigonish Review*, has the same factual quality found in Buchanan's "Emigration of the Islanders." In MacLeod's poem, the ships that sail from Rhu glide "past Rhum and / Eigg and Muck, with their prows directed / Toward the vanished pier where wail the / Vanished people" (61). The poem unfolds, as does Buchanan's work, with stress on topographical detail, with the intimacy of personal conversation, and with as much left unsaid as said: "There seems nothing left to say as there / Is literally nothing left to see. Both of / Us the descendants of those who left or / Were left. Both of us too much taken by / Those who strain their eyes and wave to / Us from the past." Consistent with Gaelic poetry conventions described by Wittig, the lines build incrementally, turning "round and round," creating "a series of exact pictures, each adding some fresh detail – with never a repetition" (189):

They climb higher and higher as the vessels
Move out, farther and farther; waving and

Crying to the departing sails, straining
Their eyes to see the familiar clothing
Of those they love. Those who are left,
Weeping and waving to those who have left.
The leaving and the left, leaning and yearning
Toward each other.

These bardic rhythms, circularities ("waving," "crying," "straining," "weeping," "waving," "leaving," "leaning," "yearning"), echoes ("the left"), and understatements are the same conventions that inform MacLeod's prose style, so that the orality of his first-person narration in his fiction sounds like the rhythmic recounting of the bards and *seanaichies* who make up the collective unconscious of Gaelic culture. Or, as the narrator puts it in *No Great Mischief*: "And if the older singers or storytellers of the *clan Chalum Ruaidh*, the *seanaichies*, as they were called, happened to be present they would "remember" events from a Scotland which they had never seen, or see our future in the shadows of the flickering flames" (64–65). The simplest events in the fiction become part of the fabric of Gaeldom's cultural identification, recreating through memory, music, folklore, and the naming of events the oral and interwoven fibre of the Gaelic diaspora. If there is any true hallmark of postmodern culture in our time, notes David Williams in "From Clan to Nation," it is our awareness of painting as *painting*, and writing as *writing*" (61). But as MacLeod integrates a traditional world of orality into his modern narrative, he writes *against* this postmodernist grain, evoking a sense of the collective unconscious in his fictions based not on literary texts but on ancestral memory and an imagined history. This is artifice, Williams argues, because ultimately "an oral narrative strains at the seams of the printed book" (64). But MacLeod none the less pulls his listener into this oral process, insisting, as he did in a book review in *The Globe and Mail* in 1976, on the narrator's having "the single-mindedness of the Ancient Mariner encountering the wedding guest":

'Look,' he says, 'no wedding for you today because I am going to tell you a story. And I am going to hold you here and not with my hand nor with my "glittering eye" but by the very power of what I have to tell you and how I choose to tell it. I am going to show you what I saw and heard and smelled and tasted and felt. And I am going to tell you what it is like to be abandoned by God and by man and of the true nature of loneliness and of the preciousness of life. And I am going to do it in such a way that your life will never again be the same' (Rubinsky 19).[4]

MacLeod's introductions to his short stories and *No Great Mischief* confirm this strategy of pulling the listener into a visceral process of seeing, hearing, smelling, tasting, and feeling. Speaking in the present tense, the *seanaichie* cum narrator captures the listener with his opening lines: "There are times even now, when I awake at four o'clock in the morning with the terrible fear that I have overslept" ("The Boat" 129); or, "It is an evening during the summer that I am ten years old and I am on a train with my parents as it rushes toward the end of eastern Nova Scotia" ("The Return" 89); or, "Once there was a family with a Highland name who lived beside the sea" ("As Birds" 118); or, "I don't remember when I first heard the story but I remember the first time that I heard it and remembered it" ("Vision," *As Birds* 128); or, "As I begin to tell this, it is the golden month of September in southwestern Ontario" (*No Great Mischief* 1).

MacLeod's "historicized discourse" (Nicholson, "Regions" 130) then unfolds, building on the bardic / *seanaichie* patterns of oral story telling that define Gaeldom's sense of itself. As Gaelic singer Mary Jane Lamond has pointed out, until she began to explore Gaelic culture, she did not truly understand what the word "tradition" meant. "In modern western society," she notes, "we equate artists and creativity with innovation. It is the polar opposite that is treasured in Gaelic society. This is an atmosphere where you are considered to be talented if you can recite a tale exactly as you heard it from previous generations. A good singer is not a person with a fine vocal quality, but one who has as many verses in the same order as they have been sung for generations. Even within the context of newly created stories and songs, those that are admired are the ones which are closest to tradition" ("Celtic Spirit"). Of course, it is the erosion of these singing traditions that confounds Archibald in "The Tuning of Perfection" and concerns the narrator in "The Closing Down of Summer." In fact, there is a clear shift in the tone of the stories between the publication of *The Lost Salt Gift of Blood* in 1976 and that of *As Birds Bring Forth the Sun* in 1986. In 1976, the narrator in "The Road to Rankin's Point" can affirm the continuity of the Gaelic tradition (and, indeed, Lamond's remarks) by observing, "My father and my uncles and aunts take the violin from its peg and play the complicated jigs and reels gracefully and without effort. All of them grasp the bow in the same spot and in the same manner and bend their wrists in an identical way. It is a style older than any of our memories and produces what we call 'our sound'" (180).

By the time of the second collection of stories, however, published after MacLeod had been a visiting Canadian writer at the University of Edinburgh, there is a greater sense of edginess in the stories about the endurance of language, folklore, and the natural world (especially animals) in preserving the traditions that Lamond has identified. The result, notes Ken MacKinnon, is that the second group of stories, compared with those in the earlier book, "are even more culturally and spiritually relevant to the world they evoke. They are more explicitly Celtic, more resourceful in the use of oral and folk materials, and more given over to observation, humour, and implied comment" (3). Thus, gazing at the bedraggled and drunken roisterers on his porch at the end of "The Tuning of Perfection," Archibald can see in the young men both the destruction of traditional culture and yet the same reckless energy that took his ancestors onto the battlefield of Culloden in 1745. And in the reiteration of the legends of the *cu mor glas a bhais* (the great grey dog of death) in "As Birds Bring Forth the Sun" and the dogs of the *Calum Ruadh* in *No Great Mischief* as unifying motifs in his fiction, MacLeod points to the same qualities of cultural continuity that Archibald glimpses on his midnight doorstep. The death of the narrator's parents on the ice in *No Great Mischief* is described in the context of the *cu*'s faithfulness, descended as she was from the original *Calum Ruadh* dog, "the one who swam after the boat when they were leaving Scotland." "It was in those dogs to care too much and to try too hard," notes Grandpa early in the novel (57), and the phrase is repeated verbatim by his clansmen in Moidart years later with the description of the emigration of the *Calum Rhuadh* MacDonalds to Cape Breton hundreds of years before. "Just as certain members of the clan have distinctive physical attributes (red hair and dark eyes)," notes Hal Jensen in the *Times Literary Supplement* review of *No Great Mischief*, so the scenes in the story "work by echoing each other, adding thin layer on layer to one central story" (22).

It is this reweaving, recircling pattern typical of bardic presentation that sustains the illusion of one history, one collective unconscious, and oral verisimilitude in MacLeod's construct of the universal region of the *Gaeltacht*. This sense of the Gaelic diaspora is also reinforced by the sensuousness of MacLeod's prose, for he writes, as he reads and speaks, with the rich cadences of Gaelic-inflected English:

Sometimes they would take the lids off the kitchen stove to provide more light and then the actual flames would flicker and flare in constantly changing patterns of orange and red and black, constantly changing patterns of colour and shadow within the stove and emanating from it to the surrounding walls and the dusky overhead ceiling. Sometimes those gathered would merely watch the fire and its shadows, but at other times it seemed to move them to tell stories of real or imagined happenings from the near or distant past. And if the older singers or storytellers of the *clan Chalum Ruaidh*, the *seanaichies,* as they were called, happened to be present they would "remember" events from a Scotland which they had never seen, or see our future in the shadows of the flickering flames (64–65).

There is a rhythm in passages such as this one as the subject is turned round and round (Wittig 188) ("would flicker and flare in constantly changing patterns of orange and red and black, constantly changing patterns of colour and shadow within the stove and emanating from it to the surrounding walls and the dusky overhead ceiling"). The visual is described here in every nuance – first the fire, then the flame, then the flicker, then the colour, then the pattern of the colour, then the shadow, then the colour and shadow together on the wall, and, finally, the reflection on the dusky ceiling. The subject is limited, but it is described in all its possibilities until it is exhausted (Wittig 188). The result is a sonorousness, a visual picture, and a complexity of immediacy (Wittig 189) that can be compared with the intricate design of Celtic jewellery (Wittig 189).[5]

The illusion of orality is further heightened by MacLeod's use of paratactic sentence structure, creating a series of clauses linked by "and," with the phrases rising, in a sense, in a written illusion of musical crescendo. Moreover, the frequent allusion to colour found in the stories (black, white, red, orange), the intimacy of the natural world (including horses and dogs in stories such as "In the Fall" and "Winter Dog"), and the preoccupation with the immediate intensify the effects that make MacLeod's Gaelic-inflected speech evocatively atypical of literary English narrative found elsewhere in Canadian literature. Nor can this richly-inflected narrative prose be identified as regional to Cape Breton, for nowhere else do Cape Breton writers – from Ann-Marie MacDonald to Lynn Coady – write with the same rich sense of Gaelic-infused orality that makes MacLeod's narrative tone so instantly recognizable. This is the illusion of spoken Gaelic, wrapped in an English print version of what Williams calls the "search for some means of integrating these communal structures of personality, marked by traits of orality, into the more individualistic and introspective structures of personality shaped by writing" (48). "I do think that a lot of the language I use, a lot of the images I use, and a lot of the perceptions that I have are, how shall I say this, things that have been around me for a very long time," notes MacLeod; "that language is almost given to a person, and what I try to do is to articulate that language. I read my things aloud to myself, or hear how they sound, and if they work aurally, I find that persuasive" (Nicholson, "Signatures" 98). When that cadence of intonation and rhythm also becomes a keening for a dying culture, adds Colin Nicholson, the Scottish allusions function like "a kind of choric threnody" co-existing with what he identifies as MacLeod's "lyrical celebration of living" (98).[6]

As the miners of "The Closing Down of Summer," introduced at the beginning of this essay, convey sprigs of spruce from Cape Breton to Africa to define who they are, they are invoking the affirmation of tree and sap, the centuries-old symbol of chieftain and clan in Gaelic tradition. It is an image realized to this day by the varieties of heather and heath that grow "in beds of moss, in cracks and crevices in the rocks," in pockets of Nova Scotia, for in 1749 and in 1775 and in all the subsequent wars when Highland soldiers in the post-Culloden years took the King's shilling, young men such as the miners of MacLeod's story shook out on the shores of New Scotland the mattresses of heath and heather that they had brought from the hills of chieftain, clan, and home (DeVilliers 4). And it is the further affirmation in *No Great Mischief* of the great central spruce – cut at its trunk but branches holding it upright and immovable – that informs Catriona's comment: "All of those people with their black and red hair. Like you and me. All of them intertwined and intermarried for two hundred years here in Canada and who knows for how many years before. In Moidart and Keppoch, in Glencoe and Glenfinnan and Glengarry" (*No Great Mischief* 234–35). Or, as her grandmother says shortly before her death, "Blood is thicker than water" (268). What MacLeod encodes here is a sense of a universal Gaelic diaspora, transcending the landscape of the regional, and, in the words of Colin Nicholson, asserting "a wider collective experience" that "reconnects the disconnected and re-roots the displaced; not in a sentimentally recuperated Scotch mist but in a painfully resilient Canadian text" ("Regions" 131).

NOTES

1 Conversation between Alistair MacLeod and Gwendolyn Davies on 26 January 2007. See also Cope.
2 MacPhee, "Proposal for a Thesis."
3 For a discussion of "Vision," see MacPhee, "Highland Culture" (38–43) and Davidson (39–41).
4 Also quoted in MacPhee, "Highland Culture" 44. I wish to thank Dianne MacPhee for providing me with a copy of the Rubinsky interview.
5 Wittig draws a comparison between Gaelic poetry and Gaelic sculpture. See also Jirgens, 88.
6 See also Buchan, who notes that once folk literature becomes part of an accepted cultural discipline studied by universities, "The subject has a particular value for small nations which have stood in a minority relationship to a larger and have been strongly affected by the language and mores of the majority culture, since in these cases it is often the folk tradition which has maintained the language and other distinctive expressions of the indigenous culture." His observations underpin the importance of folklore and Gaelic conventions to MacLeod's development of a sense of the Gaelic diaspora.

WORKS CITED

Buchan, David. *The Ballad and the Folk*. London and Boston: Routledge and Kegan Paul, 1972.

– *Scottish Tradition: A Collection of Scottish Folk Literature*. London, Melbourne and Henley: Routledge & Kegan Paul, 1984.

Cope, Michael. "Lament for Cape Breton's disappearing Gaelic." The Halifax *Chronicle Herald* (23 December 1989): A7.

Davidson, Arnold E. "As Birds Bring Forth the Story: The Elusive Art of Alistair MacLeod." *Canadian Literature* 118 (1988): 32–42.

De Villiers, Marq and Sheila Hirtle. "Subtle and Subdued? No Way." *The National Post* (6 May 2000), Weekend Post, 4.

Dunn, Charles W. *Highland Settler: A Portrait of the Scottish Gael in Nova Scotia*. Toronto: University of Toronto Press, 1953.

Guilford, Irene, ed. *Alistair MacLeod, Essays on His Works*. Guernica: Toronto-Buffalo-Lancaster (UK), 2001.

Jensen, Hal. "Red Calum's clan." *Times Literary Supplement* (11 August 2000): 22.

Jirgens, Karl E. "Lighthouse, Ring and Fountain: The Never-Ending Circle in *No Great Mischief*." In Guilford, 84–94.

Lamond, Mary Jane. "Celtic Spirit." The Thistle & Shamrock Newsletter, http://www.npr.org/programs/thistle/features/lamond_art.html (first published in January 1999).

– The Thistle & Shamrock. http://www.npr.org/programs/thistle/features/lamond_int.html.

MacAulay, Donald, ed. Modern Scottish Gaelic Poems. Edinburgh: Canongate Classics 55, 1976.

MacDonell, Margaret. The Emigrant Experience: Songs of Highland Emigrants in North America. Toronto, Buffalo, London: University of Toronto Press, 1982.

MacKinnon, Ken. "Alistair MacLeod's Fiction: Long Homeward Journey From Exile." Atlantic Provinces Book Review 13.2 (May-June 1986): 3.

MacLeod, Alistair. "As Birds Bring Forth the Sun." As Birds Bring Forth the Sun and Other Stories. Toronto: McClelland and Stewart, NCL, 1986 [repr. 1992]: 118–27.

– "The Boat." The Lost Salt Gift of Blood. Toronto: McClelland and Stewart, 1976: 105–25.

– "The Return." The Last Salt Gift of Blood. Toronto: McClelland and Stewart, 1976: 89–105.

– "The Road to Rankin's Point." The Lost Salt Gift of Blood. Toronto: McClelland and Stewart, 1976: 126–56.

– "The Road to Rhu and Cairn an Dorin (The Cairn of Sorrow)." Antigonish Review (Spring 1985): 7–8.

– "Vision." As Birds Bring Forth the Sun and Other Stories. Toronto: McClelland and Stewart, NCL, 1986 [repr. 1992]: 128–67.

– No Great Mischief. Toronto: McClelland and Stewart, 1999.

MacMhannain, Calum Bàn (Malcolm Ban Buchanan). "The Emigration of the Islanders." In MacDonell, 105–30.

MacPhee, Dianne. "Highland Culture As the Essence of Being in the Short Stories of Alistair MacLeod." Unpublished BA thesis, Acadia University, 1994. Supervisor: Dr. Gwendolyn Davies.

– "Proposal for a Thesis to be Entitled Out of Regionalism into the Gaeltacht: Alistair MacLeod as 'Seannachie'." Submitted to Dalhousie University English Department, December 1999, 14 pages.

Martin, Sandra. "I think you carry a landscape within you." The Globe and Mail (29 April 2000): D9.

Nicholson, Colin. "Regions of Memory: Alistair MacLeod's Fiction." British Journal of Canadian Studies 7.1 (1992): 128–37.

– "Signatures of Time: Alistair MacLeod & his Short Stories." Canadian Literature #107 (Winter 1985): 90–101.

Rubinsky, Holley. "An Interview with Alistair MacLeod." *Brick* 36 (Summer 1989): 19–28.

Williams, David. "From Clan to Nation: Orality and The Book in Alistair MacLeod's *No Great Mischief.*" In Guilford, 43–71.

Wittig, Kurt. *The Scottish Tradition in Literature*. Edinburgh: James Thin, Mercat Press, 1978.

MARTA DVOŘÁK

Of Cows and Configurations in Emily Carr's The Book of Small

A cow yard with a cud-chewing red-and-white song-loving cow. Clothes that live in a camphor-wood chest which has sailed from England round the Horn. Horse-drawn carriages, chamber pots, flour barrels in the pantry and wooden tubs in the kitchen. Bear coats and brick houses. Oil lamps, ox teams, pie socials, and sleighs. Stiff Sunday clothes, fox farms, screened porches, and gramophones. Hot chocolate poured out of pink-and-white china pots in velvet-draped hotel tearooms. Chronotopic spaces in which time thickens (Bakhtin, 84) and takes on texture, made tangible by homely, quotidian objects drenched in history. Time spaces refigured by modernist and postmodern writers from Emily Carr[1] and Ernest Buckler to Mavis Gallant, Margaret Laurence, Alice Munro, or Margaret Atwood,[2] who stage across a gulf – through hybridized primal or second-hand recollections – the vanished worlds of Imperial and post-imperial Canada from Vancouver Island and small town Manitoba and Ontario to Montreal's Sherbrooke Street and rural Nova Scotia. These are refigurations of temporal experience, a practice which, as Paul Ricoeur has pointed out, is the cornerstone of all narrative configurations (*Le Temps raconté*, 9). But generic developments have reflected or affected the shifting hierarchization of these spatio-temporalities. Our readings of these texts benefit by a heuristic distinction Mikhail Bakhtin makes between, on the one hand, the epic's distanced stance from a completive, absolute past of founding fathers and heroes, and, on the other hand, the novel's radical move to the open-ended present of the utterance, of the narrating self, as starting point and centre (34–38; 218). The shift – adopted by other genres – sets up a hiatus and a dynamic of tension between the distanced image of the represented object and the enunciative stance grounded in personal experience and interrelating with a fluid, extratextual, contemporary reality, the Third Space of enunciation in which the negotiation and translation of cultural differences is articulated (Bhabha). The short fiction writers I have evoked in effect configure and reconfigure the pre-existent conventions of 17th- and 18th-century life writing,[3] as well as those of the baroque novel and 19th century travel literature.[4] These involve a loose metonymic mixture of anecdotal sketches, descriptions, portraits, and essays. The reconfigurations – combinations of different codes and deviations from the inherited configurations of a common cultural matrix – can be situated on a double plane: sociocultural and aesthetic.

Owing to the limited scope this paper allows, I shall focus primarily on post-impressionist painter/writer Emily Carr's *The Book of Small*, first published in 1942, exemplary of the indigenous story cycle of place[5] spawned by the early travel and immigrant literatures constructed in a mode of seriation geared to anticipated reader response. The composite is all the more valuable to study as it overlaps with the cycle of character through a binary structure that focuses on the origins of selfhood at the same time as it focuses on the origins of community and nation – double dimensions of the process of individuation and identity construction. Emily Carr was born in 1871 in an interstitial geopolitical and temporal space framed by Empire and Republic[6]: the Vancouver Island where West meets East,[7] the very year that British Columbia joined the new Confederation of Canada. We encounter a syntagmatic, metonymic axis with which Carr chooses to chronicle the growth and development of a colonial outpost into a capital city – from the plank sidewalks and wooden stockade with bastions of a Hudson's Bay fort to the stone copper-roofed Parliament Buildings of the administrative capital of British Columbia. This referential, mimetic axis addresses the phenomena of migration, acculturation, and indigenization submitted to chronotopic contingencies, from the dual – and ambivalent – stances of witness and participant. Yet, from cow yard and wild lily field to prim English garden, there co-exists – in an apparently exceptional fashion – a strong metaphorical, paradigmatic axis involving superimpositions and substitutions which recurrently suspend the referential function of language and set up a state of contemplation. As Ricoeur has judiciously remarked, the mimetic function of story, which operates within the temporal values of the field of action, is discrete from metaphorical description, which operates within the field of sensorial, pathic, aesthetic, and ethical values (*L'Intrigue et le récit historique*, 12). While these two axes do intermingle in modes of poetic discourse, the testamentary dynamics of *The Book of Small* refiguring a recognizable world seem on the surface at odds with the compressed genre and clusters of images conforming to a modernist aesthetic, particularly that of Imagism.[8] Yet I shall demonstrate how Carr harnesses the tension between event or chronotopic experience and the unfurling of symbol. She conflates the forms of oratory concerning past, present, and future, fusing instantaneity and remembrance. Simultaneously, by atomizing, she paradoxically generates a metaphorical and ultimately metaphysical unifying system. This system finds itself superscribed onto the discursive strategies of identity politics in an overcoding which confers veracity – the veracity inherent to an ontological stance.

I began this paper with a cow yard and a cow. To begin to convey their multiple resonances and roles in Carr's configurations, I shall resort, incongruously but appropriately, to L.P. Hartley's *The Go-Between* as mediator. Its opening sentence, "The past is a foreign country: they do things differently there," is so notorious that in his equally notorious essay "Imaginary Homelands," Salman Rushdie could not resist a playful refiguration. Foregrounded by a cleft clause, his inversion – "it's my present that is foreign, and … the past is home" (9) – reflects the "migrant's-eye view" stemming from the "uprooting, disjuncture, and metamorphosis" (394) he identifies as the increasingly commonplace diasporic condition (responsible for Carr's cow being where it is). Rushdie prolongs the subversion by arguing that "the past is a country from which we have all emigrated" (12), in other words a common loss, whereas the loss may be more intense for "the writer who is out-of-country and even out-of-language" (12) owing to the disjunction of time and place, or an asynchronic landscape which I could term an elsewhere present. Just as he naturalizes the equation of time and place, so too do his neologistic compounds posit a holistic symbiosis of place and language which brushes aside a disquieting hiatus in settler societies. He nevertheless admits that migration is one of the richest metaphors of our age, involving, well beyond issues of national borders, the notion of metamorphosis – the transformation of ideas, and the migration of ideas into images (278), which we effectively encounter in Carr's painterly, sensual, and playful depiction of the expansion of a crown colony. Migrants and mutants (210), hybridization, mongrelization (394), cultural transplantation, cross-pollination (20): Rushdie's lexicon, organic, biological/genetic, and metaphorical – concretizing the contact zone between the familiar and the unfamiliar – calls to mind one of Carr's apologues: the hen that hatched ducks and sulked when they swam off, allowing the naïve child protagonist to address notions of becoming, of the Same and the Other, of outside and beyond: "if the hen hatched ducks, why couldn't the cow have a colt?" (19) The semantic field of hybridization in these two texts separated by half a century resonates with the epistemological and aesthetic experimentation triggered by modernism and its subsidiaries (futurism, cubism, Imagism, surrealism), all striving to defamiliarize, deconstruct, atomize, decentre, and show by making strange.[9]

♦

"All our Sundays were exactly alike," begins *The Book of Small*. Just where, when, and who is 'we'? The non-compound opening sentence of the story cycle effectively presents a space-time devoid of any traces of an historical era and grounded in a repetitive cyclicity through the voice of a speaker whose intimate confessional mode is offset by the first person plural pronoun suggesting the merging of the individual with a larger regulated and regulating community. Whose past is this? Is it 'foreign' or 'home'? The opening sentence of the second section of the book, "A Little Town and a Little Girl," makes explicit Carr's dual focus on the self and the world. This first sketch entitled "Beginnings" begins with the grammatical and echoic parallelism of a binary periodic sentence. The mounting protasis stages the external, real-life chronotope, and the descending apodosis occupying the final, strategic position asserts the internal, intimate sphere of the subjective consciousness: "Victoria, on Vancouver Island, British Columbia, was the little town; I was the little girl" (75). Elsewhere, Carr establishes a fictionalized distancing from her autobiographical self by recurrently shifting from first person to third,[10] and by calling the other two middle sisters of the large Carr family and herself by the nicknames Bigger, Middle, and Small, respectively. None the less, while fictional devices such as these do generate tension between undisguised autobiography and invention, the autobiographical pact[11] determining the mode of readership – one linked to literary realism, and involving an even stronger readerly trust in the veracity of the refiguring of a recognizable world – is implicitly present. The fact that the author, narrator, and main protagonist are one and the same is made manifest in "Beginnings" when the narrator introduces herself to one of her mother's old acquaintances: "I am Emily Carr's daughter, Emily" (76).

In an earlier story entitled "The Cow Yard," the reader has already divined that Carr is double voicing so as to provide more effectively the fractured perceptions and distorted space-times of a small child and her unreliable temporal measurements rooted in the sensory pleasure principle.[12] An additional chronotopic indeterminacy is generated through the simulacrum of synchronicity between event and narrative positioning. The older narrating I is manifest in the recurrent flash forwards of explicit ellipses or in the collision of flashbacks and fast forwards.[13] Carr's I simulates an almost complete erasure of the enunciative split and a quasi-fusion between narrating I and narrated self: "*Now* that I *am* eight, the same age that Lizzie was when the party happened, and *am getting* quite near to being grown-up, I can see how shamed poor Lizzie must have been of me then" (59). The present of enunciation encroaches into past time territory, the time deixis 'now' misleads, and a hyperbolically distorted perspective[14] produces a disorienting immediacy. All simulate a presencing of selfhood which negotiates what Homi Bhabha terms "the condition of extra-territorial and cross-cultural initiations" (9), even if Carr is not what Rushdie terms 'out-of-country' (12). These initiations involve the child's relocation of homeliness from the "prim and carefully tended" Old World garden of hawthorn hedges, primroses, and shrubberies, "all from imported English stock," in the new soil of which her parents "had buried a tremendous homesickness [which] had rooted and sprung up English"(77, 76 respectively), to the (forever) New Field "left Canadian," surrounded by an indigenous snake fence and carpeted with what Carr pointedly appropriates as "*our* wild Canadian lilies" (77). The descriptive pause which follows is rife with the rhetorical devices of personification and celebration which operate within the sensory field of the affect. The lilies are

> the most delicately lovely of all flowers – white with bent necks and brown eyes looking back into the earth. Their long, slender petals, rolled back from their drooping faces, pointed straight up at the sky, like millions of quivering white fingers. The leaves of the lilies were very shiny – green, mottled with brown, and their perfume like heaven and earth mixed. (77)

In her praise, Carr overcodes the aesthetic value judgment with a social and axiological hierarchy (the good and the homely are what is valuable). She also superimposes a metaphysical dimension (the grateful joy of prayer, in the dual sense of adoration and reflection).

In essence, Carr shifts gears between the diachronic, horizontal axis of narrative/dramatic scene and the synchronic, vertical axis of the pause. As Bhabha has remarked, descriptive pauses function within the time lag of the socially ordered sign or symbol, and are suffused with political agency (193). In Carr's case, the political agency strongly involves "the attitudinal identification with a particular locale" (New, 117).

Conforming to this paradigm is the incipit of "A Little Town and a Little Girl," just discussed: "Victoria, on Vancouver Island, British Columbia, was the little town; I was the little girl." (75) Here too, the expected horizontal, mimetic narrative of displacement promised by the opening single-sentence paragraph is suspended by a metaphorical freeze frame, timeless locus of meditation:

> It is hard to remember just when you became aware of being alive. It is like looking through rain onto a bald, new lawn; as you watch, the brown is all pricked with pale green. You did not see the points pierce, did not hear the stab – there they are! (75)

The reader thus encounters in a stereoscopic manner Carr's vision of emergence, which I do not use in the exclusive acceptation of Bhabha's emergence of a national perspective (143–44), but as the inscape of individual identity-construction grounded in the dynamics of place, which W.H. New has described as the "belonging to place" involving "a determination of self through a relationship with site"[15] (117). Alongside the extended simile blending the abstract and the concretely homely, we can note a highly effective stylistic combination. First, the use of the inclusive second person pronoun positing universality. Then, the shift to the immediacy, permanence, and timelessness conveyed by the concluding synoptic present tense which surges dramatically out of the binary enunciative present/diegetic past. And finally, the rhetorical device of exclamation serving to foreground the emotive function of language centred upon the speaker. Readers can divine that the individual life-sequences Carr presents to them are, to borrow Bakhtin's terms, "mere bas-reliefs on the all-embracing, powerful foundation of collective life" (218). Like the protagonists deployed by the early colonial writer Susanna Moodie,[16] or a century later by Ernest Buckler or Mavis Gallant, with their abundant recourse to antonomasia and apologue,[17] Carr's protagonists are representatives of the social whole, and the events of their lives take on their full significance on the social, not individual, plane.

The writer takes care to include indigenous figures as well as representatives from the various epochs and stages of transplantation and sedimentation. She wields social antithesis masterfully, providing accurate phonetic transcriptions of mangled grammar or distorted pronunciation so as to offset, and at times gleefully mock, geographical or socio-economic appurtenances or pretentions.[18] A parade of portraits furls by, in which she alternates meliorative antonomastic figures (individuated synecdoches of those who have learnt to renegotiate inherited relational notions and attitudes to property, production, propriety, and power) with pejorative figures (essentially the dysfunctional migrants who cannot or will not adapt[19]). The little stories in "Characters," for instance, are in point of fact a series of loosely-connected portraits of the different types making up the collective whole, insisting on its misfits ("there lived a most astonishing family," "another human derelict was ...," "another familiar figure of our school days," "then there were ..." [127–31]). The dysphoric portraits are on the whole gently ironic. In the description of a brother-and-sister couple mincing up Birdcage Walk like "elderly fowls" (131), the simile serves to confer a physical and moral ridicule inviting readerly distance. Elsewhere, Carr suggests an amused distancing from metropolitan values through fallible narration. Having always equated Queen Victoria with the queens of fairy tales, the child ingenuously confesses: "I had never known that she was real, only that she owned Victoria, Canada, the twenty-fourth of May, the Church of England, and all the soldiers and sailors in the world" (135–36). The hyperbolic, chaotically enumerated errors of the naïve narrated self effectively de-naturalize the givens of imperial *doxa*. But nowhere is Carr's New World axiological positioning clearer than when she adopts a caustically ironic distance. The short piece "Schools," which moves fluidly back and forth between essay and anecdote, anticipates Mavis Gallant's biting satire of the imperial mindset on class and gender roles in a story like "Varieties of Exile" (few of the genteel English youths in exile "being fit to do much of anything, being well schooled but half educated, in that specifically English way" [748]). Carr manifests the same control of periodic structures, rhetorical antithesis, and syllepsis, along with the technique of blaming while seeming to praise:

Politeness-education ladies had migrated to Canada, often in the hope of picking up bread and butter and possibly a husband, though they pretended all the while that they had come out on a

very special mission – to teach the young of English-born gentlemen how not to become Canadian ... So young ladies whose papas
had sufficient means learned English manners – how to shut a
door, how to bow gracefully, how to address people of their own
class and how a servant, how to write a dignified letter in beautiful script, how to hold their heads up, their stomachs in and how
to look down their noses at the right moment. For all this the old
ladies were very handsomely remunerated and the girls' brains remained quite empty. (*Book of Small*, 116)

Antonomasia clearly participates in a modernist strategy of fragmentation, engaging in the metonymical contiguity of narrative. Yet,
like the descriptive pause, it brakes/breaks narrative speed for the
metaphorical stratification of substitution, a layering process of permutation from the particular to the general, and from the textual to
extratextual spheres.

This finally brings me to our cow in the Cow Yard, munching sweet
hay and listening to Bong's falsetto Chinese songs as he milks (16). Or
Small's noisy cow-songs "boiling over like the jam kettle" (31). Or the
cow chewing with delighted slobbering and half-closed eyes the first
pussy-willows of spring (18), placidly reigning over all the other creatures in her yard. But also the other cows, allowed to roam loose in the
streets and turn unfenced flowers into milk (90), which "preferred to
walk on the plank sidewalks rather than dirty their hooves in the mud
by the wayside," so that it was "the woman-lady, not the lady-cow
who had to take to the mud and get scratched by the wild rose bushes
that grew between sidewalk and fence" (90). The cow as town-planner.
For "it was the cows *who* laid out the town, at least that portion of it
lying beyond the few main streets. Cow hooves hardened the mud into
twisty lanes in their meanderings to and fro – people just followed in
the cows' footsteps" (95, my emphasis). The cow as the measurement
of progress, cow control (they are eventually impounded if they roam
the streets) equated with a vertiginously accelerated modernization:
"You never knew when new lumber might be dumped on any piece of
land and presently the lumber was a house and someone was moving
in" (151). A proteiform figure operating on the boundaries of fable
and metaphor, with overtones of the objective correlative so dear to
the modernists[20] and in particular the Imagists, the cow is clearly at
the heart of Carr's semiotics of representational space.[21] It participates
in the spatial structures, geometric configurations, and symbolic,

value-laden spatial allusions which Bill New has identified in the book *Land Sliding*, which, by an interesting coincidence, harbours a cow on the cover: Barbara Klunder's playful "Laura Secord's Udderly Patriotic Cow" (reminding us once again of the historically close relations between cows and Canadian nationhood).

The cow yard, site of overlapping and displacement of selfhood and nationhood, participates in the tradition of allegorical *topographia*. Its connections with the three Carr daughters born on New World soil represent three stages of negotiated dislocation and re-location, spatially foregrounded through emphatic paragraph breaks:

> Of the three girls who played in the Cow Yard, Bigger tired of it soonest ... The garden rather than the Cow Yard suited her crisp frocks and tidy ways best, and she was a little afraid of the Cow.
>
> Middle was a born mother, and had huge doll families. She liked equally the tidy garden and the free Cow Yard.
>
> Small was wholly a Cow Yard child. (15)

Carr's cow is of course a universally perceived image of contentment, a concrete example which replaces the expression of an abstract idea, and which involves the dynamics of emphasis. In the delightfully distorting manner of caricature, her cow also materializes the notion of "belonging to place." It actually configures both place and process, nowhere more overtly than in the extended opening simile of the piece "Father's Store":

> Victoria was like a lying-down cow, chewing. She had made one enormous effort at upheaval. She had hoisted herself from a Hudson's Bay Fort into a little town and there she paused, chewing the cud of imported fodder, afraid to crop the pastures of the new world for fear she might lose the good flavours of the old to which she was so deeply loyal. Her jaws went rolling on and on, long after there was nothing left to chew. (95)

The performative nature of the cud-chewing simile as process of cultural translation in this piece figures a historically transformative period of events and actors from the temporal and perspectival distance of a spectator. In other stories, the cultural sign configures a negotiation of differential identities in which the speaker finds agency "in a form of the 'future' where the past is not originary, where the present

is not simply transitory" (Bhabha, 219) In "Singing" the cud-chewing metaphor figures a symbiotic process between little girl and cow
(yard): "The harder Small sang, the harder the cow chewed and the
faster she twiddled her ears around as if stirring the song into the food
to be rechewed in cud along with her breakfast " (29). Significantly,
the image superscribes additional layers of meaning when it is reiterated and rewoven contrapuntally into the dovetailing closing narrative
of the piece. This in turn is feather-stitched to the sterile cud-chewing sequence of Victoria the cow. Its very repetition and permutation
identifies a common reducible dimension by highlighting, as Gilles
Deleuze suggests in *Différence et repetition*, both a qualitative order
of re/semblance and a quantitative order of equivalence. A reversing
mirroring device translates place and character from the child in the
cow yard to the mother and a lady friend in the drawing room, whose
nostalgia for the England they left behind leads them to launch into
the old songs of their youth:

> Here were two ladies nearly fifty years old, throwing back their
> heads to sing love songs, nursery songs, hymns, God Save the
> Queen, Rule Britannia – songs that spilled over the drawing-room
> as easily as Small's cow songs spilled over the yard, only Small's
> songs were new, fresh grass snatched as the cow snatched pasture
> grass. The ladies' songs were rechews – cudded fodder. (33)

To be remarked is that complex form of analogy, the proportional
metaphor, positing a multilateral system of interconnections in which
the mothers' resuscitated old songs are to Small's original musical im-
provisations what imported, cudded fodder is to new, fresh grass, clearly
signifying that creative reinscriptions rooted in new territory take ascendancy over stale mimeticism and monocultural replications. In anticipation of Rushdie's assertion that newness emerges through the hybridization of migrants turned mutants (Rushdie 210), the duck hatched by the
hen, which jumps into the water and swims off, may well be a figure of
Small and of the translation from garden to cow yard.
   Metaphor is acknowledged to be the most elaborate as well as the
most condensed form of imagery. The examples I have hitherto fo-
cussed on moreover simultaneously contain the ramifying discursive
dynamics habitually carried by metonymy,[22] and are sites of cultural resistance grounded in indigenized axiological stances. These, of
course, commingle with inherited mindsets which critics such as, most

recently, Linda Morra,[23] have not failed to dwell on. Yet, as I suggested in my introduction, Carr's images do much more than adroitly figure empirical chronotopic experience and metamorphosing belief-systems. Her clusters of images and sensory (ap)perceptions, which explore and de-naturalize the very process of seeing, are more sensorial and less cerebral than Gertrude Stein's notoriously cubist approach to writing,[24] and participate in the aesthetic frame of literary impressionism practised by modernist writers such as Katherine Mansfield.[25] Carr, like Mansfield, is attached to poetry's traditional, metaphoric trope, readopted almost militantly by Ezra Pound and the Imagists, who claimed that the adequate symbol rested always in the natural object,[26] which is autotelic, gaining meaning from itself. Pound's definition of an image as "that thing which presents an intellectual and emotional complex in an instant of time" (*Gaudier-Brzeska* 143), anticipating T.S. Eliot's assertion that an objective correlative is the only artistic way of articulating emotion,[27] identifies it as the precise site of the power that poetry has in rendering social language mysterious, and "delivering the word as simple signifier back to its numinous position as object" (Barbour 32). Calling to mind Mansfield's recurrent recourse to plants and flowers as agents of transformation and of blurring,[28] but devoid of the New Zealand writer's ambivalent, often ironic dimension,[29] Carr's images of the uncultivated, unordered lily field are semantic and do signify, but denote nothing in epistemological terms, for metaphor, like prayer, is neither true nor false.[30] None the less, her iconic descriptions of the indigenous or home-grown flowers and berries are *ekphrastic*[31] vehicles of thought, of the "pondering [even ordering] of experience" which Richard Chadbourne finds generic to the essay (149), but which dovetail with the aesthetic movement of Vorticism launched by the avant-garde painter-writer Wyndham Lewis and Ezra Pound. When in a neighbour's garden Small comes "face to face" with a significantly capitalized Orange Lily, the entrance to its trumpet "beyond sentinelled doors" 56) suggests access to the mysteries of origins accentuated by the religious running metaphor:

What was in the bottom of Lily's trumpet? What was it that the stamens were so carefully guarding? Small pushed the stamens aside and looked. The trumpet was empty – the emptiness of a church after parson and people have gone, when the music is asleep in the organ and the markers dangle from the Bible on the lectern. (56–57)

Disappointed by the gift of pinks in lieu of the lily,

> in her heart she hugged an Orange Lily. It had burned itself there
> not with flaming petals, not through the hot, rich smell. Soundless,
> formless, white – it burned there. (58)

This complex conceit for the unnameable joins the abstract and the
concrete (heart/hugged), combines the conjunctive and disjunctive
forces of preterition (not with/not through), synaesthesia (hot, rich
smell), and paradox (orange/white/formless). It channels the opposite
dynamics rife in Carr's writings,[32] and distances itself from the static
stillness Pound felt imagism had come to. The whirling energy concentrated here calls to mind Pound's vortex, a "radiant mode or cluster,"
a point of maximum energy "through which, and into which, ideas
are constantly rushing" (Pound, *Gaudier-Brzeska* 92). The remarkable fusion of stillness and dynamism calls to mind Wyndham Lewis's
claim that the "Vorticist is at his maximum point of energy when still-
est" (Lewis, *Blast* 1, 148). A comparable vorticist aesthetic drives the
preceding short piece entitled "White Currants," which begins with a
hermetic iterative binary (the subject pronoun being enigmatically an-
tecedent-less): "It happened many times, and it always happened just
in that corner of the old garden" (53). The description of the ripening
of the white currants is in point of fact a paean to life and a quest for
essence or Idea, or *quidditas*, what James Joyce's protagonist Stephen
Dedalus called the whatness of things (Joyce 193):

> The riper they got, the clearer they grew, till you could almost see
> right through them. You could see the tiny veins in their skins and
> the seeds and the juice. Each currant hung there like an almost-
> told secret.
>   Oh! You thought, if the currants were just a wee bit clearer, then
> perhaps you could see them *living*, inside. (53)

The scene develops into a vibrant monadic moment of Emersonian
"ex-stasy" in which the universe waits to be known and accounted
for. The dynamics strain toward the *noumenon* or absolute supersen-
suous Unity,[33] (which interestingly evoke Carr's painterly style – and
which she herself describes meticulously in notably two of her journal
entries[34]):

Everything trembled. When you went in among the mauvy-pink flowers and the butterflies you began to tremble too; you seemed to become a part of it – and then what do you think happened? Somebody else was there too. He was on a white horse and he had brought another white horse for me.

We flew round and round in and out among the mauvy-pink blossoms, on the white horses ... In and out, round and round we went ... Everything was going so fast – the butterflies' wings, the pink flowers, the hum and the smell, that they stopped being four things and became one most lovely thing, and the little boy and the four horses and I were in the middle of it, like the seeds that you saw dimly inside the white currants. In fact, the beautiful thing *was* like the white currants, like a big splendid secret getting clearer and clearer every moment- just a second more and – (*Book of Small* 54, original emphasis)

The small girl's fantasy is evocative of Coleridge's concept of the secondary Imagination which "struggles to idealize and to unify" and which is "vital" while "objects (*as* objects) are essentially fixed and dead" (*Biographia Literaria* 452, emphasis in original). The whirling movement accelerates metamorphically in an aesthetic which shapes and confers value. Carr's dynamic textual imagery is comparable to her painterly intentions and techniques of movement, which she exposes in her journals:

From the land, the movement sweeps out over the sea and up to the air. Its movement and its speed are one, and the more complete the movement, the more complete the picture. *When you find the thing's direction in space, you find its key.* (*Opposite Contraries* 70, my emphasis)

Just so, her verbal images mediate yet transcend the experience of human, material reality, also attempting to express that which lies *beyond* common logic and common language – corresponding to what Paul Ricoeur terms the existential function of the metaphor (*La Métaphore vive* 313).

This essay has demonstrated that *The Book of Small's* episodic axis of scattered events – consubstantial with the hybridized short genres of essay, sketch, fable, portrait, and self-portrait – is (suf)fused with a configurational dimension.[35] Early colonial mindsets are blended into a cultural continuum mingling mimeticism, appropriation, and even an indigenization involving totem transfer, which Carr frankly admits to in her journal when discussing her famous early paintings of Indian villages and totems: "The old Indian pictures expressed the Indians. There was only an insignificant splatter of me. They made the cake and I only had to cut it and hand it around. Any fool could do that" (*Opposite Contraries* 100). Simultaneously, I have argued that the writer strives to construe a significant whole out of the scattered narratives and images. She reconfigures diachronic aesthetic stances ranging from Romanticism to the various currents of modernism, along with certain neo-platonic interrogations and monadic stances. These are reminiscent of Coleridge's declaration that "the beautiful, contemplated in its essentials, that is, in *kind* and not in *degree*, is that in which the many, still seen as many, becomes one" (*On the Principles of Genial Criticism* 443, original emphases). The artist's eye guiding the writer's pen struggles to produce a full representation of the world, to disclose "the inner burstings of growth showing through the skin of things" (Carr, *Hundreds and Thousands* 295). The textual space, complementing perhaps the surface of her canvas, attempts to accede to a valued, higher order of meaning, and to explore and celebrate the numinous dimension of both world and language.[36] Interestingly, this idealist, even religious, vision positing one essentialist suprareality participates – albeit two decades later than her English and American counterparts – in the early manifestations of Modernism which, prior to the First World War, were still in quest of truth and meaning. Carr's re/configuration is old as well as new. In spite of the indigenized, de-doxifying axiological stances that suffuse her tropes, her revisiting of paths trod on from the Greece of Antiquity to the England of the Romantics is a figuring backwards, an acceptance and a return.

NOTES

1   Carr's conflation of time and space is consubstantial with her acculturation, as we can see in certain antithetical parallelisms such as the following: "I did not want to go to the Old World to see history, I wanted to see *now* what was out here in our West. I was glad Father and Mother had come as far as the West went before they stopped and settled down" (*The Book of Small* 85, Carr's emphasis).

2   Notably the short fictions in Carr's *The Book of Small*, Buckler's *Ox Bells and Fireflies* and *Thanks for Listening*, Gallant's Linnet Muir sequence in *Home Truths*, Laurence's *A Bird in the House*, Munro's *Dance of the Happy Shades*, and Atwood's *Bluebeard's Egg and Other Stories*, respectively.

3   Notably the works of Walton, Pepys, Johnson, and Boswell.

4   Tobias Smollett's *Travels through France and Italy*, Laurence Sterne's *A Sentimental Journey*, or Bougainville's *Voyage autour du monde* to name but a few examples.

5   For discussions of cycles of place and cycles of character, see Helen Hoy and Gerald Lynch.

6   Just "across the line" from Victoria was San Francisco. Carr confides that the Americans "thought English and Canadian people as slow and stupid as [the Canadians] thought the American people uncomfortable rushers – makers of jerry-built goods that fell to pieces in no time." While Victoria residents "preferred to wait ages for [their] things to come by sailing ship round the Horn from England rather than to buy American goods," they did consent to "go to the other side" to save their lives, in other words, to be operated on in San Francisco rather than sail back to England and "either die before they got there or else get well and forget what the operation was for" (*Book of Small* 93).

7   The timeless use of the present tense in her concluding sentence assigns permanence to the Island"s liminality: "so stands tranquil Victoria in her Island setting – western as West can be before earth's gentle rounding pulls West east again" (Carr, *Book of Small* 168).

8   While Gerald Lynch interestingly posits that a resistance to causal or chronological narrative is inherent to the very genre of short fiction, which he alleges is closer to lyric poetry in its systematic use of suspended, metaphorical moments (22), I find that before the advent of Modernism the short fiction genres were in no way averse to such narrative, Maupassant's carefully crafted stories (see in particular "Boule de Suif" and *La Maison Tellier*, 1880 and 1881 respectively) being no exceptions.

9   Rushdie himself admits the kinship in his essay "Imaginary Homelands": "those of us who have been forced by cultural displacement to accept the provisional nature of all truths, all certainties, have perhaps had modernism forced upon us" (Rushdie 12).

10 Critics such as Gérard Genette, Linda Hutcheon, or Patricia Waugh have called attention to the long-standing readerly acceptance of the first person pronoun as reflecting subjectivity and of the third person pronoun as guaranteeing objectivity.

11 See Philippe Lejeune, *Le Pacte autobiographique*.

12 The fallible narrator-protagonist reiterates a hyperbolic disjunction
    with man-made clock-time. Time slows down with desire or expectation
    ("Small had wanted a dog – she did not remember how long she had
    wanted it – it must have been from the beginning of the world" [36]; "It
    seemed years since we left home, but neither Alice nor I had had a birth-
    day" [48]; "All week we stared at the clock, but, for all she ticked, her
    hands stuck" [68]), but quickens during pleasurable activities ("What was
    Time anyway, that things could play such tricks with it? A stream could
    squeeze a whole afternoon into one minute. A clock could spread one
    minute out into a whole year" (71).) The toy watch with the hands that
    do not move proves that "play things are always truer than real" (72).

13 Ellipses are recurrent in phrases such as "Years passed" (38), or "at the
    end of fifty years we still called that piece of ground 'the new field'" (76).
    Flashbacks and flash forwards collide in sentences like the following:
    "They moved East *long before I was born*, but how was I to know, *when
    nearly grown up*, what the love of those pioneer women must have been
    for one another, for *when years later* I stood at Mrs. Bissett's door … for
    the first time … she took me to herself in the most terrific hug" (76, my
    emphases).

14 With the exaggeratedly distorted point of view of a little girl, Emily 'real-
    izes' that those giving the party were the little boy's "big brother" and "big
    sisters" who were "hundreds and hundreds of years" older than he (59).

15 New judiciously distinguishes "belonging to place," which denotes "the
    attitudinal identification with a particular locale," from "being in place,"
    which merely involves an awareness of existing in a certain spatial envi-
    ronment (117).

16 Moodie's recourse to the self-portrait, portrait, and sketch for didactic,
    exemplary purposes, is notably clear in the story "Tom Wilson's Emigra-
    tion," which establishes a socio-economic parallel between Australia
    and Canada, both targets of early 19th-century mass migration, as well
    as structural and dramatic parallels between Wilson and the Moodies.
    The quite Dickensian device of concretization (Wilson's pet monkey in
    Australia is equated with his pet bear in Canada, positing in turn an
    equivalence between the overt thievery of the convicted "rogues" in the
    former colony and the covert ruses of the average residents in the latter)
    sets up an anticipatory pattern of entropy which prepares the reader for
    Moodie's concluding moral. Tom Wilson, a "test case" of what Michael
    Peterman so rightly terms "the uneasy post-revolutionary meeting of
    English principles with American notions of ultra-republican liberty"
    (Peterman 509), with his manipulation of modals and tense sequence

("Gentlemen can't work like labourers, and if they *could*, they *won't*" [Moodie 71, my emphases]) prepares the reader for Moodie's concluding remarks, in which she explains what she has previously illustrated ("The gentleman can neither work so hard, live so coarsely, nor endure so many privations as his poorer but more fortunate neighbour" [Moodie, 489]) and confesses that her stories are meant to deter genteel English families from making the mistake of migrating to "the backwoods of Canada," which she equates with a "prison-house" (489).

17 Obeying a strategy of displacement from the one to the many, from an individual to a group or category, but also, inversely, from the particular to the general (or underlying, universal One), Buckler's reliance on antonomasia is particularly clear in the short fiction "A to Z," (*Ox Bells and Fireflies*) in which the author inventories and describes the inhabitants of a village, from App to Zeb, named after the letters of the alphabet, and so clearly marked as *exempla*. His villagers are reminiscent of the types or roles peopling Carr's story "Characters." Also see Dvořák, "Mavis Gallant's Fiction: Taking the (Rhetorical) Measure of the Turning Point," in Nicole Côté, *Varieties of Exile: New Essays on Mavis Gallant*: 63–74.

18 One can remark the contrasts drawn between the O'Flaherty brothers living in a shanty built with driftwood ("Does she seem turrible [sic] bad?" [128]), and the snobbish young Canadians freshly back from English finishing schools "'patering' and 'matering' their mother and father, saying 'Awfully jolly, don't you know,' and 'No, not rawlly [sic]!'"(118).

19 Mrs. Mitchell, an *exemplum* of the nostalgic migrant, finally returns to England only to die, unhappy, amongst strangers. One cannot fail to note how a foregrounded temporal hiatus suffuses the agency of identification with the dynamics of relocation and reinscription which are no longer in process but completed. The disapproving enunciative stance of a speaker having already undergone a process of acculturation herself is notably discernible in Carr's elegant binary period involving a triple whammy combining catachresis, syllepsis, and personification: "The journey nearly killed her, and England did quite" (137).

20 In Mansfield's New Zealand stories, the aloe is one of the notable objective correlatives – significantly preferred by Linda Burnell because it flowers only once every one hundred years, while she is condemned to bear "great lumps of children" (Mansfield, "Prelude" 77).

21 E.M. Forster pointedly used the solid, lowly cow to playfully address elevated philosophical concerns. In the opening passage of *The Longest Journey* beginning "The cow is there," Cambridge University students tackle idealism and materialism by arguing over whether a cow exists

only when there is someone there to see her. The Canadian modernist Ernest Buckler deploys the image of the cow to explain how in his short autobiographical fictions he strove to create correspondences between the homely object and the cosmos, to "underline the omnipresence of the far in the near (maps of Tasmania on the cow's brockled sides); the universal in the particular (all geometry in the owl's eye); whole galaxies in a pasture of wild flowers)" (Dvořák, *Ernest Buckler: Rediscovery and Reassessment* 71).

22 Metonymy is notably a trope implying a transfer which is based not on substitution or analogy, but on a logical link between sign and thing, implying an appurtenance or relationship of inclusion.

23 Morra argues that Carr was "patently engaged with ethnic stereotypes that were in currency in that period and that perpetuated the notion that the Chinese were "a threat to [English] [sic] cultural identity," reposing her affirmation on historian Paul Yee's statement that "White society rooted in European values was attempting to assert itself in North America. It felt that the Chinese could never be assimilated because they were of a different race" (422).

24 On how Stein's cubist perceptual method of codes of transfer effectively subverting lyrical discourse was notably a huge influence on Canadian writers such as Steve McCaffery and bpNichol, interested in the liberating possibilities of heteroglossic free-floating words, see Douglas Barbour.

25 See notably Julia Van Gunsteren.

26 The Imagist manifesto, Pound's *A Retrospect* (1918), notably recommended the direct treatment of the "thing," whether subjective or objective.

27 See Eliot's famous declaration, "The only way of expressing emotion in the form of art is by finding an objective correlative, in other words, a set of objects, a situation, a chain of events, which shall be a formula of that particular emotion," reprinted in *The Sacred Wood: Essays on Poetry and Criticism.*

28 See Dvořák, "Katherine Mansfield's Geranium Plate: or the Construction of Liminal Space": 55–67.

29 One thinks of the "tall, slender pear tree in fullest, richest bloom" standing "perfect" against the sky that the young female protagonist of "Bliss" perceives as "a symbol of her own life" (Mansfield 115); when Bertha's world collapses around her pending her discovery that her husband and her friend Miss Fulton are having a passionate affair, the pear tree ironically remains "as lovely as ever and as full of flower and as still" (124).

30 Jean-François Lyotard reminds us in *La Condition postmoderne* that Aristotle excluded prayer from denotative discourse (*apophantikos*) (Lyotard 36).

31 I take the liberty of applying the notional *ekphrasis* related to iconic poetry which involves the verbal representation of a graphic representation,
although the object of Carr's contemplation is not a real or imagined
work of art, but a recollected landscape, depicted like a picture, and filled
with the *energia* of hypotyposis.

32 The "opposite contraries" Susan Crean has foregrounded in *Opposite
Contraries: the Unknown Journals of Emily Carr and Other Writings*.

33 The small girl and the currant bush call to mind Emerson's delightful
suggestion of "an occult relation between man and the vegetable." He
adds, "I am not alone and unacknowledged. They nod to me and I to
them" (*Nature* 13).

34 "The picture must contain one movement, and the articulations of that
movement are very important. The eye must travel through the spaces
without a jot or jolt. Earth, sky, and sea must travel the same way. The
end of their journey is the same destination. Your picture must not stop
anymore than life must." (entry dated 22 April 1934, *Opposite Contraries*, 70). "There is to be one sweeping movement through the whole air,
an ascending movement, high and fathomless. The movement must connect with each part, taking great care with the articulation" (entry dated
9 February 1935, *Hundreds and Thousands* 170).

35 Paul Ricoeur also distinguishes between the episodic dimension of narrative and its configurational dimension in "Narrative Time."

36 For an earlier discussion of Carr's intergeneric, intratextual processes, see
Dvořák, "Emily Carr: Text as Illustration."

WORKS CITED

Atwood, Margaret. *Bluebeard's Egg and other Stories*. London: Virago,
1988.

Bakhtin, Mikhaïl. *The Dialogic Imagination: Four Essays*. Ed. Michael
Holquist. Trans. Caryl Emerson and Michael Holquist. Austin: University
of Texas Press, 1996.

Barbour, Douglas. "Transformations of (the Language of) the Ordinary:
Innovation in Recent Canadian Poetry," *Essays on Canadian Writing* 37,
(Spring 1989): 30–64.

Bhabha, Homi. *The Location of Culture*. London/New York: Routledge, 2001.

Buckler, Ernest. *Ox Bells and Fireflies*. Toronto: McClelland and Stewart, 1974.

– *Thanks for Listening: Stories and Short Fictions by Ernest Buckler*. Ed.
Marta Dvořák. Waterloo: Wilfrid Laurier University Press, 2004.

Carr, Emily. *The Book of Small*. [1966] Toronto: Irwin, 1986.

– *Hundreds and Thousands: the Journals of an Artist.* Toronto: Clarke, Irwin, 1966.
– *Opposite Contraries: the Unknown Journals of Emily Carr and Other Writing.* Ed. Susan Crean. Vancouver/Toronto/Berkeley: Douglas & McIntyre, 2004.
Chadbourne, Richard. "A Puzzling Genre: Comparative Views of the essay." *Comparative Literary Studies* 20, 1983: 133–53.
Coleridge, *On the Principles of Genial Criticism.* In *English Romantic Writers.* Ed. David Perkins. New York: Harcourt, Brace and World, 1967.
– *Biographia Literaria.* Ed. David Perkins. New York: Harcourt, Brace and World, 1967.
Côté, Nicole & Peter Sabor (eds.). *Varieties of Exile: New Essays on Mavis Gallant.* New York/Washington/Bern: Peter Lang, 1999.
Deleuze, Gilles. *Différence et repetition.* Paris: Presses Université de France, 1968.
Dvořák, Marta. *Ernest Buckler: Rediscovery and Reassessment,* Waterloo: Wilfrid Laurier University Press, 2000.
– "Katherine Mansfield's Geranium Plate: or the Construction of Liminal Space." In *Les Nouvelles de Katherine Mansfield.* Eds. D. Dubois, L. Lepaludier, J. Sohier. Angers: Presses de l'Université d'Angers, 1998: 55–67.
– "Emily Carr: Text as Illustration." In *Image et récit: littératures et arts visuels du Canada.* Eds. Jean-Michel Lacroix, Simone Vauthier, Héliane Ventura. Paris: Presses de la Sorbonne Nouvelle, 1993:51–76.
Eliot, T.S. *The Sacred Wood: Essays on Poetry and Criticism.* London: Methuen, 1970.
Emerson, Ralph Waldo. *Nature.* ([1836] Ed. Kenneth Walter Cameron. New York: Scholars' Facsimiles and Reprints, 1940.
Forster, E.M. [1907, 1922] *The Longest Journey.* New York: Vintage Books, Random House, 1962.
Gallant, Mavis. *The Collected Stories.* New York: Random House, 1996.
Hartley, L.P. *The Go-Between.* Harmondsworth: Penguin, 1978.
Hoy, Helen. "No Honey, I'm Home: Place Over Love in Alice Munro's Short Story Cycle *Who Do You Think You Are?*," *Canadian Literature* 160 (Spring 1999): 73–98.
Hutcheon, Linda. *The Politics of Postmodernism.* London/New York: Routledge, 1990.
Joyce, James. [1916] *A Portrait of the Artist as a Young Man,* London: Granada, 1977.
Lejeune, Philippe. *Le Pacte autobiographique.* Paris: Editions du Seuil, 1996.
Lyotard, Jean-François. *La Condition postmoderne.* Paris: Editions de Minuit, 1979.

Lynch, Gerald. *The One and the Many: English-Canadian Short Story Cycles*. Toronto/Buffalo: University of Toronto Press, 2001.

Moodie, Susanna. [1852] *Roughing It in the Bush; or, Life in Canada*. Toronto: McClelland and Stewart, 1989.

Morra, Linda. "'Like Rain Drops Rolling Down New Paint': Chinese Immigrants and the Problem of National Identity in the Work of Emily Carr," *The American Review of Canadian Studies*, Autumn 2004: 415–38.

Munro, Alice. *Dance of the Happy Shades*. Toronto: McGraw-Hill Ryerson, 1988.

New, W.H. *Land Sliding: Imagining Space, Presence, and Power in Canadian Writing*, Toronto: University of Toronto Press, 1997.

Peterman, Michael. "*Roughing It in the Bush* as Autobiography." In *Reflections: Autobiography and Canadian Literature*. Ed. K.P. Stich. Reappraisals: Canadian Writers 14. Ottawa: University of Ottawa Press, 1988: 35–43. Rpt in Susanna Moodie, *Roughing It in the Bush; or, Life in Canada*. Ed. Elizabeth Thompson. Ottawa: Canadian Critical Edition, Tecumseh, 1997: 504–11.

Pound, Ezra. "Vorticism." *Fortnightly Review* NS 96 (September 1914): 461–71 (rpt in *Gaudier-Brzeska*: 86–89).

– [1916] *Gaudier-Brzeska: a Memoir*, London: New Directions, 1960; New York: New Directions, 1974.

Ricoeur, Paul. *La Métaphore vive*. Paris: Seuil, 1975.

– "Narrative Time," *Critical Inquiry* 7.1 (1980): 169–90.

– *Temps et Récit* I. *L'Intrigue et le récit historique*. Paris: Seuil, 1983.

– *Temps et Récit* III. *Le Temps raconté*. Paris: Seuil, 1985.

Rushdie, Salman. *Imaginary Homelands: Essays and Criticism 1981–91*. London: Granta, 1992.

Van Gunsteren, Julia. *Katherine Mansfield and Literary Impressionism*, Amsterdam: Rodopi, 1990.

Waugh, Patricia. *The Theory and Practice of Self-Conscious Fiction*. London: Routledge, 1984.

NEIL BESNER

Reading Linnet Muir, Netta Asher, and Carol Frazier: Three Gallant Characters in Postcolonial Time[1]

◆

Of what possible significance can it be to remember, in the first person, and then record, with the kind of assured and confident certainty that characters in Gallant's stories most often misuse or misapprehend, that the first time I read a Mavis Gallant story was at the beginning of the summer of 1980, sitting on a short bench under a small window? It was a bright and sunny day, in the early afternoon, on the fourth floor of Buchanan Tower on the UBC campus in Vancouver, just outside of Bill New's office. While I was waiting to talk to him, I was reading the title story of Mavis Gallant's 1956 collection, "The Other Paris," in a 1974 New Canadian Library selection, *The End of the World and Other Stories*. Mavis Gallant's name was very much in the air in Canada because her finest book of stories to date, *From the Fifteenth District: A Novella and Eight Short Stories* (1979), had been published the previous fall, and, really for the first time in Canada, at any rate, her stories had begun to gain wide attention. Shortly thereafter, *Home Truths: Selected Canadian Stories* (1981) was published, and won the Governor General's Award for fiction, reinforcing, once again, one powerful and perennial Canadian notion of the functions of fiction and its connections with the exploration, location, or establishment of a national identity. That notion and its force are not unrelated to the argument which follows.

I was on that narrow bench long enough to finish "The Other Paris," and when I went in to Bill's office I told him that I'd just read it, and I thought it very good; he smiled, and twenty minutes later I left the office, having decided to think seriously about writing what Bill had described as "an exploratory thesis" on Gallant's stories. Five years earlier I'd written my Master's thesis on Saul Bellow, another writer who had left Montreal early for other parts; that connection did not occur to me then or, in any serious way, for roughly another twenty years, when I found myself living in Montreal again for a year, in 2001, for the first time since an earlier return in the early 1970s. On this most recent return, I walked every day on my way to McGill through what had been my neighbourhood on Sherbrooke Street as a six-year-old, when I'd left Montreal for the first time. The lower Westmount apartment building on the south side of Sherbrooke Street that I'd lived in as a child, and walked by now every day, was the self-same building, with a more recent generation of ivy, although now the building, nameless in my memories of the fifties, is called The Chateau Redfern. As I walked down Sherbrooke Street in 2001, I often found myself involuntarily replaying, or attending, a kind of silent film. There are some sharply visual and strongly filmic moments in Gallant's stories, and not simply because of personal associations like this one; Gallant has remarked on her related sense of one of her stories' characteristic origins in an image rising in memory. Writing about the Linnet Muir stories, for example, she comments:

> [t]here began to be restored in some underground river of the mind a lost Montreal. An image of Sherbrooke Street, at night, with the soft gaslight and leaf shadows on the sidewalk – so far back in childhood that it is more a sensation than a picture – was the starting point. ("An Introduction," *HT* xxii)

Walking, impossibly, under the selfsame trees on Sherbrooke, I found myself watching that silent film, and listening to a kind of silent voice-over, in which selected lines from the end of Gallant's Linnet Muir story, "In Youth Is Pleasure," scrolled by. The ending of this story closes on a culminating but ironic moment for Linnet, who has returned to Montreal from New York at eighteen and is trying to find out the truth about the circumstances of her father's death. Near the end of the story, she is standing on Sherbrooke waiting for the light to change when she asserts that "the Sherbrooke Street of my exile – my Mecca, my Jerusalem – was this. It had to be: there could not be two. It was *only* this" (*HT* 235). The scene dissolves, and the story closes with an older Linnet remembering her reflections as an eighteen-year-old, watching an unhappy crocodile of little girls emerging from her former school; like the Sherbrooke Street that in exile had been her Mecca, her Jerusalem, the school, which she'd remembered from childhood as "penitentiary size," was revealed to her in her eighteen-year-old present, she remembers, as "simply a very large stone house" (*HT* 236). The adult Linnet's, and the story's, closing observation is that "time had been on my side, faithfully, and unless you died you were bound to escape" (*HT* 237).

These layered perceptions and announced insights of Linnet Muir's should be situated in a wider context. One of postcolonial theory's strongest, most conflicted, and most perennial desires is the wish – articulated more objectively as an approach – to consider all of the temporal layerings, disturbances, discontinuities, ruptures, and always-incipient hauntings that attend former, emerged, and emergent colonies as they reflect on *and* suppress, summon up *and* batten down, conjure with *and* consign back to near-oblivion the insistent and troubled traces of their recent, and less recent past. Since before the middle of the last century – that is, long before the term "postcolonial" first formed itself on the lips of any critic anywhere – Mavis Gallant's stories have been performing their distinctive versions of this particularly powerful and painful operation, often without anaesthetic. One dimension of her stories has consistently given us characters like Linnet Muir amidst these kinds of engagements with the past, and of course many other less apparently assertive characters as well, among whom I will cite two more in a moment. The more extended roll call of such characters in Gallant's stories would be very long; and her stories have also ranged very widely across, and often moved in a reciprocally fissured exchange between two continents, North America and Europe, as well as farther afield.

My first contention is that Gallant's fiction, uniquely in terms of its constancy and its variety, its range and its acuity, has engaged in what George Woodcock memorably described at the very end of an essay published in *Canadian Fiction Magazine* in 1978 – he was talking principally about the Pegnitz Junction stories (1973) and her later fiction, but his comment applies to all of Gallant's fiction – as "the true rediscovery of time." I would like to add to Woodcock's observation that by its nature, and by the nature of Gallant's style, "the true rediscovery of time" is performed in her fiction as an ongoing and fluent vocation, but a vocation that is always subject to and at the same time resistant of memory's categorical interruptions, clarifications, and corrections. The tensions forming and reforming as signs of this abiding conflict are one of the principal sources of irony in Gallant's fiction; and irony is a major element that still remains mostly unaddressed in Gallant's work, although it is perhaps now overly emphasized in postcolonial studies generally, and certainly in Canada.

Returning, however, to Linnet for a moment in Montreal and the end of "In Youth Is Pleasure," my second contention is that Linnet Muir – "semi-autobiographical" as she might be (for that is finally neither here nor there, and it is only, and symptomatically, in Canada, that we would, avidly, want to dwell on how, and whether, and where exactly Linnet is or is not, and to what temperature or degree, a replication, reproduction, portrait, reincarnation, or representation of someone named Mavis Gallant) stands, like Carol Frazier of "The Other Paris," Netta Asher of "The Moslem Wife," and many other Gallant characters, as a sign of *just* how fluid and ongoing and symptomatically conflicted such a vocation *must* be. When Linnet reflects that "Time had been on my side, faithfully, and unless you died you were bound to escape," it is difficult not to gloss "bound to escape" as one indication, beginning, perhaps, at the level of a well-worn irony attending a well-worn phrase, that if a character's childhood – a childhood from which Linnet felt exiled in New York, returning to what had seemed a Mecca, a Jerusalem on Sherbrooke – is imagined as a prison (remember that memory of Linnet's of a gloomy penitentiary, her first school), then escape from that childhood prison might necessarily involve being "bound" over to another, more adult prison – into which Linnet is, in part, "bound to escape" precisely because the structure of her imagination at eighteen conceives of, for example, Sherbrooke Street as irreducibly one street, and not two – "it had to be. There could not be two. It was *only* this." Another way to put this is that Linnet at eighteen is constrained – and her readers are shown that she is constrained – by categories of memory and imagination that only allow either for a Mecca, a Jerusalem, or for *"this.* Only this." Linnet's adolescent categories shape themselves an impossible binary, around two powerful and competing desires: one, to rescue and re-inscribe a childhood remembered in double exile (i.e., in New York, and over time), and the other, to obliterate or understand (perhaps the two are synonyms in this sense) that past.

These competing and conflicted desires do not occur spontaneously in nature, but in culture, and they are not genetic. They are *responses* of a kind, though, and they are characteristic. They are not the only ways to conjure with a past, and Linnet's memories, what she makes of and with them, and her concurrently powerful resolutions, are not universal or natural categories, or ur-memories. Linnet's strong determination to find the real circumstances of her father's death, like her intrepid return to Montreal itself, are forces that form around her particular circumstances; and our interest in them, in their form, their subject and style, their resonance, articulates itself as insight both into the complexities of Linnet's character *and,* arguably, into our own conditions and categories as situated readers of *this* kind of story. When we recognize the particular constraints of Linnet's categories, in other words, we are recognizing more than one eighteen-year-old's particular purchase on the past and the present. In a limited but resonant sense, we are recognizing something locally and explicitly representative: one species of return to the country of the past with which we are likely to be, if not sympathetic, then familiar, and if not conflicted, then perhaps ironically disposed. The emancipation, independence, or autonomy to which Linnet so strongly aspires might also seem familiar; and to the degree to which our recognition of the irony inflecting her last phrase also seems familiar, if not natural, we are also reading as postcolonial subjects.

◆

In the Preface to her 1996 *The Selected Stories of Mavis Gallant,* Gallant notes that "[T]he way the stories are arranged in this collection, as well as their selection, was left up to me" (xviii). Happily, and not only for the purposes of the argument here, the selection, arranged chronologically by the dates of the settings of the stories, opens the book with two celebrated stories in a section entitled "The Thirties and Forties": these two stories are set in Europe, "The Moslem Wife," "The Four Seasons" (both of these were first published in a book in *From the Fifteenth District* in 1979), while the very fine third and last story, which should be better known, and set in Montreal, "The Fenton Child," is from a more recent book, *Across the Bridge* (1993). All three of these stories are directly relevant to my contention here, but a brief comment on Netta Asher of "The Moslem Wife" will serve to illustrate the general argument. Given that this story is much anthologized, a plot rehearsal is perhaps redundant, save to say that "The Moslem Wife" is one of the most striking of Gallant's stories to poise two reconstructions of the recent past against each other – Jack Ross's

and Netta Asher's: one, Netta's, formed by her dark and direct experience of the war as waves of Italians and Germans occupy her hotel, the
other, Jack's, formed by default in his oblivious absence for the same
years in North America. The story's famous ending depicts Netta giving in to Jack's happy lack of a memory and taking him back, despite
the "light of imagination" she sees dancing all over the square, and
despite the wartime ghosts she sees and hears (and that Jack doesn't)
everywhere around her.

But if the ending of "The Moslem Wife" is one of the most striking
of all of Gallant's endings – and this, the subject of Gallant's endings, is
another issue still largely unaddressed in Gallant criticism – this story is
also remarkable for its opening moment, in which, just as tellingly and
subversively, another and more general kind of obliviousness is set in
motion as the narrator advises readers in the story's first sentence that
the hotel in which Netta Asher's father is signing the one-hundred-year
lease that will extend his dominion through his daughter "Is quite near
to the house where Katherine Mansfield (whom no one in this hotel
had ever heard of) was writing 'The Daughters of the Late Colonel'"
(FFD 36). It is significant that "The Moslem Wife" opens with an allusion to this story of Katherine Mansfield's – to an allusion, actually,
to Mansfield *writing* the story, a story that, from its title onwards, is
as literal and powerful a representation, and perhaps *too* literal and
powerful, of Empire's lifelong shadow over the psyches, psychologies,
and suppressed and repressed desires of two daughters of Empire. Because at the same time the narrator informs us that no-one in the story
we are about to enter has ever heard of Mansfield, let alone read "The
Daughters of the Late Colonel," the opening begins its quietly resonant,
if submerged path under the story's more explicit and announced path.
The force of the unread story gathers in waves of reversed or arrested
momentum along the way as Netta's own character, and the narrator's
and Netta's observations, obliquely, momentarily resurrect Mansfield's
unread story. So, for example, we learn along the way that Netta, and
the story, get their mutual name, "The Moslem Wife," from the Doctor whose wife, a vicious and bigoted hypochondriac, has insisted that
the three East Indian girls sojourning at the hotel, prewar, must wear
white for their tennis lessons; the Doctor, meanwhile, is hopelessly in
love with Netta then and later. By the time the war is over, the middle
girl of the three has returned, now a "severe, tragic girl"; seeing her
prompts Netta to reflect that "Every calamitous season between now
and then seemed to descend directly from Georgina Blackley's having

said 'white' just to keep three children in their place," and, following that, "Neither the vanquished in their flight nor the victors returning to pick over the rubble seemed half so vindictive as a tragic girl who had disliked her governess" (*FFD* 66).

Because all of these reflections unfold under the silent, unread sign – really, the counter-narrative of "The Daughters of the Late Colonel" – it might seem fair to ask, what if the confident and assertive, plain-speaking Mr. Asher, for example, *had* read the story, what if some of those assembled in the hotel's business-room *did* know Katherine Mansfield? Then might Jack Ross, too, have seen the ghosts in the square, apprehended Netta's war, let memory have its say? And would Netta have had an easier time simply saying "No" to Jack? But they didn't, and Netta doesn't; she lets stand Jack's memory of the day of their reunion as the "happiest event of his life" (*FFD* 74). Linnet Muir, bound to escape from childhood, standing on Sherbrooke Street, sees firmly that there is only one street; Netta, harassed by her oblivious husband into giving up her ghosts, re-engages with Jack in another, related, ironic surrender, described moments earlier as a "powerful adolescent craving for something simple, such as true love" (*FFD* 73). Both characters sacrifice, banish, or suppress the potential for ambiguity; doubleness; irony; ghosts and chimeras; history. Both characters end up standing firmly on one postcolonial shore, while time recedes out of mind.

♦

I would like to return now, for the last time, to that narrow bench, June 1980, and "The Other Paris," and to pause over that story's American protagonist, one Carol Frazier, who at twenty-two has come to work in Paris, has fallen in love with her older American boss, Howard, and who is looking for love in all the wrong places, as they say, in the Paris of her North American fantasies. This story brings Carol Frazier into a series of collisions with the historical, daily, postwar Paris – with displaced refugees such as Felix, who is her own age; with her officemate, and Felix's companion Odile, whose family's standing has fallen postwar; with a pre-war culture and architecture that seems to her to be inexplicably, suddenly, dated; and with a small nagging loneliness and lovelessness that she can't dispel as she looks forward to married life back in Chicago. There is no exit in the world out of Carol's impasse. She cannot at once have and hold her romantic Paris *and* the everyday city, and she can't reconcile any of the other blaring contradictions that confront her. Linnet Muir could not have both Sherbrooke Streets, and Netta could not have Jack *and* her ghosts, her memories, the light of imagination, *and* her obliviously happy husband. Because Carol cannot have both the Paris she dreams and the Paris she sees – the "Other" Paris – she learns, from Harold, a storytelling art, reshaping memory, that will help her, as the story's closing makes clear, to form a "coherent picture, accurate but untrue." Here is the last sentence: "The memory of Felix and Odile and all their distasteful strangeness would slip away; for 'love' she would think, once more, 'Paris,' and, after a while, happily married, mercifully removed in time, she would remember it and describe it and finally believe it as it had never happened at all" (*OP* 30). Carol's progress, or regress in this relatively early story, is announced with all of the ironic certainty that will divide Carol's happy marriage from what would otherwise be a longer engagement with the everyday; and looking back from 2005 to that narrow bench in 1980 with all the retrospective and fictional certainty conferred by twenty-five years, the temptation, almost irresistible, is to read Carol Frazier's story as opening out another "coherent picture, accurate but untrue," of the persistently fugitive nature of Gallant's characters' engagements with time. But that would be a mistake. Less of a mistake, I think, would be a constantly forming apprehension that many of Mavis Gallant's stories invite readers to inquire, as steadily and faithfully as possible, into what we are always making of the past, in her stories as in life. If Linnet Muir cannot have only one Sherbrooke Street, if Netta Asher cannot simply take Jack Ross back, and if Carol Frazier cannot have only one Paris, mercifully removed in time, then reading and re-reading the past, provisionally, and in its perennially contemporary guises, becomes our postcolonial obligation. And no confident, certain, assertive, and loyally colonial imagination can stand much of that.

NOTES

1   I have tried to preserve some of the oral qualities of this paper's spoken form, including the use of the first person, because one of its major arguments concerns the rhetorical force in Gallant's stories of unqualified, "spoken" assertion – in the case of the character Linnet Muir, for example – and the ironies attendant upon the undermining of these assertions.

A corollary argument concerns the sinuous and rhetorically definitive forms articulated in the assertion of a memory.

WORKS CITED

Gallant, Mavis. *The Other Paris*. Boston: Houghton Mifflin, 1956.
– *The Pegnitz Junction: A Novella and Five Short Stories*. New York: Random House, 1973.
– *The End of the World and Other Stories*. Toronto: McClelland and Stewart, 1974.
– *From the Fifteenth District: A Novella and Eight Short Stories*. Toronto: Macmillan, 1979.
– *Home Truths: Selected Canadian Stories*. Toronto: Macmillan, 1981.
– *Across the Bridge*. Toronto: McClelland and Stewart, 1993.
– *The Selected Short Stories of Mavis Gallant*. Toronto: McClelland and Stewart, 1996.
Woodcock, George. "Memory, Imagination, Artifice: The Late Short Fiction of Mavis Gallant." *Canadian Fiction Magazine*, 28 (1978): 92–114.

FLORENCE CABARET

From Location to Dislocation in Salman Rushdie's East, West and Rohinton Mistry's Tales from Firozsha Baag

East, West by Salman Rushdie is a collection of short stories that were first published separately and later gathered under a thematic title, one that points to the question of geographical belonging and its legitimacy (the title implicitly invokes the familiar saying, "East, West – Home's best"). The ambivalence of the seemingly dichotomous title is reiterated in the organization of the book, which falls into three sections. The first of these sections, "East," deals with stories taking place in India; the second, "West," has to do with stories taking place in Europe (Denmark, Great Britain, Spain); while the third, "East, West," centres on comings and goings between India and Great Britain, with Great Britain as the vantage location of the stories. As for Rohinton Mistry's collection of short stories *Tales from Firozsha Baag*, it was published as a whole (although several stories were published separately beforehand) and it ultimately functions as a cycle with the main action taking place in a Parsi district in Bombay in the 1980s. Still, such a geographical unity is regularly disrupted by a number of trips within and outside the limits of the district, and also outside the limits of Bombay and India since some of the characters emigrate to Toronto and to Western Canada, a distance clearly implied by the preposition "from" in the title. So each title appears to epitomize two stylistic ways of referring to a territory. Or, to be more precise, the two titles offer two variations of the use of metonymy, a trope that has often been associated with colonial discourse in that it reduces a whole national territory to one of its traits. In Rushdie's case, we understand that he

chooses a global scale, alluding to national territories by means of car-
dinal points evocative of a nineteenth-century view of the world's division. By contrast, Mistry opts for a more immediate apprehension of
space, shaping local territory as a clearly circumscribed part of a wider
national territory. So both titles point to a synecdochic connection between the part and the whole (where the whole stands for the part in
Rushdie's case and *vice versa* with Mistry), but what I would like to
show here is that both writers re-appropriate the metonymic trope,
or colonial gaze, and variously expose its inadequacy. Thus I will first
study how the "metonymic fallacy" is undermined by an excessive
choice of partial locations in the two books (which are themselves
embodiments of textual metonymies since they are collections of short
texts composing a whole). The second way of dis-locating metonymy
is through the use of metaphor and the emphasis which is laid on displacements within the narrative plots and within the text (taking into
account both narrative and stylistic techniques). Thus metaphor in this
context may be labelled a meta-trope, though we will see that the two
writers use it in rather different – even chiasmic – ways. Indeed, Rushdie uses metaphor in order to celebrate geographical *un*belonging and
cultural *re*-location, though his celebration is not devoid of ambivalence. Conversely, Mistry uses metaphor to question the possibility of
a new geographical belonging, but his geographical orientation is also
displaced onto other "territories" (such as that of the body).

PARTIAL LOCATIONS, OR AN EXPOSITION OF THE "METONYMIC FALLACY"

Borrowing from Graham Huggan's discussion of the "metonymic fallacy,"[1] I intend to show that the use of metonymy by writers such as
Rushdie and Mistry is an appropriation of an orientalist approach of
the world so that the metonymy becomes an essential component of
short stories, i.e. texts which are parts standing for the whole of the
collection they belong to. But, in a more striking way, this form of
metonymy also triggers a language game involving such notions as
"partition" and "partiality," which appear to be part and parcel of a
certain postcolonial approach to space.

  This is what Rushdie explains about the narrator of *Midnight's Children* and his own essentially fragmentary vision as a migrant writer.[2]
He even claims the partiality of his vision by pointing to the link between the fragments and the whole they stand for, but also by under-

lining the density of the fragments when set beside the whole they are taken from.[3] So knowing that "whole sight" is impossible to achieve, he deliberately turns to "stereoscopic vision,"[4] which is rather easy to trace in the shifting viewpoints that characterize both Rushdie's and Mistry's short stories – for instance, an emigrated inhabitant of the Baag living in Toronto in "Swimming Lessons," a Catholic ayah from Goa in "The Ghost of Firozsha Baag," a retired Indian school teacher sitting under the banyan tree of his village in "The Free Radio," an Indian man emigrating to live in Great Britain in "The Harmony of the Spheres." Their different styles and ways of telling draw a composite image whose metonymic nature is also implemented by the short story as a literary genre. What is interesting here is that neither Rushdie nor Mistry, or their – respectively – British and Canadian publishers, chose the title of one of their short stories to stand as the title of the whole collection,[5] which is not a compulsory rule of course, but this decision also leaves readers face to face with their own metonymic reading of the collection and their own selection of emblematic stories.

As a foreshadowing of such a reading process, the metonymic trope used by Rushdie and Mistry appears to turn space into territories, i.e. partial places, which are easy to circumscribe and identify as they are rendered as highly typical places, immediately conjuring up associations with this or that area or country. Examples include the dusty street and the gates of the consulate of post-colonial India in "Good Advice Is Rarer than Rubies," the banyan tree of rural and so-called traditional India in "The Free Radio," and the maze-like pattern of the city of Srinagar which is described as if it were an Arabian Nights type of city in "The Prophet's Hair." But the metonymic trope is not only used as a narrative device carving up a whole country to sketch its most stereotyped sites. Indeed, the exposition of the metonymic fallacy is more explicit when the trope itself becomes the object of commentary within the narrative – as in "Lend Me Your Light," in which the narrator pokes fun at "the virtuosi of transatlantic travel" (182) for their metonymic and tourist-like apprehension of "Toronto's Gerrard Street known as Little India" (181). It is of course much more blatant when the metonymy is the central object of the narrative and is suddenly denounced as a fraud. Such is the case in "The Collectors," where the collected stamps of Dr Mody, which stand for all the foreign countries he is in touch with, lose their power of attraction with the young protagonist and are soon ravaged by cockroaches and white ants (102–103) so that they are turned into meaningless and worthless fragments.[6]

The last two examples reveal another tendency of metonymy, which is to sever the part from the whole it allegedly represents, so that the object of the metonymy could be described as being uprooted and totally cut off from its original context. This is clearly a stance Mistry opposes when he describes the "insular world" of the Parsi housing complex of Firozsha Baag as an *apparently* self-contained space, out of post-colonial time. But the reader is quickly given to understand that this fortress-like territory is the result of a mapping out of India by colonial history and that, as Jakobson would have it, the connection between the part and the whole cannot be overlooked since the main characteristic of metonymy is contiguity and closeness.[7] In "The Collectors," the "massive iron gate" which separates the district from surrounding areas is described as the gate which protected the Baag from the Shiv Sena riots, as well as from the beggars and riff-raff, not to mention the Bombay Municipality's attempt "to appropriate a section of Baag property for its road-widening scheme" (82). Similar connections operate inside the Baag with the striking hierarchy classifying the buildings, the flats within each of them, and the other remaining places such as the compound, back yards, and parking lots.

Of the two writers, Mistry is probably the one who makes the most thorough use of metonymy as an emblematic trope questioning one's sense of belonging to a particular place. This is quite in keeping with the frequent depiction of Mistry as a skilful "miniature painter" (Ramaswany 55) using a style that emphasizes details, bits and pieces, parts and fragments. Somehow this taste for detail helps him set into relief his characters' dilemmas when they confront foreign and unknown territories, for it entails a subtle sense of apparent disconnection within and between each story. Thus, in "Swimming Lessons," the protagonist learns about Canada bit by bit, i.e. in a fragmented and synecdochic way. For example, at first the only leaves he recognizes are maple leaves, undoubtedly thanks to his knowledge of the Canadian flag (241); he starts learning French from bilingual labels at the supermarket (235); when he finally decides to strike up a friendship with the old man in his building, he looks for the white plastic letters on the entrance board but discovers that the letters are not there ("just the empty black rectangle with holes where the letters would be squeezed in," 249) and realizes that the man has just died. In a more symbolic way, "Squatter" tells about Sarosh's inability to use Western toilets in the Western way, which stands for his failure to adapt fully to the Canadian way of life: "If he could not be westernised in all respects, he was nothing but a failure in this land – a failure not just in the washrooms of the nation but everywhere" (162). In this short story, metonymy oversteps its restricted territory to invade the protagonist's space and daily activities: "working hours expended in the washroom" (163), "whole days went by seated on the toilet" (163).

Still, behind the obvious symbolic meanings of such spatial metonymies, the way Mistry uses the trope sometimes enables the reader to hear one of its archetypal abusive uses – that of racist speech, since racist speech makes a systematic use of the metonymic device to justify its rhetoric of the invasion of the whole by the part. In "Squatter," for instance, Sarosh is identified as a foreigner through parts of his body which betray his inadequate way of using western toilets.[8] In "Swimming Lessons," the narrator's parents, who have just been reading the collection of stories we also read, fear that their son's depiction of the Baag may stand as a portrayal of the whole Parsi community and that it may be used to misrepresent them.[9] But of course, by having the figures of the parents assert the partial nature of his metonymic style, Mistry compels the reader to be wary of such a reading of these stories. Such a strategy can easily be compared to Rushdie's use of metonymy to denounce the fanatic purpose it may serve. If this is an experience he made as the writer of the notorious *Satanic Verses*, we find relevant examples of the possibly devastating power of metonymy in "The Prophet's Hair," where the hair in question is turned into a relic that spreads madness and death in a family where it is accidentally introduced. A similar device is at work in "At the Auction of the Ruby Slippers," where the slippers of the heroine of *The Wizard of Oz* are staged as the metonymic relic of a secular world ready to trespass into the protective territory around the famous pair of shoes just to touch them: "We do not know the limits of their powers. We suspect that these limits may not exist" (88). Here again, the metonymic part (i.e. the slippers) is described as an apparently small-scale territory whose potential extension is actually unfathomable. Still, what is also worthy of note in this last example is Rushdie's propensity to convert metonymy into metaphor, so that he chooses a pair of shoes which are not made to tread on solid ground but which are said to allow their owner to fly into an imaginary world. This is why, in stories mainly dealing with migration, the issue of belonging to this or that geographical location is often metaphorized, i.e. displaced onto other kinds of territories.

DIS-LOCATION, OR THE METAPHOR AS META-TROPE

This displacement is quite characteristic of writers who have used the genre of the short story as a temporary location in their literary career. Rushdie was already famous for his novels when, in 1991, he published *East, West.* As for Mistry, he was launched into the literary world with this collection of short stories published in 1989, after which he turned to the writing of novels. So the short story appears to have been a momentary resting place for Rushdie and a starting place for Mistry, but neither remained in these textual locations. What is more, the way the collection of short stories is designed, i.e. as a gathering of typographically isolated texts, prompts readers into practising a double reading of such a whole – not only a metonymic reading as I have already indicated, but a metaphoric reading as well, since they constantly shift from one text to another as they read. All readers of short stories are familiar with the final impression of par- tially overlapping stories once the reading is over.[10] But in the cases of *East, West* and *Tales from Firozsha Baag,* such a process is enhanced when the notion of territory is questioned by the recurrence of places of transition or by the characters' inability to remain in one place and consecrate it as a territory.

Rushdie is undeniably best known for favouring the "experience of 'migrancy' and unbelonging" (Ahmad 152) as he himself claims in "The Location of *Brazil*," when he states that mass migrations result in "the creation of radically new types of human beings: people who root themselves in ideas rather than places, in memories as much as in material things" (Rushdie 1991: 124–25). Turning a potentially trau- matic predicament into a delightful experience, he dubs the metaphor the arch trope of the migrant, playing with both its figurative and literal meaning as he constantly puns on its etymological origin, shift- ing from the Greek word to its Latin version, which is no other than the word "translation," to its English interpretation, "borne across." As he declares in "Imaginary Homelands," "Having been borne across the world, we are translated men" (Rushdie 1991: 17). From then on, Rushdie's representation of territories is constantly mediated by dis- placement and by the metaphor as meta-trope.

Of course, it is easy to notice that all his stories deal with characters on the verge of leaving or coming back, and that these movements encompass a wide variety ranging from transatlantic travels to textual borrowing and rewriting, to imaginary travels. But if we take a look at the first and last stories of the collection, we also realize that they can be read as bridges leading in and out of the collection rather than as doors opening and closing the collection. "Good Advice Is Rarer than Rubies" concerns a young ayah who finally decides to refuse to leave for England where she is supposed to get married, while "The Courter" tells of the narrator's former ayah who follows his family to England but eventually goes back to India. In both stories, most of the action is situated in transitory places (near the gates of the British Consulate, in the stairs of their English flat, in the porter's flat), and the plot revolves around a metaphorical shift (the expected story of a would-be emigrant's attraction to London is replaced by the story of a man's attraction to a woman, the porter is literally turned into a courter by a woman's accent when speaking English). Some characters may also be read as the embodiment of the metaphor on account of their ability to move from one place to another. For instance, in "The Free Radio," Ramani the rickshaw-wallah is depicted as a dying metaphor, one who becomes burdened by the widow he marries, and who is eventually emptied when he is sterilized. But we may also wonder whether the storyteller is not a dead metaphor himself, stuck as he is under the banyan tree, no longer listened to, agreeing to be replaced by the white caravan of the sterilization program and turning a deaf ear to what was happening inside this mobile place of death (24). In "Christopher Columbus and Queen Isabella," the history of the Western origins of colonization is re-written through the character of Columbus who is presented ironically as a "foreigner" (107), i.e. an Italian trying to win the favours of the great Spanish queen. This characterization leads to another one – "foreigners can be very brazen" – when the narrator plays word games with the literal and metaphorical meanings of words as illustrated in the sentence "Foreigners forget their place (having left it behind)" (108). Such a play on language and referent is all the more ironic as Columbus is also known as one of the most famous misnamers of the era of Western empires, the person who confused India and America. This original transfer of words supposed to identify territories is construed here as the epitome of the linguistic flaw and of language's fate to name nothing but "places of the mind."

Now what strikes me when I compare Rushdie's collection of short stories with Mistry's is the density, the variety, and the extension of Rushdie's use of metaphor, whereas Mistry appears to employ it in a much more discreet and circumscribed way. The temptation then is to extol Rushdie as a cosmopolitan writer and to marginalize Mistry as a sort of local writer. Or, if we take up Jakobson's characterization of literary schools according to the predominance of metaphor or of metonymy,[11] Rushdie could stand along romantic and surrealist writers favouring the imaginative leap that metaphor entails, while Mistry could seemingly be classified as a realist writer. I have already tried to show that this would misread his use of metonymy, but it would also be a misreading of his no less telling use of metaphor.[12] The fact that Mistry eventually conceived his collection as a cycle with recurring characters and places undoubtedly helps establish the impression of unity and textual stability conveyed by the whole. It is also true that the concentration of the time line and the focalization on indoor scenes or scenes taking place within a clearly delineated space may stand as another obstacle to the free play of metaphor. But the performative power of metaphor does not rely on quantity – its effectiveness is rather a question of textual location. So that, for instance, when scenes taking place in Toronto are described in pretty much the same way as scenes taking place in Firozsha Baag (with an obvious partiality for places such as flat, hallway, corridor, parking lot, swimming pool, and toilet), the reader experiences a sense of defamiliarization. Such a description displaces the rather conventional depiction of Canada as a land of open spaces and great distances; it also leads the reader to draw a parallel between the two places, whereas narratives of migrancy tend more traditionally to underscore differences between places. So when Mistry depicts intimate and small-scale territories as sharing similarities, he at the same time questions the trope of geographical displacement as representative of the migrant's situation.[13] Ironically, he displaces the issue by internalizing it within the body of the migrant, electing the metaphor of intestine transition as emblematic of the migrant's digestion of his new territory. This subdued metaphor appears in the first story of the collection, which opens when Rustomji comically bursts out from the leaking toilet of his Indian flat and admits that "his bowels were recalcitrant in strange surroundings" (7). Then the metaphor is taken up in "Lend Me Your Light" when the narrator remembers taking the plane to Toronto and having the feeling he was "being swallowed up into its belly" (181). It is then fully expanded in "Squatter" and displaced in "Swimming Lessons," which are two stories dealing with the training of an Indian man's body to master Western ways of living. The choice of metaphors is not innocent either and is quite representative of Mistry's ironic mood, as "squatter" is also an insult which stigmatizes a person by suggesting that he illegitimately occupies someone else's territory. Moreover, while the metaphorical use of the migrant's body is not specific to Mistry's writing, it appears to reduplicate a group characteristic, at least in the last narrator's representation of his Parsi community. Indeed, in "Swimming Lessons," Mistry's narrator depicts the Parsis as an elected people who are plagued by osteoporosis,[14] a disease which is usually regarded as typical of Western aging populations and which is obviously a physical symptom of the privileged relation the Parsis entertained with the English in colonial times.[15] So Mistry's more internal use of metaphor is also a way of looking into a community whose dis-location first occurred within India before its members eventually started to emigrate.[16]

TEXTUAL RELOCATION: FROM COMMON PLACES TO IMAGINARY HOMELANDS

The consequence of these two different approaches of the notion of "territory" is that we may be tempted to say that textual and imaginary relocation is much more central in Rushdie's writing than in Mistry's. As Rushdie wrote in an essay on literary influence, the only ground beneath his feet that he is looking for is made of the texts he writes: "Like the figure in the fairy-tale who must spin straw into gold, the writer must find the trick of weaving the waters together until they become land: until, all of a sudden, there is solidity where once there was only flow, shape where there was formlessness; there is ground beneath his feet." (Rushdie 2002: 69)

The title of his story collection is proof enough of his desire to locate his work within English culture and its most common places or hackneyed tropes. Indeed, the title of his collection also alludes to Kipling's poem, "The Ballad of East and West," which opens: "Oh, East is East, and West is West, and never the twain shall meet." According to two diverging interpretations of the poem, this line may point either to the irreconcilable nature of the two territories or to their possible merging thanks to the relationships between people from the two areas,[17] so that once again ambivalence and impossible choice lie at the heart of the covert quotation. Thus Rushdie constantly plays on grounds that are excessively familiar to the reader (relying on characters as types, famous landmarks of both Anglo-Saxon and Indian high and low culture, of colonial and postcolonial history, characteristic ways of speaking English by Indian characters[18]) and offers an unexpected version of these "common places." But at the same time, the truncated quotation of his title is also a way of dislocating – so that the reader is led onto less familiar grounds. This dislocation is achieved as early as the first story, "Good Advice Is Rarer than Rubies," which wrong-foots the reader and relocates the saying of the title by having an Indian speaker rephrase it ("Now I will go back to Lahore and my job," Rushdie 1991: 15). "Yorick" may also be read as a caricature of this eagerness to dis-locate and relocate famous texts of English culture (*Hamlet, The Life and Opinions of Tristram Shandy, Alice in Wonderland*).

Still it appears to me that Mistry's narrators are no less tempted by imaginary homelands than are Rushdie's, and that we must not be misled by the relative unobtrusiveness of his hints. The narrator of "Squatter" thus stages his protagonist as mimicking the magniloquent style of the moor in *Othello* so as to underscore the parallel and discrepancy between the two men's fates: "When you shall these unlucky deeds relate, speak of me as I am; nothing extenuate, nor set down aught in malice: tell them that in Toronto once there lived a Parsi boy as best as he could. Set you down this; and say, besides, that for some it was good and for some it was bad, but for me life in the land of milk and honey was just a pain in the posterior" (168). More generally, famous heroic figures of Western culture are often summoned up to create an effect of bathos through which both the legendary character and the more common character of the story are debunked. This is typically the case in "Lend Me Your Light" when the narrator, suffering from conjunctivitis on the day of his departure for Toronto, portrays himself as a Greek tragic hero: "Half-jokingly, I saw myself as someone out of a Greek tragedy, guilty of the sin of hubris for seeking emigration out of the land of my birth, and paying the price in burnt-out eyes: I, Tiresias, blind and throbbing between two lives, the one in Bombay and the one to come in Toronto ..." (179–80). All these examples are emblematically borrowed from fictitious literary universes and they keep interposing in the memory of the narrator in "Swimming Lessons," when he tries to imagine what he will remember as an old man "in this country," i.e. Canada (244): "all I will have is thoughts about childhood thoughts and dreams, built around snowscapes and winter-wonderlands on the Christmas cards so popular in Bombay; my snowmen and snowball fights and Christmas trees are in the pages of Enid Blyton's books ... My snowflakes are even less forgettable than the old man's, for they never melt" (244). The Indian landscape is superseded by the remembrances of cheap cards depicting European winter landscapes which he actually never saw but whose power over time and mind is therefore even more enduring than memories of a "true" landscape. Imaginary homelands clearly find their way through the minutely delineated places of India and Canada where the characters happen to live their lives – pointing to their crucial role in the competition between locations taking place in Mistry's short stories. As the conflict between Nariman the story-teller and one of the inhabitants of the district shows, telling stories at the entrance of A Block is immediately metaphorized into the challenging occupation of a common territory: "Two days in a row, whole Firozsha Baag gathers here! This is not Chaupatty Beach, this is not a squatters' colony, this is a building, people want to live here in peace and quiet!" (164). Could there be a more metaphoric way of referring to a metonymic place which happens to be the stage where stories and imagination reign supreme?

NOTES

1   "All India is there": "This metonymic fallacy, already identified by Edward Said as a classic Orientalist strategy, has been parodied by many an Indian writer, of whom Rushdie and Seth are merely among the best-known examples" (Huggan 75).

2   "It may be that when the Indian writer who writes from outside India tries to reflect that world, he is obliged to deal in broken mirrors, some of whose fragments have been irretrievably lost" (Rushdie 1991: 10–11).

3   "It was precisely the partial nature of these memories, their fragmentation, that made them so evocative for me. The shards of memory acquired greater status, greater resonance, because they were *remains*; fragmentation made trivial things seem like symbols, and the mundane acquired numinous qualities" (Rushdie 1991: 12).

4   "Indian writers in these islands, like others who have migrated into the north from the south, are capable of writing from a kind of double perspective; because they, we, are at one and the same time insiders and outsiders in this society. This stereoscopic vision is perhaps what we can offer in place of 'whole sight'" (Rushdie 1991: 19).

5   The US publishers retitled Mistry's book *Swimming Lessons and Other Stories* for American distribution.

6   "He let his hands stray through the contents, through worthless paper scraps, through shreds of the work of so many Sunday mornings, stop-

ping now and then to regard with detachment the bizarre patterns created by the mandibles of the insects who had feasted night after night
under his bed, while he slept ... It was doubtful if anything of value remained in the trunk" (Mistry 103).

7   For a discussion of the difference between metonymy/contiguity and
    metaphor/similarity, see Jakobson 1956: 91–96.

8   "The absence of feet below the stall door, the smell of faeces, the rustle
    of paper, glimpses caught through the narrow crack between stall door
    and jamb – all these added up to only one thing: a foreign presence in the
    stall, not doing things in the conventional way" (Mistry 156).

9   "He should have found some way to bring some of these wonderful facts
    into his stories, what would people reading these stories think, those
    who did not know about Parsis – that the whole community was full of
    cranky, bigoted people ... " (Mistry 245).

10 This is caricaturally "mis en abyme" in the short story entitled "Yorick."
    Here the constant shifts in the narrative regime and narrative fragmenta-
    tion that ensues also dramatize the question of displacement – self-inter-
    ruptions of the opening, interruptions on the part of a fictitious audience
    (65), dialogue in a theatrical scene (67–70), skipping paragraphs of the
    vellum (71), lists of body parts or of meals for a banquet (71, 72).

11 For a discussion of metonymy and metaphor as the two stylistic oppo-
    sites framing the whole of literary production throughout the centuries,
    see Jakobson 1956: 91–96 and Jakobson 1960: 375.

12 After all, if Rushdie is often described as a magic-*realist* writer (pointing
    to his complex use of metaphor, among other stylistic traits), Mistry may
    well be described as a realist-with-a-pinch-of-salt.

13 Cf. in "Lend Me Your Light," he makes fun of Indian returnees and their
    never-ending conversations about plane companies: "The evening would
    then become a convention of travel agents expounding on the salient fea-
    tures of their preferred carriers" (182).

14 "We are the chosen people where osteoporosis is concerned. And divorce.
    The Parsi community has the highest divorce rate in India. It also claims
    to be the most westernised community in India. Which is the result of the
    other? Confusion again, of cause and effect" (Mistry 230).

15 Cf. in "The Ghost of Firozsha Baag," the Christian ayah's description of
    the Parsi community where she found a job when a teenager (46).

16 "The near-total alienation from postcolonial India has pushed more and
    more Parsis into a Western Diaspora" (Bharucha 26). Cf. the Baag's deal-
    ings with the nearby districts: in "Auspiciou Occasions," two trips out of
    the Baag ends up in disaster and immediate retreat to the Parsi district; in

"One Sunday," the nearby poor district of Tar Gully is constantly associated to the spitting of its residents falling on well-off passers-by (31, 32), i.e. it is reduced to a synecdoche which is also a metaphor: "the menacing mouth of Tar Gully" (33), "Tar Gully and its menacing mouth" (16).

17 Cf. Porée & Tadié 165.

18 Cf. "Ces nouvelles remettent en cause attitudes répertoriables et opinion reçues" (Porée & Tadié 166–68).

WORKS CITED

Ahmad, Aijaz. *In Theory*. London: Verso, 1992.

Bharucha, Nilufere E. "Rohinton Mistry's Fiction as Diasporic Discourse." In Dodiya: 23–32.

Dodiya, Jaydipsinh, ed. *The Fiction of Rohinton Mistry*. New Delhi: Prestige, 1998.

Huggan, Graham. *The Post-Colonial Exotic. Marketing the Margins*. London: Routledge, 2001.

Jakobson, Roman, & Morris Halle. "Two Aspects of Language and Two Types of Disturbances." In *Fundamentals of Language*. The Hague: Mouton, 1956.

– "Closing Statement: Linguistics and Poetics." In Thomas A. Sebeok (ed.), *Style in Language*, Cambridge, MA: MIT Press, 1960: 350–77.

Mistry, Rohinton. *Tales from Firozsha Baag*. London: Faber and Faber; Toronto: Penguin, 1987; rpt. Toronto: McClelland and Stewart, 2000, afterword by W.H. New, 263–69.

Porée, Marc, and Alexis Massery (Tadié). *Salman Rushdie*. coll. Les Contemporains, Paris: Seuil, 1996.

Ramaswany, S. "Local Colour in *Tales from Firozsha Baag*." In Dodiya: 54–60.

Rushdie, Salman. "Imaginary Homelands." 1982; rpt in *Imaginary Homelands*. London: Granta, 1991: 9–21.

– "The Location of *Brazil*." 1985; rpt. in *Imaginary Homelands*. London: Granta, 1991: 118–28.

– *East, West*. London: Jonathan Cape, 1991.

– "Influence." 1999; rpt. in *Step Across This Line*. London: Jonathan Cape, 2002: 69–76.

Said, Edward. *Orientalism. Western Conceptions of the Orient*. 1978; rpt. London: Penguin, 1995.

ORALITY AND SCRIPTURALITY: QUESTIONS OF CULTURE AND FORM

ISABEL CARRERA SUÁREZ

Epistolary Traditions in Caribbean Diasporic Writing: Subversions of the Oral/Scribal Paradox in Alecia McKenzie's "Full Stop"

Caribbean literatures have a long history of using Creole in writing, and more markedly in orature, although the scope and reception of this use has varied, with acceptability and more confident practice growing in the final decades of the twentieth century. One of the pioneering and persistent subgenres associated with orality and the use of Creole is the epistolary exchange or series of epistolary monologues, where a persona, often female and using humour, writes home relating impressions of the new land to family or friends, or abroad to inform émigrés of the state of affairs "back home." The literary form of these exchanges has overwhelmingly been poetic, usually a dramatic monologue which demands performance or "voice" for full appreciation. Paradoxically, letter-writing, a scribal and prosaic genre by definition, became the vehicle for orality and poetry, framing the personal and reflective components of the epistolary mode.

Caribbean literature offers relatively few examples of the epistolary genre in prose, despite abundant writing from and on exile. Perhaps the overdetermined European genre of the eighteenth-century epistolary novel, whose context differed so radically from that of Caribbean diasporas, has acted as a deterrent, or it may be that the formal limitations of the genre have discouraged its use, as they seem to have done in other twentieth-century writing. Given the popularity of dramatic monologues in poetry and the development of the short story in the Caribbean, however, it is slightly surprising that the short narrative, better suited to the epistolary form than is the novel, provides relative-

ly few texts structured by means of an exchange of letters,[1] although
instances of epistles embedded in stories are more abundant. Among
the notable exceptions is Alecia McKenzie's "Full Stop," in which the
author·fully exploits the narrative possibilities of the genre, both in
linguistic terms and in plot and characterization, making intelligent
and efficient use of multiple codes for this purpose. This story gains
strength from the subversion of stereotypes effected in language and
character, particularly in the central figure of the grandmother, whose
letters constitute the main body of the text.

The popularity of the epistolary dramatic monologue in Creole
can be traced back to the beginning of the twentieth century, when
Michael McTurk and Edward A. Cordle published a series of poems
in the vernacular in the newspapers of their respective colonies, the
Argosy in Guyana and the *Weekly Recorder* in Barbados. McTurk
used the persona of "Quow" (a term meaning albino or light-skinned)
who addressed his friend "Jimmis"; Cordle used the female "Lizzie,"
who wrote to her friend "Susie" about marriage and various daily
encounters, but also, like "Quow," on social and topical matters, with
a critical and satirical edge. Although a multiple impersonation was
taking place here (the authors did not belong to the social class, colour
or – in Cordle's case – gender associated with the language used) and
the texts contained a strong element of caricature, these series were
very popular, being representations of a social group usually excluded
from print. Their portraits established persistent gendered stereotypes
of "ordinary people" as "quarrelsome and outspoken, the men unfaithful, the women domineering and jealous" (Burnett xxxvii). The
search for an appropriate literary form, however, is still very incipient,
with Cordle using a regular four-line rhymed stanza, of great popular
appeal through the familiarity of hymns, but hardly in tune with the
African cultural and linguistic component.

The· major landmark for the oral and poetic epistolary genre was
the work of Jamaican folklorist, performer, and writer Louise Bennett, whose huge popularity from the 1940s onwards did not grant
her entrance into the literary establishment (including anthologies)
during the first two decades of her fame. Recognition, in fact, had to
wait until the use of Creole had gained acceptance against middle-
class prejudice in the 1960s,[2] and became consolidated in the 1980s.
Bennett's "Miss Lou" letters showed some continuity with the Cordle
and McTurk genre, but were more directly the heritage of Claude
McKay's fluent use of Creole in *Constab Ballads* (1912), expanded

and strengthened by her own deep knowledge of folk culture, song, proverb, and cadence. Bennett's very successful career as a performer included an early spell in Britain where, aside from study at the Royal Academy of Dramatic Art and work for the BBC, she performed widely, returning to Jamaica in 1955. A relevant consequence of this exile period were the popular "letters home" of her Miss Lou persona. There had been a precedent for this form of descriptive-critical missive from abroad in the work of another well-known Jamaican poet, Una Marson. "Quashie comes to London" (1937) presents the perspective of an islander in the "motherland" with critical humour and the same reaffirmation of Jamaicanness in language and affections that marked Bennett's epistolary verse. The theme of this piece, as Donnell and Welsh have noted (120), anticipates Bennett's famous "Colonization in Reverse," although Marson's use of Creole is more tentative. Despite these precedents, it is Louise Bennett's public figure, and her witty powers of observation and expressive language, that first encouraged Caribbean women writers in their proficient use of Creole (Mordecai xx-xxi), while at the same time establishing the epistolary Creole monologue as a subgenre suited to migrant experience.

The diasporic trope of letter writing captured the imagination of a number of male Caribbean-British poets in the 1980s, James Berry's *Lucy's Letters and Loving* (1982) being the most directly intertextual with Bennett's: the name "Lucy" and the reference to "labrish" (gossip) in the opening of the first poem are evident links. The ten dramatic monologues that constitute "Lucy's letters" to her friend Leela in the village "back home" convey a humorous, satirical view of 1970s–80s England through the eyes of an interstitial citizen, an immigrant whose children ("From Lucy: New Generation") are British and behave as such. In the final poem, Lucy speaks of "we women in Brit'n" with a telling inclusiveness. The subjects of the missives range from the Queen to the Royal Wedding, from London carnival to London violence, and display certain nostalgia for the Yard and a desire to return "home." Berry's poetic form and language are also part of the Caribbean-Britain continuum, or Creole-Standard English, whilst making use of West Indian Bennett-inspired rhetorical devices, such as the proverbs that conclude all poems.

Other versions of letter-writing monologues in these years were produced in the U.K. by Linton Kwesi Johnson ("Sonny's Lettah. Anti-Sus Poem," 1979), Fred D'Aguiar (*Mama Dot*, 1985) and David Dabydeen ("Coolie Son [the Toilet Attendant Writes Home]," 1988). The most dis-

seminated of these, because of its recordings and the author's popularity
within the Black British and musical contexts, is "Sonny's Lettah," a politically loaded text in which a young man writes to his mother from Brixton
prison, explaining how random police brutality towards his brother led
him to intervene and get charged with murder. The text breaks radically
with the tradition of humour and of observer-speakers of earlier monologues, and makes thorough use of Creole and of rhythm, rhyme, and
music for dramatic effects. Johnson's measured, low-key performance, to
effective background music, powerfully enhances the pathos. In contrast
to most monologues, the letter also begins and ends with realistic epistolary formulas in near Standard English: "Dear Mama / Good Day. / I
hope dat wen / deze few lines reach yu, / they may find yu in di bes af helt"
... "till I hear fram you. / I remain your son, Sonny" (27–28). The epistolary form here serves as a vehicle for social comment within the urban
resistant aesthetics of an author whose poetry, in Fred D'Aguiar's words,
"represents a cluster of emotions geared to black life, youth experience in
the inner cities and international socialism" (2002: 12).

D'Aguiar himself was to follow in the steps of earlier West Indian
writers and create "Mama Dot," a correspondent more readily immersed in the scribal, Standard English traditions: "You are a traveller
to them / A 'West Indian working in England', / or Friday, Tonto or
Punkawallaw / Sponging off the state. Our languages / Remain pidgin
like our dark, third / Underdeveloped world" ("Letter from Mama
Dot"). "Mama Dot," though, also uses Creole, in the linguistic shut-
tling to and fro characteristic of the Caribbean. In this central figure,
D'Aguiar builds on the elegiac mood of mother / grandmother texts,
ever-present in a society where women so often head the household.
The third example, "Coolie Son," is part of David Dabydeen's *Coolie
Odyssey*, a collection on the diasporic experience on the India-Guy-
ana-England route, spanning a thematic variety of dramatic and
celebratory subjects in Creole. The poem, again in the form of a letter written from the U.K., merges contemporary social comment (immigrant employment in Britain) with the ironic bravado of a "coolie"
toilet attendant describing himself for the home crowd as "Deputy
Sanitary Inspector," telling of the arrival of the most European of
seasons, "The Spring," and asking about affairs at home. Dabydeen's
lively use of Creole is paired with humour in this particular poem, but
the lightness is counteracted by its juxtaposition with the preceding
piece, "Coolie Mother," where Jasmattie works her life away to make
her son's education possible.

These three poets show the expansion of Creole in the 1980s, offering examples of the epistolary along a linguistic and aesthetic continuum, firmly grounded in the oral, urban British Creole in the case of Johnson, a more Caribbean-oriented and "syncretic" language in Dabydeen, and closer to the written codes, albeit with much switching, in D'Aguiar. In fact, all texts described so far, as well as their reception, are closely related to the fate of Creole throughout the twentieth century, and show that the watermark in range of use and acceptability took place after the development of a regional post-independence poetics, which privileged indigenous (particularly African) forms and folk traditions. Kamau Brathwaite's active argument in favour of geographically and linguistically located cultural forms and the use of Nation Language is extremely influential, and the cornerstone of a literary evolution which later linked with the huge popular appeal of reggae and dub. Thus, the status of Creole, limited to conceptions of the humorous and the popular when Claude McKay or Louise Bennett first wrote, changed to the point of turning into a marker of regional authenticity, becoming a near-canon itself. Creole was revalued by linguists and literary theorists, and a growing number of writers employed the continuum more consistently. Despite this general climate of attention to the oral,[3] however, tensions between the oral/written aspects of texts persisted at certain levels. While the performative, oral, gestural and sometimes musical side of the texts gained ground, its dissemination and reception through traditional channels (criticism, publication, universities world-wide) was complicated precisely by the difficulty of conveying the oral and performative aspects. Orality and Creole were far more extended in poetry than in prose. Despite Sam Selvon's pioneering use of Creole for narrative and descriptive sections in his prose (i.e., going beyond its common usage in dialogues or monologist stories), full narrative texts without such devices are comparatively rare, and critical texts in Creole, aside from some of Kamau Brathwaite's interventions and Carolyn Cooper's text on Sistren (1989), are practically non-existent. Creole continued to be most consistently the language of characterization and orality in prose texts, although the calculated use of code-switching is a recurrent structural device.

Jamaica seems particularly active in the use of Creole. And one of the authors who has most skillfully employed the range of the continuum to (re)produce voice and to represent social matters is the Jamaican/Canadian writer Olive Senior, whose stories often structurally depend on the contrast between the voices of the characters. Their speech conveys a wealth of social information, from rural background to the aspiring snobbery of hypercorrection, from street language to the codes of formal education, identifying stereototypes or defining individual development. A couple of Senior's stories contain instances of letter-writing embedded in the text. "Ascot," as Velma Pollard has pointed out (243), shows the parallel evolution of language and social aspiration in the protagonist, who migrates to the U.S.A. and writes erratic letters home to his mother boasting of his progress. Lorna Goodison adopts a parallel strategy in her story "Bella Makes Life," where Bella's personal change is reflected in the difference between early and later letters:

> Dear Joseph,
> What you saying? I really sorry that my letter take so long to reach you and that the Post Office seem to be robbing people money ... I don't write as often as I used to because I working two jobs. (76)

> Dear Joe Joe,
> I know you're mad with me because you didn't want me to come back to the States, but darling, I'm just trying to make it so that you and me and the children can live a better life and stop having to box feeding outta hog mouth. (80)

Relatedly, Olive Senior's "Bright Thursdays" reflects the huge gap between social classes by contrasting the language and the literacy of correspondents. Miss Myrtle, mother of an illegitimate child by a rich man, writes to his family in the following terms:

> Dear Miss Kristie
> Greetings to you in Jesus Holy Name I trust this letter will find that you an Mister Dolfy ar enjoin the best of helth. Wel Miss Kristie I write you this letter in fear and trimblin for I am the Little One and you are the Big One but I hope you will not take me too forrad but mr Bertram little girl now nine year old and bright as a button wel my dear mam wish you could see her ... (40)

The reply, in prim Standard English, returns with its own distancing (and faintly formulaic) language: "Dear Myrtle, / In response to your call for help we are sending you a little money for the child, also a parcel which should soon arrive" (41). These examples are in keeping with Senior's habitual use of codes or code-switching for characterization. Her stories are mostly polyphonic texts, peopled by voices as much as by characters, often using folk structures as organizing principles ("Ballad"), and exploring the written as well as the oral registers in relation to social class, particularly through personal relationships. Many of her stories are fully in Creole, although told through intradiegetic narrators who become characters in their own right.

Senior is one of a number of Caribbean women writers who established their reputation in the 1980s, a generation that includes other diasporic authors such as Jamaica Kincaid in the U.S.A., Grace Nichols in Britain, or Dionne Brand in Canada, to name only paradigmatic examples. Coming shortly after this generation, Alecia McKenzie presents a somewhat less canonical case of migration, having published her collection *Satellite City* while residing in Brussels in 1992, and currently living in Singapore. Her territory of exile is thus less fixed, less historically marked or community-based, and her stories are set in her "home territory," the Caribbean. *Satellite City* explores issues in 1980s Jamaican society and includes two stories that share the characters of Grand Ma Scottie, Richie, and Carmen, "Jakes Makes" and "Full Stop," the striking epistolary text which opens the book. The subversiveness of this story is apparent in its language and characterization, and in its adaptation of epistolary form. It is perhaps significant that one of the few Caribbean writers to create another "epistolary" story, exile Jamaica Kincaid, also subverts readers' expectations rather dramatically: "The Letter from Home" (*At the Bottom of the River*, 1978) is a monologue, but has no explicit letter-structure, context, or writer, and moves from descriptions of daily chores to an oniric and symbolic world (characteristic of the collection) that departs completely from the epistolary tradition described for poetry. It has been argued that the canon/s of Caribbean literature have tended, in recent history, to render women's writing invisible (Donnell and Welsh 219, 293), partly because of the privileging of certain themes (public, political, nationalist) and genres (like the male-dominated dub scene). As Jean Binta Breeze pointed out with respect to dub, a new, liberating form can become as restrictive as an old pattern (the paradigmatic iambic pentameter) if flexibility and innovation disappear and prescription prevails (498). McKenzie's "Full Stop" is heir to a number of tropes and practices in Caribbean writing, and simultaneously destabilizes

many of these. Some of these subversive elements are related to gendered perspectives, others have been seen as generational, while still
others may be traced to the non-orthodox diasporic trajectory of the
author or merely her individual world-view.

McKenzie's work has not quite been incorporated into a canon of
Caribbean / Jamaican literature, partly because her production is not
(yet) abundant, but also because its parameters lie beyond certain
patterns: the narrower version of oral, Nation Language canon; the
migrant subject as narrated from the metropolitan centres of London,
Toronto, New York; the recent emphasis on (and sometimes posing
as) the working-class, popular perspective; the canonical male voice of
nationalism and/or postcolonialism. McKenzie, like the character of
her story "The Grenada Defense League," is a journalist abroad with
a strong connection to the island and a piercing social view, inevitably
filtered through "middle class migration," the migration of study or
professionalism, and cosmopolitan life. Her narrative perspective is
also frequently woman-centred, with a political and social awareness
unconstrained by doctrine. The jacket for *Satellite City* presented her
in 1992 as part of "a new generation of writers ... [moving] away
from Jamaica's colonial times" and tackling broad contemporary
themes in Jamaican society. A review by Kwame Dawes welcomed this
"confidence in the validity of [Caribbean] society as fitting and substantial fodder for fiction writing" and its movement away from "the
Manichean and polemic constraints of 'postcolonial' discourse," but
almost immediately diminished her writing by comparing it with V.S.
Naipaul's supposedly superior choice of a first-person child narrator,[4]
thus exemplifying the rather arbitrary use of canonical male writers
as a way of measuring women's writing. Nevertheless, the quality of
a story such as "Full Stop" did subsequently grant her some degree of
canonicity through inclusion in the 1996 *Penguin Book of Caribbean
Short Stories*, and merited special mention by Bruce King who, in a
review of the anthology for *Wasafiri*, praises editor E.A. Markham
precisely for this choice (55). The story, therefore, is situated on the
borders of canon in the decade of the 1990s, a decade which saw an
important development in theorizing on, and by, Caribbean women's
writing (Boyce Davies and Savory Fido; Cooper, 1993; O'Callaghan),
and which was able to build on a substantial body of literature by
women writers who in the previous decade had used Creole.

"Full Stop" is structured as letters between a young Caribbean
woman living in New York and her grandmother living "back on

the island." The first three exchanges are briefly framed – "My grandmother writes without commas or full stops She writes ..." ... "And I write back saying" ... "She writes back saying ..." After that, the alternating letters appear without comment. As the dialogue takes place between grandmother (Grand Ma Scottie, aged 73) and granddaughter (Carmen, "almost 30"), with frequent references to the absent mother, who migrated to England in Carmen's early childhood, the scene seems set for the autobiographical, elegiac mode of much Caribbean writing and the feminist inscribing of a (generally positive) female genealogy. We also seem to be contemplating the usual oral/scribal dichotomy, the quintessential divide between Creole and Standard (Jamaican) English, portrayed in the contrast between the grandmother and the granddaughter's language and writing skills. But the text soon gives signs of far more complex characterization, plot, and linguistic structure, as the grandmother is gradually revealed as a witty, intelligent, but highly manipulative matriarch, one who challenges her granddaughter on her scribal condescension: "I got your letter yesterday Why are you writing me without punctuation Don't you know better is that what I worked hard and sent you to school for Don't let me down like this" (1).

Carolyn Cooper has argued, in a different context, that "[i]t is important to distinguish between actual letters and diaries written by women, and the literary use of this sub-genre as fictional frame. For the artifice of these feminist narrative forms is that they are artless" (1989: 49). McKenzie's text embodies this distinction, and contains an intra-story example in the "artless" discourse of Grand Ma Scottie, apparently unable to use punctuation until the crucial moment at the end of the story. The letters advance the plot in carefully calculated measures, creating suspense and using many devices from oral tradition, particularly their additive, repetitive structures and contrapuntal form. Each letter, returning to a limited number of topics and including significant litanies on the part of the grandmother ("Write your mother," "Kiss your hubby for me"), builds up the reader's knowledge of the correspondents' lives: the grandmother's ever-shifting use of the money sent by Carmen, the state of affairs on "the island," and ultimately, the truth about the mother's apparent lack of interest in her children, raised by Grand Ma Scottie. Each letter also has a cumulative linguistic effect, as we become increasingly familiar with the two idiolects: on the one hand, Grand Ma Scottie's conversational style, interspersed by proverb and Creole idiom, always framed – we might say, constantly punctuated – by religious preaching rhetoric, and always betraying some ulterior motive: "Greetings in Jesus Precious name Its so nice hearing from you The time doesn't matter as long as we are in each others thoughts Well Im here still holding on praying for a better way of living myself We just have to keep hoping our sweet Saviour helps us take one day at a time" (1). This pattern is counterpointed by Carmen's caring, honest, though often ironical notes, mostly in Standard English, revealing a world view two generations and many miles removed: "Please don't go painting at your age. Enclosed is $100 to pay a painter. Remember the last time you painted the house you fell off the ladder? God didn't catch you then, and you spent weeks in the hospital and hated it" (2).

The story portrays the historical migration patterns of three generations of women: the older generation at home, the mother's generation of the working-class diaspora, who travels to Britain for survival jobs, and the granddaughter's migrating to the U.S.A. for professional (and culturally determined) reasons (Senior 1991: 108). The main focus of the story, however, lies in the personal relationship between them, a relationship only marginally determined by this pattern, for it is through the triangular connection between the women, with the grandmother as mediator, that history is viewed. The story both affirms and disclaims, inscribes and deconstructs female diasporic genealogies. While it centres on domestic relationships, it does so not to eulogise the matrilineal continuities of the diaspora, but to show a break-up in trust and good faith within them. The ending reveals that the grandmother has effectively kept the children away from their mother by deception. "Full Stop" thus defamiliarizes the mythical nurturing (grand)mother figure (and the idealized extended family relations) by individualizing her into a resourceful, contradictory woman, whose wit engages the sympathy of readers while gradually showing a capacity for betrayal hidden behind her sacrificial self-narrative. The text refuses to reduce the figure to a stereotype, and gives her an agency achieved in a great measure through her conscious manipulation of language. Her use of religious discourse to justify her desires ("My Dear Carmen Whats wrong with you The Lord said be fruitful and multiply Stop wasting time I would like to see your children before Our Saviour call me onto him," 6), as well as to preach what she does not practice ("Forgive and forget"), is also the source of much humour: "The Sweet Lord has spared my old shack [from thieves] But let anyone try to break in and see if I don't chop him up with this machete I keep under my bed" (3),

"Your mother [had a good voice] too before she met the no good boy your father I forget his name May he rest in peace" (5). Its self-justifying function reaches its peak in her final explanation to Carmen:

My Dear Carmen Your mother was always a snake in the grass don't believe a word she says She and your father were not fit to raise you so The Good Lord appointed me guardian He did not want you to be raised in England so he gave you onto my care And look how fine you've turned out. (8)

The fact that this sentence ends with the only full stop used by Grand Ma Scottie in her writing, and that the rest of the letter abandons the forbidden subject, is not simply a clever literary device giving the story its ironic structure and title. It also disrupts the illusion of the relative (il)literacy of the character, who ultimately has the authority over what is said. Her skilled use of religious and proverbial language in her letters crosses the oral-scribal divide, denies the limitation of the use of orality / Creole, and, more crucially, powerfully subverts the Western / Northern stereotype of the subaltern, victim nature of the "illiterate, Third World" woman. Far from being the victim she often stages herself as (although without denying her obvious economic marginality), Grand Ma Scottie possesses a skill for wielding power through language, handling register and story-telling devices to favour her family strategies. The character speaks, more clearly than much theory, of the need for a different, more complex reading of the "back home" figure of the "matriarch," idealized and eulogised by many male and female authors,[5] whether in mythical, symbolic contexts or in recuperative feminist genealogies. McKenzie does offer, as her early publicity and reviewers observed, a step forward from earlier and necessary postcolonial and cultural reconstruction. While it is obvious that the diasporic and family patterns described are related to colonialism, they are contemplated as a present historicized reality, rather than as encumbering remnants of the past. The granddaughter, on meeting her mother in New York, describes her presents as "all that old British stuff" (7), an expression that seems to show an attitude not limited to the bedspreads and tablecloths.

The text thus falls, in many aspects, within the poetics identified by some critics as recurrent among Caribbean women writers, but inevitably transcends its borders. It touches on the themes of diaspora and home, survival, community, extended family, religion, and prayer, and definitely offers an "unsentimental catalogue of ordinary life" (Mordecai xxvi); it centres on recurring themes of education, sexuality (or its repression), and mothering (O'Callaghan); it makes efficient use of the Creole and the oraliterary continuum (Cooper, 1993, Mordecai), and emphasizes the connection between the personal and the political through close attention to the first. It does so by creating a disquieting, though profoundly enjoyable, text. Its relation with the poetic epistolary tradition is also illuminating, and shows the continuities and the innovation of McKenzie's use of the subgenre. The paradoxically oral aspect of the epistles of the poetic tradition, which mostly ignored the written and formulaic conventions of "realistic" letter-writing in favour of capturing oral speech for performance, is here inverted to foreground both the formalities of the epistolary mode (letters end "Love, Carmen," "Same Grand Ma Scottie"), and the biblical origins of so much oral speech, reproduced in the resonant language of the grandmother, increasingly overridden with religious discourse as her need to justify her actions grows. Crucially, the story presents the converse paradox to the dramatic monologue of poetry: the "illiterate" woman is making use of the literate genre of letters to present herself in the most favourable strategic terms, the written form allowing her not only to wield power but to invent herself.

McKenzie presents in this epistolary story a decidedly "literary" and written version of the genre and of Creole. But it is one that helps deconstruct the oral/scribal binary at different levels: through the juxtaposition of spoken and written codes in the discourse of the two characters, particularly the grandmother; through the use of the oral, conversational tradition of epistolary language next to formulaic conventions of non-literary letter-writing; and most subversively, through the characterization of the grandmother as the falsely-illiterate, falsely-subaltern whose performance in letters reverses the oral performance of the poetic epistolary tradition.

NOTES

1 A notable exception is Harry Narain's "A Letter to the Prime Minister," a politically committed critique in the shape of a letter to the PM of Guyana, written in Creole and signed "Rice Farmer."

2 Mervyn Morris's "On Reading Louise Bennett, Seriously," published in *Jamaica Journal* in 1967 revalues her writing in literary terms, pointing

out its strengths and explaining her exclusion in terms of a middle-class eager to separate themselves from the vernacular.

3 The 1980s were to see much work on the Creole in the West Indies, and also on orality at an international level: Walter Ong's influential (though contested) study *Orality and Literacy* (1982) put forth a theory on the thought of oral cultures as additive, aggregative, redundant, close to the human lifeworld, agonistically toned, empathetic and participatory (37–57).

4 These two statements are rather puzzling, considering that the review is posted on a CACLALS page (a "postcolonial" association) and that the collection simply is not a short story cycle with a unified narrator, child or otherwise. Other qualifying devices (they are "quite" moving pieces, she is "sometimes" such a powerful writer, there are "some" positive elements to her work) riddle the review, despite the fact that most of the concrete description is positive.

5 Among the numerous examples, too many to discuss, Brathwaite's "Mother Poem" and Goodison's pieces in *I Am Becoming My Mother* are two ends of this spectrum. Jamaica Kincaid offers more ambiguous renderings, and women writers, in particular, have also presented critical views of these quasimythical matriarch figures, as Bringas López and other critics have discussed.

WORKS CITED

Berry, James. *Lucy's Letters and Loving*. London: New Beacon, 1982.

Boyce Davies, Carole. *Black Women, Writing and Identity: Migrations of the Subject*. New York and London: Routledge, 1994.

Boyce Davies, Carole, and Elaine Savory Fido, eds. *Out of the Kumbla: Caribbean Women and Literature*. Trenton, NJ: Africa World Press, 1993.

Brathwaite, Kamau. *Mother Poem*. Oxford: Oxford University Press, 1982.

– *Roots*. Michigan: University of Michigan Press, 1993.

Breeze, J. Binta. "Can a Dub Poet be a Woman?" *Women. A Cultural Review*, 1:1 (1990): 47–49. (Quoted from Donnell and Welsh, eds. 498–500).

Bringas López, Ana. *Muller e literatura na sociedade caribeña anglófona*. Vigo: SPU Vigo, 2000.

Burnett, Paula, ed. *The Penguin Book of Caribbean Verse*. Harmondsworth: Penguin, 1986.

Cooper, Carolyn. "Writing Oral History: SISTREN Theatre Collective's *Lionheart Gal*." *After Europe: Critical Theory and Post-Colonial Writing*. Ed. Stephen Slemon and Helen Tiffin. Coventry: Dangaroo, 1989. 49–57.

– *Noises in the Blood: Orality, Gender and the 'Vulgar' Body of Jamaican Popular Culture*. London and Basingstoke: Macmillan, 1993.

Dawes, Kwame. Review of *Satellite City and Other Stories*. http://www.unb.ca/CACLALS/chimo28.html#_Book_Review:_Alecia (Accessed 15 January 2006)

Dabydeen, David. *Coolie Odyssey*, London: Hansib-Dangaroo, 1988.

D'Aguiar, Fred. *Mama Dot*, London: Chatto and Windus,1985.

– "Chanting Down Babylon." Introduction to Linton Kwesi Johnson, *Mi Revalueshanary Fren: Selected Poems*. London: Penguin, 2002. Ix-xiv.

Donnell, Alison and Sarah Lawson Welsh, eds. *The Routledge Reader in Caribbean Literature*. London and New York: Routledge, 1996.

Goodison, Lorna. *Baby Mother and the King of Swords*. Harlow: Longman, 1990.

Johnson, Linton Kwesi. "Sonny's Lettah. Anti-Sus Poem. *Forces of Victory*, 1979. (Quoted from L.K. Johnson, *Mi Revalueshanary Fren: Selected Poems*. London: Penguin, 2002: 27–29)

King, Bruce. Review of *The Penguin Book of Caribbean Short Stories* and *The Pressures of the Text: Orality, Texts and the Telling of Tales. Wasafiri*, 27 (1998): 54–56.

Kincaid, Jamaica. *At the Bottom of the River*. London: Picador, 1984.

McKenzie, Alecia. *Satellite City and Other Stories*. Harlow: Longman, 1992.

Mordecai, Pamela. Introduction. *From Our Yard. Jamaican Poetry since Independence*. Kingston: Institute of Jamaica. 1987. xiii-xxvi.

Morris, Mervyn. "On Reading Louise Bennett, Seriously." *Jamaica Journal*, 1: 1 (1967): 69–74.

Narain, Harry. *Grass-Root People: Thirteen Stories on One Theme*. Havana: Casa de las Américas, 1981.

O'Callaghan, Evelyn. *Woman Version: Theoretical Approaches to West Indian Fiction by Women*. London and Basingstoke: Macmillan, 1993.

Ong, Walter. *Orality and Literacy: The Technologizing of the Word*. London: Methuen, 1982.

Pollard, Velma. "Mothertongue Voices in the Writing of Olive Senior and Lorna Goodison." *Motherlands: Black Women's Writing from Africa, the Caribbean and South Asia*. Ed. Susheila Nasta. London: The Women's Press, 1991: 238–53.

Senior, Olive. *Summer Lightning and Other Stories*. Harlow: Longman, 1986.

– *Working Miracles: Women's Lives in the English-Speaking Caribbean*. London: James Currey, 1991.

WARREN CARIOU

"We Use Dah Membering": Oral Memory in Métis Short Stories

Métis stories are something like the Rigoureau, the shape-changing wolf-man character which often appears in those stories. The Rigoureau is an amalgam of European werewolf legendry and Oji-Cree shape-changer narratives, and perhaps because of this it is a creature of liminality, a dangerous passe-partout, a trickster, a traitor, a folk hero, an outsider. In other words, it is the perfect metaphor for the slipperiness of Métis identity itself. I grew up hearing Rigoureau stories, and I was even told once that my Uncle Vic *was* a Rigoureau, but I was never certain that I would know a Rigoureau if I saw one. The same is true of this elusive sub-genre of the Métis short story, which may or may not exist, depending on how one looks at it. Part of the problem is defining the term Métis itself, a question which has been debated for generations without any satisfactory conclusions. This problem of definition goes back to latter half of the nineteenth century, when Canada's first Prime Minister, Sir John A. Macdonald, effectively decreed that the Métis did not exist as a people. In his House of Commons speech of July 6, 1885, just after Louis Riel's surrender, Macdonald says:

Now, every half-breed in the North-West, if he does not claim as an Indian and has not accepted as an Indian, belonging to an Indian band and enjoying all of the advantages of an Indian, and they are great, because the treaties are liberal, the annuities are large, the supply of implements, cattle, seeds, and so on, is very generous, on the whole – and any half-breed who says I will be considered a white man has all the privileges of a white man; he can get his 160 acres, and after three years' cultivation he gets his land. (qtd. in Bowsfield 126)

In this statement Macdonald allows the Métis to choose between two normative racial identities, but they are not given the option of claiming their hybridity as a place of belonging. The Red River resistance of 1885 was in some ways a battle against the solidified categories of nineteenth-century racial ideology, which we can see demonstrated in Macdonald's speech. Métis people are accustomed to being considered as problems of classification, so it should perhaps be no surprise that their stories pose similar difficulties.

Another point of complication is that Métis writers, like many First Nations writers, seem to be relatively unconcerned about the niceties of Euro-American genre distinctions. Métis poetry tends toward the narrative; Métis prose tends toward what Lee Maracle calls "oratory," a term which she characteristically refuses to define in generic terms. "Oratory," she writes, "place of prayer, to persuade. This is a word we can work with" (3). This focus on working with words, and especially working collectively with words, is what most characterizes Métis stories, especially the ones collected and translated by Maria Campbell under the title *Stories of the Road Allowance People*. These stories are written in a Métis dialect of English, and stylistically they imitate the speech patterns, the circumlocutions, and the code-switching practices that are characteristic of oral storytellers in other aboriginal traditions. What most interests me in these stories is the ways in which they represent a particular kind of work: the work of memory in the creation and perpetuation of community. This process is described by the narrator of the story "Jacob," who contrasts the "white" and the Métis ways of remembering through language:

Dah Whitemans
he can look back thousands of years
cause him
he write everything down.
But us peoples
we use dah membering
an we pass it on by telling stories an singing songs.
Sometimes we even dance dah membering. (88)

Stories do memory-work, according to this narrator, and different kinds of stories have different strengths and weaknesses. The written stories of "dah Whitemans" are acknowledged to have a particular power to reach far into the past, to enable a connection with distant people and events. But the Métis way, "membering," is shown to have its own strengths, or at least to represent a distinct and viable alternative to the use of books. "Membering" is a communitarian kind of memory, one that connects recollection with the idea of *member*ship in a larger whole. An oral story cannot be told in isolation, and a dance (at least a Métis dance) cannot be danced in solitude. "Membering" here is a performance of social bonding. Stories of "membering" involve the body, physical proximity between teller and listener, and the creation of a community of remembering. They are a living connection to traditions and to the past.

As such, it is appropriate that stories of "membering" also often express alternative versions of history. For example, in the story "Joseph's Justice," also collected in *Stories of the Road Allowance People,* the narrator disputes the official number of Métis men fighting at Batoche:

> Oh I know dah history books dey say we was two
> hundred an fifty.
> But you gotta member
> dey write dah history books.
> My ole Uncle Alcid
> he was dere
> an he say dere was less den a hundred at Batoche. (123)

We can see here a quintessential tension between a literate way of understanding the world and an oral way. "You gotta member," the narrator says, and his statement has the ring of a moral imprecation. In one sense, this is a classic battle of the media, something that Walter Ong sees in many cultures, and something that Walter Benjamin also notes in his paean to the lingering presence of storytelling sensibilities in the stories of Anatoly Leskov. For both Ong and Benjamin, oral modes are associated with communitarianism, while the literate mode (or the novelistic for Benjamin) is associated with individualism. However, both Lee Maracle and Maria Campbell have very interesting things to say about the ways in which Métis stories complicate this oral-literate paradigm.

In Lee Maracle's essay, "Oratory" is not contrasted specifically with literacy but rather with theory. To her, theory is static, merely descriptive, and therefore dead. She argues in favour of oratory as an activity, particularly a collective activity, that to her is alive with possibility. She writes "We believe the truth of a thing is in the doing. Doing requires some form of social interaction and thus, *story* is the most persuasive and sensible way to present the accumulated thoughts and values of a people" (3). We can see here the same idea that the narrator of "Jacob" put forward in his description of "membering": the notion of story as a medium and a mechanism of community cohesion and perpetuation – in other words, story as community work.

Maria Campbell characterizes her own art as a writer in precisely these terms: as community work. In *The Book of Jessica* she says, "My reason for doing anything, is that it's for my community. I am a community worker, the work has to be useful to the community, has to be healing" (69). This focus on the collective use-value of stories, and on the pedagogical and therapeutic values of story-making, is common among Métis writers. Gregory Scofield, for example, in his memoir *Thunder Through My Veins,* describes his aesthetic as one of community work, and at a climactic moment in the book, his dying mother praises him for doing this kind of writing, saying "You're going to do so much for our community, for the lost ones like Grandpa and me" (186). By "lost ones" she means the many Métis who chose to pass as white or as treaty Indians during the Métis diaspora that followed the defeat at Batoche in 1885.

In the context of this dispersal, this vast space of forgetting into which generations of Métis history was placed, Gregory Scofield asserts that the way to re-connect with the past of Métis culture is through story. Story becomes the nexus of belonging, the medium of transgenerational memory, the way of reconnecting to one's lost identity. But of course, during a time of cultural trauma such as the post–1885 period for the Métis, orally-based storytelling traditions also become all the more vulnerable. This is because, as the narrator of "Jacob" suggests, using "dah membering" depends upon physical proximity, performance, and a shared communitarian experience. Thus it is much more difficult to recover a storytelling tradition after an interruptive event than it is to recover a literate tradition.

The Canadian government knew this about oral cultures. From the late nineteenth century to the middle of the 1960s, the government made various attempts at interrupting the transmission of aboriginal oral cultures in order to "civilize" or rather deculturate First Nations people. The Métis were not as easily targeted by governmental mechanisms of assimilation such as residential schooling and forced adoption, largely because they wouldn't hold still; they kept moving around. They had no land, after all. They came to be known as the Road Allowance People because so many of them lived on the sides of public roads. But even though the Métis sometimes escaped the sharpest end of colonial policy, it seems clear that the defeat at Batoche and the loss of their land accomplished many of the same governmental goals.

The diaspora after Batoche resulted in many stories being lost, or at least driven underground, suppressed. The loss of land meant that the communities disintegrated, and thus the very basis for the transmission of the stories became endangered. It is in fact quite remarkable that I heard the Rigoureau stories at all when I was growing up. But of course, I was never told that they were Métis stories. I had to find that out for myself, long after I heard them.

Many aboriginal storytellers talk about their fears that their own particular storytelling traditions will soon be lost. They have seen the results of the many assaults upon oral culture that have occurred in the last few generations. Many of them believe that some of their stories will die with them, or perhaps with the next generation. Anishinaabe storyteller and writer Basil Johnston expresses these fears in his essay, "One Generation from Extinction." He is talking mostly about the loss of indigenous languages here, but he also expresses concern about the loss of stories. He says that those who have lost their languages (and by implication their stories) "will have lost their identity, which no amount of reading can ever restore" (100).

This "reading" to which Johnston is referring, this insufficient replacement for oral culture, seems to be a particularly anthropological kind of reading, the kind which constructs Native cultures not as living communities but as ethnological specimens, preserved in the formalin of academic prose. But none the less, Johnston's essay reveals an interesting contradiction or disjunction that merits further consideration. Johnston says that "no amount of reading can ever restore" that lost identity once the language is gone, and yet Johnston has devoted much of his life to writing down the stories of his people and publishing them. He is by no means unusual among aboriginal storytellers for writing his people's stories down, or having them transcribed by others. Okanagan storyteller Harry Robinson, for example, allowed and encouraged anthropologist Wendy Wickwire to record, transcribe and then publish his stories.

This is the context in which we can place Maria Campbell's collection of Métis stories, except that the *Stories of the Road Allowance*

People exist in a particularly unstable place in relation to both orality and literacy. While they display many of the attributes of oral stories, they are also self-consciously literary objects. They are written by a woman who, by her own admission, is a master more of text than of oral storytelling, but is certainly very highly qualified in both. They resonate between the poles of the oral and the literate, and this ambiguity is particularly interesting in the way it is related to constructions of memory.

The *Stories of the Road Allowance People* are, in fact, not strictly speaking Maria Campbell's stories at all. The preposition in the title connotes a kind of community ownership and perhaps also a sense of community responsibility toward the stories. Campbell is listed as the translator rather than the author of the book, and in her introduction, she makes it clear that she has undergone the necessary training process and asked for the proper community permissions in order to be able to present these stories for publication. So while her name is beside the copyright symbol on the title page, she is very careful to remind her readers that she is not the owner but rather a kind of custodian of these stories.

Campbell brings up an unexpected metaphor in relation to the process by which these stories have come to reside in her memory. She writes,

> with the stories, I have had lifetimes of "stuff" put into my memory. I am not even sure what it is but the teachers say, "Don't worry about it, just think that your brain is the computer you use and we are the people typing it in. When you need it, or you have had the experience to understand it, your spirit will give it to you." I have learned to trust them. It is in this spirit that I share these stories with you. (2)

The computer metaphor here represents the story as a medium of memory – of "lifetimes of stuff" – and the apprentice storyteller is portrayed as simply a repository for that information, rather than a master of it or a creator of it. This idea of the storyteller as a living computer, a storage system of oral culture, is compelling; yet it is also clearly attached to a particularly modern or even postmodern idea of technological literacy. Campbell's teachers go on to complicate the metaphor further by adding the spiritual dimension, saying "your spirit will give it to you." Thus, they are pointing out that information is not the same thing as understanding. The "it" to which the elders

refer is not simply the text of the stories, but rather something else that
the words might allow access to: something that requires the hearer
to reach a state of readiness before it will be given. A person might
have the stories recorded in his or her memory, but the most powerful import of these stories might not be given to this person for many
years, if ever.

After bringing up this computer metaphor and its complication,
Campbell then makes the step of handing the stories over to us, her
readers, and again she brings up the idea of spirit. "It is in this spirit
that I share these stories with you," she writes. The repetition of this
word here suggests that Campbell regards our reading in a kind of
ceremonial context, perhaps analogous that of a listener to an oral
story in the Métis tradition. Even though we don't have to do the kind
of listening that a hearer of an oral story does – because the book does
some of the "work" of remembering for us – this does not mean we
will have ownership of the stories or mastery over them. This is an
extraordinary oral way of describing story and its ceremonial, ethical
and aesthetic effects upon us *as readers*. It could be said that Campbell
is attempting to "oralize" the medium of writing here.

Helen Lock discusses a very similar deployment of oral modes within written texts in the case of African-American literature, especially
the work of Toni Morrison, Paule Marshall, and David Bradley. She
says of these writers,

> Their aim, as African/American writers, is not to exclude either tradi-
> tion [ie, the oral or the written] but to energize the dialectic between
> them by reasserting – through the medium of the written word – the
> value of an orally derived perception of the workings of memory. (1–2)

Lock focuses on the ambiguous relationship between oral and print
modes in these novels, claiming that the interaction between the two
is the product of a transitional phase between oral culture and "evolving" (3) literacy in African-American communities. This rhetoric of
transition and evolution might be overly skewed toward a teleology
of modernity and literacy, but none the less, Lock's examination of the
oral-literate nexus in African-American novels is very useful in relation to the issue of memory.

The most compelling example Lock gives of memory in these texts
is her discussion of "rememory" in Toni Morrison's *Beloved*. In that
novel, rememory is a kind of oral memory that bursts through peri-

.odically into the zone of literate modernity, or that in a sense exists simultaneously with the strategies of remembering and forgetting that literate modernity employs. Lock writes that rememory "is both subjective and intersubjective" (3) and she goes on to say, "rather than a solipsistic remembering subject, Morrison envisions a remembering community of overlapping and interlocking, sometimes interdependent, consciousnesses" (3). This is an apt description of the kind of memory that is represented in the Métis conception of "membering," as the narrator of "Jacob" defines it. This should not be a surprise, because Métis people have since their very beginnings been enacting the negotiation between the oral ways of the Cree and Anishinaabe and the literate ways of the English and French. But that negotiation is not merely a transitional phase; it is instead a way of life.

The story "Jacob" is a good illustration of how such negotiation between orality and literacy have come to be an integral part of Métis culture. It is a story about memory interrupted by colonial intervention, and about aboriginal identities literally being erased. The eponymous character Jacob is not born with that name. It is given to him in a residential school, and he eventually forgets his original name. This renaming strategy – part of the Christian conversion process – is applied to almost everyone in the community, and it has a devastating effect not only upon individuals but also upon storytelling traditions. The narrator gives the example of his own grandfather, whose very identity becomes disconnected from the storytelling traditions after his name is changed to "Jim":

> Once long ago
> I could 'ave told you dah story of my grandawder Kannap
> an all his peoples but no more.
> All I can tell you now
> is about Jim Boy
> an hees story hees not very ole. (89)

When Jacob returns to his community after residential school, no one knows who he is or who he belongs to. He is welcomed none the less, and he re-integrates himself into the community, but many years later, while trying to prevent his own children from being sent to residential school, he makes a horrifying discovery. After complaining to the priest that he does not even know who his own father is, the priest looks it up in a book and gives Jacob this crucial information, thus closing the gap that had been opened in oral culture, using the power of literacy to reach back beyond the living generation. But the book does not bring healing to Jacob. Instead it brings a magnified trauma. Jacob's wife hears the priest reading the name and she runs away and kills herself. Her father was the same man as Jacob's father.

The story does not end at this point, however, with the tragic effects of literacy. It goes on to recount Jacob's efforts in his old age to prevent this tragedy from ever happening again. He does this by writing in a book – a registry of the "old" indigenous names and the "new" Christianized names of all the community's members. One might think that this ending represents the triumph of print, of the colonial mindset, but another interpretation is possible. It seems more likely that Jacob's use of the book is not a simple abandonment of the oral for the literate world, but rather an attempt to hold the two worlds together, to use print as a medium through which oral ways of knowing can be preserved and expressed. This is exactly what Campbell does in her translation of the *Stories of the Road Allowance People.*

WORKS CITED

Benjamin, Walter. "The Storyteller." *Illuminations: Essays and Reflections.* Trans. Harry Zohn. New York, Schocken, 1968.

Bowsfield, Hartwell, ed. *Louis Riel: Selected Readings.* Toronto: Copp Clark, 1988.

Campbell, Maria, ed. & trans. *Stories of the Road Allowance People.* Penticton, BC: Theytus, 1995.

Campbell, Maria and Linda Griffiths. *The Book of Jessica: A Theatrical Transformation.* Toronto: Playwrights Canada, 1989.

Johnston, Basil. "One Generation from Extinction." *An Anthology of Canadian Native Literature in English.* Second Edition. Ed. Daniel David Moses and Terry Goldie. Toronto: Oxford University Press, 1998: 99–102.

Lock, Helen. "'Building up from Fragments': The Oral Memory Process in Some Recent African-American Written Narratives." *College Literature,* 22:3 (October 1995): 1–12.

Maracle, Lee. *Oratory: Coming to Theory.* North Vancouver, BC: Gallerie Publications, 1990.

Ong, Walter. *Orality and Literacy: The Technologizing of the Word.* New York: Methuen, 1982.

Scofield, Gregory. *Thunder Through My Veins: Memories of a Métis Childhood.* Toronto: HarperCollins, 1999.

JEAN-PIERRE DURIX

Myth in Patricia Grace's
"Sun's Marbles"

Among the tropes most frequently used in postcolonial fiction, the allegory looms large. According to Fredric Jameson in "Third-World Literature in the Era of Multinational Capitalism," all Third-World cultural constructions are national allegories and serve to contest colonialist representations. Mythic elements have been used for allegorical purposes by major writers from Kenyan novelist Ngugi wa Thiong'o to Maori novelist Witi Ihimaera. In his novel *Weep Not Child* (1964), Ngugi notably includes the story of Mumbi and Gikuyu, the primordial Gikuyu parents, anchoring his characters in a primordial setting where divine sanction guaranteed the people's secure possession of their land (later expropriated by British settlers). In Ngugi's fiction, the myth is made to serve as a blueprint for the recovery of lost tenure and national pride.

Similarly, in the epigraph to his novel *Tangi* (1973), Ihimaera evokes the myth of the primordial parents Rangi, the Sky-father, and Papa, the Earth-mother:

> The first parents, who clasped each other so
> Tightly there was no day. Their children
> Were born into darkness ...

In mythical Maori times, parents and children lived in a fusional embrace, a blessed situation of harmony. Ihimaera's narrator suggests that this situation was comparable to the experience of the rural Maori who, until recently, preserved the values of "aroha, love and sympathy for each other." The modern individualism and selfishness of life in the cities is implicitly deplored. Paradoxically, Ihimaera highlights a communal ethic of rural solidarity at a time when, after the Second

World War, most Maori had already abandoned their old ways to look for work in the cities. To a certain extent, *Tangi* belongs to the "culture clash" genre common in the early days of postcolonial national literatures. Far from being exclusively Maori, it shares conventions with similar works from different parts of Africa. All these fictions express some measure of nostalgia for a past which is supposed to have vanished after the introduction of white civilization.

In Ihimaera's epigraph, the myth stops at the stage where parents and children are still indissociable. It re-emerges only at the end of the last chapter, just before the short epilogue. After repeating the lines in the epigraph, the narrator ends with the primordial children finally breaking free from their parents' embrace:

> Their children were born into darkness. They lived among the shadows of their mother's breasts and thighs and groped in blindness among the long black strands of her hair.
>
> Until the time of separation and the dawning of the first day. (204)

Nothing is said concerning the circumstances of the separation or the part played by Tane, the son, who ripped his parents apart from each other. It is as though the operation had come naturally, almost without trauma, and the children were simply born into another existence, just like the protagonist in *Tangi* who is faced with the prospect of walking in his dead father's footsteps, returning to the country to look after his family instead of continuing his successful city existence with a good job and a white girlfriend. The mythic story which underlies the novel enables the protagonist to give meaning to the hard decision he has to make. The future appears wide open and he can envisage continuing with the age-old family tradition as though nothing had changed. This blissful denegation of history has led critics to call this novel a Maori "pastoral."

The story of Rangi and Papa, which plays a central role in Ihimaera's *Tangi*, became a central motif in Maori literature and art during the last three decades of the twentieth century. It enabled the Maori to give shape to their experience of social uprooting and uncertainty by finding a mythic precedent in their own tradition. For these rural people transplanted to the cities, the new environment had caused an erosion of values and self-respect. Yet there is no sense that the new life might result in hybrid compromises, and in *Tangi*, the organization of place and people remains inherently Manichaean. The narrator seems to hanker after an idealized, edenic Garden, evoked in terms of the primordial myth.

The examples cited here must not give the wrong impression that myths are omnipresent in postcolonial fiction. When they appear, they do not generally constitute the main storyline and critics often ignore them.[1] Myths are even deemed suspect by a category of readers who believe that postcolonial literature should deal primarily with social reality and not with imaginary creations, which are thought to distract people from their "true" condition. In these circles, myths are interpreted in the sense of representations which are wrongly believed to be true.[2]

Myth fulfils different functions depending on whether one adopts the perspective of the anthropologist or that of the literary critic. In the nineteenth and early twentieth centuries, the former started to use the term to study so-called "primitive societies." According to Mircea Eliade in *Mythes, rêves et mystères*, myths are not only stories which enable a group of people to declare their identity by gaining an ordered view of their origin; they also constitute a moral reference and serve as a foundation on which to build social structures in the present. For Bronislaw Malinowski, who writes from a functionalist point of view, "it is a tradition explaining essential sociological features" (243). In postcolonial literatures the problem is complicated by the fact that indigenous myths, in the versions in which they are known today, were often collected and translated by Western scholars. These mediators produced written reinterpretations of stories which are the object of religious belief in so-called "traditional" societies.

Maori myths were classified and written down by observers such as Sir George Grey, one of the first governors of New Zealand in the 1840s, and Elsdon Best in the 1920s. While myths often supposedly tell of the origins of life and culture, these are only imaginary representations concerning an inaccessible "beginning." Any discourse about this supposed genesis is constantly revised and modified by those who retell it. One cannot therefore trace any "authentic" version of a myth, although myths of origin are supposed to legitimize the existence of societies and regulate the lives of people.

When postcolonial writers use myths belonging to their original culture, they are both insiders and outsiders. Their agenda may be to defend values eroded by the colonial encounter but they rarely consider myths as the bearers of religious belief to which they adhere completely. Instead of having ontological value, as is the case in "traditional societies," myths therefore work as tropes, as figurative expressions of situations closer to the experience of the artists concerned.

◆

Patricia Grace uses myth very sparingly in her short fiction. She makes more use of it in her novel *Potiki*, published in 1986, at a time when the debate concerning Maori land rights[3] was rife in New Zealand and the author felt the need to reassert the specific cultural values implicit in myths.[4] In the first lines of "Sun's Marbles," the author seems to use a candid, almost simplified rhetoric of the kind people expect to find in volumes classified as "the myths and legends of ..." Usually such literature is produced for a child readership and little attempt is made to link the myths concerned with the societies in which they originate. The main purpose is generally to captivate the readers with wonderful stories about supernatural heroes who perform fantastic feats. Patricia Grace's apparent adoption of this genre is deceptive, as her subsequent subversion of conventions indicates.

As I have already noted, the Maori myth concerning the separation of Rangi and Papa, the original Sky Father and Earth Mother, has been abundantly used in Maori literature and painting since the "Maori Renaissance" of the 1970s and 1980s. In "Sun's Marbles," it forms the backbone of the story, but a reader who is not well-versed in Maori mythology is likely to miss its presence and consider the story as just an imaginary tale about fantasy characters. The primordial parents are referred to in capital letters as "Earth" and "Sky" but in a form which is not at first recognizably Maori or even conspicuously mythical. Knowledge of Maori mythology adds value to this story, but is not essential for the understanding of the basic plot. None the less, some of the enigmas will make little sense to someone with no knowledge of the mythical reference.

Grace's elliptic allusion to "Conflict, being a metaphor for People" (13) refers to the dispute that broke out between the children of Rangi and Papa over what course of action to take towards their parents' desire not to relinquish their embrace, thus maintaining their children in perpetual darkness between their clasped bodies. According to an Arawa version of the myth reported by Margaret Orbell in *Maori Myth and Legend* (195), Tawhirimatea, the god of the winds, disagreed with his brothers when they resolved to separate their parents. He stayed with Rangi, his father, and sent storms to the earth to punish his brothers. The earth-mother did her best to protect her offspring from the fury of the winds. Originally, there was supposed to have been no female creature, so Tane fashioned an image of himself with earth and breathed life into it, thus giving birth to Hine-ahu-one. Tane then mated with her and they had a daughter, Hine-titama, with whom Tane later committed the first incest. When she discovered who the father of her children was, Hine-titama fled to the underworld in shame and became Hine-nui-te-po (the great lady of darkness). The brief allusion to solo parenthood in Patricia Grace's story probably refers to the fact that, before disappearing into the world of darkness, Hine-titama asked Tane to look after their children.

"Sun's Marbles" places more emphasis on the demi-god Maui than on the primordial parents. Maui's decision to slow down the course of the sun forms the opening episode of the story. In her allusions to myths, Patricia Grace takes up some of the elements she developed in the text she wrote for the volume entitled *Wahine Toa* (1984).[5] According to the version of the mythical story offered in *Wahine Toa*, Maui was abandoned as a miscarried foetus to the waves of the sea by his mother, Taranga, who had wrapped him in her topknot of hair. Because of his exceptional gifts, this child, whose father was a god and whose mother was human, managed to survive.

Maui always proved a mischievous character. Among his feats, this Promethean hero played with fire: since fire had been lost to the world, Maui went to ask his grandmother Mahuika, who kept fire in her fingernails, to give him one of her magic nails. After inadvertently putting out the flame she had given him, he went back to Mahuika for more. The same action was repeated until, after giving him the last of her fingernails, Mahuika became cross with Maui and set fire to the world around him. In the general conflagration that followed, Maui changed into a hawk to try and escape the blaze. He eventually asked his ancestor Tawhirimatea (god of the winds) to send torrential rain. A flood engulfed the fire at ground level, but it sought refuge in the topmost branches of some of the largest trees where it survived.

The opening sentence in "Sun's Marbles" sums up a spectacular and violent action meant to strike the reader. Non-specialists will probably notice the slapstick effect of Maui clobbering Sun over the head in what looks like a cross between an oral story for children and an episode in a comic cartoon. The tone is almost farcical or carnivalesque. If one ignores the mythical status of Maui, one might just mistake him for a hero in an action film set today. The vocabulary used ("booby-trapped," "clobbered") belongs to colloquial idiom and everyday life. The anachronistic reference to 'daylight saving' refers to the modern concern about making the best possible use of energy. However, the phrase may well prove to be an allusion to an earlier text, that of Sir Peter Buck's classical study, *The Coming of the Maori*.[6] Readers well versed in Maori culture will recognize the mythic episode in the course of which Maui, the trickster, asked his ancestress Muriranga-Whenua for her magical jawbone of enchantment and knowledge, which Maui later used to make a fishhook with which he fished up the North Island of New Zealand. He also wielded the jawbone to club the sun over the head before trapping him in his net in order to slow his journey across the sky and make the days longer.

In "Sun's Marbles," Patricia Grace resorts to all the techniques familiar to an expert storyteller. The action is reported in rhythmic language. Following the rules of the genre, Grace does not spare any element in an enumeration[7] when this is meant to retain the attention of the audience. She also makes deliberate use of alliterative patterns such as "So the offspring of Sky and Earth began trying to move the parents away from each other, pushing, pulling, prising ..." (13). While in postcolonial writing, the evocation of myths often serves as a reminder of the deep roots of national pride and frequently takes the form of epic discourse in which the heroes assume extraordinary stature, Grace does not operate within that sort of framework. At the beginning of this short story, the tone is deliberately light-hearted. The narrator does not appear to consider the mythic figures involved with any particular reverence other than what is suggested by the capitalization of their names. Even the episode in which Maui beats up the sun turns to farce. This process of deflation corresponds to a no-nonsense attitude towards life very commonly found in New Zealand. Similarly, the colloquial language used is in keeping with the country's particular fondness for the unpretentious ordinary person.

In her deliberate strategy of deflation, Grace uses double-entendre in such a way that one cannot help hearing allusions to popular culture when she mentions the fact that the sun's marbles "went skittering out to stardom" (11). When she writes "here was no room to swing a cat's ancestor," the author resorts to a colloquial expression that refers to one of the most sacred values in Maori culture, the respect for ancestors. The possibility of making jokes based on such fundamental principles indicates the degree of freedom Patricia Grace enjoys when she alludes to specific Maori values without feeling in any way restrained by political correctness.

A former primary schoolteacher, Grace adopts a style of storytelling which is accessible to the young and uninitiated; she avoids rare words and privileges colloquial expressions. Yet she never talks down to her readers and instead shows them the potential for double-entendre that common expressions have. In order to facilitate the non-specialist reader's task, Grace occasionally resorts to the logic of the glossary, a question which caused heated discussions among early African authors in the 1960s. When evoking the terms "teina"[8] and "tuakana,"[9] she does not hesitate to translate them, thus emphasizing the particular respect enjoyed by older siblings, a characteristic not so often found in Western families today.

Her narrative strategy involves telling the story through the medium of a third-person narrator who pretends to act as a safe guide. The characters mentioned never express themselves directly but always through the mouth of the narrator or, at best, in free indirect style. The effect of this choice is to privilege the narrator's voice with its idiosyncrasies, particularly her use of colloquial, sometimes even trivial language. A complicated storyline based on mythic material thus becomes accessible to a wide reading public. The narration appears deceptively simple, but far from simplistic.

Among the distinctive features of this story, the use of abstract terms (such as nothingness, otherness, powerlessness, hiddenness) evokes philosophical notions whose complexity contrasts with the apparent simplicity of the storyline. Patricia Grace's use of such terms is also based on Maori myths of origin. These generally start with the void, which is not, however, described as complete absence but as a form of emptiness pregnant with possibilities. From that initial state, life and the elements gradually emerge. Thus, what may appear as inconsequential terms to the uninitiated readers of Patricia Grace's story evokes original myths to someone versed in Maori tradition.

Some of the notions, such as "Darkness," are capitalized. So are other words such as "Creatures," "Wind," "Plants," "Water," "Light," "Space," which represent the different elements in the universe. In the retelling of Maori myths, such capitalization is often used by anthropologists, Elsdon Best in particular. Sir Peter Buck indicates in *The Coming of the Maori* that traditional storytellers "arrang[ed natural phenomena] in an ordered sequence, and recit[ed] them in the same way as a genealogical table of human descent" (433). The elements are thus personified and considered as common ancestors on a par with human beings. Based on the convention that an initial capital letter graphically signifies a proper name, this might initially appear as an odd use of the uppercase, but the capitalization takes on a new dimension in the context of the Maori tradition. However, Grace is not content with merely reproducing a reverential attitude towards such sacred values. When her narrator talks of "Conflict, being a metaphor for People," one suspects that the reader is meant to take such references with humorous distance too.[10] Obvious tongue-in-cheek attitude is perceptible when Grace's narrator talks of "Perspective" and "Dimension." The implication is that humour is just as acceptable as a more respectful attitude when evoking mythic figures, even when they belong to a body of knowledge which very nearly disappeared with the imposition of British culture. This appears to be the price to be paid for these myths to retain some of their relevance in the contemporary world.

Far from advocating a return to regressive conceptions of myth, the story may be an allegory of the situation of the contemporary Maori who have taken their fate into their own hands at the cost of abandoning the comfort of their safe idealized conception of their own society. Besides referring to such preoccupations, the story also evokes the more general problem faced by people who live in a traditional environment and are tempted to move into another complex world in which notions of identity and Maoriness may well rest on processes of ever-changing hybridization. Some prefer to retreat behind the safety of unchanging mythical versions of the Garden and refuse any alteration while others run the risk of simply living, that is, of adapting to the established order. Like the children of Rangi and Papa who are prepared to face uncertainty and chaos for the sake of knowing what light and freedom are, the modern Maori may well have to re-examine their tradition and give up their nostalgia for a lost past. The old mythical pattern serves to articulate Grace's suggestion that living in the light with one's eyes wide open may be less comfortable than staying in the cosy darkness of past cultural certainties. Yet there may not be any other solution to avoid cultural annihilation.

The plot of this story is arguably based on a pun interpreted literally. The universe which seems to have "lost its marbles" has no origin in myth and is simply the result of Grace's linguistic inventiveness. The suggestion here is that the "marbles" chipped off the sun's head can prove to be dangerous material when it falls into the hands of irresponsible people. In the context of the South Pacific in the early 1990s, this cannot fail to remind the reader of the heated debate in Australia and New Zealand over nuclear tests in Polynesia. In New Zealand, denuclearization became associated with the fight for Maori rights. Some allusions in the story to populations which had to be moved from their original lands to escape becoming ill or dying echo the enforced displacement of people who lived in the Micronesian islands where the first American nuclear tests took place. The same displacement happened later in French Polynesia.

The Maori myth of origin is also playfully interpreted in terms of the difficult relationships between parents and children and the clash between generations. Wisdom does appear to be on the side of indulgent parents who would like to prevent their children from committing irremediable acts but are trapped in their convictions on the virtues of permissiveness. Unfortunately, what the parents feared most happens. In the contemporary world, this finds echoes in the frequent discussions about delinquent Maori youths in poorer suburban districts. The parallel drawn between the original Maori gods and the growing-up problems of young people today playfully illustrates the relevance of myths.

The story starts in the form of an oral narration and ends in the style of a letter to the editor of a women's magazine questioning parental behaviour. The story's mythic background seems completely integrated in ordinary contemporary discourse with a pseudo-psychological purpose: this tends to prove that children cannot help trying to find out their parents' secrets. They are not content until they test for themselves the extent of their knowledge; they wish to discover how much their parents have kept hidden. The potential destructiveness inherent in human beings is playfully attributed to the fact that they are spoilt brats indulged by their parents because, like Potiki, they were the last to be born. This allegation does not quite fit in with the fact that, in the myth, Maui was abandoned at birth to the sea by his mother and only survived thanks to a miracle. But Grace chooses to ignore this part of the myth here. The implicit conclusion is more general, and the narrator seems to suggest that it is wise to trust older people's experience before behaving in a brash way.

Still, this reduction of godly feats to very ordinary human behaviour is not to be taken too seriously. It simply forms part of the deflation process, of the author's desire to show that heroes and demi-gods are not above humanity but are supposed to have behaved like human beings whose failings they share. Following Sir Peter Buck, Grace is probably convinced that Maori gods do not constitute a world apart which must be revered and preserved as a sacred untouchable corpus. Both are very much aware of the fact that, far from being the creators of human beings, as most mythologies suggest, gods were created by human beings in their own image and to serve their own interests. Myths are not sacred texts which suffer no modification. The author makes a living and joyful use of myths while addressing more particularly those readers who, because they share her cultural knowledge, will be able to laugh at her in-jokes.

◆

Patricia Grace parodies the light entertaining style of stories found in collections of "myths and legends." The use she makes of these conventions is subverted since the author turns a purely escapist tale into one with a moral purpose. However, what appears to be of relevance only to the Maori proves to be applicable to human beings in general. This serves to reassert the fact that the Maori are part of humanity and their experience can also be of use to other populations outside New Zealand, an interesting reversal of the colonial situation in which the people of Europe and North America are supposed to have the privilege of universality. Paradoxically, for people who believe in the sacredness and inviolability of myths, this story suggests that the Maori original myth can be the prototype of any evolution which has taken place in Maori society since the beginning. Far from being a guardian of orthodoxy, the myth becomes a blueprint for the necessary evolution and adaptation of society in order to meet the requirements of today.

The story ends with apparently naïve questions which bring the mythic content back to everyday reality. The narrator refrains from providing answers and this might frustrate readers who consider Patricia Grace to be a committed writer who, they believe, should offer solutions to the problems encountered by the Maori. The humorous question marks which punctuate the inconclusive end of the story raise questions rather than provide answers. Patricia Grace's refusal to oversimplify complex matters and to give in to the attraction of nostalgia is perhaps a sign that Maori literature has reached its maturity, found a territory of its own, which is not fossilized within the frontiers of essentialised myth. "Sun's Marbles" is an example of creative heteroglossia in which various levels of language, myths, and contemporary reality are made to respond to one another in a fruitful confrontation with an open-ended issue. The Maori does write back, but with a sense of each discourse's relative merit in producing tropes about a reality which always fails to let itself be captured absolutely.

NOTES

1 Significantly there is only one brief occurrence of the term "myth" in Bill Ashcroft, Gareth Griffiths and Helen Tiffin's *The Empire Writes Back* and none at all in the same authors' *Key Concepts in Post-Colonial Studies*.

2 For some West African critics in particular, who demand that the writer be a moral guide to the people, myths appear to be merely escapist.

3 The Waitangi Tribunal was set up by the New Zealand government in 1985 to examine Maori land claims. The movement for Maori sovereignty which had made a public breakthrough in the early 1980s was well-established by the time Patricia Grace wrote "Sun's Marbles," which came out in 1996.

4 See my own discussions of the myth of Maui in *Potiki* in "Patricia Grace's *Potiki* or the Trickster behind the Scenes" in Hena Maes-Jelinek et al., eds., *A Talented Digger*, 436–41; "The Breath of Life/Stories" in Marc Delrez and Bénédicte Ledent, eds., *The Contact and the Culmination*, 281–92; "The Modernity of Maori Tradition" in Marc Maufort, ed., *Union in Partition*, 241–53.

5 The title "wahine toa" means "strong women." This book, illustrated by the painter Robyn Kahukiwa, stresses the importance of women in Maori culture, and develops a feminist interpretation of a tradition generally considered as male-oriented. Little of the feminist rhetoric contained in *Wahine Toa* appears in "Sun's Marbles," however.

6 "Maui ... belonged to a much earlier period as evidenced by his snaring the sun in the first instance of daylight saving" (440).

7 "There was no 'above' and 'below' in those days. No direction was different from any other – no 'vertical', 'horizontal' or 'diagonal ...'" (11).

8 Younger brothers and sisters.

9 Older brothers and sisters.

10 One is reminded of the way in which the Indian novelist G.V. Desani makes fun of the pseudo-philosophical use of such capitalization by would-be gurus and charlatans in his novel *All about H. Hatterr.*

WORKS CITED

Ashcroft, Bill, Gareth Griffiths and Helen Tiffin. *The Empire Writes Back*.
    London/New York: Routledge, 1989.
- *Key Concepts in Post-Colonial Studies*. London/New York: Routledge, 1998.
Best, Elsdon. *Maori Religion and Mythology*. 1924; rpt. Wellington:
    Government Printer, 1982.
Buck, Sir Peter, *The Coming of the Maori*. 1949; rpt. Wellington:
    Whitcoull's, 1977.
Delrez, Marc and Bénédicte Ledent, eds. *The Contact and the Culmination*.
    Liège: L3, 1997.
Desani, G.V. *All about H. Hatterr*. London: Aldor, 1948.
Eliade, Mircea. *Mythes, rêves et mystères*. Paris : Gallimard, 1957.
Grace, Patricia. "Sun's Marbles," in *The Sky People*. Auckland: Penguin,
    1994: 9–16.
Ihimaera, Witi. *Tangi*. Auckland: Heinemann, 1973.
Jameson, Fredric. "Third-World Literature in the Era of Multinational
    Capitalism." *Social Text* 15 (1986): 65–88.
Kahukiwa, Robyn and Patricia Grace. *Wahine Toa*. Auckland: Viking
    Pacific, 1984.
Maes-Jelinek, Hena et al., eds. *A Talented Digger*. Amsterdam/Atlanta:
    Rodopi, 1996.
Malinowski, Bronislaw. *Magic, Science and Religion*. 1948; rpt. London:
    Souvenir Press, 1974.
Maufort, Marc. *Union in Partition*. Liège: L3, 1997.
Orbell, Margaret. *Maori Myth and Legend*. Christchurch: Canterbury
    University Press, 1996.

GERALD LYNCH

Mariposa Medicine: Thomas King's *Medicine River and the Canadian Short Story Cycle*

Thomas King's first book of fiction, *Medicine River* (1989), is marketed as a novel. It is not a novel. King himself has said that he prefers "to think of *Medicine River* as a cycle of stories," and he agreed with an interviewer's suggestion that his first novel has a place in the continuum of Canadian short story cycles (Rooke 63–64), the fictional form that occupies the generic space between the miscellany of short stories and the novel (see Ingram, Lynch 2001). King also claimed that such features as the episodic structure and repetitions of *Medicine River* derive from Native story-telling traditions, but I would suggest that such Native narrative influences are more relevant to King's short fiction subsequent to *Medicine River*. Moreover, those features of orature expressed in *Medicine River* are some of the distinctive literary features of the short story cycle. In oral composition, repetition serves a predominantly mnemonic function, whereas in *Medicine River* repetition is more accurately described as recurrent development in plot and character. Pertinently, recurrent development is *the* distinctive narrative dynamic of the story cycle as the genre was originally analyzed at book length by Forrest L. Ingram (1971).

In *The Truth About Stories* (2003), King addresses the anthropologically and linguistically complex issue of the meanings of the oral and the written. He distinguishes between the two by comparing the Judeo-Christian creation myth and a Native version, arguing that "these strategies [the written and the oral] colour the stories and suggest values that may be neither inherent nor warranted" (22). But soon he cannot resist specifying these values in the binary manner he usually dismisses: "the elements in Genesis create a particular universe gov-

erned by a series of hierarchies – God, man, animals, plants – that celebrate law, order, and good government, while in our Native story, the
universe is governed by a series of co-operations – Charm, the Twins,
animals, humans – that celebrate equality and balance" (23–24). But
even in King's own terms, I am not persuaded by his "rhetoric" (115).
I believe the subtly tendentious King was closer to the truth when he
first said that such values are "neither inherent nor warranted" in the
mode of telling. Later (96–98), King again accords the oral and the
written equal status, declaring that his interest is in the power of story
per se (though here, too, I remain puzzled at just how a legendary lost
Aztec library in Mexico could have preserved oral works).[1] In his "Afterwords," King attempts yet again to distinguish, this time less invidi-
ously, between the oral and the written as between the public and the
private performance respectively (134). But by this point King must
concede, in a rhetoric intended to forestall criticism, the untenability
of his position: "So I'm probably wrong."

Undoubtedly many aspects of the literary story cycle itself derive
from older traditions, some of them exclusively oral: a people's heroic
myths and legends, the folk tale, and such cyclical forms as liturgical
calendars, medieval miracle plays, and sonnet sequences. As undoubtedly, *Medicine River* could be said to mimic other features of Native
oral story-telling, as in, for example, the genealogy that begins chapter
five (52). But even here King's mapping of all Big John Yellow Rabbit's
relations is a mock-genealogy, a simultaneous deflation and validation of pretentiousness and family ties that had already been done to
perfection a number of times by the quintessential nineteenth-century
English comic novelist, Charles Dickens (see especially the opening of
David Copperfield). In short, King's purported indebtedness to Native
oral traditions in the matter of mock-epic genealogies is again a technique more literary than oral.

Specifically for present purposes: the language and form of *Medicine
River* – its literary tradition – is the English-Canadian short story cycle.
Medicine River is no more *written* under the predominant influence of
an oral tradition (and note the unavoidable oxymoron in saying this[2])
than is the first Canadian short story cycle, Duncan Campbell Scott's
In the Village of Viger (1896). Strange as it must appear to that growing body of readers who are aware only of Scott's so-called Indian
poems and his controversial role as Deputy Superintendent General of
Indian Affairs, it could be said that his *Viger* has the more legitimate
claim to the influence of Native oral traditions, and said so not entirely

facetiously or provocatively. More than any contemporary writer, the long-serving Scott was exposed to Native cultures in conditions less influenced/contaminated by literary culture.[3]

◆

Readers interested in the Canadian short story cycle can find its formal predecessors in the works of early writers of epistolary novels, collec-tions of letters, and books of loosely linked sketches: Frances Brooke's *The History of Emily Montague* (1769), Thomas McCulloch's *Letters of Mephibosheth Stepsure* (serialized 1821–23), the first series of Thomas Chandler Haliburton's *The Clockmaker* (1836), and the collections of linked nature and character sketches by the likes of Catharine Parr Traill, Susanna Moodie, Anna Brownell Jameson, and many other ambitious sketch-artists of the nineteenth century. From about the mid-nineteenth century onwards, such linked series of shorter works were likely influ-enced by Charles Dickens' *Sketches by Boz* (1836) and *Pickwick Papers* (1837). Dickens' very popular first books would have been an important influence not only on the Canadian short story cycle – especially for Moodie and Stephen Leacock – but on the development of the story cycle in English literature generally. A lesser claim can be made for Ivan Turgenev's *A Sportsman's Sketches* (1852), the book that Sherwood Anderson, author of the first modern American short story cycle, *Wines-burg, Ohio* (1919), considered "one of the great books of the world" (qtd. in Ingram 148, n.12), and which Frank O'Connor enthusiastically described as perhaps "the greatest book of short stories ever written." O'Connor goes further, thinking perhaps of the work's coherent form: "Nobody, at the time it was written, knew quite how great it was, or what influence it was to have in the creation of a new art form" (46).

As stated, the Canadian short story cycle then came into its own in Scott's late nineteenth-century story cycle of a small town in Western Quebec, *In the Village of Viger*, and, a little later, found fulfillment in Leacock's humorous treatment of small-town Ontario, *Sunshine Sketches of a Little Town* (1912). *Viger* and the *Sketches* were the first to weave for literary artistic purpose the various strands of the nineteenth-century nature sketch, character sketch, anecdote, tall tale, local colour writing, fable, and romantic tale that preceded the forma-tion of the Modern story and story cycle. Scott's *Viger* is in fact a *tour de force* of those nineteenth-century story forms (Dragland 12), while Leacock's sketches expertly parody many of the same types.[4]

Throughout the twentieth century, the story cycle continued to be well suited to the concerns of Canadian writers intent upon portraying – or documenting, in Dorothy Livesay's identification of *the* Canadian mode – a particular region or community, its history, its characters, its communal concerns.[5] In addition to providing opportunities for a conventional documenting of place and character, the story cycle also offers formal possibilities that allow its practitioners the opportunity to challenge, whether intentionally or not, the totalizing assumption of the conventional novel of social and psychological realism. (And I emphasize here the adjective *conventional*, aware that there are many contemporary novels, such as *Medicine River*, that are patently short story cycles advertised as novels by timid, presumptuous publishers.[6]) Canadian writers who have been inspired to compose something more unified than the miscellaneous collection of stories and who do not wish to forgo the documentary aspect of the realistic novel, but who are themselves wary of the traditional novel's grander ambitions – suspicious of the implications of its totalising, coherent plot, linear chronology, and resolute drive towards closure – have found in the story cycle a form that allows for a new kind of unity in disunity, reflecting a fragmented temporal sense, and incorporating a more authentic representation of modern sensibilities.[7]

But even such late-nineteenth and early-twentieth-century cycles as Scott's *Viger* and Leacock's *Sunshine Sketches* already portray the struggles of small communities for coherence and continuance under contrary pressures from metropolitanism and modernity, in this form, the story cycle, that figures the tension between cohesion and a kind of entropy, solidarity and fragmentation, essentialism and contingency – between things holding together and things falling apart. In this regard, it is worth noting Alistair Fowler's generic version of McLuhan's "the medium is the message." "Genre," Fowler asserted, "primarily has to do with communication. It is an instrument not of classification or prescription, but of meaning" (22). After Leacock, such writers as Frederick Philip Grove, Emily Carr, Margaret Laurence, and Alice Munro would explore the formation of character in this form that simultaneously subverts the impression of completion, of closure and product, suggesting that selfhood may be as much an illusion in fact as in fiction. Considered in this way, in the deeper disparities between its form and its subject, the story cycle can thus be seen to display a critical tension between its "outer form" and "inner form," as those determinants of distinctive genre were first termed by Wellek and War-

ren (231). At the close of the present essay, I will have something to say
about possible reasons for the enduring attraction that the short story
cycle holds for Canadian writers; for now, I turn to an analysis of some
of the ways King's *Medicine River* fits into this Canadian continuum.

◆

Medicine River is composed of eighteen chapters that can stand alone
as short stories, if as individual stories whose meanings are most fully
appreciated in the context of the whole cycle. King obviously exploits
one of the chief features of many short story cycles: parallel structuring, where paired stories in the sequence comment on each other. In
Medicine River this technique is mainly used within individual chapters that often tell two apparently unrelated stories. "Apparently"
because the paralleling is always being deployed to focus the interdependent relation between past and present, whereby a remembered
event assists protagonist Will to understand his present or to keep him
from repeating a mistake. For example, this arrangement can be seen
most clearly in the running stories of former girlfriend Susan and current love-interest Louise Heavyman, with the juxtaposition serving to
caution Will about the dangers of even his mild machismo and, more
generally with regard to some of the fiction's central themes, the vexed
(and pointedly Native?) questions of possessiveness and ownership.
With respect to Will's coming to know where he comes from and who
he is as a mixed-race character, the present event as often serves to help
him better understand his past.

    This paralleling (sometimes alternating) of stories is another sophis-
ticated literary technique, and was used effectively by such writers as
Scott in *Viger* and Emily Carr in *Klee Wyck*. In the fairly obvious art
of *Medicine River*, King none the less sometimes employs paralleling with a subtlety that would demand a great deal indeed of only a
listening audience. One further example will have to serve. In chapter
fourteen's parallel stories of the retarded girl Maydean and the ersatz
Native activist David Plume (this pairing is not the subtle aspect), King
implies much about the dangers of wanting too earnestly to belong
(189–200). The parallel technique allows him to comment indirectly
on the unacceptability of violence as a means to Native ends, and it
serves as well as a memory lesson to Will about the perilous attrac-
tiveness of easy answers to difficult matters of individual identity in
relation to group membership. Finally, it might be observed that *Medi-*

cine River's repeated paralleling of past and present stories to these pedagogical purposes expresses a predominantly conservative, and arguably Canadian, temperament, as characteristic of Haliburton as it was of Scott and Leacock.[8]

The eighteen stories of *Medicine River* are unified primarily by the continuing presence of the protagonist Will and the dominant setting of the titular small city and the reserve of Medicine River. What could be overlooked is that for mixed-race Will, his identity quest is at least as much a grappling with the non-Native half of himself, which was contributed by an absent father, as it is to find a home in the Native community. Consider the close of the opening chapter/story, where photographer Will contemplates an old photograph of his mother and father:

> And I remember the picture of the two of them. My mother with her dark hair and dark eyes, the pleated skirt spread all around her. She was looking back, not turned quite far enough to see the man behind her. His hand lay on her shoulder lightly, the fingers in sunlight, his eyes in shadows. (10)

In *Medicine River*, place and identity, home and self, are connected in a complex evolving, even revolving, process. But from the start Will, raised by his full-blooded mother, better knows who he is as a Native man: it's those non-Native eyes of the father, in shadows, that he must attempt to integrate into who he was and is, how he sees himself, even if the absent father's purpose is to show him what not to be as a man.

But such a cautionary reading is none the less to simplify events, because Will must also come to see that his non-Native father loved his mother, which is why *Medicine River* opens with the address of a decontextualized letter: "*Dear Rose...*" The letter (whose first recipient is of course named for the floral symbol of romantic love) and its message are eventually received, and better late than never for the child, Will, conceived in the relationship: if love had not had something to do with his birth, then Will would be a pathetic product in wilful process indeed. In typical King fashion, this knowledge of the absent father's love for the mother mitigates the damning view of Will's father. And that too is in accord with King's hopes for an "associational" Native literature that "devalues heroes and villains in favour of the members of a community, a fiction which eschews judgements and conclusions" ("Godzilla" 14). King doesn't shirk apportioning responsibility to the bad fathers of *Medicine River* (see 43–51 on the complex way in which the Native community deals with a wife-beating that leads to the murder of the husband), but, for the sake of communal health, he shies from assigning blame unequivocally.

A key sign of the success of Will's self- and social-integration as partner to Louise and surrogate father to her child, South Wing, is the framing symbol of a child's toy top, with framing being another of the major structural features of the short story cycle. A top was supposedly sent to Will and his younger brother as a Christmas present from their absent father, but it never arrived (it was probably never sent). In the penultimate paragraph of the story cycle that is *Medicine River*, Will has purchased a similar top for South Wing, thereby signalling his acceptance of the role of father, the role that his own father eschewed. Notably, the biological non-Native father was a rodeo rider who chose a life of irresponsible adventure that is more in keeping with the American myth of rugged individualism than the conservative, communal Canadian myth given earlier expression in such story cycles as *Viger* and *Sunshine Sketches*. Alone at Christmas in the last story of the cycle, the domesticated Will sets the toy top spinning and it makes "a sweet, humming sound, the pitch changing as it spun in its perfect circle" (260–61). Literally come home, and securely home alone, in this story cycle Will has more truly willed himself into the perfect circle of a surrogate family and Native community (a healing circle, or what Scott called *The Circle of Affection*). What Will does here in reconstituting and redefining family and its roles at the end of the violent twentieth century – by remembering creatively and taking action – is different only in historical time from the choice made by the eponymous Paul Farlotte in the return story of Scott's *Viger* towards the end of the disruptive nineteenth century[9] or, with different emphasis, what the narrator aboard "The Train to Mariposa" is admonishing at the end of *Sunshine Sketches*.

Of course, just about any informed Canadian fiction of the small town written after 1912 cannot avoid owing much to Stephen Leacock's *Sunshine Sketches of a Little Town*. And Thomas King's *Medicine River* shares an indebtedness to that earlier Canadian short story cycle that is at least as striking as those of Alice Munro's *Who Do You Think You Are?* (1978) and George Elliott's *The Kissing Man* (1962). In fact, King's debt to Leacock's masterpiece may well be the most remarkable. I offer the following parallels/echoes as a kind of conclusive, intertextual evidence of what Northrop Frye termed an "imaginative continuum" ("Conclusion" 250) in Canadian literary culture, and as ersatz evidence that the Canadian short story cycle possesses what Mikhail Bakhtin conceived of as "genre memory" (see Morson and Emerson 89).

To begin broadly, other than King I cannot think of a Canadian comic writer since Leacock whose tone and authorial attitude are so "kind" – Leacock's term for the humour of communal identification, of *kin*ship, which is similar to what King means by his title *All My Relations* – and whose narrator's irony persists so trickily. Decoding the deceptively simple narration of such comic writers as Leacock and King often necessitates extra-textual trips. Notably, then, King has stated that he feels protective towards the Native communities about which he writes, even to the extent of not disrespecting his fictional Natives with what he considers foul language (Rooke 72–73), just as Leacock in his preface to *Sunshine Sketches* insists on his affection for the originals that make up the composite Mariposa and its characters (xviii). Here obviously are two Canadian writers of story cycles, separated by numerous differences of origin, time and place, who are eager to clarify that they cherish the communities they document and anatomize with humorous satire.

Less evidently similar is the way in which comedy is always threatening to turn into tragedy in both story cycles, or the way in which seriously dangerous matters are laughed into farce – the way in which Leacock and King are always rescuing their characters and readers from catastrophe.[10] For example, "The Mariposa Bank Mystery," wherein a rumoured murder is slowly degraded (or upgraded) to the level of the comically ludicrous (110–12), is echoed in *Medicine River's* handling of an episode involving AIM (American Indian Movement), where a rumoured murder dissolves into the story of an Indian having fallen on a bottle he carried in his pocket (254), which then becomes a problematic use of the drunken Indian stereotype. And to take but one more example of this authorial predilection from among the many revealing parallels and echoes between the two story cycles, *Medicine River* has its own Mariposa Belle scene, where Will and his mother and brother find themselves sinking in a boat and seriously fearing death by drowning in what turns out to be a few feet of water (246–47; the scene is itself paralleled in Will's and Harlen Bigbear's misadventure in a canoe, which must be another Native in-joke).

Most strikingly parallel of all are the ways in which *Sunshine Sketches* and *Medicine River* privilege the connections between place as small town, home, and identity by continuously repeating and developing those tropes in a manner that is the essence of a short story cycle's movement. *Sunshine Sketches'* return story, "L'Envoi: The Train to Mariposa," first cautioned Canadians, in the figure of its interlocutor the city-dwelling Mausoleum Club member, about the dangers to identity of not returning home periodically (by "L'Envoi," which takes place outside of Mariposa, this return is clearly meant figuratively with respect to all that "Mariposa" has come to represent of Canadian origins, traditions, and communities). In *Medicine River* it is Harlen Bigbear, the *spiritus loci* of the Native community, who repeatedly insists (in a castigating, seemingly irrational reference to drinking and Native basketball competitions) on a real and present physical connection between place of origin and identity, suggesting that place enables the performance of a true self. Harlen says to the players he coaches, "'That's why you miss them jump shots. That's why you get drunk on Friday night and can hardly get your shoes tied on Saturday. That's why we lose those games when we should be winning … cause you don't know where you are'" (15). The implication for the greater Native community of winners and losers needs no presumptuous elaboration from this non-Native critic.

But where you need to be to know where you are is "home." *Home* is a word that King plays on and repeats with almost as many ironies and typographical qualifications of quotation marks and inverted commas and italics as does trickster Leacock himself in the first few paragraphs of "L'Envoi" (141). The following scene is presented some eighty pages after Harlen Bigbear's admonition to the basketball players, so again asks much even of the reader, let alone a projected listener, who is to remember Harlen's earlier poignant address on place and identity. (I don't think it germane to argue for the purportedly superior memorial abilities of oral cultures: *Medicine River* is written for a contemporary readership.) This second scene occurs earlier in narrative time, however, when Harlen was presumptuously trying to convince Will to return to Medicine River:

Harlen turned the radio down a bit. "Can't see Ninastiko from Toronto," he said. "So, when you think you'll be moving back home?"
"Here?"
"Sure. Most of us figured that, with your mother and all [just buried], you'd be coming home soon."
There was no logic to it, but my stomach tightened when Harlen said *home* …

"... You see over there," Harlen said, gesturing with his chin. "Ninastiko ... Chief Mountain. That's how we know where we are. When we can see the mountain, we know we're home." (93)

In *Medicine River*, and in Medicine River, to know where you are and where you belong is to be in sight of the reifying landmark Ninastiko, Chief Mountain, which seems here to be suggestively and appropriately identical with Harlen and his pointing chin. Good medicine indeed (which really does sound better than talk of a metaphysical signifier). And this is the same generic medicine that's been prescribed by Canada's Carlylean literary physicians-of-the-age from pre-modern Scott and Leacock to postmodern Alice Munro and King. Most pertinently for present purposes, this Canadian literary healing continues to be practised often in the form of short story cycles.

Such continuity of form and attitude to subject (and even of the ubiquitous ironic tone) from Haliburton to Scott and Leacock to Munro and King should argue at least that the form of the short story cycle has proven itself adaptable over some two centuries to the literary needs of both genders and various racial groups. I am not saying that King can serve for all Native or ethnic Canadians, even if he is conveniently of mixed race ("a native writer of Cherokee, Greek and German descent," as his book bio describes him), only that *Medicine River* provides another compelling example of the short story cycle's continuing adaptability. King is certainly not the only available contemporary writer of Native or ethnic heritage to employ it in ways strikingly reminiscent of its uses since the beginnings of Canadian literature. For as much as the short story cycle served the needs of such writers as Grove and Carr earlier in the twentieth century, it continues to serve writers from the diverse groups that make Canadian communities and Canada (see Davis 7–9). Short story cycles are especially well suited to documenting and anatomizing places (small towns and variously defined communities), and to conveying a character's fragmentary experiences, so the immigrant's experiences as s/he struggles to adapt to a new home are readily amenable to treatment in such a form because of the immigrant's divisions of loyalty and consciousness, identity issues, losses, novelty, and the episodic nature of those experiences.

After the generically necessary elements of an independent-interdependent arrangement of short stories and the dynamic of recurrent development – features shared by the generic family of story cycles from

James Joyce's *Dubliners* to American Native writer Louise Erdrich's
Love Medicine – the return movement that concludes many story
cycles distinguishes the Canadian practice in the genre. Indeed, *Medicine River* could be described as a short story cycle composed entirely
of return stories (recalling in this respect Grove's *Over Prairie Trails*).
W.H. New writes in *Land Sliding* that "Canadian writing recurrently
takes characters on journeys home; far from the standard American
model of eternal progress – 'you can't go home again' – Canadian
writing advises that you must return, in order to place the past apart,
to read its other-centred rules in a fresh way, and to make the present
and future home, whatever its relationship with a distant childhood,
your own" (159–60). George Willard of the American Anderson's
Winesburg, Ohio lights out from home like Huck Finn before him;
such Canadian characters as Leacock's silent interlocutor in "L'Envoi"
and King's Will yearn to return home. In his own way Will forgoes
what Leacock's "L'Envoi" narrator calls "money-getting in the city"
(Toronto, named in *Medicine River* if unnamed in *Sunshine Sketches*)
and returns to proximity with his Albertan reserve community – his
home – and there finds accommodation with self and other, with past
and present, and with the Native and non-Native within himself.

I am arguing, therefore, that the short story cycle not only performs
the cross-generic, literary, cultural, and even nationalist work that I've
ascribed to it elsewhere (2001) but also that the form can be viewed as
something of a hybrid genre in postcolonial terms. What I've described
as the story cycle's middle-way form between the miscellany and the
novel, and its definitive tension between the one and the many, may
form a large, if subconscious, part of its attraction for the writers of a
country, Canada, that developed out of the tensions between the conservatism of both England and Royalist France, and the liberalism of
its enterprising neighbour to the south (and later post-Revolutionary
France). The distinguished Canadian short story in its extension to the
story cycle can also be figured as mirroring the distinctive yet closely
linked regions of Canada, constituting a kind of fictional linkage of
abiding bonds and creative gaps *A mari usque ad mare* as opposed to
the attempt to write a continuous totalizing story *E Pluribus Unum*.
Such overreaching, not to say bombastic, speculation may help to explain the continuing presence in Canadian culture of what Priscilla M.
Kramer has called the "cyclical habit of mind" (qtd. in Ingram 24), a
habit that we see expressed in such diverse genres as explorers' journals, sketch books, and documentary long poems from the eighteenth

century onwards, and in the shaping of interdependent short stories into patterns of recurrent development whose movement is cyclical, excursus and recursus, as in Thomas King's *Medicine River*.

NOTES

1   I cannot resist speculating that *The Truth About Stories*, which began as a series of lectures, must have 'worked' much better in the auditorium than on the page, which is not to say that it's an unrewarding read (King tells some good stories). Only that this book itself provides evidence of what King is often at pains to deny: namely, that the literary/written demands more of its readers than the oral of its listeners; that, not to put too fine a point on it, the literary is the more sophisticated art; and that, to out with my own subject position, I prefer the printed page to the recitation, the published essay to the conference paper.

2   King (1990, 13) uses the term "interfusional" to describe "that part of Native literature which is a blending of oral literature and written literature." I think, though, an earlier statement in the same article demonstrates the Orwellian sin against plain speaking – from the usually plain-writing King – that occurs when he discusses the nomenclature for Native literature's indebtedness to Native oral traditions: "If we are to use terms to describe the various stages or changes in Native literature as it has become written, while at the same time remaining oral, and as it has expanded from a specific language base to a multiple language base, we need to find descriptors which do not invoke the cant of progress and which are not joined at the hip with nationalism." Cant aside, see Hertha D. Wong (172–74) for an illuminating discussion of the relation between short story cycle form and Native oral traditions. Wong proceeds to focus her discussion on the American Native writer Louise Erdrich's "short story sequence" *Love Medicine* (1984). *Love Medicine*, revised and expanded in 1993, is part of a much longer sequence of stories, a tetralogy of books; and it has a more legitimate claim to connection with Native oral traditions, if only for the fact that its stories, often the same stories, are told by a multiplicity of narrators.

3   See King on Scott (*Truth* 132–33): "Duncan Campbell Scott, the deputy superintendent general of Indian affairs (among other things), speaking candidly in 1920 of Canadian Indian policy said, 'Our object is to continue until there is not a single Indian in Canada that has not been absorbed into the body politic and there is no Indian question, and no

Indian department.' Hocus-pocus! Indians. Now you see them. Now you don't." No question, Scott was an assimilationist. But King none the less decontextualizes Scott at his most racist. It's at least worth adding that Scott, representatively wrong as he was in this, was envisioning hundreds of years into the future, that he wrote differently about Natives for different readerships, and that his view changed over the years of his growing contact with Native cultures. In the remarks quoted, he's writing in bureaucratese to an administrative readership about government policy (see Lynch 1982). Or as Orwell would have put it, Scott is writing to defend the indefensible, and his language shows it. In the "Afterwords" to *The Truth About Stories* (153–54), King himself will insist upon the importance of context in the matter of transcribing Native stories: "So when Native stories began appearing in print, concern arose that the context in which these stories had existed was in danger of being destroyed and the stories themselves were being compromised." As King often repeats, we are made of stories – whether Native myths or Scott's stories of Indians – though (*pace* Orwell yet again) some contexts would appear to be more equal than others.

4 In American literature, Sarah Orne Jewett's *The Country of the Pointed Firs*, like *Viger* published in 1896, holds the distinction of being the first short story cycle, a fact which at least discredits the notion of a Canadian cultural lag in the new form's development.

5 Regions and communities as diverse as the world of working women in the Montreal of J.G. Sime's *Sister Woman* (1919), the multi-cultural Montreal of Hugh Hood's *Around the Mountain* (1967), and the working-class Jewish community of Mordecai Richler's *The Street* (1968); the dust-bowl prairies of Sinclair Ross's suggestively cyclical *The Lamp at Noon and Other Stories* (1968); southern Ontario small town life some fifty years after Mariposa in George Elliott's *The Kissing Man* (1962); the eccentric west coast islanders of Jack Hodgins' *Spit Delaney's Island* (1976) and the spiritedly impoverished Cape Bretoners of Sheldon Currie's *The Glace Bay Miner's Museum* (1979) in the 1970s; the mostly women's lives of Sandra Birdsell's semi-rural residents of the fictional community of Agassiz, Manitoba, in *Night Travellers* (1982) and *Ladies of the House* (1984), and the Albertan Pine Mountain Lodge (an old folks home) of Edna Alford's *A Sleep Full of Dreams* (1981) in the 1980s; Thomas King's strikingly Leacockean portrayal of native community life in *Medicine River* (1989) and Derek McCormack's fictional depiction of homosexual life in *Wish Book: A Catalogue of Stories* (1999) in the 1990s. Other story cycles, such as Margaret Laurence's *A Bird in*

the House (1970), Clark Blaise's *A North American Education* (1973), Alice Munro's *Who Do You Think You Are?* (1978), Robert Currie's *Night Games* (1983), Isabel Huggan's *The Elizabeth Stories* (1984), and McCormack's *Dark Rides: A Novel in Stories* (1996), focus on the growth of a single character in a particular community, illustrating in the story cycle the interest in individual psychology since the rise of modernism. And any survey of high points of cyclical story form in Canada must accommodate such unacknowledged innovators in the genre as the Frederick Philip Grove of *Over Prairie Trails* (1922), the Emily Carr of *Klee Wyck* (1941), and the Hugh MacLennan of *Seven Rivers of Canada* (1961), the last of which employs the serial-cyclical form to take in the whole of Canada through its main rivers.

6   See Robert Luscher (153): "The form's development has been spurred not only by Joyce and Anderson but also by the possibilities of unity demonstrated in American regional collections and by more recent experimentation with the novel"; and Dieter Meindl (17): "Considering that the modern novel is above all characterized by a dissolution of consecutive temporal structure, by the breaking up of plot and story line, the short story cycle, which radicalizes this trend, becomes a key modernist genre"; and Barbara Godard (27): "discontinuous narrative modes are privileged in contemporary English-Canadian literature where anecdotes are strung together in extended patterns that stretch the traditional story. They occur in two modes which have generally been considered to form distinctive genres, the short story cycle and the long poem."

7   See Sherrill Grace (448): the short story series "retains the fragmentation of experiential reality while allowing the artist to shape and control material unobtrusively."

8   No less an authority than Northrop Frye observed that "the prevailing tone of Canadian humour ever since" Thomas McCulloch (1776–1843) has been "deeply conservative in a human sense." Frye added that Canadian comic writing of the nineteenth century was distinguished from the American by providing not just a series of jokes but a "vision of society," and that this larger purpose also became characteristic of Canadian comic writing (Frye ix).

9   Farlotte gives up his life's dream of returning to France and his dying mother in order to assume responsibility for his neighbour's destitute children. Scott's many Indian poems most often present a situation of mother and child, often a sick child, with no father in the picture. The implications for the future of Native peoples, in Scott's mistaken view, are obvious. But it should be remembered that the French-Canadian fam-

ilies of the village of Viger are in a similar state of disruption and transition, and frequently portray women and children left without protective
paternity.

10 See King (Rooke 65): "There is a level of disaster in each of those epi- ·
sodes that I feel helpless to prevent."

WORKS CITED

Alford, Edna. *A Sleep Full of Dreams*. Lantzville BC: Oolichan, 1981.
Anderson, Sherwood. *Winesburg, Ohio*. 1919. Rpt. Ed. Malcolm Cowley.
New York: Penguin, 1976.
Birdsell, Sandra. *Ladies of the House*. Winnipeg: Turnstone, 1984.
– *Night Travellers*. Winnipeg: Turnstone, 1982.
Blaise, Clark. *A North-American Education*. Toronto: Doubleday, 1973.
Carr, Emily. *The Complete Writings of Emily Carr*. Vancouver/Seattle:
Douglas & McIntyre/University of Washington Press, 1993.
Currie, Robert. *Night Games*. Moose Jaw, Sask: Coteau, 1983.
Currie, Sheldon. *The Glace Bay Miner's Museum*. Ste. Anne de Bellevue, PQ:
Deluge, 1979.
Davis, Rocio G. "Negotiating Place: Identity and Community in M.G.
Vassanji's *Uhuru Street*. *Ariel* 30:3 (1999): 7–25.
Dragland, S.L. Introduction. *In the Village of Viger and Other Stories*, by
Duncan Campbell Scott. Toronto: McClelland and Stewart, 1973.
Elliott, George. *The Kissing Man*. Toronto: Macmillan, 1962.
Erdrich, Louise. *Love Medicine*. New York: Holt, Rinehart & Winston,
1984; rev. New York: HarperPerennial, 1993.
Fowler, Alistair. *Kinds of Literature: An Introduction to the Theory of
Genres and Modes*. Cambridge: Harvard University Press, 1982.
Frye, Northrop. "Conclusion to *Literary History of Canada*." 1965. Rpt. *The
Bush Garden: Essays on the Canadian Imagination*. Toronto: Anansi,
1971. 213–51.
– Introduction. *The Stepsure Letters*, by Thomas McCulloch. New Canadian
Library 16. Toronto: McClelland and Stewart, 1960.
Godard, Barbara. "Stretching the Story: The Canadian Story Cycle." *Open
Letter* 7 (Fall 1989): 27–71.
Grace, Sherrill. "Duality and Series: Forms of the Canadian Imagination."
Canadian Review of Comparative Literature 7:4 (Fall 1980): 438–451.
Grove, Frederick Philip. *Over Prairie Trails*. 1922. Rpt. Toronto: McClelland
and Stewart, 1991.
Haliburton, Thomas Chandler. *The Clockmaker, or the Sayings and Doings*

of Sam Slick of Slickville. 1836. Rpt. Series One, Two and Three. Ed. George L. Parker. Ottawa: Carleton University Press, 1995.

Hodgins, Jack. *Spit Delaney's Island* 1976. Rpt. Toronto: Macmillan, 1987.

Hood, Hugh. *Around the Mountain: Scenes from Montreal Life.* Toronto: Peter Martin, 1967.

Huggan, Isabel. *The Elizabeth Stories.* 1984. Rpt. Toronto: HarperCollins, 1990.

Ingram, Forrest L. *Representative Short Story Cycles of the Twentieth Century: Studies in a Literary Genre.* Paris: Mouton, 1971.

Jewett, Sarah Orne. *The Country of the Pointed Firs and Other Stories.* 1896. Rpt. Garden City: Doubleday, 1954.

Joyce, James. *Dubliners.* 1914. Rpt. Markham, ON: Penguin, 1977.

King, Thomas. "Godzilla vs. Post-Colonial." *World Literature Written in English* 30:2 (1990): 10–16.

– ed. *All My Relations: An Anthology of Contemporary Canadian Native Prose.* Toronto: McClelland and Stewart, 1990.

– *Medicine River.* 1989. Rpt. Toronto: Penguin, 1995.

– *The Truth About Stories: A Native Narrative.* Toronto: Anansi, 2003.

Knister, Raymond. Introduction. *Canadian Short Stories.* 1928. Rpt. Freeport NY: Books for Libraries Press, 1971. Xi-xix.

Kramer, Priscilla M. *The Cyclical Method of Composition in Gottfried Keller's Sinngedicht.* New York: Lancaster, 1939.

Laurence, Margaret. *A Bird in the House.* 1970. Rpt. Toronto: McClelland and Stewart, 1989.

Leacock, Stephen. *Sunshine Sketches of a Little Town.* 1912. Rpt. A Canadian Critical Edition. Ed. Gerald Lynch. Ottawa: Tecumseh, 1996.

Livesay, Dorothy. "The Documentary Poem: A Canadian Genre." 1969. Rpt. *Contexts of Canadian Criticism.* Ed. Eli Mandel. Patterns of Literary Criticism 9. Chicago: University of Chicago Press, 1971. 267–81.

Luscher, Robert M. "The Short Story Sequence: An Open Book." *Short Story Theory at a Crossroads.* Ed. Susan Lohafer and Jo Ellyn Clarey. Baton Rouge: Louisiana State University Press, 1989: 148–67.

Lynch, Gerald. *The One and the Many: English-Canadian Short Story Cycles.* Toronto: University of Toronto Press, 2001.

– "An Endless Flow: D.C. Scott's Indian Poems." *Studies in Canadian Literature* 7:1 (1982): 27–54.

– *Stephen Leacock: Humour and Humanity.* Montreal-Kingston: McGill-Queen's University Press, 1988.

Lynch, Gerald and Angela Robbeson, eds. *Dominant Impressions: Essays on the Canadian Short Story.* Ottawa: University of Ottawa Press, 1999.

MacLennan, Hugh. *Seven Rivers of Canada.* Toronto: Macmillan, 1961.

McCormack, Derek. *Dark Rides: A Novel in Stories.* Toronto: Gutter, 1996.
– *Wish Book: A Catalogue of Stories.* Toronto: Gutter, 1999.
McCulloch, Thomas. *The Letters of Mephibosheth Stepsure.* Halifax: H.W. Blackadar, 1869. CIHM Microfiche no. 49067.
Meindl, Dieter. "Modernism and the English-Canadian Short Story Cycle." *RANAM* 20 (1987): 17–22.
Morson, Gary Saul and Caryl Emerson. *Mikhail Bakhtin: Creation of a Prosaics.* Stanford: Stanford University Press, 1990.
Munro, Alice. *Who Do You Think You Are?* Toronto: Macmillan, 1978.
New, W.H. *Land Sliding: Imagining Space, Presence, and Power in Canadian Writing.* Toronto: University of Toronto Press, 1997.
– *Dreams of Speech and Violence: The Art of the Short Story in Canada and New Zealand.* Toronto: University of Toronto Press, 1987.
O'Connor, Frank. *The Lonely Voice: A Study in the Short Story.* 1962. Rpt. London: Macmillan, 1963.
Rooke, Constance. "Interview with Thomas King." *World Literature Written in English* 30:2 (1990): 62–76.
Ross, Sinclair. *The Lamp at Noon and Other Stories.* Toronto: McClelland and Stewart, 1968.
Scott, Duncan Campbell. *The Circle of Affection.* Toronto: McClelland and Stewart, 1947.
– *In the Village of Viger.* 1896. Rpt. Toronto: McClelland and Stewart, 1996.
Sime, J.G. *Sister Woman.* 1919. Rpt. Ottawa: Tecumseh, 1992.
Wellek, René, and Austin Warren. *Theory of Literature.* 3rd ed. New York: Harcourt, Brace, Jovanovich, and World, 1962.

ALEXIS TADIÉ

Under the Banyan Tree:
R.K. Narayan, Space, and the Story-Teller

'The Raj' by itself is meaningless. It could be prefix or suffix to a
proper name. You may say 'Raja' (king or ruler) or 'Rajya' (kingdom) in any Indian language. The Raj in its present form is a
vacuous hybrid expression neither Indian nor British, although the
OED (which is a sacred cow for us in India, while other dictionar-
ies are useful, they are not necessarily revered as the OED) has admitted it for a definition. (Narayan 2001: 480)

The beginning of R.K. Narayan's essay, "After the Raj," spells out
his view of the English Empire, of the colonial period, of the language
that one might use in reference to it. Although to my knowledge Narayan, the creator of Malgudi, did not use the expression, this essay
comes close to defining his "postcolonial" position. He addresses here
the craze for the Raj that was exemplified through a number of films,
including *Passage to India*.[1] All pictures of India, Narayan explains,
are by essence fragmented, piecemeal; and whoever attempts to encap-
sulate India, or generalize about India, is doomed to failure. Narayan's
criticism of colonial representations of India not only derides their
proponents, such as E.M. Forster or Rudyard Kipling, who he says
had only a limited view of their subject, but he shows how even works
such as theirs are travestied in the portrayal of India that is peddled in
international entertainment.

The analysis of colonial and postcolonial India that Narayan offers
in other essays, such as "When India was a colony," underlines further
the perspective of the writer. In no sense does he offer a broad theory
or even a description of the colonial state; his is the oblique view, the
incidental, ironic perspective on the workings of the colonial state.
The domination of England over the Indians is likened to the work-

ings of wild elephants in his southern province, "where wild elephants are hemmed in and driven into stockades by trained ones, and then pushed and pummelled until they realize the advantages of remaining loyal and useful, in order to earn their ration of sugarcane and rice" (Narayan 2001: 471). He portrays the Governor of a province with gentle irony ("His Excellency generally divided his time between horse racing and polo, golf and swimming" [Narayan 2001: 473]); the visit of the Viceroy ends in a rather stilted way ("When pudding was to be served the band in attendance should always strike up 'roast Beef of Old England'" [475]). Narayan does not attack in sweeping theories, nor does he generalize. His is the delicate ironical touch, preferring to expose contradictions, such as those of the distinguished British historian who, hearing Narayan complain that Indian history was written by British historians, replied: "'I'm sorry, Indians are without a sense of history. Indians are temperamentally non-historical'" (478).

This position vis-à-vis colonialism has, of course, not precluded a complex, profound relation with the English language and its literature: "Through books alone we learnt to love the London of English literature" (Narayan 2001: 465). But he remains aware, at the same time, of the impossibility, and indeed of the futility, of writing Anglo-Saxon English. Some time before Salman Rushdie voiced a similar concern, Narayan wrote: "The English language, through sheer resilience and mobility, is now undergoing a process of Indianization in the same manner as it adopted US citizenship over a century ago, with the difference that it is the major language there but here one of the fifteen" (Narayan 2001: 467). But having noted this, the writer, as usual, retreats calmly, to suggest that, as far as he is concerned, the English language has served his purpose "of conveying unambiguously the thoughts and acts of a set of personalities, who flourish in a small town named Malgudi supposed to be located in a corner of south India" (468).

These few remarks and notations remind us of the tone of Narayan's writings, and suggest ways in which we should, or should not, approach his texts. What makes them both fascinating to read and difficult to analyze, is precisely this, mentioned by Narayan in the last quotation: they only seem concerned with a set of personalities, somewhere in south India. The deceptive simplicity of the stories, the delicacy of tone, the subtle irony are all features of his writings that are central to his art, and most difficult to analyze. This is even more apparent in the short stories, a form for which Narayan had a particular fondness.

THE SHORT STORY AND THE STORY-TELLER

Throughout his career, Narayan asserted the importance of the short story. This predilection appears in the number of stories that he wrote over the years, as well as in the (rare) theoretical statements that he offered on the subject – rare, because Narayan believed that all theories of writing are bogus. In his view, the short story provides the author with more freedom in the treatment of themes, and more variety in the wealth of topics than can be touched upon in the longer form. Paradoxically, Narayan finds the novel more constricting because the form imposes upon the writer a certain amount of concentration on a central theme, whereas short stories do not have to leave anything out, they "can cover a wider field by presenting concentrated miniatures of human experience in all its opulence" (Narayan 1985: viii). They can spring from chance encounters, conversations overheard on a bus, personal acquaintances, scenes observed. The short story enables the narrow focus as well as the change of scale. It concentrates on fugitive moments in the life of individuals as much as on history, it looks through the semi-darkness that envelops the Astronomer ("An Astrologer's Day"), as clearly as it reconstructs the history of the Municipality of Malgudi, it stops in on the corner of a street in Malgudi, or it overlooks India. The opening of "A Horse and Two Goats" exemplifies perfectly the peculiar perspective offered by the story: "Of the seven hundred thousand villages dotting the map of India, in which the majority of India's five hundred million live, flourish, and die, Kritam was probably the tiniest, indicated on the district survey map by a microscopic dot, the map being meant more for the revenue official out to collect tax than for the guidance of the motorist, who in any case could not hope to reach it since it sprawled far from the highway at the end of a rough track furrowed up by the iron-hooped wheels of bullock carts" (14). We have moved in one sentence from the map of India to the mark left by the bullock cart on a rough track.

To Narayan, the short story presents distinct advantages over the novel: "The short story rather than the long novel has been the favourite medium of the fiction-writer in India, because, it seems to me: (1) the short story is the best-suited medium for the variegated material available in the country, (2) the writing of a short story takes less time" (Narayan 2001: 458). The last reason he gives is familiar, it was also Raymond Carver's excuse (if he needed one) for not writing novels. Narayan's first point echoes in reverse the practice of some contemporary Indian novelists (Rushdie, but also Seth or Mistry) who have tended to view the great big novel as a means of encapsulating India and the Indian experience. For Narayan, on the contrary, the possiblity of moving from theme to theme, of varying the perspective and constantly coming back to the same set of personalities, makes of the short story (or any sequence of stories) the perfect means of approaching the variety of India. In an essay that was first published in the *Times Literary Supplement* and later reissued as the preface to his *Picador Book of Modern Indian Literature*, the novelist Amit Chaudhuri reiterated the preference for the shorter form (Chaudhuri 2002). In Narayan's work, it is not the singularity of form, but the multiplicity of points of view, the juxtaposition of characters, the heterogeneous composition of the collection of stories that offer the more complex way into the world. In allowing the reader to come back to Malgudi in story after story, to review the characters or the place, to walk down familiar streets or peep down unknown alleys, Narayan constructs a world which is based on the detail of the story as well as on the larger perspective. If the short stories focus on singular events, they become remarkable because they belong to the history of Malgudi. As we read of surprising characters such as the Green Blazer ("Trail of the Green Blazer"), or of indifferent characters such as the Ayah whose name is unknown ("A Willing Slave"), we form a picture which relies on the juxtaposition of the stories within the collection and is built on the reader's awareness of the progression of the life and the history of Malgudi. The varied and complex perspective which the short stories allow rests indeed on a complex movement. Each individual story may choose its field of literary investigation with utmost freedom; considered as a unit, the collection of stories provides the reader with a fragmented, complex, heterogenous picture. Narayan's stories further suggest endless combinations, rearrangements, new anthologies that readers are free to construct in their libraries or in their memories.

Narayan's stories are usually based on a character who faces some kind of crisis, but this character is rarely the narrator. Stories where the first person is also the main character are rare in the collections.[2] On the other hand, a number of stories are narrated in the first person, by a discreet, silent observer, who has seen it all, and may at times be identified as "The Talkative Man." More often than not, the narrator remains in the background, but may come forward with an introduction or a conclusion (Narayan 1965: 10). It is the experience of the narrator rather than his knowledge which is brought to the fore. The narrator of "The Roman Image" for instance can deliver his story because "Once, he says, I was an archeologist's assistant" (Narayan 1985: 31). "Once" signals the end of the process, and the distance in time; and the function once occupied by the narrator implies, in its subaltern presence, observation, as well as inclusion in the events to be recounted. The gentle modalization of some of the openings or descriptions implies further the unobtrusive presence of the narrator. It establishes his presence, as well as his slightly retiring position: for instance, "he had a most curious occupation in life" (Narayan 1985: 96) opens "The Evening Gift." This is one of the characteristics of irony in Narayan's stories.

Although the passage of Time is acknowledged, and the distant turmoils of History can sometimes be felt – "Another Community" addresses the issue of Partition – the perception conveyed to the reader is rather one of timelessness. This does not mean that Narayan's characters or stories are "timeless," but that the perception of time does not rely on the unfolding of elaborate strings of events. On the contrary, his stories tend to focus on one event, whose importance is to be judged by the characters, perhaps by the narrator, and which is sometimes a defining moment in the life of the protagonist: the child who bites the burglar, the man who goes down a well to recover a bowl, the boy who captures a cobra. Frequently, the central character is a child, for whom the event represents a form of rite of passage, such as Dodu earning four annas or the heroism of Swami. In this sense, the stories are not concerned with time, but with the experience gained in such moments of crisis. Sometimes, they can ironically constitute non-rites of passage, such as the fortieth birthday of Rama Rao in "Fruition at Forty": "He suddenly felt that he had not been growing and changing. It was an illusion of his appearance caused by a change of dark hair into grey hair, and by the wearing of longer clothes. This realization brought to his mind a profound relief, and destroyed all notions of years; at the moment a birthday had no more significance and fixity than lines marked in the air with one's fingers" (Narayan 1985: 168). Here, clearly, the story renounces linear unfolding time, rejects its most significant human marker, the birthday, and insists on the contrary on a lack of change – although the characters do, of course, gain experience, which the narrator imparts and readers in turn apprehend.

These stories are caught in the everyday fabric of village or small town life in South India. They dwell on the little trades, on the economic fragility of the shopkeepers, on the life of the small employees, even on recognizable types (such as the miser in "Half a Rupee Worth"). They inhabit the universe of the small town because the narrator belongs to this world: he has first hand knowledge of the events, or of the people he is parading for the reader. He is a local craftsman, one who "knows the local tales and traditions" (Benjamin 84). He knows the characters and can introduce them with a certain amount of irony, if the story demands it: "Dodu was eight years old and wanted money badly" (Narayan 1985: 61). But above all, he is not one to sit down and write his stories: he prefers to stand and tell his tale. This is obvious in the recurrent figure of the Talkative Man. It is felt in stories such as "Chippy" that begins with "I cannot give a very clear account of Chippy's early life" (Narayan 1985: 77). Of course the fact that Chippy is a dog suggests further irony. The reliance on experience, his own or that reported by others, the subtle ear for dialogue, the importance of memory, the accuracy of things rather than interpretation, the relevance of the episode, the moral of the story, all signal a narrator who is immersed in orality rather than writing. The whole story relies on his ability to convey the tale, on the simplicity of his language, on his authority. The narrator of Narayan's stories is, as I have been trying briefly to sketch him, a story-teller.[3]

SPACE AND THE SHORT STORY

In his introduction to the collection of stories entitled *Gods, Demons and Others* (1965), Narayan investigates the world of the storyteller. He shows him to be part and parcel of the Indian village community, a man who has aged with wisdom, and who retains in the midst of the villagers an aura that comes from the enchantment he can impart. There are, of course, as Walter Benjamin once explained, two types of story-tellers. There is the seaman, who has travelled the world and comes back to his village to tell of far-distant lands, and there is the tiller, who never moves from his field (Benjamin 1970: 84). Narayan's story-teller clearly belongs to this second category: "a grand old man who seldom stirs from his ancestral home on the edge of the village, the orbit of his movements being the vegetable patch at the back and a few coconut palms in his front yard, except on some very special occasion calling for his priestly services in a village home" (Narayan 1965: 2). And his home is the focal point of the village, after the day's work – it gives the village a sense of community, of belonging, of not missing anything. Narayan's story-teller knows the value of rituals, being a religious man. He dresses and prepares himself for the recitation, he begins the session with a prayer, he tells of ancient times, of legends and myths, and imparts his wisdom through the moral significance of the story. The narratives have been passed down through the centuries, and "each tale goes back and further back to an ultimate narrator, who had, perhaps, been an eye-witness to the events" (Narayan 1965: 7).[4] Narayan, in describing the world of the story-teller, relies on his own observation and attendance. Benjamin's story-teller is a theoretical construct, and a perceptive one; Narayan's is an empirical and majestic human being. In presenting the tales of *Gods, Demons and Others*, Narayan indeed explains: "I have made my selection after listening to the narratives of several storytellers such as I have described, and checking them again by having the originals read out to me by a Sanskrit scholar." So that Narayan himself becomes the great story-teller, the great discreet but towering presence of the story-teller. Benjamin wrote: "And among those who have written down the tales, it is the great ones whose written version differs least from the speech of the many nameless storytellers" (Benjamin: 84).

Narayan insists that the reference for story-telling in India lies in religious tradition: "Our minds are trained to accept without surprise characters of godly or demoniac proportions with actions and reactions set in limitless worlds and progressing through an incalculable time-scale" (Narayan 2001: 466). His *Gods, Demons and Others* testifies to this, as does his retelling of the *Mahabharata* and of the *Ramayana*. The character of Muni, in "A Horse and Two Goats," tells at great length to the foreigner how he has come to learn all the stories: "When we were young we staged at full moon the stories of the avatars. That's how I know the stories; we played them all night until the sun rose ..." (Narayan 1985: 26). Narayan directs our gaze more perceptively, and more discreetly, to the performance, to the conditions for utterance, where the story relies on the story-teller.

The world outlined by the short stories of Narayan is diverse and variegated, and it conjures up the complexities of India. One might detect a tension here, for the universe he describes is at the same time confined to the small towns and villages of South India. There is indeed a strong sense of place in Narayan's stories, and perhaps more fundamentally a sense of space that is constructed, apprehended, and restored to the reader/hearer. Places range from Malgudi of course, where the majority of the stories are set, to small villages such as Kritam, mentioned above, or the village Somal, "nestling away in the forest tracts of Mempi" (Narayan 1985: 187). From story to novel, the topography of Malgudi bears recurrent features, such as street names and a river. The short story acknowledges the landmarks, Market Road or the Oriental café. But what matters most to the short story is not so much the sense of place, the would-be realism of the location, but rather the creation of a space and the perception that is imparted to the reader. Some stories generate the immediate sense of space through travel – not, of course, great distant travel, but perhaps travel to the temple, which in these southern villages is akin to an expedition, or the incessant travels up and down the county of the failed archeologist. These travels do not offer great exoticism, although the unexpected may occur during one of the journeys: the possibly surreal apparition of "Old Man of the Temple" occurs in the middle of a taxi journey, some twenty miles from Malgudi. In this sense, they give the story an environment where the event may unfold. They generate a distance, a sense of a different place from what is familiar to the audience. The story-teller may have seen the distant place, may have experienced this journey himself, but the listener is suddenly caught up in a different world. Narayan does not need extraordinary settings for this, and the protection from the rain afforded by a banyan tree by the roadside is enough to give two characters, a former married couple, the opportunity to confront their past.

The stories sometimes take place in a recognizable environment, one that the audience will conjure up immediately: the little shop in the market where Subhia sells rice (Narayan 1985: 175), or the provision stores once set up by the talkative man, some way away from Market Road, in Malgudi (43). Even some of the villages where the stories take place, a little out of the way, recall the village where the audience is perhaps listening to the story. The function of space is also to make sure that the event which the story-teller recounts is, in many ways, familiar to the audience. The majority of stories are set in a place which is immediate in its simplicity: the house across the road, the bungalow, the corner of the town hall veranda. The introduction of these elements is done through a generic marker ("the bungalow" for instance), which makes them both recognizable and exemplary. The story "Ranga" opens on an infinity of possibilities, suggesting the freedom of the story-teller: "Ranga was never certain what he was going to do next" (Narayan 1985: 157). This is immediately translated in spatial terms: "He set out of his little home in Kabir Lane, and by the time he turned the corner at Market Road, he always found some odd

job coming his way. Today a very peculiar task offered itself as he sat
near the Market Fountain." When the central character of "A Breath
of Lucifer" (who has temporarily lost his sight) is taken out of his familiar space, the experience is traumatic. In this sense, the audience for
Narayan is immediate. He is concerned with the Indian reader, and not
with the international public – there is no need for him to assume that
the village or the small town might be unknown to his audience.

At the same time, Narayan cherishes the larger dimension of his
world: "All I can say is that [Malgudi] is imaginary and not to be
found on any map (although the University of Chicago has published
a literary atlas with a map of India indicating the location of Malgudi).
If I explain that Malgudi is a small town in South India I shall only be
expressing a half-truth, for the characteristics of Malgudi seem to me
universal" (Narayan 1972: ix). "I can detect Malgudi characters even
in New York," he adds: "for instance, West Twenty-third Street, where
I have lived for months at a time off and on since 1959, possesses
every element of Malgudi, with its landmarks and humanity remaing-
ing unchanged – the drunk lolloing on the steps of the synagogue, the
shop sign announcing in blazing letters *Everything in this store must
go within a week. Fifty per cent off on all items*, the barber, the dentist,
the lawyer and the specialist in fishing hooks, tackle and rods, the five-
and-ten and the delicatessen ... – all are there as they were, with an air
of unshaken permanence and familiarity" (Narayan 1972: ix).

The function of this "local" treatment of space is threefold. It gener-
ates for the reader or for the audience a background against which
they can perceive the events, for that background is at the same time
familiar and different. It creates a setting for the story which is sufficiently confined for the tale to unfold in its entirety, and sufficiently
abstract for the reader not to be distracted by the arrangement, nor
for the story-teller to be tempted to indulge in description. Finally, it is
essential because it connects with the space of the story-teller himself.
If we remember the ritual which Narayan conjured up in his portrayal
of story-tellers, if we remember the village audience sitting, listening to
the story-teller, we can see how the mention of space, in its recognizable topography (the streets of Malgudi), in its familiar abstraction (the
bungalow, the shop), in its remote proximity, immediately connects the
physical world where the audience has sat with the story-teller, to the
world of the story. The mention of space at the beginning of the stories
is a form of narrative shifter that leads the audience into a fictional
world. And the tension between the imaginary and the real, between

the familiar and the abstract, between the close and the remote comes to define the work of fiction in the tale, and hence in the short story. Fiction generates a hesitation in the reader, for whom space is both immediate and distant, singular and generic, recognizable and strange. It would be wrong to read Narayan's stories as documents on the life of a small south Indian town, but it would be equally wrong to view them as pure invention disconnected from any kind of reality. Their purity springs from their ability to make the reader sit with the village audience to listen to the story-teller or marvel at the Talkative Man's musical past (Narayan 1947: 134), only to remember Malgudi while walking down the streets of New York.

UNDER THE BANYAN TREE

There are privileged places for the telling of a story, at privileged times: tales are narrated "to everyone in childhood by the mother or the grandmother, says Narayan, in a cosy corner of the house when the day's tasks are done and the lamps are lit" (Narayan 2001: 466). They can be enacted at full moon by the children in the village. But stories are told, as exemplified by the title of a collection of stories, which takes its title in turn from the last story in the collection, "under the banyan tree."

The village where the story is set lies out of the way. It is small, not very well looked after: Narayan describes it as "a village to make the heart of a rural reformer sink" (Narayan 1985: 187), (the irony being directed, of course, not at the village, but at the rural reformer). The squalor with which it is enveloped is probably not noticed by the population because of an enchanter, a story-teller who has lived through the ages. The story-teller is the main character of the story, and Narayan portrays him as he did the story-tellers of the preface to *Gods, Demons and Others*. Of course the story-teller is illiterate, and Narayan explains the process simply: "he could make up a story, in his head, at the rate of one a month; each story took nearly ten days to narrate" (Narayan 1985: 187). He lives in the temple, thereby testifying to the link between story-telling and religion in India. His days are spent by the temple, under the banyan tree, which is the point of focus for him and for the villagers: "the banyan shade served as a clubhouse for the village folk" (Narayan 1985: 188).

The ritual of story-telling is conjured up. Narayan juxtaposes the description of the ritual for worship on Friday evenings with the evocation of the arrangements for story-telling: "On the nights he had a story to tell he lit a small lamp and placed it in a niche in the trunk of the banyan tree" (188). The story-teller himself meditates inside the temple before moving to his audience, and at the end of a story, "the whole gathering went into the sanctum and prostrated before the Goddess" (188). The world conjured up by the story-teller is one inhabited by ancient kings, in ancient times, in ancient capitals. Part of the skill, or the magic, of the story-telling lies precisely in the story-teller's ability to construct space: "Opening thus, the old man went on without a pause for three hours. By then brick by brick the palace of the king was raised. The old man described the dazzling durbar hall where sat a hundred vassal kings, ministers, and subjects; in another part, ..." (Narayan 1985: 189). In the evocation of these scenes, Narayan concentrates on the members of the audience, on their reactions and participation, on their involvement in "that world which was created under the banyan tree" (189). Stories are more than a recreation, and the craft of the story-teller is essential to its life. The space that the story-teller inhabits is clearly marked in the village and is connected to the sanctuary. It is a meeting place during the day, it is a place of communion of the village in the evening. The banyan tree defines this space, and embodies the ways in which the story-teller is dependent on his audience, on the social structure of the village, as much as he creates the unity of their dreams: "The villagers laughed with Nambi, they wept with him, they adored the heroes, cursed the villains, groaned when the conspirator had his initial success, and they sent up to the gods a heartfelt prayer for a happy ending" (Narayan 1985: 189).

One day, as those who have read the story will never forget, the man loses his inspiration, loses his memory, loses his voice. The world of the story-teller which was at a great distance from everyday life, which was beyond the reach of time, has suddenly succumbed to the dictates of time: "For the first time he realized that he was old" (Narayan 1985: 190). And realizing that he has been deserted by divine inspiration, that there is no use struggling, he decides to tell his greatest story yet, the story of the story-teller who stops speaking: "the rest of his life was one great consummate silence" (192).

This story captures the essential moments of story-telling. It suggests divine inspiration or a link to the deity; it stages the social relevance of stories and the essential relation between the story-teller and the village; it conjures up the enchantment of the audience without which there is no story-telling; it shows, in this man for whom "the written word was a mystery," the powerful nature of orality; it evokes the ability of stories to build dreams. Hence the discreet but tragic end that confronts the end of stories and the beginning of silence. Once the story-teller has stopped talking there is nothing left but the empty repetition of the rituals of daily life: at first, "when he felt hungry he walked into any house that caught his fancy and joined the family at dinner" (Narayan 1985: 188), but now "when he felt hungry he walked into any cottage and silently sat down for food, and walked away the moment he had eaten" (Narayan 1985: 192).

♦

Narayan's stories rely on the figure of the story-teller, who is forever discreet, signals his presence on occasion, and takes centre stage only when he is about to fall forever into silence. This indirectness suggests the necessarily elusive character of story-telling, the difficulty in analyzing it, the impossibility of providing a theory. Narayan's story-teller informs all of his story-writing: the short stories are akin to oral tales, or rather they suggest the importance of orality. But they are obviously written stories, in which the author does not stand in awe of the written word.

The story-teller inhabits a space which is the condition for story-telling to take place, because story-telling is a ritual. At the same time, the condition necessary for his story-telling to be efficient, performative, is to build the space where the story will take place. And if this is an accurate analysis of the role of the story-teller in the short story "Under the Banyan Tree," it is also a reflection on the workings of the stories of Narayan himself.

So that we are back to tropes and territories, where the territory of the short story, in Narayan's works, is marked by shade. It is a place of rest, a place of shelter from the rain, a place of meditation, but also a social place, the clubhouse of the village, before turning, in the evening, into a place of magic and enchantment. And this is where, I suspect, lies the mystery of Narayan's stories, not in the complex workings of a theory of writing, but in the simplicity of the space they inhabit, under the banyan tree.

NOTES

1   Such films, such romance as these films present, are more than inad-
    equate descriptions of the realities not only of India, but of colonialism:
    "The Raj concept seems to be just childish nonsense, indicating a glam-
    orized, romanticized period piece, somewhat phoney. The Briton did not
    come to India for his health or to try on 'crown and jewel.' He came on
    serious business; empire building was no light job" (Narayan 2001: 480).
2   They usually rely on a specific device. "Uncle's Letters" takes the form of
    a collection of letters written by an uncle to his nephew, and the juxtapo-
    sition of the letters defines the irony as well as the passage of time. The
    absorption manifested by the narrator of "At the Portal" who misses a
    meeting because of his fascination for a couple of squirrels requires first-
    person translation of the dialogue between the squirrels.
3   This analysis relies on Walter Benjamin's analysis of the story-teller (Ben-
    jamin 1970).
4   Cf. "Storytellers tend to begin their story with a presentation of the cir-
    cumstances in which they themselves have learned what is to follow, un-
    less they simply pass it off as their own experience" (Benjamin 1970: 91).

WORKS CITED

Benjamin, Walter. "The Story-Teller." In *Illuminations*, trans. Harry Zohn.
    London: Jonathan Cape, 1970.
Chaudhuri, Amit, ed. *The Picador Book of Modern Indian Literature*.
    London: Picador, 2002.
Narayan, R.K. *An Astrologer's Day, and other stories*. London: Eyre &
    Spottiswoode, 1947.
– *Lawley Road and other Stories*. London: Heinemann, 1956.
– *Gods, Demons and Others*. 1965; rpt. London: Vintage, 2001.
– *A Horse and Two Goats and other stories*. London: Bodley Head, 1970.
– *Malgudi Days*. 1972; rpt. London: Heinemann, 1982.
– *Under the Banyan The Banyan Tree and other stories*. 1985; rpt.
    Harmondsworth: Penguin, 1987.
– "After the Raj." In Narayan, *The Writerly Life: Selected Non-fiction*. Ed. S.
    Krishnan. New Delhi: Viking, 2001: 480–83.
– "The Problem of the Indian Writer." In Narayan, *Writerly Life*: 457–63.
– "When India was a colony." In Narayan, *Writerly Life*: 469–79.

READING PRACTICES:
TROPES, TERRITORY,
TEXTUALITY

CHRISTINE LORRE

The Tropes and Territory of Childhood in The Lagoon and Other Stories by Janet Frame

In an essay entitled "Beginnings," Janet Frame explains how she opted for "this imaginary world whose characters were drawn from objects and people I met in my daily life, with occasional intrusion of characters from fiction" (44–45). It gradually appeared to her that "that world" – the world of the imagination, dreams, and words, the world of art – was the only possible alternative to her inability to cope with "this world" – the material world of real life, which to Frame also meant the isolating and imprisoning world of the mental hospital. She has described her writing as a way of "making designs from [her] dreams" ("Beginnings" 46), thus delineating a poetics of reverie, of the ethereal, but her stories also have remarkable power to evoke the real world, as many of her readers have pointed out. The New Zealand novelist Barbara Anderson remembers when she read *The Lagoon*, Frame's first short story collection, shortly after it came out in 1951, when Anderson was living in Swanmore in England. She considers Frame as the writer "who put the real world into a book" – and by "the real world" Anderson means "the real world nobody knew anything about in Swanmore but me. A country of childhood shared by millions but never before given the authority and permanence of print" (107, 108). One may be tempted to infer from Anderson's statement that Frame's stories are realistic, and her writing mimetic,[1] but her stories are not evocative of the real world for New Zealanders only. The Canadian critic W.H. New observes that Frame's stories "stir recognition across boundary lines ... because her words have shadows. Because, repeatedly, the shadows take you back to the rippled slate pools of private memory, and guide you to the edge that still stands there, undercover, in the middle of the dark pool" ("Glimpses" 40, 41–42). Anderson's and New's comments suggest that Frame's stories tap into the archetypal material of the Jungian journey, the mythical dimension of dreams and fantasies from which tropes referring to a collective unconscious are developed, and at the same time graft a specific culture onto that material, thus appropriating a language, and defining an imaginary territory that will have particular resonance for readers personally familiar with Frame's background.

In Frame's first collection, children are the privileged explorers of uncharted territories,[2] whether a new beach, new words, the past, or the world of adults – the "childhood stories" of the collection are among Frame's most luminous, epitomizing as they do her enterprise of making new beginnings with language.[3] They are also part of a "persistence of the child's point of view in New Zealand writing," to quote Lydia Wevers, which has been functioning as a metaphor for a relation of dependence to the parent culture, and in Frame's writing in particular marks "a recognition of difference" which foregrounds her subsequent work (281). As for the genre of the short story, it has been suggested, to quote Wevers again, that "short fiction is peculiarly marked and characterized by cultural preference, that its very brevity speaks for the absence of other, larger certainties, encoding the problematic context of colonial and post-colonial literatures" (245). This was particularly true of the early 1950s, when *The Lagoon* was published, a period marked in New Zealand by gradual progress in the transition from literary and cultural dependence to increased independence.

This paper will focus on a selection of short stories from *The Lagoon* told from the viewpoint of child narrators or narrators looking back at childhood, and its aim is to examine, in Gaston Bachelard's terms, the "dynamics of the imagination" at work in these narratives, by studying the "links between original complexes and cultural complexes."[4] In other words, the point is to show how Frame captures both a sense of the place where she grew up – "place" including how people *relate* to place through the whole complex of what amounts to their culture – and the emotions of childhood, which are often associated with a place. She especially relies on the potential of tropes to transport us to a different place, a different time of one's life. In classic rhetorical theory, tropes – from the Greek word for "turn" – are "rhetorical figures in which words are used in a way different from their standard or literal usage to mean something else" (Harvey 647), the two main tropes being metaphor and metonymy, and other tropic figures including irony.[5] But contemporary theoreticians insist on the dynamics at work in the making of tropes, and which Bachelard already underlined. Thus Barthes, when writing about metaphor, focuses on "transport": "no matter what meaning is conveyed, no matter what the terms of the journey are; what counts – and what creates a metaphor – is *the transport itself.*"[6] In a more general sense, the word trope is also used to mean a figure or motif. The following study will focus on territory, first in a literal sense, through the study of landscape tropes, and secondly in a more figurative sense through the study of tropes that have to do with culture and history, that is to say how one relates to place. The third and last part of the development will step back and consider the impact of tropes on the stories as narrative units, from a stylistic and generic viewpoint.

REVISITING FAMILIAR LANDSCAPE TROPES

Like other countries that used to be part of the British Empire, New Zealand has often relied on its original landscapes and its native fauna and flora in asserting an identity of its own, while trying to loosen the colonial bond to the metropolis. In literature, especially, these markers, beyond their literal, referential value, have become motifs, also called tropes, for the country as a separate entity, to the point of becoming conventions. Harry Orsman and Roger Robinson mention the opening paragraph of Katherine Mansfield's "At the Bay," which establishes an unmistakably New Zealand setting for its English readers, as an example of conventional characterization through native flora and local language: "Very early morning. The sun was not yet risen, and the whole of Crescent Bay was hidden under a white sea-mist. The big *bush-covered hills* at the back were smothered. You could not see where they ended and the *paddocks* and bungalows began ... [T]he silvery, fluffy *toi-toi* was limp on its long stalks, and all the marigolds and the pinks in the bungalow gardens were bowed to the earth with wetness."[7] Because these motifs present the risk of remaining clichés signifying a New Zealand setting, their treatment has come to represent a challenge for writers.

In Frame's collection of stories, motifs referring to New Zealand landscapes – the omnipresent bush, the beach, the eponymous lagoon – represent such points of entry into a specific world, and Frame uses these liminal spaces – between land and sea, between nature and culture – as entries into her own imagined New Zealand topography. But while relying on these motifs, she also turns them away from their literal meaning towards the world of her imagination, thus expanding trope beyond its value as conventional motif, making it a creative metaphor.[8] The analysis in this section will approach several tropes by focusing on their semantic functioning as words in two narratives, "Swans" and "The Lagoon."[9]

The trope of the beach is a central one in "Swans." The word "beach" evokes first of all the seaside as "a place of enjoyment or recreation" (Orsman 38) and stands for amusement, family, other children to play with, "merry-go-rounds and swings and slides" (Frame, *The Lagoon* 59). Thus "the Beach" is anticipated by the Mother and her two small daughters as the goal of a family outing, a scene of familiar socializing between mothers and their children, an extension of the secure environment of the home, in which mothers and fathers know how to bring comfort. But this is a new beach, one they have never been to before (the word is capitalized), and it is a weekday, so they are the only ones going there, which seems strange. The mother is confused about whether the beach they go to is the right one, and whether she has followed the father's instructions correctly. Unfamiliar sounds, as opposed to familiar sights, add to the prevailing puzzlement, and the children are "eager to turn the desolate crying sound of sea to the more comforting and near sight of long green and white waves coming and going for ever on the sand" (58–59). The trope of the beach, both familiar (as a place) and strange (the new "Beach"), thus fulfils its role, on a figurative level, and in the characters' minds, as "a conventional site on which competing forces fight for power"[10]; in this case the struggle is the personal one of a child: it opposes antagonistic impulses of confident joy and fear, between which the narrator keeps wavering. When first seen, the sea turns out to be "true sea" (59), presenting the familiar signs of a friendly sea to play at: white on the sand, seagulls, shells, seaweed, a crab. Doubt creeps back in when the children can't find the usual places to undress and get ice-creams: "It was the wrong sea" (60). But the seaweed the children are used to play with makes up for that: "So it was all right really, it was a good sea ... They felt proud. It was a distinguished sea, oh and a lovely one, noisy in your ears and green and blue and brown where the seaweed floated. Whales? Sharks? Seals? It was the right kind of sea" (61). Doubts about whether the sea is the right or the wrong one are dismissed, in a gesture which mimics the mother's constantly stated confidence that "things would be all

right, ... as if she knew, and she did know too, Mother knew always"
(55). On unfamiliar ground, the Mother acts as a role model, even
though she too doubts whether this is the right place, and even though
the adult narrator's voice is heard making a momentary reservation
about the mother's certainty ("as if she knew"). The precariousness
of the beach as a cultural construct imposed on nature is reflected in
the felt fragility of the world of childhood and its ephemeral security.
Doubts about the meaning of this trope (as motif) paves the way for
further elaboration of meaning.

    At the end of the day, the mother and her daughters go back to the
station the quicker way, walking across the lagoon over a strip of land.
In contrast with the beach and its endless activity, the lagoon is a place
for reflection. A liminal space between sea and land, it is a location of
mystery and ambivalence: it evokes the dark unknown of the future,
the sense of loss that is foreshadowed, and yet an impression of peace
prevails. The exploration of a different beach, familiar yet strange, the
day's adventure into the unknown, in which the children try to identify familiar bearings, add up to an experience in growing up, and the
children feel secure walking across, accompanied as they are by the
comforting presence of their mother. The beach is where discovery is
played out – the discovery of familiar elements as well as of new ones.
But the lagoon, as a bridge between the new Beach and home (via the
train station), is a symbolic space where the new experience is taken
in with confidence, a temporary bridge between childhood and adult-
hood, where the sense of loss that the adult narrator experiences later
is foreshadowed.

    The trope of the lagoon is charged with figurative meaning, and
the eponymous swans which inhabit it act as the instruments of the
narrator's final epiphany. The birds appear as the children and their
mother cross the lagoon:

> It was dark black water, secret, and the air was filled with mur-
> murings and rustlings, it was *as if* they were walking into another
> world that had been kept secret from everyone and now they had
> found it. The darkness lay massed across the water and over to
> the east, thick *as if* you could touch it, soon it would swell and
> fill the earth ... They looked across the lagoon then and saw the
> swans, black and shining, *as if* the visiting dark tiring of its form
> had changed to birds, hundreds of them resting and moving softly
> about on the water. Why, the lagoon was filled with swans, *like*

secret sad ships, secret and quiet ... no other sound but the shaking of rushes and far away now it seemed the roar of the sea *like* a
secret sea that had crept inside your head for ever. And the swans,
they were there too, inside you, peaceful and quiet, watching and
sleeping and watching, there was nothing but peace and warmth
and calm, everything found, train and sea and Mother and Father
and earwig and slater and spider. (64)

As the family crosses the lagoon, various images appear. Three of
them are introduced by "as if" (italicized in the passage quoted),
which establishes a relation of similitude ("as") immediately made
hypothetical, indeterminate ("if"), like something that might or could
be, something imagined. Two more images are introduced by "like"
("like secret sad ships," "like a secret sea"), which establishes a tighter
relation of similitude. The final image is not introduced by a connector but establishes a direct relation of contiguity between the narrator
and the swans, as well as with the reader, through the second person
address: "And the swans, they were there too, inside you ..." The narrator thus retraces the process of how a trope emerges to capture the
elusiveness of a memorable moment of childhood. The swans stand as
a metonymy for the experience taken in that day, the mixed feelings of
confidence and doubt, joy and fear, discovery and mystery. As ships,
they figure the outward journey, but they are ships safely harboured
in the lagoon, close to home, along the strip of land that links up sea
to land, beach to home. The swans stayed "inside you" as a luminous
memory of the feeling of having gone beyond the limits of the familiar world of childhood, into the unknown, and headed back, feeling
enlarged. The tropes of the beach (as motif), of the lagoon and of the
swans (as metaphor) overlap, and the motif of the beach finds itself
revitalized through this contiguity.

Because of the mythical associations they convey, the swans also
have the value of symbol. But the meaning they convey is renewed
through inversion – they are black, not white. They contrast with the
standard associations of light, sun, gracefulness, and purity of the symbolic white swans which are found in Western culture, and as actual
birds, in the Northern Hemisphere. The associations brought up by
the antipodean black swans are an inversion of those the Northern
Hemisphere white swans evoke: as peaceful observers, the black swans
bring together the light and the dark sides of the mind, feelings of
touching upon the uncharted territory of the uncanny while being on

seemingly familiar ground. As a central figure of the story, they result from the rewriting of the symbol of the (white) swan, which is also a symbol for the poet and the force of poetry. A quiet, darker, powerful poetry is at work where the (black) swans live.

The title story, "The Lagoon," takes up the motif of the lagoon as liminal space between land and sea from a different angle from "Swans," because the adult narrator shifts back and forth between present and past. The opening paragraph is a poetic description of the lagoon by the narrator's grandmother that hints at the mystery of the past. Although the grandmother is later characterized as a story-teller, she never tells her granddaughter the story of the lagoon. The latter hears it years later, after the grandmother's death, during a visit to Picton relatives. She then hears from her aunt that her great-grandmother, the Maori princess, pushed her unfaithful husband into the lagoon, drowning him. The telling of this story strengthens the female lineage all the way back to the Maori great-grandmother. This continuity is reflected in the opening and closing paragraphs of the story: the grandmother's words which the story opens with are faithfully echoed at the end in her granddaughter's voice, which by then has taken over: "At low tide there is no lagoon. Only a stretch of dirty grey sand" (7). And this same voice – remembering play, quoting children's words – closes the story, or rather, leaves it open: "I remember we used to skim thin white stones over the water and catch tiddlers in the little creek near by and make sand castles. This is my castle, we said, you be Father I'll be Mother and we'll live here and catch crabs and tiddlers for ever ..." (7). By the end of the story the narrator has appropriated her grandmother's voice, giving it a new direction by adding her own memories of the lagoon to the narration, adding another layer of history to the land, on which children's ephemeral sandcastles are the most permanent construction. At the same time, the introduction of the Maori princess character has echoes of fairy tales at least as much as it has historical value as far as family history is concerned. The motif of the Maori princess is part of the romantic and fabulous world imagined by Pakeha writers in their retelling of Maori myths and legends in the late nineteenth and early twentieth centuries.[11] The appearance of this motif indicates that Frame's narrator is unreliable, especially since her aunt is also an unreliable narrator who, having told the two versions of how the grandfather drowned – one the official record of an accident, the other the family lore of a murder of passion – admits her preference for the latter. The fact that the aunt and her niece have been looking at family pictures adds to the atmosphere of family legend being imposed onto mute images that cannot speak for themselves. The mingling of voices, in Bakhtinian polyphonic fashion, and the narrator's implicit reservations about the truthfulness of the story reported by her aunt, are echoed in her question: "Was it my aunt speaking or was it my grandmother or my great-grandmother who loved a white lace dress?" (7). By establishing a genealogy that is part legend, the narrator inscribes her feelings of belonging in subjective rather than historical discourse, suggesting none the less that the former may be as valid as the latter, if not more so.

The accumulation of family history anchored in a specific landscape reflects the changes that affect the land over time. The Picton of the "grandmother who could cut supple-jack and find kidney fern and make a track through the thickest part of the bush" (1) is an image of the settler dominating the bush, but is none the less a rewriting of colonial history, the settler being female, history becoming her-story in the process. In contrast with that period, the new Picton is less wild and has been taken over by people. The lagoon is where the narrator comes back to take stock of these changes and of time passing, to link up with relatives and family stories. In other words, the Picton lagoon acts as her *turangawaewae* – in Maori, literally, "a place for the feet to stand," a place where she can stand on her own two feet because she belongs to this piece of land which reflects her history, her identity.[12] She feels she belongs, as did her grandmother, and when her grandmother died, "all the Maoris at the Pa came to her funeral" (1). But the forms of belonging, like the land, have changed, for the Maoris too, most of whom have gone from the Pa, the Maori village.[13] They don't sing Maori songs anymore, but imported American old favourites such as "You are my sunshine" and "South of the Border." Cultural intermingling is at work, which is reflected in the land through the mingling of native and non-native plants: "there was gorse mixed up with the bush" (4). The trope of the eponymous lagoon, a fluctuating space, reflects the ephemerality of land occupation: land appears and disappears, generations of children come and go, including those nurtured on British children's literature – "Christopher Robins with sand between the toes" (6) – and words also vanish, be they English or Maori: after the 1960s, the Pa of the grandmother's days would have been talked of as marae, a different kind of Maori village in different times. By mingling the motif of the tidal lagoon with the openness of story-telling, the narrator inscribes herself as a recorder of change in the landscape.

Landscape tropes are central in "The Lagoon" and "Swans." Their significance raises questions and doubts, yet without a destabilizing effect: displacement occurs through shifts in the meaning of words, but the protagonists' organic link to the landscape is not challenged, unlike their cultural relation to place.

CULTURE, HISTORY AND IRONY

Landscape tropes are used by Frame as a springboard into a redefinition of a sense of place, a process of rewriting in which the colonial past becomes a palimpsest, a layer of history. The redefinition of the relation to place is also done through a revitalization of language based on tropes having to do with culture and history, which are two dimensions of one's relation to place. The following section aims to examine some of the ways in which Frame performs this revitalization. It focuses on tropes and the semantics of discourse, that is to say how tropes participate in a system of meaning with the text as whole (Ricoeur 87–128). The analysis will consider how dead metaphors inherited from British culture are treated ironically by Frame in "Miss Gibson – and the Lumber-Room"; how phrases are appropriated and revitalized by children, becoming fresh metaphors in "My Cousins – Who Could Eat Cooked Turnips"; and how, in "A Note on the Russian War," tropes fail to turn words away from their meaning, because history cannot be ignored.

"Miss Gibson – and the Lumber-Room" consists of a hypothetical letter that a former student, just turned twenty-one, writes to Miss Gibson, the eponymous school-teacher, to confess an old lie. Years before, having been read, as a model, the story of a man's "thoughts on entering the old lumber-room" (132), the schoolgirls were asked by Miss Gibson to write an essay on that theme. With the trope of the lumber-room as starting-point and stimulus for the imagination, the girl narrator wrote an essay amounting to a series of romanticized, upper-class British cultural stereotypes, because what passed as an exercise of the imagination was in fact an exercise in mimicry the girls were asked to perform. And because, as Homi Bhabha points out, "Mimicry *repeats* rather than *re-presents*" ("Of Mimicry" 88), the result was not a representation of the world of the girl narrator, but a fake, dishonest contemplative fancy. The girl's essay reads as an ironical caricature of what has been called pathetic fallacy, "disclos[ing] the ambivalence of colonial discourse" and "also disrupt[ing] its authority," to quote

Bhabha again (88). Through this essay, which verges on parody, the authority of the teacher, the imagination-deprived representative of official culture, is undermined. The pathetic fallacy of the essay mirrors the decay of metaphor – not only the specific metaphor of the lumber-room, but also of metaphor as a rhetorical and poetic device. This phenomenon can be dated back to the first half of the nineteenth century, according to Paul Ricoeur, by which time metaphor had become reduced to "a mere ornament."[14] The term "pathetic fallacy," first used by John Ruskin in 1856 in a negative way, testifies to a similar distaste at that time for predictable tropes, in which human feelings are ascribed to the inanimate.

In "Miss Gibson," the irony is based on the fact that the metonymy of the (British upper-class) lumber-room fails to be revitalized through appropriation by a local (poor colonial) speaker and becomes even more of a dead trope. Going by Pierre Fontanier's definition, metonymies, or "tropes by correspondence," "consist in the designation of an object through the name of another object which, like the first one, makes a completely separate unit, but which owes the first object, or to which the second object itself owes more or less, either for its existence, or for its way of being."[15] In the metonymy of the lumber-room, the correspondence between the lumber-room and the memories of the past does not function because the second term of the metonymy (the memories) does not "owe anything" to the first term, in fact the second term does not have a referent – the girl declares triumphantly at the end of her letter, "and Miss Gibson, if you really want to know, we didn't even have a lumber-room" (136). Eventually, revitalization of language is achieved, not through correspondence, but through rupture with dead (supposedly poetic) tropes imported from (and imposed by) the "mother country." In this case, metonymy completely fails to perform its rhetorical trick.

The girl's subsequent vehemence, years later, in confessing the lies that she had written shows her urge to reject the fake culture imposed on her – even though her mimicry was so blatant that her schoolteacher judged the story "highly improbable" (135). The only way out for the grown-up girl, "a sort of student at university" (135), is through a radically different form of writing, and the antidote to dead metonymies is found in reducing the gap between signifier and signified as much as possible, through a prose as bare as can be. This writing, first, needs to be honest, to dispose of previous fake writing through negations, and to replace the cultural pretenses with genuine culture:

"I didn't have a sleeping doll, only a rag one ... and all I read at six years old was *My Favourite Comic, Terry and Trixie of the Circus, Rin-Tin-Tin the Wonder Dog* ... and even later all I read was *Bunch of the Boarding School, the Sneak of the Fourth, The Princess Prefect,* anyway it wasn't Shakespeare" (135–36). Secondly, it is writing that deals with reality in a direct, unadorned way. The world of childhood is immediate and doesn't call for elaborate (and inadequate) tropes imported from another place to stand between the world, the writer, and the reader. The urgency of the final passage gives it the freshness of truth and life, and contrasts with the stiltedness of dead tropes: "I had a little place to live in. I had a mother who cooked for us, and she cooked nicely too, and my father dug the garden in the weekend, and he planted pansies, ... and I liked being alive and I didn't care twopence about the past it was the present that mattered" (136). The simplicity and concision of the description, the child-like breathlessness of the prose, the immediacy of the present time and space for the child, all have a liberating effect on the writing – and the writer. It is only when lies have been confessed that a beginner's fresh, lively prose can be inscribed. However, one can equally doubt the truthfulness of this account, which after all sounds too perfectly innocent to be true, especially when coming from a narrator who identifies herself from the start as a liar, and whose status is subsequently ill-defined ("a sort of student").[16] The story leaves the reader with the impression that it is a delusion on the protagonist's part to believe that an entirely fresh start is possible; one's past does have to be reckoned with.

As in "Miss Gibson – and the Lumber-Room," the narrative dynamic of "My Cousins – Who Could Eat Cooked Turnips" is based on the distance between two different worlds, but it doesn't end in rupture and the dismissal of dead tropes. The opening sentence, "For a long time, I couldn't understand my cousins in Invercargill" (41), sets out an opposition between two worlds, two families, "they" and "us," and takes the reader into the familiar situation of parents and their children on a week-end visit to relatives. The manners of the narrator's family are cruder and ruder than those of her cousins' family who, to put it in a nutshell, "were Cultured" (42). Mavis and Dot are two clean, polite, refined children, whose ways contrast with the rougher Bill, Elsie, and Nancy, the narrator. The trope of the cooked, as opposed to raw, turnips contained in the story title sums up these differences. Nancy and her siblings couldn't eat cooked turnip: "we didn't eat it at all, and we didn't like it, it didn't seem to have the good earthy taste raw turnip had, and we weren't eating it outside the garden with the cow looking approval over the fence and ... everything being alive and natural and uncooked" (43). It is hard to resist pointing out that the raw and cooked turnips binary trope anticipates so precisely the same metaphoric binary terms used by Claude Lévi-Strauss in his *The Raw and the Cooked*, first published in French in 1964, to express the transition from nature to culture. Nancy and her siblings are first intimidated by their cousins' ways, and this cultural gap is unbridged by language for a long while: "we didn't ever talk to our cousins" (44). They see Auntie Dot's house as "an alien world ... all so sad and strange" (45). Although the garden is slightly more appealing than the house, with a swing and "nice trellis-work too, with dunny roses growing up it" (41), the children are so uncomfortable at first that they want to go home. Their feeling of alienation comes not from the geographical distance – one may presume the narrator's family also lives in the South Island of Frame's childhood, where Invergargill is – but from socio-cultural differences.

Something changes when the children do end up eating cooked turnip, like their more civilized cousins. By adopting similar manners, they begin to share the same code, and words start flowing, bringing Nancy and Mavis together. They share words and mimic adult talk, sociability, and formulaic politeness: "And we played house together, Mavis and I, and we drank tea out of little china cups, and we said really is that so just fancy, and we swung, all day we swung as high as the dunny roses" (47). What are supposedly exclamations of surprise have been turned by adults into formulas of marked (polite) interest in someone else's speech, as the absence of punctuation and the effect of accumulation suggest ("really is that so just fancy"). When used by the two cousins, these clichés are appropriated and become words free to transport new meaning, eventually acting as a metaphor for the two girls' delayed but genuine joy at being together. They may thus be seen as metaphor at its purest, if one bears in mind Roland Barthes's understanding of that word: "no matter what meaning is conveyed, no matter what the terms of the journey are; what counts – and what creates a metaphor – is *the transport itself*." The two cousins start understanding each other when they find a common language which projects them beyond their usual one. The possibilities offered to them by play-acting, mimicking adults, and finding new meaning for words, open up onto a new friendship, a feeling of increased confidence in themselves, and a sense of freedom to explore the larger world – that of adults and other children. Culture, through the tropes of the cooked turnips or the polite words, stops being simply an odd and intimidating ornament and turns into a set of codes and manners through which the child narrator relates to the world and to others.

"A Note on the Russian War," like the two stories examined already, is based on the opposition between two worlds and deals with the complex links between culture and emotions, but the latter are approached from a different angle: the story reads like a tale imagined by a child, but in which the adult narrator's voice cannot help interfering, a fantasy vainly trying to keep the reality of war at bay, a song helplessly attemping to cover undesirable sounds. The narration is based entirely on a strategy of diversion which relies on tropes: the title introduces the narrative as a historical commentary or thought ("a note"), but the story turns out to be a childhood narration. Similarly, the announced "Russian War" turns out to be neither Russian nor war. This strategy of diversion is based on the faith that tropes should have the power to turn words away from their meaning, but it fails, and the narrator eventually has to acknowledge that some realities stand beyond the power of words and cannot be denied or alleviated.

The narrative opens with an insistent characterization of the setting, the Russian Steppes, where sensuous memories of childhood are located. The word "war" slips into a sentence early on, almost unnoticed, without, in this first occurrence, inflecting the sense of the sentence or diminishing the joy it conveys: "we went outside under the trees to sing a Russian song, it went like this, I'm singing it to myself so you can't hear, tra-tra-tra, something about sunflowers and a tall sky and *the war* rolling through the grass, tra-tra-tra, it was a very nice song we sang" (137–38, italics mine). Another subsequent main false note in the narration is contained in the words of the mother, which sound incoherent, or at least follow a disrupted logic, as if adult talk didn't quite make sense: "There are no lands outside, they are fenced inside us, a fence of being and we are the world, my mother told, we are Russian because we have this sunflower in our garden" (138). The narrator then reasserts her control over the narration by regressing to the viewpoint of a child, which is clearly marked by her physical size: "[the sunflower] was too tall for us to see properly, the daisies were nearer our size" (138). The world of childhood is depicted as seen from a child's perspective, and time is the psychological time of children, of seemingly endless days, a feeling conveyed by the anaphoric repetition of "All day on the lawn, we made daisy chains ... All day on the lawn, don't you remember ..." (138). It is the time of the experience of the senses: "we made daisy chains and buttercup chains, sticking our teeth through the bitter stems ... don't you remember the smell of [the new white daisies]" (138), vividly brought back to memory through the second person mode of address.

When war arrives, its dramatic connotations are muffled. Although the word "War" is capitalized, as if in a newspaper headline, or as if stressed for emphasis by adults gravely discussing the matter among themselves, it appears as the natural, seasonal follow-up to the days of joy previously evoked: "And then out of the spring and summer days the War came" (139), thus being part of a natural chain of events. Its dramatic potential is further deflated in the following sentence: "An ordinary war ..."; no uppercase letter this time, and no principal verb in this sentence, as if the tone were casual. This war is tamed by being compared to other wars known through history lessons – "like the Hundred Years or the Wars of the Roses" – or through family history – "or the Great War where my father went and sang Tipperary" (139). But that is yet another false note in the narration of a happy childhood, which causes a shift in the narrative voice, from the voice of the child to that of the adult narrator, marked by the rewriting of the last sentence on the Great War to introduce a self-correction: "All of the soldiers on my father's side sang Tipperary, it was to show they were getting some-where, and the louder they sang it the more sure they felt about getting there. And the louder they sang it the more scared they felt inside" (139). The repetition ("and the louder they sang it") and the contradic-tion it introduces ("the surer they felt" / "the more scared they felt") dismisses the rhetoric of war which then prevailed, based on the utter confidence in the power of the Empire. The soldiers' song, with lyrics about going home, is meant to dispel fear, like the children's "Russian song"; the story, as a "note," mirrors the dynamics of the soldiers' sing-ing and its attempt at turning away from fear, and turning fear away. But the memory of the wartime songs and the fear they vainly tried to dispel impose themselves, hushing the sound of the children's Rus-sian song to a quiet "tra-tra-tra" by the closure of the story. By then, the notion of war has been erased from the child narrator's imaginary country of Russia, but not from real life, the setting of which can now firmly be identified with Frame's South Island, signaled earlier by the "cow-byre" (138),[17] and where the two World Wars felt both remote and close. The diversion at play in the narrative reflects a dual attitude towards war in the first half of the twentieth century: on the one hand, the strong feeling of patriotism of New Zealand and of Empire, and on the other hand, the experiencè and memory of the horrors endured in the worst of battles.[18] But the narrator's strategy of diversion through tropes ("the Russian song") fails to eliminate war from life.

In the three stories examined, Frame relies on tropes to redirect the meaning of words and challenge various aspects of New Zealand culture, mostly in terms of its link to British culture. Literature and writing, manners and language, and the perspective on history have all been under colonial influence, and Frame casts a fresh look at these various ways of thinking of oneself, whether ironically or with controlled emotion. But tropes have even deeper impact on her stories.

THE POETICS OF TROPES AND FRAMES

It is striking that at the beginning and the end of most of the childhood stories of *The Lagoon*, a recurring trope appears, framing the narrative – this pattern can be observed in all of the stories analyzed in this paper.[19] These tropes signal boundaries which delimit the circumscribed world of childhood, the feeling of security associated with it, and at the same time the sense of its being on the edge of the larger world, the presence of which is suggested by a slight evolution, a subtle change that is marked between the first and the second occurrence of the trope. This narrative structure is also at work in *Owls Do Cry*, Frame's first novel, in some chapters which may be read as poems.[20] I would like to focus on the impact of this pattern on the short stories as narrative units.

In several stories, the second term of the frame – the second occurrence of the trope – opens up the story and has a liberating effect, conveying a feeling of the protagonists' having grown up and gained self-confidence. In "My Cousins – Who Could Eat Cooked Turnips," the dunny roses in Auntie Dot's backyard frame the story. At first they appear as a decorative element in Auntie Dot's garden: "They had a nice trellis-work too, with dunny roses growing up it, you *could almost* touch the roses *if* you were swinging high enough" (41, italics mine). Metaphorically, the roses also stand for unaccomplished potential and possibility ("could almost," "if") as the narrator's aspirations are projected onto them. By the end of the story, the narrator has accomplished her hopes (the final sentence is in the performative mode), as the two girl cousins have become friends. The roses then transport new meaning, being associated with the two girls' delayed but genuine joy at being together; Nancy's world has expanded, upwards, towards the sky, as she and Mavis "sw[i]ng as high as the dunny roses" (47).

"Swans" is also about children exploring the larger world. It is framed by Gypsy, the family cat, about whom Totty keeps worrying at the beginning of the story, as the family is ready to leave, because she thinks that she is dying. The cat is a bearing in the child's familiar world, a sign of security, like the insects in the wash-house, and as such, acts as a foil to the black swans. When the family comes back from the beach, the cat is dead. Yet its death doesn't unsettle the feeling of confidence gained from the day and the inclusion of new bearings in the children's world view. It is mentioned as if in afterthought: "And Gypsy? But when they got home Gypsy was dead" (64), and its death is silent proof that the mother does not always know: she was wrong about the cat being all right. On that day the children began learning that adults can also be lost in the world, although they pretend they are not, that the familiar world is not protected from loss, but also that the bigger world need not be feared, but explored.

As in "Swans," the trope which delimits the children's worlds in the story "My Father's Best Suit" also points to adult shortcomings. The trope of the father's suit frames the story, the opening sentence reading: "My father's best suit was light grey and somehow it had got a tear in one of the coat sleeves, and anyhow the pants were threadbare and shiny so my father sent my sister and I down town to get a reel of grey mending cotton" (97). The two sisters go downtown and look in vain for the right coloured thread. In the course of the story, as she remembers this incident, the first-person narrator also recalls how poor the family was at the time, in the days of the Depression, but still, what prevailed was the fun she had with her sister, not through owning things, considered as "ethereal gadgets" (99), but through inventing stories, pretending, playing roles together. The sisters' imagination and friendship is what rescued them from daily hardships. They were inseparable, and the family's difficulties are left behind in the narrator's mind – and on the page – as her memories of endless sisterly play build up and fill up the final passage: "We did plenty of fighting. We had Wars. We wrote in invisible ink with lemon, and we wrote spidery writing with green feathers, and we wrote with the blood of dahlias. And still my father wore his light grey suit on Sundays to the Union meetings" (99). By the end of the narration, the father's "best suit" that "was light grey" has become "his light grey suit." Although it is still the best suit he owns, in fact it is probably the only one he owns, so it cannot really be compared as his "best," and it cannot even be called good anymore either, being so threadbare. The illusion of having something that could be seen as one's best suit has vanished, but in the course of the story the suit has been eclipsed by the vividness of the girls' play and complicity. The trope of the suit delimits the world of childhood, but by the end of the story, this space has been trespassed so that the child's world has expanded, not through venturing very far – the outings are the simple ones of childhood – but rather through the discovery of the kinds of lies that lurk in words taken as absolutes – "My father's *best* suit."

Other framing figures have the effect of hinting at loss, the unreliability of a narrator, or the fragility of memory. In "Miss Gibson – and the Lumber-Room," the motif of the lumber-room is introduced very abruptly by the narrator at the beginning of the story: "It's about the lumber-room" (131). Her tone is that of someone intent on settling accounts and who claims frankness at the end of the story, ending her letter with: "and Miss Gibson, if you really want to know, we didn't even have a lumber-room" (136). The tone of the letter is vindictive and by the end of it the narrator thinks she has the upper hand, but in the process she has revealed herself to be a liar – or perhaps an underconfident writer. "The Lagoon" is framed not by a recurring word, but by a remembered childhood formula: "I remember we used to skim round white stones over the water, and catch tiddlers in the little creek near by, and make sand castles on the edge. This is my castle, we said, you be Father I'll be Mother and we'll live here and catch crabs and tiddlers for ever" (2). It is repeated almost word for word in the closure: "I remember we used to skim thin white stones over the water, and catch tiddlers in the little creek near by, and make sand castles. This is my castle, we said, you be Father I'll be Mother and we'll live here and catch crabs and tiddlers for ever" (7). The slight variations – "thin" instead of "round" stones, the omission of "on the edge" – may hint at the alteration of memory. The three dots instead of a period at the end of the last sentence leave room for the nostalgia of childhood, or the sense of loss left by the death of relatives. Time passes, altering words and people, and yet, overall, within the terms and images that frame the story, the narrator's vivid memories, related in direct speech, make an ephemeral moment of childhood eternal.

The framing tropes of Frame's short stories function almost as chiasmatic figures and evoke Homi Bhabha's words about the volume he edited entitled *Nation and Narration*: "The representative emblem of this book might be a chiasmatic 'figure' of cultural difference whereby the anti-nationalist, ambivalent nation-space becomes the crossroads to a new transnational culture. The 'other' is never outside or beyond us; it emerges forcefully, within cultural discourse, when we think we speak most intimately and indigenously 'between ourselves.'"[21] The framing tropes of Frame's stories are chiasmatic figures of their own sort: the inversion of form which characterizes a chiasmus (*ab … ba*) is replaced by minor alterations in the terms of the framing trope, which leads to a displacement or partial inversion of meaning ("my father's best suit" / "his light grey suit"). The quasi-systematic adoption of this chiasmatic pattern gives a certain unity to the stories, making them poetic. Furthermore, the short length of the stories – three to twelve pages, about six pages on average – contributes to their density. All these elements suggest that the narratives may be considered as much prose poems as short stories.

Although the form of the prose poem is ill-defined, some characteristics can be identified. It is "a composition printed as prose, but distinguished by elements common in poetry, such as elaborately contrived rhythms, figures of speech, rhyme, internal rhyme, assonance, consonance, and startling images" (Cuddon 750–51). The prose poem emerged at the end of the nineteenth century and was part of a general movement toward free verse, as turn-of-the-century Modernists aimed at making art "an intensification of reality" and "wanted meaning to reside in the process of experience," to quote Clive Scott (349). Scott further examines the interplay between prose and poetry in the prose poem, observing that prose is able to "compress many tones, by liberating or challenging the resourcefulness of the voice," while rhythmic means and cadences can "mak[e] the voice full of event, by variation of tone, pitch and speed … Cadences become poetic when we find ourselves regularly returning to a particular one until we feel it controlling our reading; it assumes the proportions of an overseeing will, enveloping the narrative with an aura of absoluteness and depriving it of the capriciousness of a fiction" (350, 352). In Frame's stories, this poetic cadence is achieved by the focus on tropes, the use of repetition, motifs and metaphors that frame and control the narratives.

The context Frame's stories were written in further claims for a poetic reading of them. That period, between 1945 and 1960, was when New Zealand poetry was undergoing a major shift, from being dominated by neo-Romanticism to being influenced by Modernism. In contrast with the neo-Romantic poet, Elizabeth Caffin writes, "the modernist poet ... regards the poem, the creation in words, as an object of interest in itself. The elements of language, sounds, words, phrases, sentences, and all their multifarious possibilities are seen afresh, made new" (457). Bearing in mind these developments, Frame's prose can be seen as a personal poetic response to the literary concerns of her time.[22] "A Note on the Russian War" is a particularly convincing instance of Frame's playing between the genres of prose and poetry,[23] and of her using a chiasmatic figure based on displacement or inversion of meaning. The juxtaposition of passages which are connected as well as possible, in an effort to mend the text and give it unity and sequential flow results in an effect of frames that are not properly linked to one another, which adds to the surrealist effect of the collage of "Russian" and New Zealand elements. The slight disjunctions of the narrative and the narrator's contradictions, like so many false notes, defeat her attempt at describing the children's pastoral world and bring to an end the narrative, which, like the children's Russian song, is thwarted by the sound of war "rolling through the grass." What is effectively taking place in the story / poem is a contest between two forms (short story / poem), between two songs (the children's / the soldiers'), which the children eventually lose, while neither form wins. The sunflower trope which opens the story – "The sunflowers got us, the black seeds stuck in our hair" (137) – fails to guard the world of childhood and innocence because it contains dark seeds itself. When it reappears at the end it is overshadowed by the black sun of war: "We had sunflowers by the fence near where the fat white cow got milked ... We were just Russian children in the Steppes, singing tra-tra-tra, quietly with our mother and father, but war comes whatever you sing" (139). Prose, like poetry, turns out to be impotent, and the closure is marked by a change of tense from past historic to present, making war a permanent possibility that cannot be controlled, either historically, because it recurs, or textually, for the narrative poem fails to contain it.

The experience of the First World War was at the core of the Modernists' search for new artistic forms adequate to their times, and "A Note on the Russian War" shows that Frame shared their personal and aesthetic preoccupations. Her creativity with the form of the short story, which she takes in the direction of the prose poem (by relying on tropes, rhythms, brevity, musicality, repetition ...) and thus places between genres, reflects the fact that she writes from a place that feels both on the edge of the world and of it, a double dynamic which is epitomized in the chiasmatic figure.

In the childhood stories of *The Lagoon*, Frame is first and foremost a (re)creator of words, that is to say a poet. The language she inherited presented her with words that had been taken from one territory to another. She takes them further, into "that world," the world of the imagination, causing further displacement of meaning and the ensuing emergence of new tropes. Like the poem described in her essay entitled "Departures and Returns," these figures and the stories that serve as their nurturing soil "go [...] right to the heart of the place" (87). These dynamic movements of the imagination and language take us back to the world of beginnings, the liminal space of childhood, on the edge of the adult world, from where possibilities – including a range of possible ways of using words and of looking at the world – can be glimpsed. To take us there, Frame relies on poetic devices, in short stories akin to prose poems.

NOTES

1   Many reviewers perceived it as such when *The Lagoon* came out – probably because of its power to evoke New Zealand realities. For the opposite viewpoint, see for example Vincent O'Sullivan's argument in "Exiles of the Mind": "Frame's view of language is the reverse, then, of mimetic" (28).

2   See Delbaere 18: "Because they are explorers of new or forbidden territories – New Zealand's other island, the country of the dead, the mental hospitals, the antipodes – her visionaries are rejected by the supposedly 'normal' people."

3   Many of the stories of *The Lagoon* may be identified as "childhood stories" that can be contrasted with more openly autobiographical stories ("The Secret," "Keel and Kool," "Child," "Treasure"), fantasies ("Spirit") and "stories of outcasts" whose protagonists are often the insane and the simple ("The Bedjacket," "Snap-Dragons," "A Beautiful Nature," "On the Car," "Jan Godfrey," "The Park," "My Last Story").

4   "La critique littéraire qui ne veut pas se borner au bilan statique des images doit se doubler d'une critique psychologique qui revit le caractère dynamique de l'imagination en suivant la liaison des complexes originels et des complexes de culture" (27).

5   According to 16th century rhetoreticians, the four main classical tropes were metaphor, metonymy, synecdoche, and irony (Harvey 647–48). Other theoreticians consider that the two main tropes are metaphor and metonymy (Molinié 328–29).

6   "peu importe le sens transporté, peu importent les termes du trajet : seul
    compte – et fonde la métaphore – *le transport lui-même*" (127). In con-
    trast, as Paul Ricoeur remarks, Pierre Fontanier's early nineteenth century
    definition of metaphor focuses on the figure itself (a word or an idea)
    rather than the transport (between two ideas) it implies – which Ricoeur
    sees as a reason for the decline of rhetorics at that time (76–77).

7   Robinson and Orsman 80–81, italics mine; Mansfield 205. On landscape
    in New Zealand literature, see also Cooper.

8   Ricoeur describes the cyclical process through which metaphors are pro-
    duced: a metaphor is first innovation, then becomes current metaphor,
    then turns into cliché, and then has to be invigorated with new meaning,
    or else is threatened with becoming dead metaphor (156).

9   The analysis of metaphor and the semantics of words is one of the vari-
    ous approaches to metaphor defined by Ricoeur. See the chapter entitled
    "La métaphore et la sémantique du mot" (129–71).

10 See W.H. New, "Reading the Understory," p. 275 of this volume.

11 See McRae 349–50: "From Maori tribal stories, the [Pakeha] rewriters
    have taken the romantic or the valient ... Late-nineteenth-century and
    early-twentieth-century Pakeha writers often combined the tasks of sto-
    rytelling with ethnographic reporting, sometimes awkwardly ... Regional
    versions of myths and legends, localised stories of the fabulous, and pic-
    turesque events of tribal history" were also common in that "literature
    of retelling." See also King about Pakeha writers of Maori life in the late-
    nineteenth and early-twentieth-centuries: "These men depicted romantic
    Maori figures – noble heroes, beautiful and tragic heroines, unrequited
    love – through a haze of poetic imagery. The figures they created bore
    little relation to life and conditions in twentieth-century Maori communi-
    ties, and for the most part they made no distinction between Maori of
    different regions and tribes – distinctions that would have been crucial in
    Maori eyes" (373).

12 Definitions quoted and adapted from Orsman 865.

13 On the Pa, see Orsman 561: "Originally, a fortified Maori settlement, a
    stronghold. In a weakened sense, a Maori village or settlement; in mod-
    ern (post c1960) English use replaced by marae, occasionally by kainga."

14 "Le déclin de la rhétorique résulte d'une erreur initiale qui affecte la
    théorie même des tropes, indépendamment de la place accordée à la
    tropologie dans le champ rhétorique. Cette erreur initiale tient à la
    dictature du mot dans la théorie de la signification. De cette erreur on
    n'aperçoit que l'effet le plus lointain : la réduction de la métaphore à un
    simple ornement" (64).

15 "Les Tropes par correspondance consistent dans la désignation d'un objet par le nom d'un autre objet qui fait comme lui un tout absolument à part, mais qui lui doit ou à qui il doit lui-même plus ou moins, ou pour son existence, ou pour sa manière d'être. On les appelle métonymies, c'est-à-dire, changements de noms, ou noms pour d'autres noms" (70).

16 On "deception as a rhetorical strategy" in Frame's writing, see Oettli-van Delden 52.

17 "Cowbyre," from "byre" in Scottish dialect, is used in the southern South Island (Otago-Southland) and is synonymous with "cowshed" (Orsman 125, 175).

18 See King, "Baptism of Blood?" (284–304) and "At War Again" (391–409), in particular John A. Lee's memory of the climate at the time of the Great War: "That was the spirit ... [Folks] sang patriotic songs and they cheered ... [They] talked of the great sacrifices of young men that would be made" (294).

19 On the role of frames in Frame's fiction, see New's "The Frame Story World of Janet Frame" and in particular the conclusion: "to read Frame's stories is not merely to be invited to meet a set of characters and a range of strange events, but also to be drawn into framed narratives where *the structures of the prose are themselves the means and metaphors of perceptual understanding*" (188–89, italics mine).

20 See chapter 2 – "Their grandmother was a negress who had long ago been a slave ..." / "Francie, Toby, Daphne, Chicks, drink up your cabbage water or you shall lose two legs, like your grandmother" (10) – and chapter 16 – "Hard cash. Toby Withers unrolled his bundle of ten shilling notes and put them down in a layered and crumpled confection of soft rust upon the table that was small and shaped like a cell of black honey" / "Toby is a man, thirty-two, newminted from adolescence and the twenties, a gold coin, silver coin, copper coin, ten shilling note of rust lying upon a black cell of honey" (54–55).

21 "Introduction" 4. Warm thanks to Héliane Ventura for bringing this reference to my attention.

22 It can also be pointed out that Frame wrote poetry, of which a volume, *The Pocket Mirror*, was published in the late 1960s. She also liked to think of herself as a poet. See, in "Departures and Returns," how she humorously contrasts the (best-selling) "writer" and the "poet."

23 It is worth noting that the poet Bill Manhire included "A Note on the Russian War" in his *100 New Zealand Poems* (37).

WORKS CITED

Alley, Elizabeth, ed. *The Inward Sun: Celebrating the Life and Work of Janet Frame*. Wellington: Daphne Brasell, 1994.

Anderson, Barbara. "The Mind and the Words." *The Inward Sun: Celebrating the Life and Work of Janet Frame*. Ed. Elizabeth Alley. Wellington: Daphne Brasell, 1994: 105–10.

Bachelard, Gaston. *L'eau et les rêves*. Paris: José Corti, 1942.

Barthes, Roland. "Abou Nowas et la métaphore." *Roland Barthes par Roland Barthes*. Paris: Seuil, 1975. 127.

Bhabha, Homi. "Introduction." *Nation and Narration*. Ed. Homi Bhabha. London and New York: Routledge, 1990: 1–7.

– "Of Mimicry and Man: The Ambivalence of Colonial Discourse." *The Location of Culture*. London and New York: Routledge, 1994: 85–92.

Caffin, Elizabeth, "Poetry. Part Two: 1945–1990s." *The Oxford History of New Zealand Literature in English*. Ed. Terry Sturm. Auckland: Oxford University Press, 1998: 447–524.

Cooper, Ronda. "Landscape." *The Oxford Companion to New Zealand Literature*. Ed. Roger Robinson and Nelson Wattie. Melbourne: Oxford University Press, 1998: 296–98.

Cuddon, J. A. *The Penguin Dictionary of Literary Terms and Literary Theory*. 3rd ed. Harmondsworth: Penguin, 1992.

Delbaere, Jeanne. "Introduction." *The Ring of Fire: Essays on Janet Frame*. Ed. Jeanne Delbaere. Sydney: Dangaroo, 1992: 13–21.

Fontanier, Pierre. *Les figures du discours*. 1821-1830. Paris: Champs Flammarion, 1977.

Frame, Janet. "Beginnings." *Landfall* 73 (March 1965): 44–45.

– "Departures and Returns." *Writers in East-West Encouters: New Cultural Bearings*. Ed. G. Amirthanayagam. London: Macmillan, 1982: 85–94.

– *The Lagoon, and Other Stories*. 1951. London: Bloomsbury, 1997.

– *Owls Do Cry*. 1961. London: Women's Press, 2002.

– *The Pocket Mirror*. 1967. Auckland: Vintage (NZ), 1992.

Harvey, Elizabeth. "Trope." *Encyclopedia of Contemporary Literary Theory: Approaches, Scholars, Terms*. Ed. Irena R. Makaryk. Toronto: University of Toronto Press, 1993: 647–49.

King, Michael. *The Penguin History of New Zealand*. Auckland: Penguin (NZ), 2003.

Lévi-Strauss, Claude. *Le cru et le cuit*. Paris: Plon, 1964.

Manhire, Bill, ed. *100 New Zealand Poems*. Auckland: Godwit, 1993.

Mansfield, Katherine. "At the Bay." *The Garden Party*, 1922. *The Collected Stories*. Harmondsworth: Penguin, 1981: 205–45.

McRae, Jane. "Maori myths and legends retold in English." *The Oxford Companion to New Zealand Literature*. Eds. Roger Robinson and Nelson Wattie. Melbourne: Oxford University Press, 1998: 348–51.

Molinié, Georges. "Trope." *Dictionnaire de rhétorique*. Paris: Le livre de poche, 1992: 328–29.

New, W.H. "The Frame Story World of Janet Frame." *Essays on Canadian Writing* 29 (Summer 1984): 175–91.

– "Glimpses: Shadow, Pool." *The Inward Sun: Celebrating the Life and Work of Janet Frame*. Ed. Elizabeth Alley. Wellington: Daphne Brasell, 1994: 39–42.

Oettli-van Delden, Simone. *Surfaces of Strangeness: Janet Frame and the Rhetoric of Madness*. Wellington: Victoria University Press, 2003.

Orsman, H.W., ed. *The Dictionary of New Zealand English: New Zealand Words and their Origins*. Auckland: Oxford University Press, 1997.

Orsman, Harry, and Roger Robinson. "Bush." *The Oxford Companion to New Zealand Literature*. Ed. Roger Robinson and Nelson Wattie. Melbourne: Oxford University Press, 1998: 80–81.

O'Sullivan, Vincent. "Exiles of the Mind – The Fictions of Janet Frame." *The Ring of Fire: Essays on Janet Frame*. Ed. Jeanne Delbaere. Sydney: Dangaroo, 1992: 24–30.

Ricoeur, Paul. *La Métaphore vive*. Paris: Seuil, 1975.

Robinson, Roger, and Nelson Wattie, eds. *The Oxford Companion to New Zealand Literature*. Melbourne: Oxford University Press, 1998.

Scott, Clive. "The Prose Poem and Free Verse." *Modernism. 1890–1930*. Ed. Malcolm Bradbury and James McFarlane. Penguin, 1976: 349–68.

Sturm, Terry, ed. *The Oxford History of New Zealand Literature in English*. 2nd ed. Auckland: Oxford University Press, 1998.

Wevers, Lydia. "The Short Story." *The Oxford History of New Zealand Literature in English*. Ed. Terry Sturm. 2nd ed. Auckland: Oxford University Press, 1998: 245–320.

CLAIRE OMHOVÈRE

Roots and Routes in a Selection of Stories by Alistair MacLeod

The fact is that the beginning always begins in-between, inter-mezzo. (Gilles Deleuze and Félix Guattari, *A Thousand Plateaus*)

Central to Alistair MacLeod's *Island* is the return to the original island or Highlands, phonetic closeness somehow reducing the geographical distance between the two referents. The motif is particularly prominent in four of the collection's sixteen short stories: "The Return" (1971), "The Closing Down of Summer" (1976), "As Birds Bring Forth the Sun" (1985), and "Clearances" (1999).[1] Read in conjunction, these stories make up a corpus that roughly spans Alistair MacLeod's writing life. Starting from W.H. New's remark that "the English-language vocabulary for characterizing landscape (and people's relationship with land) interconnects with the vocabulary for characterizing language and the use and function of language" (*Land Sliding* 164), I propose to analyze the functioning of pairs that combine spatial and linguistic displacement – returning and iteration, but also crossing and analogy.

Through the conjunctions and correspondences they allow, not only do iteration and analogy contribute to the stories' textual cohesion but they also confer upon Cape Breton the coherence of a literary territory within the nation's wider space. Studying the rhetorical mesh underlying MacLeod's representation of Cape Breton may then clarify the wide acclaim his writing has received. In fact, critical responses to MacLeod's work testify to an enduring interest in writing that announces its scope and concerns as universal, as if immune – or perhaps indifferent – to five decades of post-humanist critique and deconstructionist doubt.[2] Because MacLeod's stories foreground the singularity of their Gaelic protagonists and their habitat, analyzing the tropes through which the regional is made coterminous with the universal is then likely to throw light on the tacit acceptation evidenced in their reception. In his review of Irene Guilford's *Alistair MacLeod*, the only volume of critical essays so far devoted to MacLeod's writing, Lawrence Mathews pointedly wonders why "no one ever says anything about MacLeod's work that could be construed as even mildly negative ... Despite the slightness of his output ... and despite the reluctance of academic critics to examine it closely, he has been allotted a secure niche in the Canadian pantheon" (119). My hypothesis is that, in MacLeod's short fiction, the operations of iteration and analogy allow local place to enter in resonance with a national sense of space beyond the immediate insularity, or regional specificity, of their plots and setting. The consonance of MacLeod's stories with a general, indeed national, response to the particulars of place suggests that their alleged universal value may rest upon the consensual validation of their contribution to the "imagined geographies"[3] (Fiamengo 241) in which the nation, fragmented and diverse as it is, grounds its own existence.

WHAT HAPPENED?

What distinguishes the short story as a genre from the tale and the novel, Deleuze and Guattari explain, is the secret that informs its narrative development and orients it towards the past. In a short story, they add, one does not expect anything to happen for everything has *already* happened:

> It is not very difficult to determine the essence of the [short story] as a literary genre: Everything is organized around the question, "What happened? Whatever could have happened?" The tale is the opposite of the [short story], because it is an altogether different question that the reader asks with bated breath: "What is going to happen?" ... Something always happens in the novel also, but the novel integrates elements of the [short story] and the tale into the variation of its perpetual living present. (Deleuze and Guattari 192)[4]

Here lies the implacability driving Alice Munro's "The Time of Death" or Mavis Gallant's "Voices Lost in Snow." As their narratives resist the accomplishment of what has just occurred, they delineate a tear in the fabric of events even as they attempt to mend it. MacLeod's stories are no exception to Deleuze and Guattari's principle – nothing takes place in them that did not take place long ago and, one may add, far away. The characters' individual present is enfolded in the clan's collective past – the Highland Clearances which, at the end of the eighteenth century, forced them away from their home to Nova Scotia. Six generations later, the ancestral culture that was transplanted into the New World is withering under the joint pressures of poverty and progress. The secret MacLeod's characters share, but will not admit, is constrained within a double bind, staying in Cape Breton being just as impossible as leaving it. The narrative then obsessively recounts the moment of returning when the home place provisionally coincides with the characters' longing to dwell there again.

Such is the case in "The Return," an initiation story built on concentric excursions from and back to home's still centre: the return of the prodigal son and his family to North Sydney, Alex's return to his grandparents' house, the men's return from the pit, and finally the family's return trip to Montreal. About to depart for another mining season overseas, the men in "The Closing Down of Summer" are already anticipating their return to Cape Breton and the eventuality that it may be their final journey home to one of the small island cemeteries. In "As Birds Bring forth the Sun," a tremendous big grey dog, saved as a pup by the clan's ancestor, disappears and returns to cause its master's accidental death. Later on, it will reappear as the big grey dog of death that all the man's descendants glimpse at the moment of their demise. Likewise, the blanket mentioned five times in the opening of "Clearances" is a synecdoche of a narrative weaving together the past and present of the central character, an ageing widower whose property is coveted by a clear-cutter and a German couple smitten with the ocean frontage. The clashing interests of the tourist industry and those of a local population barely surviving on the island's depleted resources are set in parallel with the territorial struggles of the Second World War and the silent eviction of thousands in the eighteenth century, suggesting the constancy of the economic pressures which have beset the Gaelic community and condemned them to poverty and exile.

In all four stories, the narrative is syncopated. It points insistently beyond its own narrow scope, so that even as it explores the present, one feels the story cannot be comprehended outside its relation to the formal dimension of the past (Deleuze and Guattari 237). What happened then may account for a sense of belonging Alex "knows and feels but cannot understand" (R 91, see also 82, 83, 90), an intimation which impresses itself even more brutally upon the characters of "As Birds Bring forth the Sun." Both "The Closing Down of Summer" and "Clearances" take this investigation further as their narratives are concerned with liminality, specifically the interstitial differences and similarities through which the characters define themselves in relation to distant origins but also in respect to other close-knit communities – Highland Scots (CS 185, C 418), French and Irish mining crews (CS 202), the Acadians and neighbouring Mi'kmaq (C 148). In musical terms, a syncopation occurs when the strong note is *not* on the beat.[5] These stories similarly feature a contrast between iteration, the recurrent motifs that encode territory and sustain a sense of belonging, and analogy, a syncopation which cuts short the refrain of home, distending its limits to accommodate intersubjective distance.

THE REFRAIN OF HOME

In "De la ritournelle,"[6] Deleuze and Guattari observe the territorializing function of repetitive sound patterns, whose effectiveness rests upon the pervasiveness of the sound which irresistibly includes the subject within its reception. In this respect, hearing is to be opposed to sight, a selective sense that requires a separation between perceiving subject and perceived object.[7] Both perceptual modes contribute to the tracing and shaping of territory. Visually, or from a discriminating perspective, a territory can be defined as the critical distance between two individuals of the same species (Deleuze and Guattari 319). Aurally, the approach being now inclusive, an interval is induced by expressive sound patterns that mark off space as territorial insofar as they supersede and exclude any other expressive matter: "We call a refrain any aggregate of matters of expression that draws a territory and develops into territorial motifs and landscapes ... In the narrow sense, we speak of a refrain when an assemblage is sonorous or 'dominated' by sound"[8] (Deleuze and Guattari 323). The meaning of *territoire*, in Deleuze and Guattari's analysis, then diverges slightly from the legal implications of the word *territory*,[9] the French concept containing notions of appropriation and identification associated in English with local, heterogeneous place as opposed to global, homogenous space.[10]

In their relation to place, Gaelic and, to an even greater degree, song are evident territorial markers. In "Clearances," they create the distance that ostracizes strangers and trespassers (C 428). And, when during the Second World War the central character visits the ancestral Highlands, the rustle of Gaelic, its "soft sounds" and "subliminal whispers," signals his entry into a territory where markers are aural and haptic rather than optic and distant (C 418–19). Back in Cape Breton, the young man has pups sent in from the Highlands to breed them following the instructions of a Scottish shepherd (C 421). The line of Border collies that later accompanies him into old age also embodies the territorializing function of sound. The man addresses his otherwise nameless dogs with the phrase the shepherd initially uttered to identify the animal and its territorial vigil: "*S'e thu fhein a tha tapaidh* (It's yourself that's smart)" (C 423). From the point of view of reception, the Gaelic fragment also has a definite territorializing value. The reader's ability to *voice* the inscription indexes belonging to the island/Highland sound continuum whereas those who need the translation are merely permitted provisional access to it, a limitation materialized visually in the writer's use of brackets.

The recurrence of a Celtic phrase is more ambivalent in "As Birds Bring Forth the Sun." The silhouette of the big grey dog also serves as a transition between the clan's mythic past and the narrator's present but, instead of suggesting their seamless continuation, the recurring name of the "*cù mòr glas*" impresses a punctuation denying the character escape or progress (B 312). The Gaelic refrain suggests that change, whether spatial or temporal, can be checked through the repetition of a set formula, not a language for communication, but signifiers whose musicality moves speaker and listener alike, hemming them in the voicing of territory.[11] Gaelic is then only marginally concerned with exchanging information. Instilled in infancy, it partakes of the sacred and its rituals. It is the language used in prayers, to love or to mourn, in lament and in exultation. As one of the characters puts it, Gaelic is the "reflexive" tongue that conveys and causes affects (C 418). As they come in sight of Cape Breton, his father's tears remind Alex of earlier ceremonies when listening to Celtic music had the double function of commemorating home and inculcating its significance in a child who had never been there:

> My mother does not like [my father's violin records] and says they all sound the same so he only plays them when she is out and we are alone. Then it is a time like church, very solemn and serious and sad and I am not supposed to talk but I do not know what else I am supposed to do; especially when my father cries. (R 80–81)

Focalization upon a ten-year-old's limited understanding leaves some space for the quiet humour of a mature narrator who recalls the sentimental ritual with mingled feelings; and it is hard to tell whether it is genuine concern for his father's grief, or plain boredom that predominates in the recollection. Equally ambivalent are the revelations as to filiation, masculinity, and their connection to home, that await Alex in Cape Breton. At the ferry landing, their small party is greeted by a drunkard's obscene song, causing the outrage of Alex's mother. As a genteel Montrealer, she finds the local filth – at once a class, a gender, and a regional marker – quite insufferable (R 82). A whole story, and a two weeks' lapse, will be necessary for Alex to begin to fathom what he senses but cannot understand about Cape Breton and its sway upon his family.

In both "The Closing Down of Summer" and "The Return," the traditional family plot refers both to the grave that awaits the characters in the local cemetery and to the course and purpose of their lives. One of its avatars is "the hereditary salmon net," another beautiful and cumbersome inheritance in "Clearances." The characters' names repeat those of the previous generation and it is expected of their descendants that they will replace those whose untimely death has left a vacancy down the pit, or on the fishing boats. In "The Return," the narrator's uncle died "buried under tons of rock two miles beneath the sea" (R 87). As it combines drowning with the shaft accident, the event epitomizes the suffocation that awaits the men, a prospect only liquor may blunt – male alcoholism turning into another, more insidious but just as fatal, form of drowning (R 87, B 317, CDS 207). Belonging *in* Cape Breton is rife with contradictions, the home place being at once life-preserving and suffocating as revealed in the climax of "The Return." Fresh from the ferry, Alex approaches the new environment with the references of any ten-year-old raised on a staple of boy's magazines and U.S. frontier adventures.[12] But it is contact with male dirt and toil that signals his entrance into masculinity and his Gaelic lineage:

[My grandfather] places his two big hands on either side of my head and turns it back and forth very powerfully upon my shoulders. I can feel the pressure of his calloused fingers squeezing hard against my cheeks and pressing my ears into my head and I can feel the fine, fine, coal dust which I know is covering my face and I can taste it from his thumbs which are close against my lips. It is not gritty as I had expected but is more like smoke and sand and almost like my mother's powder. And now he presses my face into his waist and holds me there for a long, long time with my nose bent over

against the blackened buckle of his belt. Unable to see or hear or
feel or taste or smell anything that is not black; holding me engulfed
and drowning in blackness until I am unable to breathe. (R 93–94)

The grandfather's gesture evokes the baptism rituals which, to Anne
McClintock, are so crucial to male land claiming (McClintock 29).
Alex experiences an earthy drowning and rebirth through the matrix
of two rough hands that impress their own mark and the physicality of
place upon him. The sensation, "almost like my mother's powder," is
associated with a gentle but definitely smothering affection. And as the
fine dust saturates the boy's five senses it causes a rapture that borders
on malaise, an excess perceptible in the insistent use of redundancies
– "pressure," "pressing," "presses" – and a string of isocolons culminating in an alliterative outburst of sibilants and plosives. Because it
implies that the embrace of kin and place is so overwhelming it is potentially lethal, the scene calls to mind the tragic reunion of the *cù mòr
glas* with the founder of the line in "As Birds Bring Forth the Sun."

As the dog's offspring have never had any contact with people, they
misunderstand their mother's boisterous joy for an attack on the man's
supine body; the wild pack then pounces on him and tears him apart
under the eyes of his helpless sons. Although the plot partly recalls the
cautionary tales in which a foundling brings disaster into the community that gave him shelter, its concern goes beyond the spatial distinctions ancient myth sought to establish between outside and inside,
hostes and *hospites* (Serres 1983, 145–52). Rather, it addresses the endurance of an archaic articulation between man and the environment
framed by the title and its echo in the denouement: "we are aware that
some beliefs are what others would dismiss as 'garbage.' We are aware
that there are men who believe the earth is flat and that the birds bring
forth the sun" (B 320). The hounds are emanations from the rock and
the sea; their conception on the strand results from the pull cosmic
energy exerts on the alternation of tides and seasons as well as on the
breeding frenzy of animals (B 312). Of the elements that concurred
in their birth, the dog's offspring has retained the colour, the rugged-
ness and, above all, a formidable force that is both life-giving and
devastating. "The ambiguous force of the *cù mòr glas*" (B 317) has the
characteristic duality of the ecosymbols through which human beings
have vested meaning in their surroundings, laying the foundations of
the "proto-landscape" (Berque 39–40 and 59–60) that predated the
advent of a Western aestheticizing gaze, and the subsequent perception

and representation of landscape as distinct because distant from the spectator who assesses his dominion over the view he beholds.[13]

Neither in "The Return" nor in "As Birds Bring Forth the Sun" is the environment quite objectified into a landscape: there is not enough distance for this between the characters and the place they inhabit.[14] In Alex's eyes, his grandparents are metonymically related to their surroundings: "My grandmother is very tall with hair almost as white as the afternoon's gulls and eyes like the sea ... My grandfather ... has a white moustache which reminds me of the walrus picture at school" (R 84). The mine is insistently described as having the characteristics of a living organism – "the black gashes of coal mines ... look like scabs" (R 82), "green hills with gashes of their coal embedded deeply in their sides" (R 97). In "As Birds Bring Forth the Sun," the big grey dog is silhouetted against a land endowed with human attributes as in the dead metaphor "the brow of the hill," used three times when the old man is crushed by his own creation (B 313–14). Generations later, as the narrator's father lies in hospital awaiting his vision of the big grey dog of death, his six grey-haired sons sitting around the bed eerily recall the six grey hounds who encircled their ancestor and devoured him, his mangled body materializing the foundation of a line in which genealogy, language, and territory are inextricably interwoven.[15]

"As Birds Bring forth the Sun" illustrates in an exemplary fashion the iterative patterns that characterize MacLeod's stories. Through them, the refrain of home is made consonant with the territory the characters inhabit. It also leads to a temporal inscription that shuns the linearity of chronological progress for the cosmic cycles that regulate life in its manifold forms, an aspect brilliantly analyzed by Simone Vauthier in the essay she devoted to MacLeod's unconventional use of the present tense.[16] At times, the refrain of home may have the weight of a burden. The emplotment of the character's future limits its accomplishment to the prolongation of a line in which genealogical, linguistic and territorial strands combine and bind the characters to the island conceived as a verbal extension of the original Highlands.

CONSERVING / CONVERSING

The continuity of the cultural practices that produce territory, for instance the fashioning of vegetal badges or the ritual sharing of drink and song in "The Closing Down of Summer," is also manifest in the characters' concern for their animals. Dogs, in particular, are tokens of permanence. Being descended from the animal companions of the first exiles, or later imported from the Highlands, they are quite literally "from another time" (B 310). Only careful breeding has ensured the preservation of their original traits requiring that they be kept "in pens during the breeding season so that they might maintain their specialness" (C 421). Here man's control of animal instincts draws a clear line between nurture and nature. No dubious cult of roots can be found in MacLeod's stories, their narrators being rather wary of the confinement ethnicity may involve.[17] In "The Closing Down of Summer," McKinnon's miners are distinguished from rival crews who will not leave their province because "they are imprisoned in the depths of their language" (*CDS* 203). Equating territorial entrapment with unilingualism,[18] the metaphor derives its ominous overtones from all the cave-ins recounted in "The Closing Down of Summer." "Clearances" similarly features a dilemma between conservation and conversation. For minorities, the preservation of their language is indeed an asset for ethnic cohesion but it is also a liability that may contribute to their exclusion from wider cultural and economic exchanges:

> But in the years between the two world wars they realized when selling their cattle or lambs or their catches of fish, that they were disadvantaged by language. He remembered his grandfather growing red in the face beneath his white whiskers as he attempted to deal with the English-speaking buyers. Sending Gaelic words out and receiving English words back; *most of the words falling somewhere into the valley of incomprehension that yawned between them.* Across the river the French-speaking Acadians seemed the same as did the Mi'kmaq to the east. All of them trapped in the beautiful prisons of the languages they loved. 'We will have to do better than this,' said his grandfather testily. 'We will have to learn English. We will have to go forward.' (C 418, my emphasis)

Once again land and language are brought together in a metaphor capturing the isolation caused by ethnic entrenchment. Here the "valley of incomprehension" which renders exchanges impossible finds its counterpart in the "chasm" cutting across generations in "The Return" (R 91). Because it is out of place in the maritime setting, the image jars and draws attention to a decision that links communication with spatial progress. Going forward is indeed emblematic of the dynamics that impel MacLeod's characters and the awareness that cultivating one's distinctiveness within the nation is incompatible with a stubborn clinging to the past.[19]

This is confirmed on two occasions when the return to the Scottish Highlands leads to an encounter with desolation and death immediately followed by the reassertion of Cape Breton's hold upon the character. In "As Birds Bring forth the Sun," one of the grown-up sons is battered to death outside a Glasgow pub by seven large, grey-haired men in a scene that reiterates his father's fall under the claws and fangs of the island's big grey dogs. In "Clearances," the soldier's excursion to his ancestors' villages holds no revelation for him either, except perhaps an intimation of his own mortality, some of the gravestones bearing his very name (C 420). The narrator's resentment surfaces in a description which refers to the discontents of the past only to foreground the constancy of the power politics that, having caused his community's eviction, brought him back to Europe five generations later, to defend interests in which he still has no part. History is presented as a crushing inevitability, the character's present a puny reenactment of past oppressions. The passage of time is then irrelevant or, at least, secondary to the territorial clashes that go on pitting individuals and communities against one another. The Highland shepherd implies just as much when he exclaims, "'You are from Canada? You are from the Clearances?' ... as if it were a place instead of a matter of historical eviction" (C 419). MacLeod then drives the point home when he has his ageing character defend his ocean frontage property against European interests whose financial pressure is presented as far more irresistible than the military expansion he fought as a young man in Second World War trenches.

It would therefore be inaccurate to confuse the narrators' concern with the fractures of long ago with nostalgia. The commemorated past is quite uninhabitable and offers little, if any, refuge against the economic uncertainties of the present. In "The Closing Down of Summer" descriptions of the drought and industrial decay combine into pervasive evocations of ruin. The representation of the island then splits into two irreconcilable extremes: the parched wasteland of the summer coast or the inland cemeteries of the torrential fall. And the slender beach where the characters are waiting for a change in the weather provides the geographical analogy of all the transitions their community is engaged in. In "Clearances," the diaphoric use of "clear" allows the narrator to collapse three distinct periods into one territorial struggle fusing the evictions, land clearing in Cape Breton and, finally, the pressure exerted on small land owners by the clear-cutting industry on the coast and the extension of the National Park to the north (C 426). The demonstration reaches its conclusion in a self-conscious doubling of the young soldier's discovery of the Highlands and their "unpopulated emptiness" when the soldier, now an elderly man, registers a similar desertion in Cape Breton (C 420 and 429).

The consequences of territorial strife – eviction, itinerant labour and, ultimately, immigration – lead to spatial displacements that assert the link between the story's agent and its action, indexing the structuring role of the search for employment and its consequence, the journey, identified by Chklovski first in the tale then in the episodic structure of early novels (Chklovski 194). And yet, for all their departures and returns, MacLeod's stories do not feature the circularity of the completed quest. Neither do they have the verticality of a picaresque itinerary, the ups and downs of the hero's fortune delaying narrative progress, exacerbating the reader's involvement, but never representing any serious threat to the ultimate social ascent of the hero. But MacLeod's narratives are not impelled by the necessity of an accomplishment. Their trajectory is characterized by its periodicity, their plot occupying the interval between a departure and a home-coming, the intermittence of resources and seasonal labour sending the characters from Cape Breton across the country into the wider world and back. Looking back but moving on, these stories therefore conjoin roots and routes in a lateral dynamics of successive crossings.

CROSSINGS

In MacLeod's stories, Cape Breton is never pictured as a self-contained, sufficient and secluded haven. Cut off from the mainland but open and exposed to Atlantic influxes, the island is first and foremost a site of exchanges. In all four stories, insularity transforms any displacement into a crossing of some significance, "a journey on the road to understanding" (CDS 197). In "Clearances" the middle-aged couple's trip to Prince Edward Island turns into a profane pilgrimage to the factory where they have been sending their wool production since the early years of their marriage: "Later his wife was to tell her friends, 'We visited Condon's Woollen Mill on Prince Edward Island,' as if they had visited a religious shrine or a monument of historical significance and, he thought, she was probably right" (C 414). The exclamation receives unexpected rhetorical relief, its iambic lilt getting amplified in the sway of the two equal-length segments that frame the preposition *on*. The wife's fervour suggests two analogies to the narrator – "religious shrine" and "monument of historical significance" – which shun the spectacular or the picturesque to elevate the prosaic and the germane into a local pride.[20] In MacLeod's stories, analogy has an informing function that goes well beyond that of decorative artifice. Because it captures an identity which is not essential but relational, the trope establishes a partial equivalence between the local, insular event and a global, plural field of reference.

In its strict Aristotelian sense, analogy fuses comparison and reason, as it formulates a ratio between four items and two sets of relations (a/b = c/d) (Borella 24). The relation therefore allows the conjunction of the similar with the different, but also the passage from one plane to another superior sphere, as implied by the idea of elevation contained in the Greek prefix *ana*.[21] Mediaeval theologians then developed complex analogies to approach the ineffability of the divine through a subtle, rigorous gradation of the manifestations of the One in the many. In the secular world of MacLeod's stories, analogy – with its related forms, simile and comparison – is repeatedly used to inscribe the singular, insular experience within a wider referential frame. The *cù mòr glas*, to cite but one example, is thus related to a Scottish and a West Coast manifestation of the *genus loci*: "For a while she became rather like the Loch Ness monster or the Sasquatch on a smaller scale. Seen but not recorded. Seen when there were no cameras. Seen but never taken" (B 316). Bridging the geographical and cultural extremity of its components, the analogy isolates in both an identical response of the human mind to a space alive with intensities that have not been objectified into a stable, external spectacle.

In "The Closing Down of Summer," several references to the Zulus similarly extend the story's referential and figurative scope beyond the immediate concerns of the crew and the future of their communal lifestyle. Their impressive physicality and the mastery of skills that shake the earth are not the only traits the Zulus share with the miners. Both communities belong to oral cultures in which group cohesion is achieved through ritual. And both have adapted to a fast-changing, increasingly global world where exotic forms of authenticity are all the more valued as they are becoming extinct. In this respect, the Celtic Revival concert and the Zulu dance performance are analogous in their reception by audiences who, well-intentioned though they may be, are unable to comprehend their profound signification. Communication subsequently aborts and each group remains confined within its linguistic and cultural limits, a seclusion to which the narrator reacts with unease, as evidenced in his choice of the word "archaic," used recurrently in reference to Gaelic and its speakers.

Beyond an outward likeness, analogy then isolates an intractable core of difference into which the narrator yearns to delve. Intellectual apprehension and physical displacement are expressed in identical dynamic terms, the narrator's failure "to understand [the Zulus] more deeply" being equated with the impossibility "to enter deeply into their experience" or "to penetrate behind the private mysteries of their eyes." Tracing the occurrences of the adjective "private" in this short story will highlight the pull within a trope which, even as it brings the disparate together, will not assimilate the similar with the same: "Yet in the end it seemed *we too* were only singing to ourselves ... songs that are for the most part local and private and capable of losing almost all of their substance in translation" (CDS 196). Ultimately, the analogy between the two communities conveys to the outsider the incommunicability of local experience. And yet the trope circumvents the aporia of the untranslatable, the identity it posits being necessarily relative, circumstantial, possibly debatable:

> He looked at the land once cleared by his great-great-grandfather and at the field once cleared by himself. The spruce trees had been there and had been cleared and now they were back again. *They went and came something like the tide he thought, although he knew his analogy was incorrect.* He looked toward the sea; somewhere out there, miles beyond his vision, he imagined the point of Ardnamurchan and the land which lay beyond. He was at the edge of one continent, he thought, facing the invisible edge of another. (C 430, italics mine)

The unexpected syntactic reversal in "they went and came something like the tide" jars and throws into relief the flawed logic that would derive identity from a mere recurrence. The analogy between spruce and tide is rejected as spurious because it confuses man's intervention in the vegetal cycle with the cycle itself. In doing so the analogy naturalizes the clash between competing economic interests, and disqualifies the character's rebellion. The evocation of the Scottish coast has no elegiac, reconciling virtue. Rather it confirms the narrator's awareness of the profound, essential difference that lies between the bare Highlands and the land of trees, his commitments to the past and the challenges of the present.

Often undermined by the disparity it seeks to limit, its validity threatened by an intrinsic inaccuracy, analogy is regarded with suspicion by the mathematician and the philosopher alike. For the writer, however, analogical approximation may come close to an approach, the trope triggering the associations and correspondences that open onto the multiplicity and complexity of shared experience. In the case of MacLeod's bilingual characters, Gaelic and English are frequently paired in translation, one language cleaving into the other's necessary yet inadequate shadow: "'*M'eudal cù mòr glas*,' shouted the man in his happiness – *m'eudal* meaning something like dear or darling" (B 314). Because it engages with an intractable nucleus in signification,[22] translation may be regarded as the overarching analogy out of which all the narratorial attempts to convey the bond between the characters and the land proceed. "The Closing Down of Summer," for instance, repeatedly laments the miners' failure "to tell it like it is" (*CDS* 206). The grammatical impropriety of the conjunctional use captures well the narrator's effort to *stretch* his argument beyond the literal in order to communicate the elation of the crew's physical engagement with the elemental world:

> I suppose I was drawn too by the apparent glamour of the men who followed the shafts ... We are always moving downward or inward or forward or, in the driving of our raises, even upward. We are big men engaged in perhaps the most violent of occupations and we have chosen as our adversary walls and faces of massive stone. It is as if the stone of the spherical earth has challenged us to move its weight and find its treasure and we have accepted the challenge and responded with drill and steel and powder and strength and all our ingenuity. In the chill and damp we have given ourselves to the breaking down of walls and barriers. We have sentenced ourselves to enclosures so that we might taste the giddy joy of breaking through. Always hopeful of breaking through though we never will break free. (*CDS* 201)

The Conradian overtones of the opening signal the amplification of the miners' labour into an age-old confrontation between man and the elements. The central comparison – "It is as if the stone of the spherical earth has challenged us to move its weight and find its treasure" – initiates a prosopopeia through which Cape Breton's mining tradition is elevated into a geste of man's struggle against a stinting nature, a motif which is not without resonance in the national imagination. The final chiasmus ("breaking down ... breaking through ... breaking through ... break free"), plural abstractions and the syllabic expansion in the series "walls," "barriers," "enclosures," leads the reader to consider in this miniature mining epic the ambivalence in any confinement, at once an obstacle and an enticement to movement. The contradiction, interestingly, is also present in the formal compression that character-izes the genre, an enabling constraint in terms of narrative efficiency and reader participation.

In MacLeod's stories, intensity similarly results from the contradic-tory pull between iteration and analogy, the territorializing impulse of conservation and the deterritorializing force that operates in conversa-tion but also in literature, each participant turned towards the other, text and reader tuned to the other's reception.[23] Such is the assurance I read in Terry Eagleton's words: "It is not just experience, but language, that takes a writer away from home because there is something curi-ously rootless about writing itself which is writing only to the degree to which it can survive transplantation from one context to another" (qtd. in Simpson-Housley 123). And MacLeod's stories have survived transplantation. Territorializing refrains do bind their characters to Cape Breton. Grounded in the island/Highland sound continuum, their iterations of home register the passage of time as a mere inter-mittence, the pause before a repetition – the oscillation of the tide, the flashes of the lighthouse, the occupation of the land, the rise and fall of cultures – all of them *ritornelli*. And yet, in these stories, perma-nence is checked by their narrative's restlessness, an impatience with geographical and temporal constraints, that seeks an outlet in analogi-cal forays into the distance, and the possibilities that lie somewhere, out there. These short stories therefore rely upon a sense of liminality, an in-betweenness to which a Canadian audience is likely to respond because it is emblematic of a shared relation to both region and na-tion as borderlands, zones of contact but also of interaction (Brown; New 1998), between different communities with competing and yet complementary claims to the land.

NOTES

1   Subsequent page references will appear directly in the text after the fol-lowing abbreviations: (R) for "The Return," (CS) for "The Closing Down

of Summer," (B) for "As Birds Bring Forth the Sun," and (C) for "Clear-ances."

2 In her review of *No Great Mischief*, Dianne MacPhee typically winds up citing MacLeod's claim that "what makes things universal is that they touch a core, a storehouse of human experience and concerns that transcend regions and transcend time" (qtd. in MacPhee 167). Jane Urquhart concurs when she writes that "MacLeod's stories have been called – albeit with great admiration – traditional, even conservative, by a literary world cluttered with theories and 'isms'" (Guilford 37).

3 Janice Fiamengo uses this heading to introduce her chapter on "Regionalism and Urbanism" in the 2004 *Cambridge Companion to Canadian Literature*. The phrase, of course, obliquely refers to the communities of the imagination which, as Benedict Anderson has famously argued, underlie the formation of nations. At a second remove, it also allows Fiamengo to emphasize the vitality of regional writing in Canada and its lasting role in the definition of a Canadian canon and tradition.

4 I have amended Brian Massumi's translation and restored the word "short story" where he opted for the word "novella," presumably to foreground the idea of a recent development in the course of events, the latter being implicit in French as *nouvelle* may refer either to a short story or to a piece of news. The original reads as follows: "L'essence de la 'nouvelle', comme genre littéraire, n'est pas très difficile à déterminer : il y a nouvelle lorsque tout est organisé autour de la question 'Qu'est-ce qui s'est passé? Qu'est-ce qui a bien pu se passer?' Le conte est le contraire de la nouvelle, parce qu'il tient le lecteur haletant sous une tout autre question: qu'est-ce qui va se passer? ... Quant au roman, lui, il s'y passe toujours quelque chose bien que le roman intègre dans la variation de son perpétuel présent vivant (durée) des éléments de nouvelle et de conte." (Deleuze et Guattari 235)

5 The *OED* defines the word as "the action of beginning a note on a normally unaccented part of the bar and sustaining it into the normally accented part, so as to produce the effect of shifting back or anticipating the accent; the shifting of accent so produced."

6 The translator of *A Thousand Plateaus* entitled this essay "Of the Refrain," an approximation that does not quite capture the melodious and obsessive connotations of the *ritornello* that gave the French *ritournelle* in the original version.

7 Michel Serres explains that sound does not really take place but rather *occupies* place. "Though its source may remain ill-defined, its reception is

wide and all-encompassing. Sight delivers a presence but sound does not. Sight distances, music touches, noise besets" (Serres, 1985 53, my translation). *A Thousand Plateaus* similarly emphasizes the privilege of the ear, "Colors do not move a people. Flags can do nothing without trumpets. Lasers are modulated on sound. The refrain is sonorous par excellence, but it can as easily develop its force into a sickly sweet ditty as into the purest motif, or Vinteuil's little phrase" (Deleuze and Guattari 348).

8   "On appelle ritournelle tout ensemble de matières d'expression qui trace un territoire, et qui se développe en motifs territoriaux, en paysage territoriaux ... En un sens restreint, on parle de ritournelle quand l'agencement est sonore ou dominé par le son" (Deleuze et Guattari 397).

9   "'Territory' is a designation of claim over land, of *jurisdiction*, the power to *say the law*" (New, *Land Sliding* 21).

10 *Place* has no satisfactory equivalent in French, its translation as *lieu* lacking the oppositional articulation *place* derives from its assonance with *space* (Staszak 252–53). This may account for the reliance of French geography (and Deleuze and Guattari's geophilosophy) upon the notion of *territoire* to address the specificities of the local.

11 In "The Road to Rankin's Point" and "Vision," singing the song "Never More Shall I Return" (*Island* 158–59 and 346) has an evident metonymic function for the characters. Performing the song together is a clear substitute for inhabiting the lost land, an instance of reterritorialization in song.

12 "I do not know what I'm supposed to do until my cousins come back and surround me *like the covered wagons around the women and children of the cowboy shows*, when the Indians attack ... My almost-attackers wait awhile, scuffing their shoes on the ashy sidewalk, and then they separate and allow us to pass *like a little band of cavalry* going through the mountains" (R 89, italics mine).

13 Analyzing the ambivalence of the ancient Celts' response to the forest, Augustin Berque draws upon the constitutive duality of Gilbert Durand's archetypes, their signification being either positive or negative depending upon the diurnal or nocturnal regime in which they are envisaged.

14 I am using the word "landscape" in the restricted sense Augustin Berque has defined to distinguish the notion from any unspecified reference to the natural environment. For Berque, a landscape is not an object per se but a "médiance," i.e. the outcome of a series of mediations between a perceiving subject, perceived surroundings and a fund of cultural, social and historical representations (Berque 16–19).

15 This passage is highly reminiscent of the foundational rituals in Ancient Greece and Rome where the fragmented body of the victim was shared

by the community, giving birth to a sense of the collective, political representation and art (Serres, 1983 118).

16 Although she concentrates upon one specific story, Vauthier's valuable conclusions throw considerable light on the frequent and spectacular shifts from the preterit to the present that characterize MacLeod's writing in general. Laurent Lepaludier has also drawn attention to the iterative value of the present tense in his analysis of "The Closing Down of Summer."

17 "Second Spring," a story revolving around a young boy's dream of breeding a prize-winning calf, is a wonderfully comic refutation of ideals of purity. The boy sets off on the island's roads, determined to take his precious cow to the perfect bull which, he knows, is available in a nearby farm. Like Hazard Lepage leading his stallion on Alberta's tricky roads in Robert Kroetsch's *The Studhorse Man*, the boy will have little choice but to adjust to the vagaries of animal desire.

18 By using the adjective "unilingual," MacLeod ironically suggests that, for many, bi- or multilingualism is the norm, as in the following description: "The real estate agent stood listlessly between them while the July sun contributed to the perspiration forming on his brow. He looked slightly irritated at being banished to what seemed like a state of unilingual loneliness" (C 428).

19 For a fine analysis of the inscription of *No Great Mischief* within the wider frame of the nation, see David Williams's "From Clan to Nation."

20 The narrator's awareness and implicit refusal of the pastoral alternative is just as interesting: "This was in the time before the Anne of Green Gables craze and they did not really know what people were supposed to visit on Prince Edward Island" (C 414).

21 "La notion *analogia* ... exprime l'idée d'un rapport (*logos*) entre ce qui est haut et ce qui est en bas (verticalité), parce que ce qui est en bas est comme ce qui est en haut (répétition), avec, éventuellement l'idée d'un renversement (le plus petit comme analogue du plus grand)" (Borella 25).

22 "The transfer can never be total, but what reaches this region is that element in a translation that goes beyond transmittal of subject matter. This nucleus is best defined as the element that does not lend itself to translation. Even when all the surface content has been extracted and transmitted, the primary concern of the genuine translator remains elusive. Unlike the words of the original, it is not translatable, because the relationship between content and language is quite different in the original and the translation. While content and language form a certain unity in the original, like a fruit and its skin, the language of the translation envelops its content like a royal robe with ample folds." (Benjamin 75).

23 In this respect, it is not indifferent that the etymology of the noun
"trope" should be a Greek verb meaning "to turn," referring to the rhetorical twist given to expression to achieve greater effect and perhaps
also (this is my own interpretation) to the pull that carefully-wrought
statements exert on one's attention.

WORKS CITED

Benjamin, Walter. "The Task of the Translator." *Illuminations*. Ed. & intr.
Hannah Arendt. Trans. Harry Zohn. New York: Schocken, 1968: 69–82.

Berque, Augustin. *Les Raisons du paysage de la Chine antique aux
environnements de synthèse*. Paris: Hazan, 1995.

Borella, Jean. *Penser l'analogie*. Genève: Ad Solem, 2000.

Brown, Russell, "The Written Line." *Borderlands: Essays in Canadian
American Relations*. Selected by the Borderlands Project. Ed. Robert
Lecker. Toronto: ECW, 1991: 1–27.

Chklovski, V. "La Construction de la nouvelle et du roman." *Théorie de la
littérature*. Ed. Tzvetan Todorov. Paris: Seuil, 1965: 170–95.

Deleuze, Gilles, et Félix Guattari. *Mille plateaux: capitalisme et
schizophrénie*. Paris: Editions de Minuit, 1980.

– *A Thousand Plateaus*. Trans. Brian Massumi. London, Minneapolis:
University of Minnesota Press, 1987.

Fiamengo, Janice. "Regionalism and urbanism." *The Cambridge Companion
to Canadian Literature*. Ed. Eva-Marie Kröller. Cambridge: Cambridge
University Press, 2004: 241–62.

Guilford, Irene, ed. *Alistair MacLeod: Essays on His Works*. Toronto:
Guernica, 2001.

Kroetsch, Robert. *The Studhorse Man*. 1970. Toronto: Random House, 1988.

Lepaludier, Laurent. "The Everyday in 'The Closing Down of Summer' by
Alistair MacLeod." *Journal of the Short Story in English* (Spring 2002):
39–55.

MacLeod, Alistair. *Island*. 2001. London: Vintage, 2002.

MacPhee, Dianne. "Tales of the Seannachie." *Canadian Literature* 179
(Winter 2003): 165–67.

Mathews, Lawrence. "Atlantic Myths." *Canadian Literature* 180 (Spring
2004): 119–20.

McClintock, Anne. *Imperial Leather, Race, Gender and Sexuality in the
Colonial Contest*. London: Routledge, 1995.

New, W. H. *Land Sliding: Imagining Space, Presence, and Power in Canadian
Writing*. Toronto: University of Toronto Press, 1997.

– *Borderlands: How We Talk About Canada.* Vancouver: University of
British Columbia Press, 1998.

Serres, Michel. *Rome, le livre des fondations.* Paris: Grasset, 1983.

– *Les Cinq sens.* Paris: Hachette, 1985.

Simpson-Housley, Paul, and Glen Norcliffe, eds. *A Few Acres of Snow:
Literary and Artistic Images of Canada.* Toronto and Oxford: Dundurn,
1992.

Staszak, Jean-François, Béatrice Collignon *et al.*, eds. *Géographies anglo-
saxonnes: Tendances contemporaines.* Paris: Belin, 2001.

Urquhart, Jane. "The Vision of Alistair MacLeod." In Guilford: 36–42.

Vauthier, Simone. "Notes sur l'emploi du présent dans 'The Road to Rankin's
Point,' d'Alistair MacLeod." *Ranam* 16 (1983): 143–58.

Williams, David. "From Clan to Nation: Orality and the Book in Alistair
MacLeod's *No Great Mischief.*" In Guilford: 42–71.

W.H. NEW

Reading the Understory: David *Malouf's* Untold Tales

David Malouf's second book of short stories, enigmatically titled *Untold Tales* (1999), collects four stories only: "Buxtehude's Daughter," "The Runners," "Epimetheus or, The Spirit of Reflection," and "Ulysses or, The Scent of the Fox." The entire book is no more than fifty-eight pages long. Roughly speaking, the stories tell of a real musician's real daughter and the conditions that governed her marriage; of angels and rumours that fly through the air; of Prometheus's brother, who plays handball and is stung by "a million dark and furry bodies" (41) after he marries Pandora and she opens the box; and of Ulysses' stratagem for ending the Trojan War and getting home. Intertextual allusions abound. Yet the narratives *read* like direct statements, like 'factual' or 'documentary' accounts of lives led in history or myth. Trying to find out why Malouf shaped these stories as he did – or trying to find a way of reading the texts that would do more than just summarize topics (the word 'or' being particularly relevant to Malouf's technique) – took me to the writer's earlier and later story collections. I began to see that he has recurrently been examining alternatives to whatever it is that goes by the name of fact, whether it's history or biography or literary convention. I'm calling these alternatives 'the understory,' and in the essay that follows, I'd like to recapitulate some of this trek towards a strategy of understanding. Understanding the fact of fictionality, maybe, and/or the fictionality of fact.[1]

Malouf's two other collections are called *Antipodes* (1985) and *Dream Stuff* (2000), which gather thirteen and nine stories respectively. Each runs well over 150 pages. These numbers are less significant than is the contrast they provide with *Untold Tales*, where the shortness, the illusory flatness of narrative, and the departures from Malouf's more characteristic domestic Australian settings emphasize a kind of alterity. For the middle book, investigating the character of alternatives, somehow also enacts alternatives. Self-consciously, that is. Self-reflexively. But not exclusively. For what are "antipodes" and "dreams" if not alternatives, at least on first acquaintance? And what then do antipodes and dream stuff have to do with the untold?

Contemporary reviews of Malouf's stories do not help resolve these questions. Resounding with ambiguity about 'value,' they primarily summarize topics and look repeatedly for a term – 'essayistic piece,' 'meditation,' 'documentary' – with which to *categorize* his literary form.[2] The documentary evidence of Malouf's life writing, however, provides a different way into the stories; it takes a reader 'under the surface' in one remarkable way that the reviews do not: into metaphor, particularly that of the conventional colonial Queensland house – the wooden house that is built as though on stilts, to allow airflow beneath it: a subtropical strategy to help cool the inside, and to keep *out of the house* the snakes and insects that live more characteristically on the ground.[3] Malouf's memoirs of the house – in *12 Edmondstone Street* (1985) and "A First Place: The Mapping of the World" – treat space nostalgically, glimpsing time past and place disappeared, and then metaphorically, converting time and place into body memory and narrative form. The upstairs of the house, the living space, occupies most of his commentary. He recalls the metonymic resonance of things, a brass jardinière, a collar stud, a lost doorway. But in the area he calls 'under-the-house' lies a different world. "Down here is the underside of things: the great wedge of air on which the house floats, ever darkness; the stumps of a forest of which the house, with its many rooms, forms the branches; a place whose dimensions are measured, not in ordinary feet and inches, but in heartbeats ... or the weight of your body ..." (*Edmondstone* 46) Later, "the door our fingertips were seeking was not there because we were looking in the wrong place; it was not that door we were meant to go through. The door was in us. Our actual body is the wall our fingertips come to. We have only to dare one last little blaze of magic to pass through" (66). To go inside, in other words, go under.

In "A First Place" Malouf begins again to talk about houses – then says "It is not accident that they should have invaded a paragraph that is devoted to nature, since they are, in this place, so utterly of it, both in form and substance" (262). Houses, that is, *invade memory, invade the language of memory, permit in some way an entry into the natural.* Children learn their houses, as they learn the world, through

touch; they build maps of their houses through its creaks and silences
(264); in Brisbane their houses have an inside and an outside, a "nest
of rooms and [an] open verandah" (266); and below them lies "the
space down there ... a wedge of deepening dark" (266), a space both
"sinister and liberating" (267), "a passage out of the present into lim-
bo, where things go on visibly existing as a past that can be re-entered,
a time-capsule underworld. Visiting it is a way of leaving the house,
and the present and daylight [,] and getting back to the underside of
things" (266–67), their own and other people's bodies, for example,
guilt "or ... a great break-out of themselves" (267). While his Brisbane
image is local, he goes on to say, and consequently foreign (in its details) to outsiders, the local informs the *mindset* of any writer.[4] It might
be easy to read at once for Freud and Jung, or for sexual identity and
ethnic origin. And stop. But then Malouf adds: "it is the writer's job,
so long as we are in the world of his fiction, to make insiders of all of
us" (267). Readers are urged not to stop, but to go on.

To go under. Inside. I read these as directions into narrative line and
narrative form as well as into psyche, space, and symbol. They help get
me past the reviewers' preoccupation with surface themes and settings
and past my own uncertainty in the face of *Untold Tales*. But how to
get from this complex 'underside of things' – with its knot of associations: freedom, darkness, nature, sexuality, a breakout that is also an
invasion inwards, a past that can again be the present – how to get
from this underside of house and mind into the underside of stories?
How to read the understory? the 'untold' of told tales? Once again I
turn to *Antipodes* and *Dream Stuff* as the way in.

From this vantage point, *Antipodes* seems a kind of trial run in differentiating between the declared and the implied, and of dramatizing
this difference in short narrative form. I think Malouf went on to work
out the difference in his longer fictions as well, as in *Remembering
Babylon*, but my general premise here, keeping the focus on shorter
works, is twofold. I argue that a collection of stories reveals its themes
through setting, overt subject, stated exchanges, and stated conclusions, sometimes in the voice of a character or narrator, and sometimes
in the over-voice of an authorial figure. But that it teases out its understory by means of some pattern of reiteration, by asking the reader to
read not only for ostensible subject and pronounced opinion but also
for the implications of recurrent form. Some strategies of form are
obvious: criticism speaks readily about point-of-view and narratologi-
cal focalization, direct and indirect discourse, climax and resolution,

tonality and the incongruities that give rise to laughter. But I am interested also in repeated words and phrases, in enumeration (catalogues, lists) and repeated mechanical devices such as punctuation (dashes and ellipses, hyphens and full stops): the *patterns* of discourse and the way these patterns function as narrative signs. Sentences. Fragments. Even syllables. Aha.

The overt *subjects* of the thirteen stories in *Antipodes* deal with childhood discovery and adolescent revelation, youth and death, models of behaviour, departures from social norms, emerging identities, unexplained transitions. Revelations and rebellions have an impact on the *language* of identity, and on the form that language takes in narratives of identity. As in "Southern Skies": which begins by listing a series of forms of false respect, and closes when a boy realizes that several kinds of fondling have touched him, but touched the surface only of his world, not the reality, and are therefore irrelevant to the person he is becoming. Here, and in other stories,[5] transitions are more important than the fixities of pattern or conclusion, and taken all together, the stories in *Antipodes* read past the conventional limits of generic paradigm. There's a closet "adventure story" (28) in "A Trip to the Grundelsee," something of a ghost story in "The Empty Lunch-Tin," a traveller's tale in "A Change of Scene," assorted growing-up narratives, and a quasi-documentary in "A Medium." But it's as though Malouf were trying out the familiar narrative strategies of *representing* motion less to move his characters from pole to pole than to engage his readers in the duration of *moving between*.

So these overt subjects constitute a kind of surface filter – or haze. Malouf's characters are repeatedly caught up in the details of the surface – one of the most recurrent words in the collection is "stuff": things, spoons, attitudes – the comfortable clichéd stuff (152) that the arts officer Adrian Trisk peddles as culture to rural audiences in "A Traveller's Tale," for example; or the "usual stuff" (125) in "In Trust" – the string of attitudes that a right-wing American tourist peddles loudly to his fellow travellers at the Holocaust museum in Jerusalem, just before falling dead when he recognizes himself in a photograph. Repeatedly, however, these stories call attention *formally* to the *limitations* of the surface. Here, for example, is the opening of "In Trust":

> There is to begin with the paraphernalia of daily living: all those
> objects, knives, combs, coins, cups, razors, that are too familiar,
> too worn and stained with use, a door-knob, a baby's rattle, or too

swiftly in passage from hand to mouth or hand to hand to arouse more than casual interest. They are disposable, and are mostly disposed of without thought. (123)

Another catalogue of items follows, one of many in this story, before the narrator reflects on the survival of objects, to become rare, or preserved, or collectable, to end up in tortoiseshell cabinets or museums. In this story, of course, the California traveller who recognizes his family in Jerusalem walks as it were through "a metre of roughened museum wall and the door into another country" (125), as though re-enacting Malouf's childhood walk into his under-the-house body; the man's "fellow-travellers ... went on to the rest of the experience: images, objects, carefully worked facts and descriptions. Only that one man went right to the centre, stepping through a wall that was in the end as insubstantial as breath, and on into flame" (126).[6] The story turns from the stuff of the surface to the manner of speaking, the strategy of fiction, the untold but by no means silent half of the tale.

Other stories reiterate this notion. When "Out of the Stream" opens with the seemingly flat statement "The boy stood in the doorway and was not yet visible" (73), the rhetoric suggests rather more than the ear initially hears: suggests, for instance, the potential for becoming an object (the boy later contemplates suicide) or for becoming a living being (whose doorway choice might carry him into an appreciation of something with more meaning if less definition, something that one might call grace or love). The Belgian guide in "The Sun in Winter," who refers to Australia in the barest breath of a phrase "Ah, the *New World*"(86–87), makes the place sound far more romantic and venturesome than the young Australian traveller has ever thought; and when she goes on to show him "things" and then break away into musing, she makes a distinction that the traveller is not quite ready to understand: "mere looking," she says, gets you nowhere if you want to see the real:

"All you see then ... is what catches the eye, the odd thing, the unusual. But to see what is common, that is the difficult thing ... For that we need imagination, and there is never enough of it – never, never enough." (89)

The repetition emphasizes the inadequacy of any desire for limited borders. And repetition is the textural, the undertextual, mode of *Antipodes*.[7]

"Southern Skies" depicts another boy growing up, waiting for his life to happen – one who discovers sex as a "game" (22) that he doesn't know the rules to and cannot control – one who subsequently turns into a young man with a sense of a larger identity in the universe of the stars, which takes precedence over his susceptibility to other people's physical desires and limitations. There are ways of reading this story that would stress the sexual facts it reports, whether as wish-fulfillment, expiation, projection, denial, or some other aspect of trauma, and these ways are not *wrong*. I wish, however, in the context of what I have been arguing, to look instead here for Malouf's developing rhetoric of understory. *Antipodes* opens with "Southern Skies," and "Southern Skies" opens with the sentence "From the beginning he was a stumbling-block, the Professor" (7). Structurally the rhetoric of this sentence suggests that reversals of expectation, or at least alternatives to them, are more likely than any inevitable fulfillment of them, and when the opening paragraph continues with such words as "but," "though," and "reject," qualification is clearly in the air. To be told about the Professor that "he was what was called a 'ladies man' – though that must have been far in the past and in another country" is to be told what the first sentence enacts syntactically, that the surface *lies*, that the Professor is constructed from the beginning *in apposition*, tangential to the real story. "What he practised now," the narrator adds, "was a formal courtliness," an extreme version "of a set of manners that our parents clung to because it belonged, along with much else, to the Old Country, and which we young people, for the same reason, found it imperative to reject" (7). At the end of the story, with his own brand of youthful courtliness (a formal handshake), reject the old man is precisely what this young narrator does. Not without having been touched by the Professor (literally) and more metaphorically by a kind of fixed and Ruritanian version of a long-gone Europe (17), but he has learned how to separate himself from both. He can turn away from the "phallic grotesque[s]" (16), and the masks with "tufted hair and boar's tusks" (15), that along with fossils and souvenir figureheads sit solidly, unmoved, on the surfaces of furniture in the old Professor's rooms. Hence the young man does *not* become another item in the Professor's collection; instead, aware now of both misapprehension and "the extraordinary lightness that was [his] whole life," he "bounce[s] unsteadily over the dark tufts of the driveway and out onto the road." (25) More declaratively than in many other stories, "Southern Skies" writes transformation into a fiction of hope.

Malouf's later collection *Dream Stuff* (that word "stuff" again) emphasizes the fictionality of the speech that constructs these narratives, as in "At Schindler's," where declaring someone to be one of the family "was a manner of speaking, a temporary truth like all their arrangements down here. Rivalries, gangs, friendships existed with a passionate intensity" at holiday times "and for the rest of the year, like some of the rivers they drew in Geography, went underground, became dotted lines" or "broken continuities" (9). In the same story a character explains palaeontology by declaring that "'The body's got laws, and the bones follow 'em ... It's a kind of – grammar – syntax ... So if you've got one bit, you can work out the rest ... By logic. But also by guessing right ... You've got to think yourself inside the thing, into the bones" (11–12).[8] When one of the characters in "Dream Stuff" itself, then, reflects that the "afternoon had a shape that he came to feel was exemplary, and his readers might have been surprised to know how often the fictions he created derived their vagrant form, but even more their mixture of openness and hidden, half-sought-for menace, from an occasion he had never got to the bottom of ..." (41), then I feel that I am getting closer to *Untold Tales*.

But first, *Antipodes* again – my own rhetoric (of deferral, of delay) is, of course, a deliberate strategy: resisting linear explication, implying Malouf's resistance to fixity, the "broken continuities" to which his short stories repeatedly turn. When a character in "Sorrows and Secrets" listens to his foreman's stories, and finds them "interesting" although he can make nothing of them, he reflects that "they appeared to tell more than they told" (46). This phrase – suggesting some quality of revelation that the boy is not yet willing (or perhaps ready) to hear – also suggests the methodology I want to pursue further: the rhetoric of telling that reveals something more than overt subject declares or conventional frame resolves. In interview with Ramona Koval in 2000,[9] David Malouf makes this distinction in another way, observing: "I've come to the conclusion that in the end what people are interested in, in writing, is the actual writing. They may not necessarily say that to themselves but when they choose one writer rather than another, it's the particular music of that writer that they're responding to." Even the musical metaphor is suggestive – of the importance of rhythm, of cadence: of sound and recurrence as measures of narrative meaning, the rhetoric of the understory.

To come back to *Untold Tales* in this light, therefore, is to begin to see how the stories work, developmentally more than thematically. To

simply say 'documentary form' and treat the four stories as separate
retellings of history and myth is to miss how they cumulatively connect; and simply to rehearse their *topics* is to discover nothing more
than a list: there's a tale of the 17th-century musician Dietrich Buxtehude's daughter's marriage, a tale of angels who spread rumours, a
tale of Epimetheus who married Pandora, and a tale of Ulysses in Troy
(who tricked the Trojans by enticing Patroclus to pretend to be Achilles, which then enticed Achilles to kill Hector for killing Patroclus, and
in turn got Paris to kill Achilles, all before the Trojan Horse was pulled
through the city gates and a sort of victory sent the victors on a long
voyage home). To fasten more closely on Malouf's shifting rhetoric
gets past the illusion of objective fact and disinterested narration to
tell a different, rather more connected, and much more emotionally
engaged and humane tale.

Closer attention to the *telling*, that is, reveals that each of the stories conveys its surface narrative by means of a particular rhetoric.
"Buxtehude's Daughter" uses strategies of qualification and subordi-
nation, parenthetical modification and instructive apposition, strategies that emphasize the *formality* of performed relationships, but also
the existence of the alternatives that such formalities gloss over or
elide. "The Runners," the tale of angels and rumours, repeatedly uses
co-ordinating conjunctions – *and* and *but*, but especially *and* – a strategy that produces lists, which in turn suggest the cumulative nature,
and the gathering momentum, of meaning and of what listeners take
to be meaning.[10] The final two stories, each with its alternative title
– "Epimetheus or, The Spirit of Reflection" and "Ulysses or, the Scent
of the Fox" – clearly signal alterity right from the start: the first goes
on to undercut the rhetorical forms of logical argument (thesis, antithesis, synthesis) by means of a series of *as if* paradigms, and the second
develops through strategies of repetition and reversal, demonstrating
how paradigms (especially paradigms that have come to be accepted
as conventional or sacrosanct) can become straitjackets. When all they
produce is stasis, then (says the story) people will begin to find other
ways to act – but new ways will change old premises, and with such
changes will come different codes of understanding or recognizing
truth and value. Or, the book suggests, of recognizing and understanding the music of writing.

Untold Tales is, then, a book less about Buxtehude's daughter and
Epimetheus than about how people tell stories, and to what end. In
this case, cumulatively. For these stories interconnect. Margarethe

Buxtehude, the narrator says, thinks of her situation in fairytale terms; the next story opens with the phrase "There was a time when rumours, some of them true as it happens but too fantastical and fearful to be believed, were flying about the land from village to village and one town to the next, and so fast that no human agency could be the source of them; it was as if angelic runners had made their way over the earth ..." (25) – in other words, with a variant on the fairytale convention "once upon a time." The violence of some of the rumours ("massacre, famine, pestilence," 26) is picked up in the reference to the contents of Pandora's box in the next story; and the tale of Pandora's husband, who is advised what to do by Hermes the trickster, leads into the trickery of Ulysses in the last story, trickery that leads to change, to alternatives, to the indeterminacy of being mortal and living in time – in other words, *human* – which is, in the long run, all that Margarethe lives for and Epimetheus loves.[11] Cumulatively, the stories celebrate the music of life over the restrictiveness of received convention, the exigencies of being human over the efficient omnipotence of godlike rule, time and mortality over prescriptive performance; and by implication, then – demonstrated, I think, in the rhetoric of the understory – the capacity of storytelling to break out of the received conventions of fairytale, history, documentary, rumour, logical argument, fable, epic, and heroic myth. To distinguish again between the power of formalized lies to constrain action and imagination, and the power of fictions *nevertheless* to convey the kinetic rhythms of how people live.

Turning in more detail to the first story in *Untold Tales*, "Buxtehude's Daughter," demonstrates this process more graphically, showing how the formulas of stasis, of ostensible documentary, cover but cannot suppress the strategies of understory resistance. (Perhaps the *most* recurrent phrase in the entire book is "there was"). There *is* a history that lies behind this narrative. The real-life Dietrich Buxtehude, the Danish-born organist and composer, did live from about 1637 to 1707, and did move to Lübeck in Germany in 1668, where he established a reputation as a brilliant musician at the Marienkirche, and where he married Anna Margarethe, the daughter of the previous organist Franz Tunder. It was a condition of his appointment that he marry Tunder's daughter; and when it came time for him to seek a successor, Buxtehude required the same condition: the successful candidate would marry Margarethe. In real life, both Johann Mattheson and George Frederick Handel came as suitors (Malouf's story renders them more as quarreling partners than as potential grooms, suitors for

the post but never for the lady), and at the age of 20, Johann Sebastian
Bach made a 200-mile trip on foot from Arnstadt to Lübeck to hear
Buxtehude play (in the story Bach appeals to Margarethe more than
Handel and Mattheson do, partly because he walked, although he appears to be more interested in music than in marriage, and in any event
perhaps walked because he was young and bored by his employers
rather than because he wanted to make an impression). In real life,
too, Buxtehude died before a replacement had been named or a husband found, and shortly afterwards Margarethe married Buxtehude's
assistant Johann Christian Schieferdecker and perhaps lived happily
ever after. On the surface of it, Malouf's story just tells this narrative
all over again, with wit, sentiment, and solemn flair. But there is more.
The story keeps alluding to the form in which the historical narrative
has been constructed, and the form in which it is conventionally read:
as fairytale in particular, gendered and complete. But it also keeps revealing that alternatives to this surface totality not only exist but also
subvert – with consequences that wrestle narrative back to life.

Consider how the story begins, with two sentences of formal prose,
neatly balanced, full of adjectival phrases and subordinate clauses
– bracketed, as it were, by the identical verb *was*, the voice of documentary authority:

> In the first decade of the eighteenth century the old Hansa city of
> Lübeck in North Germany *was* the home of the finest organist in
> Europe, Diderick, or, as he is usually called, Dietrich Buxtehude.
> His greatness as a performer, but also as a composer of church
> chorales and concerti, had spread the name of the Marienkirche
> through all the German states, so that when the time came to
> consider his successor, young men from all over Germany and the
> north, even as far as Sweden, began to appear in Lübeck to declare
> an interest and show their parts, though a good many of them, out
> of pride or professional caution, gave out that their only reason for
> coming *was* to pay their respects to the master and hear him play.
> (13; my italics)

Was: the ring of unquestioned, unexceptional truth. Reinforced by
a series of absolutes: *finest, greatness, all, all over, only, master*. Except
that a string of contextualizing words simultaneously alters this picture – *first, or, usually, as a performer, but also, even as far as, began,
though*, and perhaps even *play*. "Performance" takes on two mean-

ings, and as each of the figures (now "characters") shows their "part," a disparity grows between ritualized and innovative engagements with life.

Margarethe herself, the narrative goes on, was "a talented performer ... with a high regard for music as a sacred art";

> she took great pride in her father's position, and it *was* this perhaps that saved her from what might otherwise *have been* merely humiliating, the little matter, which *was* strange in modern times, of being thrown in, as it *were*, as an extra to the main chance – or, in the darker view, which even she *was forced* to take on occasion, as an obligation to be assumed or hurdle to be got over. She *was* a strong young woman with a clear sense of her place in the world and she let the candidates, or contestants or suitors, know it, amusing herself by looking on the affair as one of those folk-tales in which a penniless beggar or soldier of fortune tries for the hand of a princess, for a kingdom too, but at the risk of his head. (14–15; my italics)

The verb *to be* again, six times (once as a passive auxiliary). And again the authority is subverted by a string of qualifiers: *perhaps*, *might otherwise*, *or*, *or*, *or*, even the filler phrase *as it were*, which declares that appearance and reality do not actually accord. In the rhetoric here, Malouf also introduces the folk-tale motif directly, with a proviso: that this version of the folktale (the wandering hero, the captive princess, the adventurous challenge, the personal danger) be read for the *or* as much as for the *was* – be heard as an aberration, rather than as a model, of how to live. Already the story has set up a tension between gender and sexuality – role-playing that re-enacts previous patterns, and real life that might not follow categories so absolutely. Phrases such as "show their parts" and "risk of his head" can be heard for their 20th-century vernacular resonance here, underlining further the nature of the relationship between the *characters* named Mattheson and Händel, the "odd pair" from Hamburg who "came in the same carriage," the elder who "took a leading part" and the younger with "the complexion, the manners too, of a girl," who "praised each other's performances" and quarrelled passionately (15–16). As for Margarethe, she found them "insufferable": "She had seen enough of her father's choir-boys to have no illusions about the nature of young men" (17). But such phrases also reiterate the hierarchical nature of the *roles* that the conventions of society and narrative superficially assigned to men and women, roles that Margarethe disputed (though she could be "overwhelmed" [17] by the power of the music that the men played). Finding a way to tolerate her role in the story is what leads her into folktale. When her talent for irony leaves her, however – as it does when the character named Bach walks into the narrative – she begins to accept the folktale as fact. Was his "coming on foot," she wonders, "not intended as a secret sign to her that he too had recognized the shape of an old nursery tale and was playing his part" (19).

Of course reality steps in, and Malouf begins his next paragraph by undercutting the paradigm: *was* Bach sending a secret sign? "In fact no such thought had entered his head" (19). In "fact," music matters more to Bach than life in Lübeck does, and in this *story* Margarethe comes to recognize how limited the folktale is and to what degree the folktale limits her. She realizes (after Malouf has provided a proleptic glimpse of Bach's musical progeny) that she does not want as children "a pool of ready copyists," "begotten ... in a shadowy way," and that "When all was said and done she cared less for music ... than for life, by which she meant her own life, the life that was in her" (20). But first she has to get past the folktale. Perhaps Bach

> was the one who most nearly fulfilled all the conditions, not only of the post but of the story; he would be appointed, they would marry, all would be well. Except that it was not well, and she began to wonder if the tale she had been telling herself was the right one after all. (19)

In due course, then, "she gave him no sign" – a declaration to which Malouf again adds a tonal disclaimer: "So she gave him no sign, and was pretty certain that if she had he would have missed it. She let her prince go on sleep-walking ..." (20). And the story comes quickly to its close: "In later years" (21) she does marry – Schieferdecker, of course – whom Malouf characterizes a little slyly as "a man of moderate talent but by no means incompetent, and he was at the same time confirmed in the vacancy" (21). But there is one more twist at least to come. Malouf writes, with an obvious gesture in the direction of fairytale convention, "They had several children and she lived happily in Lübeck till the end of her days" (21). Nice, but still not over: with the last sentence of the story, Malouf depicts Margarethe walking along the beach (that conventional site on which competing forces negotiate for power), telling stories to her grandchildren. It seems she's still lodged inside narrative. The narrative she tells to the youngest child, however, strips the story that she had been told of its conventionally gendered passivity, and reassigns the roles. She urges the child to look to Denmark, "where her father's people had come from, to listen for the song of the mermaids who lure sailors in the strait" (21).

The reader is cast by the end of this story into the role of listener – but what does the listener (or grandchild) listen for? Easy to say "life," or "celebration," "resistance," or some version of parodic reform of social or literary convention. But in Malouf's story, "life" comes with its ungodlike accompaniment, death. It's been there from the beginning, in the approaching death of Buxtehude; and it lurks throughout, in the departure of the suitors, the repeated allusions to appetite, the implicit sexuality of the relationships, and the declared "end of her days" to which the narrative moves. This is a narrative that on the surface retells or re-enacts history, one in which the details do not alter; but it is also one in which the understory addresses mortality even more – asking the listener to come to terms with mutability and variation. It is at this point that the improvisational next three stories in *Untold Tales* can begin.

In "The Runners," the angels who deliver messages are so endowed with foreknowledge that they sometimes arrive to comment on events before the events have yet taken place – hence their messages are received as rumours. For all that foreknowledge makes the angels' use of the verb *to be* unexceptionable, the listeners question all the time what the angels have to say. They doubt; they quarrel; they employ double-meanings to cause laughter (29); and they live happily – so much so that the angels might at the end of the story begin to wonder what it must be like "to be human, a child of time" (29). Pandora in the third story opens the box of mortality and tells Epimetheus that one day she will die, and he (named for hindsight) affirms that he has "always known" (42); the gift she gives him is not pestilence and famine but the realization that they can come (as the gods cannot – "all-powerful as they are": that verb *to be* qualified again) "to know one another and the world" (43).

In the final story, then, the Trojan War grinds into stalemate in part because the men, who should be acting nobly, are not acting at all; and as for the gods, well (and the stories do use from time to time this tale-teller's vernacular), the verb *to be* enacts its own version of inaction: "A god cannot be other than he is" (54). Ulysses, however, "a trickster by temperament and choice" (51) rather than a conventional hero, knows he must equivocate in order to get on with war and be free to go home – knows he must *use* trickery, to which a real hero would in honour never descend, rather than rely on the "pious fog" and "brightly lit episodes of action and noble speech that come together ... as epic" (51). He knows that no trickery

> would have a place in the official story, and there would be no place in it for him either, Ulysses the fox. If he wanted *a story* he would have to invent one of his own; not an epic about honour and force of arms but one involving a new sort of hero, whose special quality would be quickness of mind; the sort of hero who could reinvent himself to meet any eventuality, who was not fixed and contained in a single virtue like the epic hero but shifting – not to say shifty – and always on the move. (51–52; my italics)

When the war begins again, then, and when Patroclus takes on Achilles' role, and Hector kills him, Hector looks into his opponent's face, expecting to see Achilles, and discovers that he has "been taken in by a counterfeit": "The hero's part could be played" (56). Back the book goes to that performance metaphor – the music metaphor – of "Buxtehude's Daughter," and once again returns to "folk-tale" to conclude Ulysses' story: to the forms of trickery and shape-shifting (58) that permit human beings, now that the age of heroes is over, to survive. The book also makes clear that the forms of re-telling, or reinvention, that modify received patterns of tales, do so in order to celebrate the kinetic nature of living instead of the static nature of repetition. *Untold Tales* hinges on this distinction. Subversively, these stories adapt conventional forms to reveal the kinesis that churns beneath the surface of apparently fixed and "factual" surfaces. Paying attention to the understory gives life to whatever sensibilities official narratives occlude: the underhouse darkness of rhetoric and memory, and the "untold" – meaning *unlimited* – alternatives that are revealed in the untelling of tales.

NOTES

1   I want to thank Travis Mason for his diligent research assistance, which made the writing of this paper possible.

2   For instance, Sybille Smith, writing in *Quadrant* in 1985, writes of *Antipodes* that "The real poles between which the stories move are youth

and age; male and female; past and present; freedom and constraint; order and contingency. Formally, they range from fairly conventional narrative to pieces that are more like essays and notations." "Not all the stories," she adds, "are successful" (83) – but after commenting on the intent of fiction (to "evoke a life," to permit a reader "to recognise a basic order of experience," 84) and suggesting that the stories work like musical "chords" (84), she later concludes that "they belong to Malouf's best work" (85). This concern to *evaluate* marks a certain kind of criticism, of course, and the range of evaluations within this review appears to be associated with a desire for order and a puzzlement about form. This puzzlement pervades other commentaries as well. Ivor Indyk, in *David Malouf*, refers to an "essayistic piece" (54) called "In Trust" in *Antipodes*. I myself have already used the term "documentary" in this commentary. And Robert Ross, also using the term "piece" when reviewing *Untold Tales* for the American journal *Antipodes*, observes first that "The book will probably add little to Malouf's well-established reputation" but later affirms that the "'series of meditations' is inventive, charming, poetic, and challenging, a miniature testament to Malouf's rich imagination that has been so fully manifest in his novels" (75).[2] The observations are not inconsistent – but they remain on the surface of critical reading. Pausing descriptively at *topic* and *categories of form*, the review concludes in evaluative generalization. Ross summarizes the subjects of the four stories, then *classifies* the 'pieces' as a folktale, an 'abstract selection,' and two 'expansions' of Greek myths. But *why* Malouf takes on these topics and renders them as he does – and to what ends beyond mere extension-of-myth – remains unasked, and unanswered.

3   Other critics to talk about the psychological implications of Malouf's house metaphor include Gillian Whitlock and (in a jointly-written essay) Helen Gilbert and Leigh Dale.

4   Referring to himself and to other Brisbane writers – Judith Rodriguez, Gerard Lee, Rodney Hall – Malouf suggests that their "restlessness," their "delight in variety and colour and baroque effects," might be traced back "to the topography of [the city] and the physical conditions it imposes on the body, to ways of seeing it imposes on the eye, and at some less conscious level, to embodiments of mind and psyche that belong to the first experience and first mapping, of a house" (268).

5   "Sorrows and Secrets" closes with a suicide and a boy realizing that the obvious details of the case do not add up to what he now knows; "The Sun in Winter" (the only story to mention the "antipodes" (90) and mean the Australian sun) locates a coffin in the Belgian rain as the most lasting

reminder of a young man's European visit; and "In Trust" hinges on the
fact that a girl has selected, as a memoir of her great-aunt, not a "valuable" tangible keepsake, such as spoons, but an X-ray of the throat of
her great-aunt's long-dead young man. Transitions are important here,
evoked in image and often left unexplained.

6   Gillian, the unusual child in the same story, picks the x-ray of her great-
aunt's beau to keep – instead of a set of spoons, which would have been
the more conventional artifacts of inheritance – because (though she does
not yet articulate it) the picture of the young man's throat, the picture of
strength and delicacy that sees through the wall of the young man's flesh,
preserves a moment of living: "A word ... that he had intended to speak
but could not, because he had to hold his breath for the machine; a thought
that had sparked in the skull, travelled at lightning speed down that luminous cord and got stuck in his throat. It was there, still visible" (128).

7   In "A Traveller's Tale," between those two concrete artifacts of
Queensland tourism, the Big Banana and the Big Pineapple, again lies
"another country" (131) in which predetermined attitudes prove to be
insufficient measures of the reality that will, *really*, be there to meet. The
boy who takes piano lessons from Miss Katie McIntyre in "A Medium"
realizes that Miss Katie lists her degrees on the nameplate in the foyer of
her building, but that the woman who shares the fourth floor with her
lists "E. Sampson, Spiritualist" – only. Remembering his youth, Malouf's
narrator writes (with a nice ambiguity): "Miss Sampson's profession,
so nakedly asserted, appeared to speak for itself, with no qualification"
(157); he remembers that he could name piano chords easily – "It wasn't
difficult. It was simple mathematics and I had an ear" – but that "looking
through into Miss Sampson's room" allows him to see an "angelic lu-
minescence" (159), a way of seeing that alters the reality of what he has
accepted as finite and clear. "Bad Blood" phrases the existence of such an
alternative in an even more direct way, declaring: "Brisbane is a city of
strict conventions and many churches, but subtropical, steamy" (93). The
sub-tropical: the under-story.

8   In "Jacko's Reach," a child's "awe" is the route to what readers are told is
"the real story" (95); it is the power of the wild that can be pressed "under" concrete, but which will continue to live in the way people think and
remember, beyond the reach of ordinance and plan (99). And in "Dream
Stuff" itself, family history is a kind of anthology of anecdote and legend,
built on top of the shelves in the under-the-house of memory (35–36). But
such subterranean realities of fiction are slowly learned. For the character
Colin, whose guide abandons him in Greece, disappointment comes from

his sense that "Things had been moving towards some event or revelation that at the last moment, for whatever reason, had been withheld" – "But the teasing suggestion of something more to come, which was unseen but strongly felt, and had to be puzzled over and guessed at, appealed to him. To a side of him that preferred not to come to conclusions. That lived most richly in mystery and suspended expectation" (41).

9 'Books and Writing,' Radio National,' recorded in Melbourne late March 2000, broadcast 14 April 2000; www.abc.net/au/rn/arts/bwriting/stories/s117284.htm.

10 Chris Wallace-Crabbe suggests that these two stories, respectively, draw on W.H. Auden's appreciation of Buxtehude, and on Franz Kafka's story "A Message from the Emperor." I would argue that the rhetoric of these works (Kafka's 1919 parable, Auden's passing allusion to Buxtehude in "New Year Letter," 1940) differs consequentially from that which Malouf uses. My thanks to my colleagues John X. Cooper and Patricia Merivale for their thoughtful comments.

11 It is also the quality that the angels and gods {who learn about mortality *through reflection,* 43} can only watch, and that Ulysses' faithful dog will recognize even through the masks and ravages of age, even when people are caught up in preconception, expectation, and no-longer-functioning rituals of interpretation. It will be clear from the comments that follow that I disagree with Wallace-Crabbe's evaluation of Malouf's style in *Untold Tales* ("here and there I am alerted to something a little puddingy about the prose ... Lighten up, Dave, I find myself saying," 45). I argue that the deliberate formality of the rhetoric in this book calls attention to the artifice of convention *and* to the vitality of alternatives to convention – the oblique narratives of 'understory' that the rhetoric also embodies. The stories, that is, are *not* randomly collected but deliberatedly arranged, and the shape of the sentences, the choices of diction and motifs, all constitute elements in the covert narrative design.

WORKS CITED

Gilbert, Helen, and Leigh Dale. "Edges of the Self: Topographies of the Body in the Writing of David Malouf." In Nettelbeck: 85–100.

Indyk, Ivor. *David Malouf.* Melbourne: Oxford, 1993.

Koval, Ramona. 'Books and Writing,' Radio National,' recorded in Melbourne late March 2000, broadcast 14 April 2000; www.abc.net/au/rn/arts/bwriting/stories/s117284.htm.

Malouf, David. *Antipodes.* London: Chatto & Windus/Hogarth, 1985.

– *Dream Stuff*. London: Chatto & Windus, 2000.

– "A First Place: The Mapping of the World." In Tulip: 261–9.

– *12 Edmondstone Street*. London: Chatto & WIndus, 1985.

– *Untold Tales*. Sydney: Paper Bark, 1999, rpt 2000.

Nettelbeck, Amanda, ed. *Provisional Maps: Critical Essays on David Malouf*. Nedland, W.A.: Centre for Australian Studies, 1994.

Ross, Robert. Review of *Untold Tales*. *Antipodes*. 14.1, June 2000: 75.

Smith, Sybille. "David Malouf's Short Stories." *Quadrant*. July 1985: 83–5.

Tulip, James, ed. *David Malouf*. St Lucia: University of Queensland Press, 1990.

Wallace-Crabbe, Chris. "A Fistful of Fables." *Australian Book Review*. February/March 2000: 45.

Whitlock, Gillian. "The Child in the (Queensland) House: David Malouf and Regional Writing." In Nettelbeck: 71–84.

HÉLIANE VENTURA

Aesthetic Traces of the Ephemeral: Alice Munro's Logograms in "Vandals"

The "other country" which is conjured up in Alice Munro's writing evidences a mythic and mystic landscape of origins strewn with aesthetic traces, which belong in the temporal category of the ephemeral, the half-glimpsed, the transient, such as footprints dissolving on sand, or mist burning away in the sunshine. Munro creates a territory which relies on flux density, on energy and forces. Her ephemeral traces are not melancholy, they are cosmic, they move along lines of deterritorialization and reterritorialization that belong in the machinery of desire, on the surface of fluid planes. They repudiate heaviness to suggest the inchoate, transient stuff that dreams are made of.

My intention is not to provide an exhaustive survey of such loci of half-glimpsed possibilities in Munro's world but to concentrate on aesthetic traces of the ephemeral in one story only, "Vandals," the last story from *Open Secrets*, her 1994 collection. These dissolving traces are of a specific kind; they are words written on the boards of the kitchen wall with tomato sauce, which blot themselves out almost intantaneously. Because they are simultaneously of a visual and of a verbal kind, I have chosen the word *logogram*, borrowed from the visual artist Dotremont, to refer to Munro's use of a graphic imprint in her short story. Her accommodation of the verbal and the visual, which in this particular instance is highly dependent on the biblical intertext (the book of Daniel), stands out against a background of other artistic activities deployed throughout the story. In "Vandals," the presence of two types of art object can be identified. The first is a nature reserve, startlingly called Lesser Dismal and created by a taxidermist named Ladner. The nature reserve can be considered as an artistic object of its own, a construct closely linked with land art. The second element that we can regard as an aesthetic object is a devastated cabin located on the private nature reserve, which is trashed in the climax of the story by a newly married couple, the "vandals" apparently referred to in the title. The act of devastation, what with throwing flour, alcohol, and tomato sauce all over the floor and the walls, consists of a ritual activity that can be compared with action painting, informal art, and *Tâchisme*.

These two objects, the nature reserve and the devastated cabin, stand in a dialectical relationship with each other: one embodies the ordering of the world by the great architect, with the stabilized permanence of taxidermy as its most striking feature. The other object typifies the chaos of absolute destruction with the vanishing mark on the wall as its outstanding emblem. It will be the purpose of this paper to try to demonstrate that, as she often does, Munro is only pitting these dichotomies against each other so as to subvert them. She accommodates in her story an art of nature in order to question the nature of art. Through the way she exposes the falsification of nature, she highlights the authenticity of the language of fiction as a means to uncover the duplicity of human nature. She uses the nature reserve as a privileged territory or a testing ground where to try to separate the wheat from the chaff.

Apparently standing on the side of order and permanence, Ladner's garden evidences the process of reclamation of the bush generally taken to typify the colonization of Canada:

> he had bought up four hundred acres of unproductive land, mostly swamp and bush, in the northern part of the county, in Stratton Townships, and he had created there a remarkable sort of nature preserve, with bridges and trails and streams dammed up to make ponds, and exhibits along the trails of lifelike birds and animals. For he made his living as a taxidermist, working mostly for museums. (266)

This reclamation is nevertheless characterized by the falsification of nature: it consists of a counterfeit, as is immediately perceptible through the predicated "lifelike birds and animals." Ladner's bush garden produces simulacra, duplicitous images which have the semblance of life. His garden is a lethal fantasy; proposing stuffed animals in place of living ones, or even more curiously alongside living ones, almost as supplements to living ones, it requires death in order to exist.

Its vicarious and deadly quality due to presence by proxy is reinforced by Ladner's area of expertise: as a taxidermist he has made it his aim to substitute life in *imago or imagines* similar to mortuary effigies.

Ladner's bush garden is built in the semblance of the original Garden of Eden, the enclosed garden with the apple tree, but there is something rotten in this avatar: Eve's offer of the apple to Adam is displaced and recontextualized into Adam refraining from offering the bounties of the earth to Eve. More specifically, Ladner picks up mushrooms which look like decayed apples and keeps them to himself:

> and then they were in the old apple orchard, enclosed by woods,
> and he directed her to look for mushrooms-morels. He himself
> found five, which he did not offer to share. She confused them with
> last year's rotted apples. (272)

This scathingly ironic reversal might also be regarded as a way of smuggling in intertextual clues, or providing evidence of what Jean Jacques Lecercle has called "the return of the rest"[1] – that is to say what eludes the rational construction of language and erupts out of its opacity through tropes, polysemy, and unconscious slips. The name of the mushroom is morel, a word which echoes the name of a famous character in D.H. Lawrence, of an infamous one in Borges' "History of Infamy," and also that of a character in an equally well known story by Adolfo Bioy Casares entitled "Morel's Invention." In this last story, which takes place in a desolated seaswept island, a man called Morel has engineered a trap: a machine that takes people's lives away in order to replace them with an everlasting three-dimensional smiling image in their exact likeness. This fantasy about engendering a type of eternal life totally congruent with our desire is also to be found in Ladner's garden, where the animals from the wild have been safely embalmed within reach of man's appreciation. With the clandestine allusion contained in the reference to the mushroom, Munro is prodding the reader to equate Morel's and Ladner's devices for trapping men and animals into everlasting life. She inscribes Ladner's story on a paradigmatic axis of substitution as a story of falsification in which our experiential, living relationship with the world has been replaced with a fantasy based on eternal simulacra.

The possibility of substituting one story for another on account of the covert allusions encapsulated in "morel" is reinforced by the metaphor that Munro engineers for the mushroom. She makes the female character, Bea Doud, see the blossoming mushroom as a rotted apple: that is to say she creates what Paul Ricoeur calls "an impertinent"[2] association for the mushroom at the same time as she convinces us of the pertinence of the label by assigning its creation to the apparently perceptive and sensitive (although rather naive) female heroine. By allowing us to reduce the impertinence in the assignment of label, she helps us reconfigure Ladner's creation of the remarkable nature preserve along the line of entropy which accommodates rottenness and corruption. Through "the impertinent metaphor" she destabilizes the dialectic of order and permanence and stability established by Ladner in his garden to pave the way for process, change, and chaos.

This impertinent metaphor, which transforms morels into rotten apples, also accommodates another level of significance based on the consonance of the word *mor-el* in which our *mor-tal* condition is encapsulated and covertly reverberates on the nature preserve. The name of the swamp is another reminder of the dialectic between creation and destruction, of the tension between prolonging life and arresting it for eternity that is generated by the taxidermist's activity within his nature preserve. The name of the swamp is Lesser Dismal, an explicit allusion to the forested wetlands called Great Dismal Swamp Nature Reserve in Virginia and North Carolina.[3] The tension created by the opposition between Great Dismal and Lesser Dismal can be read as an ironic cultural commentary on the difference between the United States and Canada, in which the status of Canada is simultaneously heightened and diminished. It can also be regarded as a commentary on the taxidermist's operation: not only is he reclaiming the bush and making it less dismal than in the United States, although of lesser extension, but he is also addressing the grim reaper, death himself, and mitigating his devastation through taxidermy.

Munro's eloquent recourse to the duplicity of language is best illustrated through the mention of the wooden signs placed along the paths in the nature reserve. These signs read PDP: Proceed Down Path, but Kenny, the young neighbour who together with his sister Liza spends his holidays and week-ends on the nature reserve, fascinated by Ladner's operations as a taxidermist, interprets these signs as Pull Down Pants. The clashing code evidenced in the acronym works literally as a dis-covery of the reason why this natural preserve is repeatedly associated with rottenness and grimness. It clandestinely levels an accusation at Ladner: he is being revealed as a PeDoPhile through innuendo and cryptogram.

Some examples of innuendo deserve elaboration because they provide a portrait of the taxidermist as a predator. Ladner's duplicity is visually conveyed to us when he mimics Bea, the woman he lives with, without her noticing it. Ladner imitates her very gestures behind her back for the benefit of Liza, the young neighbour he is revealed to be having a sexual relationship with:

This was thrilling and shocking. Liza's face was trembling with her need to laugh. Part of her wanted to make Ladner stop, to stop at once, before the damage was done, and part of her longed for that very damage, the damage Ladner could do, the ripping open, the final delight of it. (288)

Ladner's perversity is mediated through the metaphor of the ripping open that exposes his predatory instinct and transforms him into the very wild beast that it is his job to embalm. But through the antithetical process that Freud has shown to operate in dreams and the psychic life, at the same time as he is transformed into a predator, he reverses into a stuffed animal disclosing his exploded innards:

When Ladner grabbed Liza and squashed himself against her, she had a sense of danger deep inside him, a mechanical sputtering, as if he would exhaust himself in one jab of light, and nothing would be left of him but black smoke and burnt smells and frazzled wires. (292)

The nature reserve called Lesser Dismal is a far cry from the Garden of Eden. Like the reference to the morel, with its hint of death, Lesser Dismal obliquely encapsulates evil (*mal*) and paves the way for the revelation of dis-functioning, "Dis" being the Greek name for the Land of the Underworld, the place which, in Christianity, is inhabited by the devil. Ladner's garden is indeed dis-mal: its lush cover-up barely conceals the frazzled wires of the waste land that lies underneath after it is repeatedly struck by a metaphoric lightning. The pole of order and permanence supposedly represented by the garden is in fact a perverted territory entirely dedicated to duplicity, simulacra, and fraud. It does not typify the imposition of civilization over the wilderness. It rather exposes the savage, predatory, and perverse instincts of the one who set up the garden as a cover-up for the destructive forces that well up from his inner swamp.

Ladner's predatory and perverse nature is matched by that of his partner, Bea Doud, whose instincts override her morals. Bea is first presented as a woman who, after a checkered career entailing many lovers, had settled down into "an orderly life" with a decent school teacher until she jilts him to set up home with the taxidermist. In characteristic fashion, Munro introduces Bea's betrayal of her former partner as a return to the truthfulness of instinct:

> All the things that had appealed to her and conforted her about him were now more or less dust and ashes. Now that she had seen him with Ladner.
> She could have told herself otherwise, of course. But such was not her nature. Even after years of good behavior, it was not her nature. (268)

In the nature preserve, Munro exposes simultaneously the falsification of nature through artifice and the moral failings and falsehoods of human beings who are natural. Bea's name can be regarded as short for *beata*, which means happy and blessed but also naïve and simple-minded. When living on the nature preserve with Ladner, Bea is indeed is very naïve: she turns a blind eye on his sexual perversion and depraved behaviour with the children, she refuses to "see" and to denounce. She lives a life of criminal silence in the midst of nature.[4]

The story climaxes with a double crisis: at the time when Ladner finds himself in the neighbouring hospital for a routine operation, a bypass which results in his premature death, his cabin is trashed by Liza, who seems to take her revenge on the pedophile who abused her during her childhood. I propose to consider this double crisis, the man's death and the devastation of his house, as a double occurrence that gives evidence of the return of symbolic forms derived from Antiquity and primitivity.

In other words, Liza's trashing of her victimizer's house can be regarded as a reactualization in modern times of primitive instances of possession such as evidenced in Dionysian mania or the witches' dealings with the devil. Liza herself, who is depicted as a dancer, capable of abandoning herself utterly to the rhythm of fierce music, can be regarded as an avatar of the Maenads from Antiquity, who, seized with sacred fury, set about dismembering the men who dared interfere with them. She can also be envisaged as a sorceress having the ability to injure others through occult means. Thus the representation of Ladner's death in the hospital at the time when his house is vandalized can be seen as a direct illustration of the workings of magic thought: by turning against her victimizer's house, that is to say against a duplicate image of him, Liza indirectly hits him in the heart, causing his immediate death. Like the garden he has designed, Ladner's house participates in the dialectics of substance and simulacra, of presence and proxy, and requires of us that we interrogate the meaning of the work of art or the magic that is encapsulated within it.

The A-shaped cabin can be regarded as the place where two artistic activities are conducted: it is the place where Ladner worked as a taxidermist, embalming wild beasts and ensuring their survival, and it is the place that Liza trashes in order to ensure Ladner's destruction. Her act of devastation bears a great likeness to Action painting:

> A style of abstract painting that uses techniques such as the dribbling or splashing of paint to achieve a spontaneous effect. In Action Painting the canvas is the arena in which the artist acts. The action of painting becomes a moment in the biography of the artist – the canvas becomes the record of the event. (Delahunt)

When Liza sets about overthrowing furniture and spilling whisky, vinegar, or sticky *crème de menthe* all over the floor, she performs a gestural blotching which is in keeping with Jackson Pollock throwing, dripping, and dribbling paint onto canvases fastened to the floor. Munro indirectly reinforces this equation when she speaks of Liza's husband joining in the fray:

> Warren picked up the hassock he had been sitting on and flung it at the sofa. It toppled off. It didn't do any damage but the action had put him in the picture. (282)

Through the allusion to Warren's enlistment and the simultaneous use of the words "action" and "picture' to describe it, Munro provides us with "the arena in which the artist acts" and establishes the aesthetic dimension of the occurrence. Like Pollock, who was known to attack his canvas with knives and trowels, and to bicycle over it, Liza and Warren become the agents of a ritual ceremony which seems to be simultaneously concerned with both destruction and creation:

> Liza took back the bottle and threw it against the big front window. It didn't go through the window but cracked the glass. The

bottle hadn't broken – it fell to the floor, and a pool of beautiful
liquid streamed out from it. Dark green blood. The window glass
had filled with thousands of radiating cracks, and turned as white
as a halo. (282)

What is at stake is the acting out of a religious mystery: the mystery of
a sacrifice that brings about the radiance of regeneration. According
to the workings of magic, this religious sacrifice operates on two levels
at once, the visible and the invisible. The spilling of crème de menthe
in the cabin subtends the spilling of the blood of her victimizer, who
is dying in the hospital during a simple by-pass. The magic quality of
this scene of retribution is parodically underlined by Munro when she
makes Liza take up a "magic marker" and write on the wall of the
cabin "the wages of sin is death."

As a supplementary parody, which works as a carnivalization of
action, her husband, *Warren,* inscribes *warnings* on the kitchen wall
with tomato sauce:

He found and opened a can of tomato sauce. It was thinner than
ketchup and didn't work as well, but he tried to work with it on
the wooden kitchen wall. "Beware this is your blood."
    The sauce soaked into or ran down the boards. Liza came up
close to read the words before they blotted themselves out. (282)

Far from being belittled by the recourse to tomato sauce, the writing on the wall or red logogram acquires an otherworldly dimension
on two accounts. First as a reenactment of what happened during
Belshazzar's feast, the writing on the wall is endowed with the aura
of the supernatural, an aura which is supplemented through another
biblical allusion, that of the Eucharist, parodically reversed here so
that the Holy Communion is transformed into an act of accusation,
and the blood of Christ converted into the culprit's blood.[5] Secondly,
its appearing and disappearing almost instantaneously departs from
the biblical intertext but reinforces its dramatic quality. The disappearance of the sanguinary inscription confronts us with our mortality
and transforms a burlesque gesture into a tragic form. To use words
derived from Western theatre, we seem to be moving from the *com-
media dell' arte* to the *Trauerspiel*; or to compare this process with
visual artistic movements, we seem to be passing from a conception of
art as a product to a conception of art as a trajectory. The disappear-

ing logogram testifies to the presence of informal art in Munro's text which can be likened to the experiments with dissolving traces such as "dew art" encountered on the contemporary art scene. This ephemeral aesthetic trace made of tomato sauce, which relays the inscription with the magic marker and the overall action of devastating the house or action painting can be considered as a formal gesture, a formal imprint of the kind described by Aby Warburg as "*pathosformel.*" A formula of pathos is a primitive affective form dating back to time immemorial which has the capacity to survive throughout time and to return in the actuality of contemporary forms, laden with the energy of primitive forces.

This return or "survival of the primitive" (*nachleben der antike*) takes place on the occasion of a crisis, a crisis which might be similar to those that occurred at Lesser Dismal beforehand. With the use of the comparative Munro points towards the existence of other crises that have sedimented through time. The sack of the house can be regarded as the repetition of an orgiastic mystery which highlights the link between suffering and vitality, destruction and creation. What Munro seems to highlight is the symbolic function of images and their symbolic efficiency. With this forceful logogram, this verbal image in blood appearing and disappearing, she allows the return of the primitive in her contemporary bush garden. She aligns Liza's experience on a formula of pathos that links her dismembering of the house with a remembering of the self. The sack of the house by Liza can be envisaged as a performance and a psychic process very similar to abreaction, which has a cathartic power and purges her of the traumatic events which unfolded on the premises during her childhood.

The cabin becomes the *ur*-location of the original traumas. Not for nothing is it designated as a simple A-shaped building (expanded only with later additions). The use of the letter A can be regarded as another polysemic cryptogram deployed by Munro. Because it refers to the first letter in the alphabet, it sets the scene for heroic beginnings, but it also encapsulates the possibility of intertextual allusions.

The story by Borges entitled "The Aleph" is also about the first letter in the sacred language, which signifies according to the Cabala the unlimited and pure divinity. In Borges' short story, the Aleph becomes the place that encapsulates all other places, the secret point where the unconceivable universe can be looked at. By making her female character indulge in an act of devastation in the A-shaped cabin in order to replace perverted order with organic chaos, Munro makes us participate in the creation of a "chaosmos" to use the word coined by Deleuze. She gives her character access to the point that encapsulates all points – which is to say, the mythic moment of demiurgic creation that mortals can participate in when seized by divine possession or when indulging in the act of artistic expression: in the A-shaped cabin, Action painting opens the way to the Aleph.

This demiurgic power is further confirmed by the closing paragraphs of the story. After her trashing of the house, Liza walks down into the snow over the nature reserve while her husband carefully puts a piece of cardboard over the window she has just smashed to literally cover up her action. In the nature preserve, after her fit of *mania*, she recovers her sanity and looks at one of the beech trees where her initials as well as Ladner's and her brother's Kenny had been carved. She, then, waits for her husband to join her in her contemplation of nature and starts naming the elements which constitute the world:

> "Cedar," said Liza. "You've got to know cedar. There's a cedar. There's a wild cherry. Down there's birch. The white ones. And that one with the bark like gray skin? That's a beech. See, it had letters carved on it, but they've spread out, they just look like any old blotches now." (294)

The transformation of *mania* into *sophia*, of *pathos* into *logos*, confirms Liza in her demiurgic role but it also subtends another major metamorphosis. The tree with the barklike grey skin and the blotches is strongly evocative of Ladner, who had been burned on the side of his face and neck from an exploding shell during ground fighting near Caen, when he was in the army. Through the last ironic reversal in the story, Ladner is simultaneously destroyed at the same time as his house is trashed, and allowed to be reborn as a living tree on what had been a fake nature preserve upon which wild animals were kept in glass cases.

It looks here as if Munro was again providing us with the structural and structuring polarities of her aesthetic enterprise. She simultaneously exposes the perfection of the simulacra created by Ladner as the repository of perversions and extols the blotches of creation, be they the blotches of the beech on the reserve or those of action painting in the cabin. In doing this, she is not opposing the deadly perfection of artifice to the organic defects of nature, she is subverting these ambivalent categories into figures of prodigious doubling that investigate the nature of art in the artificial nature preserve.

By finally returning Ladner to an organic life in the simulacra of his nature preserve, and by condemning Liza, the newborn Christian, to the duplicity of her unacknowleged devastation, Munro is once again proffering an *ars poetica* based on a chiasmatic figure of fundamental ambivalence. She is articulating the ingrown nature of artifice at the same time as the secret falsehood of truthfulness while subsuming both into the category of vandalism. Vandalism primarily refers to "wilful or malicious destruction or damage to works of art or other property" (OED) but it also encapsulates an allusion to the original Vandals, a Germanic people who overran part of Roman Europe.

It might be possible that this secret allusion to the invasion of a country constitutes one of the paradigms of Munro's poetics. One of the major motifs developed in her works is that of the opening up of "another country" through the mediation of art. In "Vandals," she has forced open a new territory, in a transgressive aesthetic gesture, the performativity of which is the subject of most postcolonial theory. Given Munro's delight in what Homi Bhabha calls "the figure of chiasmatic cultural difference" (4), one might posit that her ambivalent representation of aesthetic imposition – the devastation of the cabin on the nature preserve – is at the same time a repetition of colonial imposition and a liberation from it. By returning the nature preserve to its original chaos, Munro's protagonists release the land from colonial imposition. They simultaneously assert the predatory nature of art and its liberating function.

But the concept of vandalism in Munro's story should not unduly be limited to territorial imposition. The territory that Munro opens up in story after story is a psychological and a moral one rather than a political one, and her delineation of vandalism implies the existence of a retributive justice that is not retained exclusively for sexual mistreatment. Kenny and Liza have suffered from Ladner's sexual abuse. They have also suffered from Bea's passive complicity in and tacit condoning of his actions, and her criminal silence might also indict her as one of the vandals in the story. The red logogram that instantly disappears on her kitchen wall levels an accusation at her as it clandestinely encapsulates the original warning:

Mene mene tekel u-pharsin; God has numbered the days of your kingdom and brought it to an end; you have been weighted in the balance and found wanting and your kingdom has been divided and given to the Medes and Persians. (Daniel 5, 6)

The vanishing red logogram that replaces, in Munro's story, the biblical mark on the wall, constitutes at the same time an indictment of Bea's base nature and an ironic metafictional commentary on *scripta manent*. The lethal warning that dominates the story with its powerful biblical hypotext ("Beware this is your blood") is one that exists only as an ephemeral trace in the short time before it evaporates.

Thus, in her ironically chiasmatic aesthetics, Munro uses de-vastation as the foundational moment of her writing. She leans on the eternal authority of the metanarrative (the creation myths and apocalyptic narratives derived from the Bible) at the same time as she composes a metafiction that self-reflexively makes a case for the poetics of the fragment, the scattered bits and pieces, the vanishing, irretrievable, half-glimpsed, and ephemeral revelations of the minor genre (Lesser Dismal) called the short story.

NOTES

1   In his ground-breaking essay entitled *The Violence of Language*, Jean-Jacques Lecercle developed a philosophy of language based on what escapes the rational construction of language and propounded the concept of "the return of the rest" to describe irrational phenomena such as slips and unconscious puns which resurface in the tropes and the polysemy of literary discourse. Twelve years later, in his debate with Ronald Shusterman on literary experience, *L'emprise des signes*, he uses this concept again as the fourth element in a development comprising eight theses on the opacity and reflexivity of literary language:

    Thèse n° 4: "La littérature est donc le lieu privilégié du retour du reste (en italiques). Sous ce concept, j'ai tenté de nommer ce qui du langage échappe à la construction rationnelle de l'objet langue, qui est le travail de la linguistique. Les règles de grammaire même les plus strictes, admettent des exceptions. Celles-ci, loin d'être des scories de l'explication rationnelle, destinées à être éliminées par le progrès de la théorie, persistent. Elles ne disparaissent en général, provisoirement, qu'au prix d'une complication de la théorie qui incitent les chercheurs à en construire une autre. Je postule donc qu'il y a, dans le langage, du reste constitutif." (41–42)

2   Paul Ricoeur's essay on *La Métaphore vive* proposes metaphor as a means to redescribe reality. This redescription of reality is predicated upon an operation of resemblance or analogy. It consists in "seeing as": "le 'voir comme' est la face sensible du langage poétique; mi-pensée,

mi-expérience, le 'voir comme' est la relation intuitive qui fait tenir ensemble le sens et l'image" (270). This possibility of seeing something as
something else is based on a semantic impertinence which is claimed
by Ricoeur as indispensable: "En ce sens, une psycho-linguistique de
la métaphore devrait intégrer à sa théorie des opérations le concept
d'impertinence sémantique" (261).

3   Munro's misstated allusion to a virgin state can be regarded as yet another tacit reminder of Ladner's abuse, and as a further instance of her art of
the implicit.

4   Carrie Dawson's paper "Skinned: Taxidermy and Pedophilia in Alice
Munro's 'Vandals'" appeared after my paper was delivered on April 22,
2005. In it, Dawson develops a similar thesis concerning the likelihood
of Bea's "knowingness" which is "encoded in her reference to nature"
(Dawson 73). She also highlights Bea's "tacit recognition of the violence
that has taken place just outside [the vandalized house]" (73), and underlines Bea's inclination to use deception and self-deception:

> "Similarly, Bea's characterization of herself as a 'fake' whose voice is
> memorable for its 'artificiality,' combined with her suggestion that she
> has come to terms with 'what [Ladner] would say and wouldn't say,'
> intimates that she may indeed know more than she is willing or able
> to say." (Dawson 72, 73)

5   I am indebted to Warren Cariou for pointing out to me, during a discussion at the Canadian Cultural Center in Paris (April 2005), Munro's
transformation of the ritualized "this is my blood" into "Beware this is
your blood." I wish to extend my sincere thanks to him for this enlight-
ening remark.

WORKS CITED

Bhabha, Homi K. *Nation and Narration*. London: Routlege, 1990.
Bioy Casares, Adolfo. *The Invention of Morel*. Translated by Ruth L.C.
  Simms. New York: New York Review of Books, 1964. [1940]
Buci-Glucksman, Christine. *Esthétique de l'éphémère*. Paris: Galilée, 2003.
Borges, Jorge Luis. *Oeuvres Complètes*. Paris: nrf Gallimard Pléiade, 1993.
Dawson, Carrie. "Skinned: Taxidermy and Pedophilia in Alice Munro's
  'Vandals.'" *Canadian Literature* 184 (Spring 2005): 69–83.
Delahunt, Michael. http://www.artlex.com copyright 1996–2004.
Didi-Huberman, George. *L'image survivante Histoire de l'Art et Temps des
  Fantômes selon Aby Warburg*. Paris: Minuit, 2002.
Dotremont, Christian. *J'écris pour voir*. Paris: Buchet Chastel, 2004.

Lecercle, Jean-Jacques. *The Violence of Language*. New York: Routledge, 1990.

Lecercle, Jean-Jacques and Ronald Shusterman. *L'emprise des signes: Débat sur l'expérience littéraire*. Paris: Seuil, 2002.

Munro, Alice. *Open Secrets*. London: Chatto and Windus, 1994.

Ricoeur, Paul. *La Métaphore vive*. Paris: Seuil, 1975.

TAMAS DOBOZY

Fables of a Bricoleur: Mark Anthony Jarman's Many Improvisations

The short stories of Mark Anthony Jarman's collection, *New Orleans is Sinking* (published in 1998), are a species of anti-naturalism, where the deterministic forces that would control the narrators and characters (and the author himself) instead furnish opportunities for resistance. For Jarman, the scene of this resistance is language itself, particularly corporate language, which, rather than limiting opportunities for meaning, is used most oddly – in the service of ends other than those for which it was intended.

In examining the improvisatory aspect of Jarman's writing, my argument owes much to Michel de Certeau's *The Practice of Everyday Life*, particularly the term *bricolage*. For de Certeau, *bricolage* is a way of making do with what comes to hand. He introduces this term in a colonial context:

> Thus the spectacular victory of Spanish colonization over the indigenous Indian cultures was diverted from its intended aims by the use made of it: even when they were subjected, indeed even when they accepted their subjection, the Indians often used the laws, practices, and representations that were imposed on them by force or by fascination to ends other than those of their conquerors; they made something else out of them; they subverted them from within – not by rejecting them or by transforming them ... but by many different ways of using them in the service of rules, customs or convictions foreign to the colonization which they could not escape. (32)

There is, of course, no small irony in de Certeau's use of the word "Indian." Even here, the terminology designating the colonized subject reflects not his or her modality but that of the colonizing power. De

Certeau's observations on the way in which such categories are trans-
gressed, subverted, and deformed in the colonial context becomes a
model for thinking about *bricolage* within another scene: that of subjects who, in the argument of Fredric Jameson, have been colonized by
capital (48). While it is not my aim (nor Jarman's, I think) to mobilize
a Marxist critique, I do want to suggest that, like de Certeau's "Indians," Jarman's characters "often [use] the laws, practices and representations ... imposed on them ... to ends other than those of their con-
querors." While such resistance does not ameliorate power relations in
any long-term way, it is none the less a resistance, one that arises in the
absence of a firm counter-hegemonic ideology.

Whether depicting alcohol abuse, infidelity, or grievous bodily injury, Jarman's stories amplify the minimalist language of the short
story Renaissance to the point of baroque excess; they re-deploy the
epiphany against static truth, offering "sudden realizations" that die
like sparks; most significantly the stories do not end but stop – as if
excised from larger bodies of work no longer in existence – troubling
the taut construction expected of the genre. Similarly, his characters
are less the "well-rounded" men and women of psychological realism than momentary agglomerations of language, and, in this, nearly
interchangeable from story to story. The speed of Jarman's writing,
its use of disassociation and juxtaposition of detail, remarks upon the
activities of the characters themselves, who rearrange the conventions
– institutional, social, religious – that structure existence. Jarman's
characters "poach" – in de Certeau's words – on social codes to craft
personal contexts of meaning, though this process also leaves them
beholden to the system that offers them the codes upon which they
improvise. Thus, if they are faced with a kind of "capitalist sublime"
– where even the boundaries of the nation state do not contain corporate forces – then Jarman's stories – in which characters travel between
Canada and the U.S. and Europe and Asia without exiting commercial
culture – make no claim on getting outside the system. Instead, the
characters combine and re-combine the verbal artifacts of that culture
to make them serve interests "foreign" to the corporation.

Like de Certeau, Jarman acknowledges the "enigma of the consumer
sphinx" (31), paying homage to what agency remains to subjects en-
tangled in the machinery of globalization (37): "the subtle, stubborn,
resistant activity of groups which, since they lack their own space,
have to get along in a network of already established forces and representations" (18). Too expansive to be breached, too diffuse to be

summed up, too insidious to permit the relocation of the subject to a "natural" viewpoint, Jarman depicts a society in which a lost connection to a "nature" not already prefabricated and part of a sales pitch is impossible. The title story of the collection reveals the omnipresence of corporate interests where the narrator speaks of

> pastel condos in the newly bulldozed clearing and the developments labeled with cheesy cheery names: Mysty Woods, Oak Meadows, Mountain Mews, Ravensdale – places named after what they dynamited, trucked away, stripped, or burnt with diesel: Jesus weeps, what a strange admission in those pastoral names. To destroy first and then to draw attention to it as a sales pitch. But I'd do the same if it was my job. My favourite townhouse development is Whisper Green: it is not green and it's beside an Esso station and noisy intersection. Fairly raucous whispering. What a world we wander through! Can you beat it with a stick? No, you cannot. (*Orleans* 25)

The description of a landscape "dynamited, trucked away, stripped, or burnt with diesel" indicates a horror at urban sprawl. Yet this horror, Jarman's character suggests, is part of the "sales pitch." That the builders and namers of these developments highlight the type of wilderness that once stood in their places recognizes a culture that knows names are better than the reality they efface and improve upon. The names – "Mysty Woods, Oak Meadows, Mountain Mews, Ravensdale" – are memorials preferred to a razed "pastoral" landscape. Here, the pastoral, as "artifice," is fully revealed. This new "pastoral" literature that Jarman produces no longer offers nature as socially restorative, as the visible and still attainable ground against which social laws can be verified; instead, it offers the pleasing associations of nature but with all the comforts of home – nature "verified" *as* the social. For Jarman's narrator, the efficacy of the "sales pitch" embodied in the condos' names is not only a source of bafflement over the "world we wander through," but of the technology he himself employs: namely, the word. Thus, when he observes "I'd do the same if it was my job," he is in fact making his own "strange admission": that he too is involved in memorialization. The excerpt thus demonstrates the subject position theorized by de Certeau, where the redeployment of a given mode of articulation implicates the subject in that mode. The narrator does not distinguish himself from the contractors who erect the condominium monstrosities, and who perpetuate the ecological waste that precedes urban sprawl. Indeed, he relishes the paradox presented by the developments' names, even to the point of participating in a "sales pitch" predicated upon advancing itself by drawing attention to what it destroys. Thus Jarman's story is, by his own admission, fully invested in the paradoxes and contradictions of a culture of manufacture.

However, here arises the consumer "riddle." For while paradox is used instrumentally by the contractors to make real estate sales, in the narrator's hands it is used to make a very different kind of "sale." The conjunction of wonderment and cliché expressed in the last lines – "What a world we wander through! Can you beat it with a stick? No, you cannot" – partakes of the richness of these paradoxes in a way that, I would argue, disturbs the destructive economy of real estate. For what emerges from this riddle is not a desire to acquire but a satisfaction, even amusement, in the act of "acquiring" something else: an assemblage of words that, as limited as it is, recycles cliché to restore memory of a "world" so overwhelming in its artificiality that you cannot "beat it with a stick." This is, of course, not a large scale political intervention; rather, it is a turning of the language of that culture upon itself, not in the comfortable simulation and nostalgia promoted by the names of the developments, but in their complete detachment from any authenticating, "natural" reality. Jarman's use of cliché at once signals his entrapment within the linguistic modalities that determine thought at the same time as it foils the self-reinforcing ends of that modality; his use of cliché disrupts the system's generation of consumer desire. Thus, while the subject of Jarman's short stories is never free of the system that encompasses him, he none the less mobilizes memory *differently* than the names of the developments would have him remember. His playing on and with the pastoral names recalls, as wonderment rather than satisfaction, the self-enclosed discourse that eventuates urban sprawl, at the same time as it comments on the ultimate inability of his characters to think "any differently." The erased landscape reappears in the figure of the negligible, the mastered, or the irrelevant.

Jarman's story, then, demonstrates de Certeau's notion of the ways in which consumers transform cultural spaces – conceptual, physical, commercial – into a "story jerry-built out of elements taken from common sayings, an allusive and fragmentary story whose gaps mesh with the social practices it symbolizes" (102). Instead of establishing an alternative ideological space, which is the promise of the postmodern novel that, in Don DeLillo's terms, attempts to be "equal to the complexities and excesses" of its culture (290), Jarman gives us stories that, in not being homologous to the culture, cannot hope to exceed it. At best, they "mesh" with "social practices." The stories are as provisional as the subjects within them, foregrounding their indebtedness to the institutions they poach upon, that they gather materials from, in order to articulate themselves. Another story from the collection, "I Apply," told as a dramatic monologue from the perspective of a business manager in charge of hiring, further illuminates the compromised status of Jarman's characters. For the duration of the monologue, the manager sits across a desk from a prospective employee who is situated above a trapdoor whose opening and closing is controlled by the manager via a lever, upon which his hand rests while he delivers instructions. Jarman announces the invisibility of the employee/subject, whose name is suggested by the title of a story in which he or she is not permitted to speak. Instead, the entirety of the narrative focuses on the manager fingering the lever while lecturing the employee on the sort of conduct that will make him or her rise "like a shot" (64) in the business. Yet, the bureaucratic rationality of the manager is continually troubled by a poetry that has little instrumental purpose:

> In clement weather you may eat your lunch down there on the courtyard steps, glance at each other thinking vaguely about metal, statues, legs, earrings and other half-formed images just past the edge of sight, the maritime light of dreams of ships and hovering horizons, salty tears in the tea-rose gazebo, no baldness or vanity, no Abba revivals or scrofula. You may daydream about one man or woman in white whose dedication and affection is without condition or testimony, a person who truly knows you with love like relentless light, light that seems sadly absent on your shrunken lunch hour on the cracked cement steps. (64)

Here, the manager attempts to describe or catalogue the options available to employees on their lunch break. By dismissing the products of the employees' imaginations as "vague thoughts" or "daydreams," the manager turns the "gap" in the labour routine, i.e. the lunch break, into an exorcism of desires the workplace cannot fulfill. However, what the manager cannot "manage" is his own logorrhea, a language that, clause after clause after clause, threatens, like the trapdoor he controls, to pull the bottom from beneath him. His poetic monologue fragments the totality of both the business edifice – into "courtyard," "metal," "statues," "legs," "earrings," and so on – choosing from the vast assemblage a se- ries of associations that proceed to no end. Moreover, the "half-formed images" he similarly catalogues are an unrecoverable excess, a move- ment rather than a content, whose occasion is the possibility of exor- cism. Thus, another story, indeed many stories, flit like ghosts through the corporate landscape, fragmenting it, taking it apart, deforming it. For all its encompassing infrastructure, for all its rules telling the em- ployees when and for how long they can eat, where they can and cannot sit, what they can and cannot think, the corporation becomes the scene of an unaccountable desire that, moment by moment, insinuates itself into it, and which functions not only in the space meant to corral it – the "shrunken lunch hour" – but in the manager's office, and mind, as well. As de Certeau states, "The language produced by a certain social catego- ry has the power to extend its conquests into vast areas surrounding it, 'deserts' where nothing equally articulated seemed to exist, but in doing so is caught in the trap of its assimilation by a jungle of procedures ren- dered invisible to the conqueror by the very victories he seems to have won" (32). The fact is that the manager, too, for all his control, for all his espousal of the "rules," struggles to enumerate the plurality of desires that destabilize and de-realize the "conquests" of the corporation. His words, as it were, "come out of nowhere," extending the very activity they wish to delimit. Despite his fealty to the corporation, the manager is also a subject of desire, and thus resistant to the static modality of the business he safeguards. His pulling of the lever at the end of the story demonstrates the punishing rationality of the system, *and* recognizes the subject's position within it, as the manager admits in the last line of the story: "Clout, likewise, can be invisible, inexplicable, hidden. Clout can be mental or clout can be metal – cold and hard – can mean I can, with impunity, pull this lever, say in mid –" (67). While the system can "dis- pose" the subject (both in the sense of "get rid of" as well as "situate") with its "mental" and "metal" clout, doing so ultimately leaves it unable to articulate the end of its sentence. As the title suggests, this narrative is less about what the corporation makes possible than about what makes possible the corporation: its isolation as a place of power ("clout"), its articulation of itself, is dependent upon an exteriority that it "applies" to, and that "applies" to it. In the end, the corporate discourse also be- comes a short story, one that falls short of enumerating the infinite ways in which individual employees and consumers take advantage of the gaps and fissures it presents.

In keeping with an observation made by Douglas Glover, in his essay, "How to Read a Mark Jarman Story," the stories in *New Orleans is Sinking* are about the ways in which "verbal inventiveness" is mobilized in an effort to maintain "dignity" (115). However, what follows in Glover's essay is notable for its exclusive focus on language. There are no subjects as such here, if by subject we mean a consciousness identifiable through the idiosyncrasies of a particular voice. Instead, what Glover regards is an "eloquent speaking" that has "no place ... in ... [the] Republic" (120). Following through on Glover, then, Jarman's texts are about the no-place that, according to de Certeau, is the condition of subjects within the corporate "republic," within a rationality that attempts to enfold all within its own, self-generated territory, which continually assigns the places they may occupy. As Glover notes, however, Jarman's "oral pyrotechnics" (120) suggest a "play" not of certifiable meaning, but of "language itself" (121). Jarman responds to this de-situation with a language that continually exceeds specific sites of meaning, mirroring the way that subjects, similarly, cannot be constituted in one definitive "place." Instead, his stories murmur snatches of lives, of an improvisatory existence that appears differently within different moments of articulation, and which are never reducible to any given instance of saying. Like lyric poems, his stories dwell in the evanescent and provisional. These are not lives that can be encapsulated, captured as conceptual wholes by way of summary or definition or program, precisely because the individual, as a discrete entity, no longer exists in Jarman's world, because the division that makes the individual possible cannot be ascertained – because there is no "pastoral" nature to corroborate institutional and societal laws, only those laws themselves in their artificial and isolated "sales pitch." The disappearance of nature as a corroborating force is precisely what permits the escape of the subject, who, as in "I Apply," never speaks but is always spoken for, and is thus never really present. Relishing their de-situation, their non-presence, the inability to come up with a language that speaks *from* them, Jarman's characters, or, better, voices, mix the signals that surround and interpenetrate them. In this act of linguistic *bricolage* they testify to an agency in the midst of an extreme colonization, a mobility that cannot be arrested, but one which, lacking a place to stop and testify to itself, is dependent upon the materials made available to it, like ghosts on a forced march through walls meant to arrest them.

WORKS CITED

De Certeau, Michel. *The Practice of Everyday Life*. Trans. Steven Rendall. Berkeley: University of California Press, 1984.

DeLillo, Don. "The Art of Fiction CXXXV." *Paris Review* 128 (1993): 274–306.

Glover, Douglas. "How to Read Mark Jarman Story." *New Quarterly* 21:2–3 (Winter 2002): 115–21

Jameson, Fredric. *Postmodernism, or The Cultural Logic of Late Capitalism*. Durham: Duke University Press, 1995.

Jarman, Mark Anthony. *New Orleans is Sinking*. Ottawa: Oberon, 1998.

RE-READING PRACTICES

MARK WILLIAMS

On the Beach: Witi Ihimaera, Katherine Mansfield, and the Treaty of Waitangi

In F.E. Maning's *Old New Zealand* (1863) the narrator, who styles himself a "Pakeha-Maori," enters Maoriland in the 1830s by way of a hearty battle on the Hokianga shore with a tattooed warrior (28–31). Recently, Maori and Pakeha have squared off on the beach with less gusto and good humour than in Maning's account. In 2003 a judicial opinion held that Maori tribes could seek exclusive title to New Zealand's foreshore and seabed through the court system.[1] The opinion prompted a swift and negative response from Helen Clark's Labour Government, worried by the electoral implications of further pro-Maori settlements and concerned that Maori claims would threaten a treasured value of New Zealand lifestyle, ready access to the beach and its democratic pleasures. Legislation was enacted to ensure that Maori tribes could not make legal claims for private ownership of the affected public domain, although they could claim customary rights and guardianship.[2] After almost twenty years of biculturalism it was clear that the concept meant different things to the parties it supposedly joined.

In the 1980s the Labour government of David Lange had set about promoting biculturalism by entrenching Treaty principles in legislation. The powers of the 1975 Treaty of Waitangi Tribunal were extended to examine claims going back to 1840 when the Treaty was signed. Biculturalism had helped produce an efflorescence of Maori cultural activity in literature, theatre, painting and film as well as traditional Maori arts, carving, music and ta moko.[3] Yet by the mid–2000s fundamental questions about the meaning of the Treaty remained unresolved: what exactly were the obligations of the "partnership" between the two peoples who signed it;[4] how might its clauses be applied in a modern context; what were the "principles" it was said to contain and how should they be translated into action; which was the authoritative version of the Treaty; were key terms in the Maori version, rangitiratanga and kawanatanga,[5] correct translations of the English version; and above all, how to negotiate between the oral understanding of the document's meaning by its Maori signers and the textual bias of its European framers?

In this paper I wish to examine some difficulties inherent in biculturalism by way of a reconsideration of Witi Ihimaera's *Dear Miss Mansfield*, a collection of stories – or variations – loosely modelled on Katherine Mansfield originals, which appeared at a time of governmental activism in favour of biculturalism, Maori language, and recognition of the Treaty of Waitangi. The collection was published in 1989, the year after the centenary of Mansfield's birth, as a tribute to Mansfield, and Ihimaera fulsomely addresses the dead author in an epistolary preface: "may I offer you this small homage as a personal tribute to your life and your art" (9). The book is indeed a tribute to Mansfield the writer, but it is one that undermines the festive cultural nationalism of her centenary and raises knotty questions about cultural interpretation, canon-formation, and national identity that the approaching celebration of 150 years of settlement in 1990 would bring into focus. *Dear Miss Mansfield* offers a politically charged model for interpreting texts foundational to Pakeha identity.

Ihimaera's capture of Mansfield caused a small literary furore at the time, indicating that he had crossed a line of Pakeha tolerance by unsettling the possessive and reverential view of an author who had come to signify national identity for her Pakeha readers. Inserting Mansfield into a current postcolonial politics, Ihimaera challenged the notion of Pakeha exceptionalism among settler cultures, the myth of harmonious race relations, and the dominant understanding of biculturalism. *Dear Miss Mansfield* also reflects the hardening of Ihimaera's political stance in the period and his response to Maori radicals like Atareta Poananga, who had savaged biculturalism in a polemical review-essay on *The Matriarch* three years earlier: "This inextricable relationship between Maori and Pakeha is a parasitical one, blandly called biculturalism, but in reality the visitor feeding off the host" (27). Ihimaera is not dismissing biculturalism as Maori people – already bicultural – understood the term, but he demonstrates in the book how far Pakeha have to go towards its realization.

Dear Miss Mansfield extends the political consciousness of Ihimaera's writing in the 1980s. In the process Ihimaera is revising his own
work as well as that of Mansfield. "The Halcyon Summer," based on
"At the Bay," revisits "Halcyon," originally published in 1971, and
Nan Albinski notes that the later version "inject[s] a new political
consciousness into his earlier pastoral world, including direct confrontation between Maori/Pakeha" (45). The insertion of Maori material
into Mansfield's stories is not in itself a strongly political strategy. Often it is unobtrusive in the stories, merely enough to signal the Maori
presence in Mansfield's life and in national life, so easily overlooked by
Pakeha. By rewriting "At the Bay" from a Maori perspective, however,
Ihimaera unsettles the Pakeha reader for whom particularly beloved
Mansfield stories offer a highly familiar experience of New Zealand-
ness. The most directly unsettling effect is achieved not by the addition
of Maori characters but by a linguistic insertion into "The Affection-
ate Kidnappers," a revision of "How Pearl Button Was Kidnapped"
that closes with a lament by the imprisoned kuia (old ladies):

"Anei, te roimata toroa." The soft sounds of waiata swelled in the
darkness like currents of the wind holding up kuini's words. "E
noho ra. Pearl Button," Kuini said, "taku moko Pakeha." The syllables drifted like two birds beating heavily eastward into the night.
Then the light went, everything went, life went. (114)

The irony is that the words will not be understood by most of their
readers, even professional ones. As Ihimaera complains in the first volume of *Te Ao Marama*:

in our search through the published material of the decade, we
found issue after issue of publicly funded publications publishing
nothing in Maori. Literary and other institutions, still operating in
one language, were unable to identify work in Māori for us. People
who teach New Zealand literature remain unable to engage with
that literature ... The irony is that the only people who possess a
bilingual literature are the Māori people themselves. (18)

My purpose here is to revisit a book which does not seem to have
been justly dealt with either by those who emphasized its aesthetic
shortcomings or by those who focused on its political messages. I do
not wish to substitute cultural politics for literary criticism but rather

to consider the relations between literary and other kinds of reading practice in a book alert to both the symbolic function of literary language and the political dimensions of culturally-circumscribed interpretation. Ihimaera, it is clear, understands language as deeply implicated in the contestations of history and the claims to cultural power and ownership. What we see is shaped by the meaning systems built into the language we use and both the language and the meaning systems of the dominant Pakeha culture in New Zealand have exercized overwhelming authority in representing the nation. In much of that representation Maori have either been "disappeared" or turned into a decorative accoutrement of Pakeha identity. But he also acknowledges the specifically literary value of his model's writing and he has built that acknowledgment into his engagement with Mansfield and, by extension, the reader's engagement with *Dear Miss Mansfield*.

Ihimaera responds to the exercise of political power not by mounting a polemical attack but by addressing a particularly resonant concentration of cultural power in local canonical literature. Literary language has symbolic resources which allow meaning systems to be both solidified and subverted. Authors themselves come to hold symbolic resonance in cultural nationalist narratives: they are made to speak for the nation by selective readings of their work. By reassigning the accumulated symbolic associations of a familiar literary figure, Ihimaera questions the way cultures and nations invest authority in specific articulations of their collective identity. In particular, he forces his Pakeha readers to confront the blindness in their own habits of noticing and interpretation. He acknowledges Mansfield's continued force as an author and a national icon while using the power of her writing against the way in which Pakeha have enlisted her in their identity-making.

The framing narrative of the collection, "Maata," is not a revision of a specific Mansfield story or even a story as such, but a mixture of factual research and invention as Ihimaera connects Mansfield to the Maori presence in New Zealand. Ihimaera calls it a novella. Maata Mahupuku was the Maori schoolfriend of the young Kathleen Beauchamp and perhaps her lover; Mansfield began a novel named "Maata," parts of which are preserved in her manuscript collections (Scott, 237–61). In *Dear Miss Mansfield* the missing manuscript of Mansfield's novel has been entrusted to Maata, who continues writing it, keeps it with her, and eventually has it buried with her as an act of respect following Maori custom. What Ihimaera is interested in here is not a specific cultural practice so different from Pakeha understandings of ownership and so different from the fate of Mansfield's actual manuscript material after her death. Rather, he is jolting the Pakeha reader with an alien concept of textuality. Here the Maori sense of treasure or taonga means that the manuscript, resonant with Mansfield's and Maata's presence, should remain private to the two women even in death because authors and text are so intimately bound together. When Mansfield died at Fontainebleau, the narrator observes, "the manuscript [of 'Maata'], which *was* also Katherine Mansfield, became a tupakau – the dead Katherine too, and all the more *tapu* for that. It was something which, in Maori tradition, would have been returned to the tangi – like a piece of greenstone or a feather cloak" (54–5).

It is this radical concept of textual presence that establishes the book's relation to the Treaty and its interpretation. Biculturalism in the late 1980s made the Treaty active after a long quiescence. But what Maori and Pakeha understood by the brief document in two languages were quite different. For Maori, the Treaty embodies a spirit, the true intention of its framers and signers, which lies inside the words. Right understanding is required to grasp this spirit. As a Treaty of Waitangi Tribunal finding put it in 1983:

A Maori approach to the Treaty would imply that its *wairua* or spirit is something more than a literal construction of the actual words used can provide. The spirit of the Treaty transcends the sum total of its component written words and puts narrow or literal interpretations out of place. (McKenzie, *Bibliography and the Sociology of Texts* 127)

According to D.F. McKenzie, the Treaty was signed by two peoples inhabiting separate universes in terms of their understanding of textuality.[6] For McKenzie, Maori are still influenced by the oral basis of their culture, which is perhaps a way of saying that they expect the protocols of sincerity and transparency to operate in matters as important as a treaty between two peoples. McKenzie has written on the impediments to Pakeha understanding of what the Treaty means and how it should be interpreted:

That spirit is only recoverable if texts are regarded not simply as verbal constructs but as social products. Crucial to that development is Pakeha recognition of their own myth of literacy and rec-

ognition of the status of oral culture and spoken consensus. For
many Maori, the spirit of the treaty is best served by the Maori
text, in which kawanatanga means what its says (governorship, not
sovereignty), in which the taonga guaranteed by the Crown include
all that is materially and spiritually precious, in which Maori and
Pakeha share the Queen's protection as equal partners. So understood, the treaty in Maori is a sacred covernant, one which is tapu,
and with mana which places it above the law, whereas the English
versions distort its effect and remain caught in the mesh of documentary history and juridical process. (127–28)

How are we to uncover or encounter what McKenzie calls "the human presence in any recorded text" – treaty or story? (79). In *Dear
Miss Mansfield* Ihimaera does not simply open Mansfield's stories up
to accommodate a Maori presence, he inserts a different presence – or
a different concept of authorial presence – into them. Mansfield more
than any other New Zealand writer has suffered from an obsessive
reading into her work of a mythical construction of the author as
suffering, child-like, and ultimately, in spite of the betrayal of self-
exile, someone who belongs especially to the country and represents
its essential character. As the Treaty has been read by Maori as embodying a spiritual purpose which ought to govern interpretation, so
Mansfield's stories have persistently been read by Pakeha in terms of
the informing presence of *their* author. Ihimaera rediscovers Mansfield, as Mansfield in a famous passage spoke of rediscovering New
Zealand (Mansfield, *Letters and Journals* 65). But the Mansfield he
discovers has been pulled free of the author of stories of bright bays
and bourgeois children encountering metaphorical snakes in their colonial gardens. Like New Zealand itself in Mansfield's formulation, his
Katherine floats, drifting across the signifiers of national identity in a
disconcerting way.
    Ihimaera sets the scene for this re-presentation of Mansfield in
"Maata," where instead of the brooding adolescent longing to escape
colonial Wellington, we find a young Pakeha woman crossing the
boundaries of cultural and sexual propriety by her affair with Maata
Mahupuku. Ihimaera's Mansfield is not in the business of engendering
national identity, yet she notices an aspect of New Zealand, its Maori
presence, that figured in the literature of her own day mainly as orna-
mental display. To read Mansfield as a New Zealand author is to read
her pre-eminence among the late-colonial writers of Maoriland as es-

tablishing the fit beginnings of a national literature in English. Yet in
the notebooks and letters Mansfield wrote as a young woman back in
New Zealand between 1906 and 1908, we find not only a frustration
with the complacent materialism of "Young New Zealand"[7] but also
an interest in Maori words, lists of which she studiously compiled in
her travels through the Urewera district in 1907 (Scott 94, 148, 166).
To read Mansfield by way of her relationship with Maata Mahupuku
is to change utterly the notion of how New Zealand figures in her
work and of how her work has been incorporated into New Zealand.

In "Country Life" Ihimaera uses a Mansfieldian technical ploy to
remind the modern reader how much has not been noticed in the reading of New Zealand literature, history, and cultural reality. The story
focuses on a Pakeha farming family, a version of the Burnells, with
one of the daughters, Miranda, serving as a counterpart to Kezia. The
family servants, George and Heni, provide a humorous background
to these familiar lives, although George's humour is indecipherable to
Miranda. But at a crucial moment in the story, as modernity arrives
with the connection to electricity supply, Miranda has an epiphany
which is meant to apply equally to the reader:

> Heni was like a queen in blue dress and white gloves, greeting her
> Maori relatives with a dignity and unspoken authority that belied
> her everyday existence as cook for the Bell family. In a sudden
> insight Miranda realised that George and Heni, in the fluency of
> their own culture and language, were different from the George
> and Heni who worked and cooked and spoke in fractured English.
> And looking at the Maori villagers as they sat there, Miranda felt
> ashamed at the great gulf that existed between herself and them.
> She wanted to fly across to Heni and say, "Oh, Heni, I'm sorry, I
> just didn't understand –." (106)

Of course, saying sorry is not an adequate response to that gulf,
and gaining understanding does not change the circumstances that
provoked the moment of insight. Ihimaera has taken a Mansfieldian
device, the epiphany – which she developed independently of Joyce
and before Woolf – and emphasized a particular feature of her deployment of it. In Mansfield's stories epiphanies, usually experienced by
young women, are generally partial, offering not true knowledge but
anticipation of what the world has in store for someone possessed of
romantic readiness. They generally end in a knowledge that involves

both reversal and disappointment and they do not rest on authorial
sympathy for the subject of the insight. Moreover, they involve the
reader uncomfortably not only in the generation of insight but also in
its undercutting. Here Ihimaera obliges the reader not only to notice,
with Miranda, that Maori people exist outside their own culturally
shaped perceptions of caste and rank in a hidden world of meaning
and values but also that to have such a moment of recognition in itself
does not change the circumstances that provoke it.

According to the Waitangi Tribunal, Maori regard the Treaty as a
text possessed of an inner spirit that speaks its true meaning. Yet there
is a less spiritual side to Maori use of the English language that might
be brought into play here. In dealing with Pakeha, Maori have often
relied on a subversive humour that allows the language to be turned
against those who claim ownership of it. This sense is registered in
Pakeha writing if at all by way of a patronizing rendition of the cun-
ning or roguish Maori, with his broken English and tall tales. The
master of this genre is a writer a generation older than Mansfield, A.A.
Grace, who achieved considerable note in Britain and Australia as well
as New Zealand in the early 1900s for his tales of Maori life and character. Grace's most well known collection, *Tales of a Dying Race*, appeared in 1905. While Mansfield was experimenting with Oscar Wilde
and Decadence at Queen's College, Grace was exploring what he calls
the "decadence" of contemporary Maori under the impact of a stronger civilisation. There is no evidence that Mansfield read Grace but in
his novel *Atareta* there is a passage very like the key scene in "How
Pearl Button Was Kidnapped" where a small, tightly buttoned representative of Christian civilization stares at her entrancing opposite:

> The white tohunga's little daughter, in hat, pinafore, cotton skirt,
> and all those articles so dear to the heart of a pakeha mother, tod-
> dled down to the beach, and attracted by the laughter of the girls,
> found her way to the bathing-place. She reached the rock at an im-
> portant moment for all the girls came scrambling out of the water
> in a state of great excitement, and among them the little maiden
> stood in diminutive shoes and garments, the representative of civili-
> sation amid nature unadorned. (10)

In stories by Grace and Mansfield the beach is a zone where whiteness
meets Polynesia, civility loses its dress code, the cold straight lines of
Pakeha life relax into the easy warmth of the physical. Indeed, "At the

Bay" has contributed not only to the shaping of Pakeha identity but also to the powerful attachment of that national identity to the beach.

But I am concerned with another of Grace's stories, "The King's Ngerengere." The story concerns a visit by a party of Maori to a Pakeha living in England. The source of the story is the visit of King Tawhaio to Grace in England in 1884. Accompanying Tawhaio was Patara Te Tuhi, who later sat for a portrait with the painter, C.F. Goldie. At the time Goldie's memorializing of Maori subjects was seen as an essential act of preservation as the race itself died out. In an 1899 article on Goldie Patara is described as "characteristic of the old school of Maori *rangitira*," the old order which was "gradually changing and giving place to the new" ("In the Public Eye" 11). He represents those "fine old warriors [who] are passing away into the Reinga, the gloomy spirit-land" ("In the Public Eye" 11–12).

The situation was in fact considerably more complex. Sitting for Goldie's study, "Patara Te Tuhi: an Old Warrior," Patara modeled the dress and aspect of ancient nobility; yet he himself had been editor and principal writer of a Maori newspaper and was a very self-conscious "savage." A photograph of Goldie and Patara during the painting of the study shows the latter, fully garbed for the occasion, having a cup of tea with the painter (Sealy, 148). In the story that Grace wrote in response to the visit of Tawhaiao's party, the Maori take delight in shocking the natives of England. One alarms the English by a mock display of pukana, rolling his eyes and sticking out his tongue (Grace, *Tales* 169–70). The story upsets the usual hierarchy of cultural knowledge with the English more ignorant than the visitors, who make fun of the English fear of savagery. At one level a comic rendition of Maori quaintness, the story also shows the misinterpretations attendant on Maori transactions with non-Maori; here the Maori subjects with their combination of dignity, sang froid, and subversive humour gain the upper hand. They perform the stereotypical expectations of Maori behaviour to amuse themselves and to mock those who would imprison them in an atavistic fantasy. They indicate thereby their distance from the savage identity imposed upon them by empire. Similarly, *Dear Miss Mansfield* talks back to Pakeha reader, resisting the identity imposed on Maori people by colonization and the role assigned them by Pakeha nationalism. In appropriating Mansfield, Ihimaera upsets the narrative in which her work was formative in establishing Pakeha identity. His object is not to denigrate her work nor, except in a rhetorical sense, to Maorify it, but rather to destabilize the cultural nationalism that has confined one party within the savagely limited view of the other.

Mansfield and her New Zealand stories have provided a point of origin for a national literary identity, one able to be exported but also homely. Linda Hardy in "The Ghost of Katherine Mansfield" wrests the writer away from her association with cultural nationalism. She recounts the story of the young Mansfield visiting Stratford in 1903 with her wealthy colonial family. Shakespeare's birthplace was "one of their first objectives," and Kathleen Beauchamp herself "will mutate into Katherine Mansfield, will acquire, in 1988, a 'birthplace' of her own, and will perhaps assume a position, in relation to the literature of New Zealand, not unlike Shakespeare's for 'English' in general: a position of priority and pre-eminence" (416–17). Mansfield, however, was too unstable, too involved in imitating the styles of other writers rather than finding an authentically New Zealand way of writing, to serve as a model for later writers. She is too slippery a model to serve as the basis of national identity or literary origins. Ihimaera is both a celebrator of Mansfield in that he recognizes the power of her writing and a dissident in that he demurs from the purposes to which she has been put in enabling the repetition of the story of a national literature developing from its greatest Pakeha exemplar who chose most of her life to be elsewhere.

Ihimaera denies that the stories in *Dear Miss Mansfield imitate* Mansfield, yet the negative responses to the book at the time indicate that what was seen as mimicry had crossed a line (*Dear Miss Mansfield* 58). That line is the moving story of settler tolerance of Maori adaptation of modernity. *Dear Miss Mansfield* rewrites Mansfield not to capture her for the cause of biculturalism but to demonstrate that literary language concentrates the symbolic power by which dominant groups assert their cultural and interpretive authority. Language, for Ihimaera, shapes who we are. It creates the structures of feeling and affiliation we inhabit, but our own reception of those structures via language is not simply passive or one-way. Ihimaera obliges his Pakeha readers to engage in a struggle with inherited assumptions about language, meaning, and identity – and the way Mansfield has been conscripted in the making of their collective identity. He does this by making that reader uncomfortable at a point where identity should be most smoothly experienced: reading Mansfield.

NOTES

1 The Court of Appeal decision Attorney-General versus Ngati Apa
   2003 "recognised the possibility that Te Ture Whenua Maori Act
   1993 would lead to private ownership of the foreshore and seabed"
   www.beehive.govt.nz/foreshore/129bar1.pdf.

2 The Foreshore and Seabed Act 2004 asserted Crown ownership of the
   public foreshore and seabed, on behalf of all New Zealanders. Guaranteeing public access permanently while protecting customary rights. See
   http://www.justice.govt.nz/foreshore/index.html. Maori reaction to the
   government's legislative defence of public ownership was immediate and
   concerted. Not since the mid–1970s had Maori challenged the state with
   such unity. A hikoi (march) was organized recalling the Land March of
   1975, and a new political party, the Maori Party, was formed, drawing
   traditional Maori support away from the Labour Government,

3 Kapa haka is the term used for the traditional Maori Performing Arts.
   See http://homepages.ihug.co.nz/~tarrangower/kapahaka/. Ta moko is
   traditional tattoo. In 2004 Derek Lardelli was awarded one of five Lau-
   reate Awards by the Arts Foundation of New Zealand, signalling the recognition of this art form.

4 The notion that the Treaty constitutes a "partnership" has longstand-
   ing credibility among Maori, but not among Pakeha New Zealanders
   until the 1980s when it was adopted by the Labour Government. Paul
   McHugh defines the concept: "The Treaty of Waitangi therefore created
   a dynamic, ongoing relationship between Crown and tribe. The Chiefs
   entered into a 'partnership' with the Crown, giving the latter overriding
   power on international matters and recognizing its authority over the
   settler population. Tribal property rights, the authority of the Chiefs under Maori customary law (rangitirantanga) and optional tribal access to
   the benefits of European culture were recognised by the Crown," 6. This
   passage is cited in Fleras and Spoonley, 10, who refer to the concept on a
   number of occasions.

5 The most widely known terms in the Treaty. A rough translation of
   rangitiratanga – which the Treaty reserved to Maori – would be 'chiefly
   authority,' of kawanatanga – which the Maori signatories ceded to the
   Crown – would be 'governorship.' Maori sovereignty advocates claim
   that, had Maori ceded sovereignty, the correct word to have indicated
   that loss would have been mana, or power. Donna Awatere asserts in
   Maori Sovereignty that "at no stage [of the signing of the Treaty of Wait-
   angi] were any Maori willing to surrender their true sovereignty," 13.

6 "[T]he Treaty of Waitangi, witnesses to a quite remarkable moment in the contact between representatives of a literate European culture and those of a wholly oral indigenous one. It can be used as a test case for measuring the impact of literacy and the influence of print in the 1830s; and it offers a prime example of European assumptions about the comprehension, status and binding power of written statements and written consent on the one hand as against the flexible accommodations of oral consensus on the other," 79.

7 "I am ashamed of young New Zealand, but what is to be done. All the firm fat framework of their brains must be demolished before they can begin to learn," Letter to Vera Beauchamp, [? April-May 1908], *Collected Letters*, I, 44.

WORKS CITED

Albinski, Nan Bowman. "Witi Ihimaera: Glimpses of Childhood." In *International Literature in English: Essays on the Major Writers*. Ed Robert L. Ross. New York: Garland, 1991: 39–51.

Awatere, Donna. *Maori Sovereignty*. Auckland: Broadsheet, 1984.

Fleras, Augie and Paul Spoonley. *Recalling Aotearoa: Indigenous Politics and Ethnic Relations in New Zealand*. Auckland: Oxford University Press, 1999.

Grace Alfred A. *Atareta: The Belle of the Kainga*. Wellington: Gordon & Gotch, [1908].

– *Tales of a Dying Race*. London: Chatto and Windus, 1901.

Hardy, Linda. "The Ghost of Katherine Mansfield," *Landfall*, 43.4 (December 1989): 416–32.

Harris, Aroha. *Hikoi: Forty Years of Maori Protest*. Wellington: Huia, 2004.

Ihimaera, Witi. *Dear Miss Mansfield: A Tribute to Kathleen Mansfield Beauchamp*. Auckland: Viking, 1989.

– *Te Ao Marama: Contemporary Maori Writing, Volume 1. Te Whakahuatanga o te Ao: Reflections of Reality*. Auckland: Reed, 1992.

– *Te Ao Marama: Regaining Aotearoa: Maori Writers Speak Out, Volume 2. Te Whakahuatanga o te Ao: the Reality*. Auckland: Reed, 1993.

"In the Public Eye." *New Zealand Illustrated Magzine*, 1.1 (October 1889): 9–12.

Maning, F.E. *Old New Zealand: Being Incidents of Native Customs and Character in the Old Times by a Pakeha Maori*. London: Smith Elder, 1863.

Mansfield, Katherine. *The Letters and Journals of Katherine Mansfield: A Selection*. Ed. C.K. Stead. Harmondsworth: Penguin, 1985.

– *Collected Letters of Katherine Mansfield, Volume I, 1903–1917*. Eds. Vincent O'Sullivan and Margaret Scott. Oxford: Clarendon, 1984.

McHugh, Paul. *The Maori Magna Carta: New Zealand Law and the Treaty of Waitangi*. Auckland: Oxford University Press, 1991.

McKenzie, D.F. *Bibliography and the Sociology of Texts*. Cambridge: Cambridge University Press, 1999.

Poananga, Atareta. "*The Matriarch*, Takahia Wahine Toa: Trample on Strong Women, I." *Broadsheet*, 145 (December 1986): 24–28.

Scott, Margaret. *The Katherine Mansfield Notebooks*, I. Wellington: Lincoln University Press/Daphne Brassell, 1997.

Sealy, H.P. "In the Studio, Mr Goldie's Work." *The New Zealand Illustrated Magazine*, 5.2 (November 1901): 144–49.

LAURIE RICOU

The Botany of the Liar

"This is not a long story." (Douglas Coupland, *Life After God*)

The un-long story sparks a short. Highly compressed narrative gener-ates such a charge – such an overload – that a circuit breaks. A surge of energy, a sudden break, a loss of power – that's the short in short story.

Short, that is, does not satisfactorily define the length of a story: it's more tempting as an embedded metaphor of surprise. Readers, feeling happily accompanied, suddenly find themselves in the dark – and all around them crackles ambient electricity. The "short" story enacts this process: a break, a gap, and an interruption preceded and followed by a buzz and a hum. Evidence of the short lingers in a buzz and hum, but we've lost the connection: the circuit breaks. This is not a long story.

◆

A lyre vibrates and hums. It accompanies a singer; it modulates a song. The song is sometimes called a lyric: critics define the lyric as an in-tersection of subjectivity, metrical coherence, passion, particularity of image, sensuality – and brevity. Where a short occurs, you can almost not-hear the lyre humming.

In English *lyre* rhymes with *liar*. This echo is entirely accidental. A linguistic short circuit proposes a one-time connection: the lyre is a liar. It's unreliable, its form is music, it can't tell a story straight, you don't know what to believe. Have we not been noticing what we could have been hearing?

◆

Notice a plant, for example. A plant might be far more *other* than any other human being. But in enabling a human-plant connection, narrative might be a help, might shape some understanding. Readers of story cannot limit their encounters with other to other humans (Scigaj 5, 14). I've been contemplating this idea since around the time I realized that the thin silvery scrub my childhood friends and I tried to hide in was called wolf willow. How is it that after 21 years in a small Manitoba city, I did not have a name for a plant that was all around me – no name to live my stories in? And then – after I was eventually taught by Wallace Stegner's memoir *Wolf Willow* – questioning shifted: what could reading story, and plant, *together,* tell me about habitat? How might a plant figure in a story? How could I learn to listen to a plant? Or how read a plant? Posing such questions seems strained. A short occurs: this circuit is bound to fail.

◆

Ecocriticism, like Marxist or feminist criticism, hopes to be a way of reading applicable to any text. And yet, when critics want to be ecocritical, they have a difficult time saying much about William Carlos Williams' "Red Wheelbarrow" or Harold Pinter's *Homecoming.* They look first for whatever more conventionally speaks ecology – animals, plants, sometimes microbes; and often the human animal. And when they admit their topic is primarily, or unavoidably human, then they look for the human as implicated in a system of plants and other animals.

My own commitment to such practice led me to Ethel Wilson. I admire the way she so often shorts out the story in her "stories." I found geese and loons and osprey presiding "On Nimpish Lake," but there's scant story. Birds in Wilson fly continually into glass – a short indeed. "Hurry Hurry" is all marsh and birds: the *story* is confined to two sentences. Distracted by sandpiper and soldier blackbird, mesmerized by meadow lark and wounded hawk, you're surprised to realize you've witnessed a murder. Wilson, I began to conclude, is a bird watcher, but plants are usually missing. "A story has to end and this story hasn't ended yet and I don't know what the end will be" (188), she writes in "Till death do us part," coming up short.

After not finding much flora in Ethel Wilson, I went musing. How about the "distinct organic unity" of tree and tree house in Carol Windley's "Living in Trees" (148)? Well, the species is never identified and the characters show no interest in its form of being.

Amid such groping, Malcolm Lowry's "The Forest Path to the Spring" promised to engage. It opens with that foundational ecological connector: the journey along a path to find water. The narrator's daily journey, and the journey of water, shapes equally animal habitat and the growth of all plants.

But Lowry's story is not very short. In my 1987 reprint edition, it's almost 70 pages. This is not a *short* story. Except where it's shorted out. As it is when nothing happens. Or when the reader realizes that *one* story – up the path to the spring, fill canister, return to the house on stilts – repeats over and over. Lowry's writing tracks the crowded mind – exuberant, perceiving, remembering, dreaming – as it drifts somewhere above or along the forest path ... a "priest pacing in the aisles of a great cathedral ... possessed by the uprush of his extraneous thoughts" (251).

This fusing of mockery and transcendence serves, more than in any other Lowry story, to advocate or enact living in touch with the earth, alertly aware of being but one part of a biotic community. The uprush of ambulatory thoughts includes heron and oil refinery (226), jazz at the Orpheum cinema (248), and the undergrowth of "snowberry and thimbleberry and shallon bushes" (215). All of these come to be comprehended in the cycle of transpiration: "rain itself was water from the sea, ... raised to heaven by the sun, transformed into clouds, and falling again into the sea" (282). Lowry does not probe patterns of species distribution. Nor, indeed, does he examine here the naming of plants. But the story is memorable eco-fable because watershed is a key to bioregional definition, and Lowry focuses fundamentally on where and how living things get water.

◆

That the flora have limited resonance in stories by Wilson, Windley, and Lowry might caution me about the foolishness of my trying, for some years now, to write something I awkwardly call botanics. I propose to myself that if lovers of poem and story, lovers of language, lovers of earth, want to write in and out of bioregion, then they – then I – had better think about how animals and plants live, grow, spread, die, disappear and interdepend. I said "awkwardly," because I believe, at heart, such connecting is a simple matter, which we miss missing by dressing up the problem in academic study with "-ics" and "-isms." This should not be a long story.

Botanizing – essentially the usually amateur observation, categorization, and collecting of plants – has a long and intriguing history. Think of the names of James Cook, Archibald Menzies, and the amazing David Douglas – and the centralizing project of Joseph Banks. Jean-François Gaultier (1708–56), King's physician in Quebec from 1742, was an ardent naturalist, collector of seeds and plants, and corresponding member of the Académie Royale des Sciences (Boivin). European "explorations" were perhaps as much botanical as they were military/cartographic. Alfred Crosby's *The Ecology of Imperialism* is the best study of this crucial interconnect. When economic motives were less compelling, botanizing was sidelined or celebrated as essentially a *female* activity, a hobby. Perhaps still is.

Poeming and botanizing have long overlapped. Although the collecting and categorizing might have used different concepts and connections. Daffodils were at once "host" and "crowd"; somehow anonymous petals on an equally anonymous wet black bough conjured apparitions in a crowded Metro station. To write a lyric is often to sing about plants, to celebrate and sometimes to interpret the plants.

Readers and teachers seizing, usually uneasily, on the label ecocriticism, find they cannot or must not – while surrounded by accelerating extinction of species – confine their work to language and a theory of text. To read "The Forest Path to the Spring" requires reading forest and spring, canopy and forest floor, flow rates and the inhabitants of estuary. And having accepted this need, recognizing the magnitude of the gap between literary analysis and ecological analysis, and the absurdity of the gap, an aspiring ecocritic may as quickly retreat into truisms that evade ecology: in literature language refers to itself, or literature is its own justification.

Botanics, given its devotion both to observation and to reading in the *Canadian Journal of Botany,* resists a simplistic poststructuralism that concludes that all texts are self-reflexive constructions ... language about language about language infinitely receding. I have no wish to push a botanical agenda on writers. I am happy, however, to take what might be an incidental (how do I know?) unstudied (how would I be sure?) reference to "shallon bushes," and read David Douglas's journal and forestry ecologist Cindy Prescott to expand my reading of Lowry's story. I am also willing to take the retreating self-referentiality and use it as instruction in *inhabiting.* My attempt to consider the short in story might signal how little ecological connectivity we expect a short story, even the best story, to contain/convey. Conventional approaches may also describe a short in interpretive will.

We can't write or speak of the knowing or feeling of a plant in something other than the language we write or speak in. Botanics must ground itself in that inherent limitation. The inevitability of language also poses a challenge and suggests a possibility: botanics acknowledges *other*, will test the *gap* as a basis of discovery, as it is the basis of metaphor (see McKay). Botanics recognizes that the scientific is "other" to a humanist short-story critic. Admitting to that limitation will be a beginning. When science tells us that the brain rearranges itself according to the world outside itself (Scigaj 15), then environmental determinism might be worth revisiting. And botanics also remembers that the language that so sets us apart from flora and fauna, begins in the world of non-human nature (Abram).

◆

Here is an un-long story:

> Chang Tsao, in the ninth century, would
> paint trees simultaneously using his
> finger and the worn stump of a brush – one for the
> living matter, the one for the dead branches and fallen leaves.
> (Weinberger 25)

This short story, I would say, has a lot of length. The amplitude of desire: I want to see Chang Tsao's paintings; I want to watch him at work. The lengthening speculation: does some of his painting look like the finger painting we did in Grade Four? can we read in Chang Tsao's work the individuality of his finger print? are the dead and fallen not alive like the worn brush leaving. This is a lyric about trees. I would title the painting "Botany of the Lyre."

◆

I had the title for this piece before I had my abstract. And I had my abstract before my example. The lure of a trip to Paris in April can play havoc with scholarly responsibility. When it came time to write some pages, at least 17 minutes worth, to go with my title and abstract, I was frustrated – then panicked. I wanted to write about Jack Hodgins' "Earthquake" because its opening line "Do you remember the earthquake of '46?" implies such intimacy, a small community in the know.

The opening question resonates with the speaker's conviction. Here is
the story "shorting" out: *no* answer is recorded. The unwritten, un-
spoken answer is "yes," because the history is known and understood,
locally, *only* locally. But (again) there's not much botany in Hodgins'
story. Most of Hodgins' best botany fronds in *Innocent Cities* – and
at 393 pages even the boldest liar couldn't smuggle it into an essay on
the short story.

Sean Virgo's "Les Rites" might serve botanics better. In that story,
moss is a more important character than the ostensibly human characters; mosscloak is only the most botanical of the numerous compounds and portmanteau words that convey an ecology of "braid[ing]
into one another" (143); and Virgo uses the leaf-shaped verb "embran-
gling" (143), an old word that is new to me, to compress the tangle
and complexity and fecundity of ecology.

Lee Maracle's "Eunice" records a discussion among several women
writers: the politics, the marketplace, the silences. The narrator waits
and waits and waits through the womens' healing and searching conversation ... until, in the final paragraph, a plant, the only reference to
a plant, provides a sure means to communicate:

> The stones stretch and rearrange themselves into mountains. Hill-
> sides, covered with huckleberries. I imagine Eunice and me trudg-
> ing along the mountains of my birth, picking berries. I see the sun
> capture the gold and red of her hair and hear us conjure up our
> next poem, but I don't say a word. (64)

We speak now so little because we understand so much.

As its title suggests, Roo Borson's "Persimmon" makes a fruit a central character. The story is an elegy for a lost mother, for her garden,
and for two gardeners named George, and for the botanics that is
their chosen language: "little explanation was needed – as though a
tendril of ivy were itself a sentence, or a flower a burst of sentient feeling" (48). The first-person narrator is, in one sense, a liar. She evades
responsibility, deceives herself, can not or will not describe her dead
mother. Perhaps, the story hints, "[I]t's hardly worth describing ..."
her dead mother. But she can and must sing persimmon, in opulently
lyrical phrasing:

> It's against autumn's enamelled blue skies that the oval leaves be-
> gin to turn, first leathery, then increasingly brittle, as if glazed with

egg-white, while beneath the polished surface a variegated gleam, almost like that of fire opals, rises. And the fruits, the dull green of young bamboo when small, grow slowly until they are of a size to sit squarely in the palm. It's at this point that they should be picked: a frosty orange colour, with the blush of powder still on them. (46–47)

When the narrator later speculates in the final paragraph that persimmon is "overvalued," I take it to be her most blatant lie (52). Overvalued only if graded on a scale of value to humans, only if assessed as commodity to be shipped and marketed. As experience, in its own persimmonic integrity, it speaks a "deep familial connection to [its own growing] place" (52).

◆

So, I am still left with little more than a title. Where I began. With buzz and hum. With Michael Pollan's *The Botany of Desire*. I want to carry this book around with me. I want to push it on others. For me, it's like another *Seed Catalogue*, or *Autobiography of Red*, or Ethel Wilson story. It won't leave me alone. The book's jacket classifies the work as Natural Gardening and "non fiction." It's not short, it does not trope the light fantastic, its ground is imperial not post-colonial. But, undeterred, I want to claim it as short fiction, central to the title of this collection.

Pollan's subtitle is "A Plant's-Eye View of the World." Its approach he admits is "unconventional": "I take seriously the plant's point of view" (xvi). In doing so, Pollan writes some of the most happily disconcerting short stories since Edgar Allan Poe preached "deliberate care [for a] certain unique or single *effect*" (136).

"Once upon a time" Pollan writes – unconventionally, at the *end* of his story "Desire: Beauty/Plant: The Tulip" – "there were no flowers" (107). The double colon and slash in his title speaks of complicated balance, and reciprocating, and impossible to decide. To get to this "short," this assertion that beauty did not exist, and hence to remind that beauty becomes crucial to evolutionary development, he, or the narrating "I" – the plant's "I" – begins with his first flower.

The sustaining story is a discovery narrative. Pollan begins with a childhood encounter and ends with philosophical reflection, blossoming into an absurd terminal question: "Could that be it – right there, in a flower – the meaning of life?" (110) The story line follows the innocent beginning in pure materialism and, as adult, indulging utter uselessness. Or the story moves from the narrator's conviction that flowers are pointless (63) to his unreasonable passion for them. The narrative also follows from the small – a single tulip bulb – to the large: "Without flowers, we would not be" (109).

So far, this outline of narrative sounds standard. It might not convey that "Tulip" is a ripping story. The intrigue rests in a set of embedded stories – a score of personal, overheard, learned, and surely improvised tales – that enact the proliferation and profligacy of natural selection. The universal story of learning by growing also incorporates the species' biggest story, "tulipomania" – the history of the seventeenth-century obsession with exotic flowers in Holland – which Pollan analyzes as carnival, a complete inversion of norms, inversion to reappraise.

And carnival carries through to the full series of stories: "beeline" (64). Not that the book's form follows a beeline in the sense of singular, uninterrupted direct flight – but as a constant series of "turns," a move in one direction, then another, and another – one desire endlessly succeeded by another and then diverted by another sweetened lure. Unexpecteds after unexpected. Turning point after turning point (93). Pollan stories the "anomalous" (105), the "trespass," the "wayward" (106).

For the ten-year-old narrator at the beginning of the story, tulip means a job, a mesh-bag of bulbs for autumn planting, in exchange for a few coins from his parents. To him lyric is useless. Pollan tells his story as a search beyond useful to the useless, to the use of the useless. The narrative follows an apparently innocent boy – there's the lying part – in search of beauty, especially the why of beauty. And he sings the song – here to a single black tulip, the Queen of Night, sitting on his desk:.

> Six stamens – one for every petal – circle around a sturdy upright pedestal, each of them extending, like trembling suitors, a powdery yellow bouquet. (96)

Well, you might say, that's a pretty anthropocentric description for someone writing the plant's point of view. Yes, although that tautology of presenting a "bouquet" to a flower might be working some oddly ecocentric redundancy. However that might be, the botany of the liar is very much at work here. Pollan acknowledges the lie – "This is all pure speculation, I know" – he interrupts himself (69). He recognizes and acknowledges his own dependency on the lyre: you have to sing this beauty: you have to connect, as in song, at some irrational level. And you allow that excess to shift awareness to a plant's point of view. That is, the very lyrical expression is recognized as a botanical strategy. So, acknowledging his pure speculation, he continues because speculation itself sometimes seems part and parcel of what a flower is:

> I'm not sure if they ever asked for it, but flowers have always borne the often absurd weight of our meaning-making, so much so that I'm not prepared to say they *don't* ask for it. Consider, after all, that signifying is precisely what natural selection has designed flowers to do. They were nature's tropes long before we came along. (69)

Here's the bewildering "short" in Pollan's short story. A disconnect between human troping and flower troping: "how did these organs of plant sex manage to get themselves cross-wired with human ideas of value and status and Eros?" (64). Humans trope for pleasure, but also, in Pollan's stories, humans trope *for plants*, or plants trope for their own good, their own spread and perpetuation.

Pollan emphasizes the crucial evolutionary importance of the variant, the sport that does not fit the genre. One of many will be a "magic flower": in a planting of hundreds, apparently from the same bulb stock, *one* might be so "possessed" to "erupt" in brilliant contrasting colour (87). This tulip is said to have "broken" (88) and in an ordered field of uniform palette is "biological irrationality" (99) – a colour *break*. The species evolves through a series of shorts.

◆

Tropes and territory. Tulips trope to *extend* their territory – the ability of a plant to unreplicate itself, to flower (from a human perspective inexplicably) "in a sense other than that which is proper to it" (as *The Shorter Oxford English Dictionary* defines trope), allows tulips to make *more* space into *their* place.

Trope from *tropos*, Greek for turn. Pollan turns the turn. Here's the discomfiture: the primary trope in botanics is *trope itself*.

In a plant, of course, tropism means a literal turning. The plant will move or grow toward (or sometimes away from) an external stimulus.

Pollan turns such turning by asking *not* why flowers matter to people, but *how do flowers make themselves matter to people*, and how does their mattering to people make *flowers*.

This idea inheres – obliquely, by omission – in Pollan's title. In titling his book *The Botany of Desire*, Pollan is de-territorializing the human animal. The normative expectation in *The Botany of ...* let's say "The Botany of Southern Manitoba" or "The Botany of the Vercors Plateau" ... is disrupted. Not a catalogue of the plants that humans might name/identify in order to better claim a territory and a place name. Instead, something like "how do plants function in some realm of abstract yearning?" or maybe, still more ungrammatically, does desire have a botany?

> *This stands for that*: flowers by their very nature traffic in a kind of metaphor, so that even a meadow of wildflowers brims with meanings not of our making ... Sometime long ago the flower's gift for metaphor crossed with our own, and the offspring of that match, that miraculous symbiosis of desire, are the flowers of the garden. (70)

Botanics, writing from the plant's point of view, requires us to acknowledge that we're liars ... the "premise we know to be false but can't seem to shake: that we somehow stand outside, or apart from, nature" (xxv).

I take a similar approach here in short-circuiting others' approaches to the short story. If we are going to discuss tropes and territory, we had better integrate in that discussion a study of how plants trope to extend their territory. And we will need to open ourselves to the possibility that the most teacherly short-storying of the plant might be shelved in bookstore and library as "non-fiction."

The botanics I thus propose is fundamentally post-colonial in that it reaches beyond the process of human settler and settlement to ask about the dynamics of a habitat, of a larger and yet intimately local system. Post colonial will mean that after the colonial comes the *primary* colonial, the ab-original colonial that recognizes the Latin root of the word, *colere*, means both to cultivate, and to dwell. The *post*-colonial will ask how the colony ecologizes. And it will seek to transcend the premise that we know to be false, but can't seem to shake: that the form *short story* is "only" human and stands outside or apart from the plant's story.

NOTES

I would like to thank Travis Mason for suggesting stories that might illustrate my title. I would also like to thank Cindy Prescott (see page 349), Professor of Forestry at the University of British Columbia, for many conversations about forest ecology.

For a compact and informative summary of the enduring and complicated belief in the *genius loci*, see Hartman. Hartman traces the demonic and religious dimension of the figure as it becomes linked to local, to "native poetry," and to national destiny.

WORKS CITED

Abram, David. *The Spell of the Sensuous: Perception and Language in a More-Than-Human World*. New York: Vintage, 1997.

Boivin, Bernard. "Gaultier, Jean-Francois." *Dictionary of Canadian Biography*. Volume III. CD-ROM. Ed. Ramsay Cook. Toronto: University of Toronto Press, 2000.

Borson, Roo. "Persimmon." *Short Journey Upriver Toward Ōishida*. Toronto: McClelland and Stewart, 2004: 45–52.

Carson, Anne. *Autobiography of Red: A Novel in Verse*. New York: Alfred A. Knopf 1998.

Coupland, Douglas. *Life After God*. 1994; New York: Pocket Books, 1995.

Crosby, Alfred W. *Ecological Imerialism: The Biological Expansion of Europe 900–1900*. Cambridge/New York: Cambridge University Press, 2004.

Douglas, David. *Journal Kept by David Douglas During His Travels in North America 1823–1827*. New York: Royal Horticultural Society/ Antiquarian Press, 1959.

Hartman, Geoffrey H. "Romantic Poetry and the Genius Loci." In *Beyond Formalism: Literary Essays 1958–1970*. New Haven: Harvard University Press, 1970: 311–36.

Hodgins, Jack. *Innocent Cities*. Toronto: McClelland and Stewart, 1990.

– "Earthquake." *West by Northwest: British Columbia Short Stories*. Eds. David Stouck and Myler Wilkinson. Victoria, BC: Polestar, 1998: 72–80.

Kroetsch, Robert. *Seed Catalogue*. 1977. Winnipeg: Turnstone, 1986.

Lowry, Malcolm. *Hear Us O Lord from Heaven thy Dwelling Place*. 1961. Vancouver: Douglas & McIntyre, 1987.

Maracle, Lee. "Eunice." *Sojourner's Truth*. Vancouver: Press Gang. 1990: 56–64.

McKay, Don. "The Bushtits' Nest." *Vis à Vis: Field Notes on Poetry and Wilderness*. Wolfville, NS: Gaspereau, 2001: 83–106.

Poe, Edgar Allan. "Hawthorne's *Twice-Told Tales*" 1847. *Literary Criticism of Edgar Allan Poe*. Ed. Robert L. Hough. Lincoln: University of Nebraska Press, 1965: 133–49.

Pollan, Michael. *The Botany of Desire: A Plant's-Eye View of the World*. New York: Random House, 2001.

Scigaj, Leonard M. *Sustainable Poetry: Four American Ecopoets*. Lexington, KY: University Press of Kentucky, 1999.

Stegner, Wallace. *Wolf Willow: A History, A Story, and a Memory of the Last Plains Frontier*. 1955. New York: Viking, 1966.

Virgo, Sean. "Les Rites." *West by Northwest: British Columbia Short Stories*. Eds. David Stouck and Myler Wilkinson. Victoria, BC: Polestar, 1998: 136–49.

Weinberger, Eliot. "Changs and Wrens." *Harper's Magazine* 303: 1817 (October 2001): 23–25.

Wilson, Ethel. *Mrs. Golightly and Other Stories*. 1961. Toronto: McClelland and Stewart 1990.

Windley, Carol. "Living in Trees." *Visible Light*. Lantzville, BC: Oolichan, 1993: 143–74.

Index